SUSTAINABLE GROWTH AND GREEN POLICIES

Navigating Energy and Environmental Challenges

World Scientific Series on Environmental, Energy and Climate Economics

Series Editor: Richard S J Tol (*University of Sussex, UK*)

Published

Vol. 4 *Sustainable Growth and Green Policies: Navigating Energy and Environmental Challenges*
edited by Farhad Taghizadeh-Hesary, Naoyuki Yoshino, Nawazish Mirza and Muhammad Mohsin

Vol. 3 *Asian Mitigation: Insights, Mitigation Actions, Strategies and Policies for Asian Economies*
edited by Hongbo Duan

Vol. 2 *Climate Change Economics: Commemoration of Nobel Prize for William Nordhaus*
edited by Robert Mendelsohn

Vol. 1 *Climate and Development*
edited by Anil Markandya and Dirk T G Rübbelke

Volume 4 World Scientific Series on
Environmental, Energy and Climate Economics

SUSTAINABLE GROWTH AND GREEN POLICIES

Navigating Energy and Environmental Challenges

Editors

Farhad Taghizadeh-Hesary
Tokai University, Japan

Naoyuki Yoshino
Keio University, Japan

Nawazish Mirza
Excelia Business School, France

Muhammad Mohsin
Jiangsu University, China

World Scientific

NEW JERSEY • LONDON • SINGAPORE • BEIJING • SHANGHAI • TAIPEI • CHENNAI

Published by

World Scientific Publishing Co. Pte. Ltd.
5 Toh Tuck Link, Singapore 596224
USA office: 27 Warren Street, Suite 401-402, Hackensack, NJ 07601
UK office: 57 Shelton Street, Covent Garden, London WC2H 9HE

British Library Cataloguing-in-Publication Data
A catalogue record for this book is available from the British Library.

World Scientific Series on Environmental, Energy and Climate Economics — Vol. 4
SUSTAINABLE GROWTH AND GREEN POLICIES
Navigating Energy and Environmental Challenges

ISBN 978-981-98-1277-6 (hardcover)
ISBN 978-981-98-1278-3 (ebook for institutions)
ISBN 978-981-98-1279-0 (ebook for individuals)

For any available supplementary material, please visit
https://www.worldscientific.com/worldscibooks/10.1142/14302#t=suppl

Desk Editor: Venkatesh Sandhya

Typeset by Stallion Press
Email: enquiries@stallionpress.com

https://doi.org/10.1142/9789819812783_fmatter

ACKNOWLEDGMENTS

This book has resulted from a collective effort by numerous senior experts in energy economics, finance, and policy, all committed to enhancing our understanding of sustainable growth and green policies. Several chapters in this volume are adapted from papers originally published in a special issue of *Climate Change Economics*.

We extend our heartfelt gratitude to Professor Robert Mendelsohn, Editor-in-Chief of *Climate Change Economics*, for his invaluable support throughout the development of the special issue. Our thanks also go to World Scientific Publishing for proposing the idea of transforming the special issue into this book, thereby making these insights accessible to a broader audience. Lastly, we sincerely thank all the contributors who generously shared their expertise and perspectives, enriching the analyses and discussions presented within these pages.

https://doi.org/10.1142/9789819812783_fmatter

ABOUT THE EDITORS

Dr. Farhad Taghizadeh-Hesary is Associate Professor at Tokai University's Research Institute for Environment and Sustainability (TRIES) in Tokyo, Japan, and Vice-President of the International Society for Energy Transition Studies (ISETS). He serves as Chief Economist of Climate Finance Asia and Editor-in-Chief of the *Journal of Environmental Assessment Policy and Management.* In 2023, Japan's Minister of Education awarded him the Medal and Commendation for Science and Technology for his work in renewable energy finance. Recognized as a *Highly Cited Researcher* by Clarivate Analytics, he has authored over 400 academic papers and chapters and 30 books. Dr. Taghizadeh-Hesary has led numerous international consulting and capacity-building projects. He holds a Ph.D. in Economics from Keio University, which he earned with a MEXT scholarship.

Dr. Naoyuki Yoshino is a distinguished economist with expertise in public finance, infrastructure development, and financial systems. He is the Chief Advisor at the Financial Research Center of Japan's Financial Services Agency and Professor Emeritus at Keio University. From 2014 to 2020, he served as Dean and CEO of the Asian Development Bank Institute (ADBI). Dr. Yoshino earned his Ph.D. from Johns Hopkins University under the mentorship of Sir Alan Walters. He has been a visiting scholar at MIT and has held visiting professorships at institutions worldwide. His research focuses on infrastructure financing, SME development, and green finance, and he has authored over 100 publications, including books and academic journal articles. Recognized for his contributions to sustainable finance, Dr. Yoshino received the International Green Finance Lifetime Achievement Scientific Award from the Central Bank of Hungary in 2021.

Dr. Nawazish Mirza is Professor and Director of Academics for M.Sc. in International Corporate Finance at Excelia Business School, France. He is Editor-in-Chief of the *Journal of Risk Finance* and *Review of Accounting and Finance.* Dr. Mirza obtained his Ph.D. in Finance from the University of Paris Dauphine in 2010. He has more than 15 years of experience in consulting and teaching in Australia, Singapore, the United Arab Emirates, and France. His teaching and research interests include sustainable finance, financial intermediation, financial valuation, investments, and financial risk management. Before his academic career, Dr. Mirza worked in investment banking, asset management, and credit ratings. He regularly contributes his opinions to popular media like Bloomberg, CNBC, and China Daily.

Dr. Muhammad Mohsin is Associate Professor at Jiangsu University, China's School of Finance and Economics. His research expertise spans energy economics, green finance, low-carbon policies, and banking, focusing on sustainable economic growth. Dr. Mohsin has published over 100 scholarly works, including journal articles and book chapters, earning recognition as a *Highly Cited Researcher* by Clarivate Analytics. His widely cited research has significantly contributed to energy transition and financial sustainability. He earned his Ph.D. in October 2018 from Nanjing University of Aeronautics and Astronautics under the prestigious Chinese Government Scholarship awarded by the Chinese Scholarship Council (CSC).

https://doi.org/10.1142/9789819812783_fmatter

INTRODUCTION

FARHAD TAGHIZADEH-HESARY*,¶, NAOYUKI YOSHINO†, NAWAZISH MIRZA‡ and MUHAMMED MOHSIN§

*Tokai University Research Institute for Environment and Sustainability Tokai University, Tokyo, Japan

†Keio University, Mita, Minato, Tokyo, Japan

‡Excelia Business School, La Rochelle, France

§School of Finance and Economics, Jiangsu University, Zhenjiang, Jiangsu, P. R. China
¶farhad@tsc.u-tokai.ac.jp

The dual challenges of achieving sustainable growth and addressing environmental degradation have taken center stage in global policy discussions, particularly in the aftermath of the COVID-19 pandemic. This unprecedented global crisis disrupted economies, exposed vulnerabilities in financial systems and energy markets, and underscored the urgent need for resilient and sustainable development strategies. As nations endeavor to rebuild their economies, green policies and innovative financial mechanisms have emerged as pivotal drivers for sustainable recovery, carbon neutrality, and long-term economic stability.

Sustainable Growth and Green Policies: Navigating Energy and Environmental Challenges offers a timely, in-depth examination of how green finance, energy transition, and sustainable policies can synergistically address today's pressing environmental and economic issues. The book is structured into two sections: "Green Policies for Sustainable Growth and Carbon Neutrality" and "Green Finance and Economic Recovery". It comprises ten chapters that provide empirical research, innovative frameworks, and actionable policy recommendations.

Section I: Green Policies for Sustainable Growth and Carbon Neutrality

The first section presents five chapters that explore policies promoting sustainable growth and carbon neutrality across diverse regions and economic contexts. These chapters emphasize the importance of inclusive policy frameworks and innovative strategies.

Chapter 1: Yoshino *et al.* investigate the role of small and medium-sized enterprises (SMEs) in ASEAN countries' carbon neutrality efforts. The study reveals SMEs'

significant contributions to CO_2 emissions. They propose green finance initiatives and revised lending practices to enhance their role in green growth.

Chapter 2: Liu *et al.* examine the interplay between financial development and greenhouse gas mitigation in BRICS economies. Using the generalized method of moments (GMM) approach, they highlight the critical role of financial development in reducing emissions and recommend robust climate financing frameworks to promote sustainable investments.

Chapter 3: Rahmani *et al.* analyze behavioral determinants influencing private investments in renewable energy. Their findings identify key factors, including perceived risks, attitudes, and norms, that drive individual willingness to invest in renewable energy projects, emphasizing the need for policies that reduce investment risks.

Chapter 4: Cheng *et al.* focus on carbon market design in China, proposing a multi-criteria scheme for carbon allowances based on equity, efficiency, and feasibility principles. Their insights provide guidance for emerging economies aiming to implement effective carbon markets.

Chapter 5: Zhu *et al.* analyze China's socioeconomic progress and environmental impact, finding CO_2 emissions tied to GDP and energy use, while renewable energy and improved utilities reduce emissions. It highlights the need for policies supporting renewable energy, sustainable tourism, and better access to utilities for sustainable development.

Section II: Green Finance and Economic Recovery

The second section delves into the role of green finance in fostering economic recovery, particularly in the post-COVID-19 era. The five chapters in this section examine financial mechanisms, market dynamics, and macroeconomic policies that support green recovery and energy transition.

Chapter 6: Karim *et al.* conduct an empirical study to assess the interconnectedness between clean and conventional energy markets in regional stock markets. Their findings reveal significant market spillovers, particularly during crises, and they propose policies to enhance clean energy investments.

Chapter 7: Zhao *et al.* explore renewable energy financing's role in mitigating climate change and supporting economic recovery in Asia and ASEAN, highlighting the need for adequate funding. It emphasizes the importance of financial institutions in enhancing energy efficiency and achieving sustainable development goals.

Chapter 8: Lu *et al.* assess green financing's impact on carbon intensity using advanced quantile modeling. They show that advancements in OECD countries boosted non-fossil energy use and reduced carbon intensity. However, the effects are inconsistent and depend on strong government policies.

Chapter 9: Liu *et al.* investigate the impact of fiscal policies on greening China's economy. The results show that increased fiscal spending led to modest reductions in carbon emissions, mainly by reducing reliance on fossil fuels like natural gas and coal, while promoting a gradual shift toward green economic activities, with a positive correlation between fiscal policy and enhanced green economic efficiency.

Chapter 10: Huang *et al.* develop a framework linking macroeconomic policies, national expenditures, energy use, and CO_2 emissions in EU countries, utilizing the cross-sectional autoregressive distributed lag method to address long- and short-term relationships. It explores the interplay between monetary policy, energy consumption, and environmental impacts within the context of EU pollution reduction efforts.

What sets this volume apart is its holistic approach to integrating green finance, energy policy, environmental sustainability, and economic growth. While much of the existing literature focuses on isolated aspects of green growth, this book bridges the gap by examining the interconnectedness of financial tools, technological innovations, and policy interventions. Employing advanced econometric models, quantitative methods, and regional case studies, the chapters provide fresh insights into the complexities of sustainable growth in both emerging and advanced economies.

Combining diverse regional and sectoral analyses, *Sustainable Growth and Green Policies: Navigating Energy and Environmental Challenges* offers policymakers, researchers, and practitioners evidence-based strategies to foster a resilient and sustainable future.

https://doi.org/10.1142/9789819812783_fmatter

CONTENTS

https://doi.org/10.1142/9789819812783_0001

FOSTERING GREEN GROWTH IN ASEAN BY STRENGTHENING SME CONTRIBUTIONS TO CARBON NEUTRALITY

NAOYUKI YOSHINO*, EHSAN RASOULINEZHAD†, HAN PHOUMIN‡, FARHAD TAGHIZADEH-HESARY§ and LILU VANDERCAMME¶

School of Economics, Keio University, Tokyo, Japan

†*Faculty of World Studies, University of Tehran, Iran*

‡*Economic Research Institute for ASEAN and East Asia Jakarta, Indonesia*

§*Tokai Research Institute for Environment and Sustainability Tokai University, Tokyo, Japan*

¶*Tokai University, Japan*

In numerous Asian nations, small and medium-sized enterprises (SMEs) are pivotal to economic growth, yet often remain beyond the reach of environmental regulations, which predominantly target larger corporations. This research investigates the link between SME activities and carbon emissions in ASEAN countries from 2010 to 2020, utilizing a fully modified ordinary least squares (FMOLS) model. The analysis reveals that SME operations substantially contribute to CO_2 emissions, indicating a disconnect between environmental protection efforts and sustainable development goals. To guide SMEs toward carbon neutrality, the study recommends implementing specific green finance policies, expanding environmental regulations to encompass SMEs, and overhauling banking lending practices to promote sustainability based on SMEs' environmental performance. These strategies aim to incorporate SMEs into ASEAN's broader green growth and sustainable development agenda.

Keywords: Small and medium-sized enterprises; green growth; sustainable development; carbon neutrality; ASEAN.

1. Introduction

Small and medium-sized enterprises (SMEs) play a critical role as the backbone of economic development in different countries, particularly in ASEAN countries, where they account for a significant share of employment and GDP (Gherghina *et al.*, 2020). Their role has been highlighted by numerous experts in the field, as well as economic policymakers (Singh, 2022). SMEs play a significant role in an economy from different perspectives, including employment, innovation, and the ability to adapt to market changes, which make them critical to fostering sustainable economic growth.

Unlike large corporations, with broad organizational structures and slow operations, SMEs have organizational agility and the capacity to seize economic opportunities more efficiently (Koçyiğit and Akkaya, 2020). Additionally, SMEs are labor-intensive enterprises (Liu *et al.*, 2022). Hence, they are critical in employment generation, especially for skilled and capable labor. In developing countries, where brain drain poses a considerable challenge, expanding SMEs can provide job opportunities for highly skilled individuals, thereby mitigating elite migration (Oliinyk *et al.*, 2021). Furthermore, SMEs contribute to broader economic transformations by driving the growth of market-oriented systems. Their development facilitates the expansion of the private sector, promotes globalization, supports trade liberalization, and enhances the overall business and investment climate.

Conversely, such enterprises' operations often fall outside the scope of strict environmental regulations, leading to significant greenhouse gas (GHG) emissions. This discrepancy underscores the pressing need to integrate SMEs into the broader framework of green policies and carbon-neutral strategies.

Despite the numerous positive aspects of SMEs' development, the post-COVID-19 era presents challenges and opportunities for such enterprises to navigate the dual imperatives of environmental sustainability and economic recovery. The pandemic temporarily reduced global GHG emissions due to decreased industrial production, transportation, and energy consumption (Liu *et al.*, 2020). This decline initially sparked optimism about achieving sustainable development, characterized by conditions that ensure a clean and habitable environment for future generations. Sustainable development refers to achieving the desired conditions for human life: a clean environment (Ruggerio, 2021).

Sikarwar *et al.* (2021) highlighted that reduced urban traffic, air travel, and transportation were key contributors to the decline of environmental pollution during this period. Similarly, Alava and Singh (2022) noted that the temporary shutdown of manufacturing plants and reduced energy consumption have reduced energy consumption and decreased global emissions. However, these gains were short-lived, as emissions have already begun to rebound, jeopardizing long-term climate targets (Li and Li, 2021). In this context, SMEs are pivotal in the push toward carbon neutrality, particularly as ASEAN nations pursue green economic recovery strategies.

Despite various support programs, such as the ASEAN Strategic Action Plan for SME Development (2016–2025) and the EU's Green Action Plan (GAP) for SMEs, the pandemic has exposed numerous vulnerabilities within the SME sector. Studies by Dai *et al.* (2021) and Ozanne *et al.* (2022) reveal that the widespread lockdowns implemented during early 2020 caused the temporary closure of over 80% of SMEs in China. With limited financial resilience, many SMEs struggled to sustain operations during the economic shock, forcing some to shut down permanently.

Beyond the immediate financial challenges, SMEs face structural and institutional barriers to adopting sustainable practices. Limited access to green financing, reliance on outdated technologies, and insufficient government incentives significantly hinder their alignment with environmental objectives. Overcoming these barriers requires innovative and targeted interventions. Policy frameworks that promote access to green financing, investment in clean technologies, and tailored incentives for SMEs can help bridge the gap between economic growth and environmental sustainability in the post-pandemic era (Chien *et al.*, 2021). Addressing these issues will ensure that SMEs contribute meaningfully to the region's climate and sustainability goals.

This study examines the relationship between SMEs' activities and carbon emissions in the ASEAN region from 2010 to 2020. A fully modified ordinary least squares (FMOLS) model is employed for analysis. The study thoroughly examines the role of SMEs in achieving sustainable development, particularly carbon neutralization (achieving a green economy or zero carbon). Contradictory debate on this topic revolves around whether these enterprises contribute to carbon dioxide (CO_2) emissions and environmental pollution. However, SMEs are pivotal to the global economy, constituting approximately 90% of all businesses and employing around 70% of the global workforce (World Economic Forum, 2023a).

It is essential to highlight that their environmental impact is substantial. In Europe, SMEs are responsible for up to 70% of industrial pollution (OECD, 2023). In Southeast Asia, SMEs emit approximately 29.7 million tons of CO_2 annually (Schaper and Wong, 2021). Recent reports highlight that 35% of Asia-Pacific SMEs cite financial barriers to adopting environmental, social, and governance (ESG) initiatives (Statista, 2023). Sage (2023) found that SMEs in the United States struggle with sustainability reporting standards. Similarly, the World Economic Forum (2023b) noted that resource and knowledge limitations hinder SMEs' participation in ESG efforts. Ergo, it is essential to acknowledge the misalignment of environmental protection goals and sustainable development objectives despite the advantages of SME development. Therefore, there is a need for policymakers to pay more attention to emphasizing the need for targeted green finance policies, the revision of environmental regulations to include SMEs, and the restructuring of bank lending mechanisms to incentivize sustainable practices based on SMEs' environmental performance to integrate SMEs into the broader framework of green growth and sustainable development in ASEAN.

Studying the relationship between SMEs and environmental pollution in the context of ASEAN (the Association of Southeast Asian Nations) countries is a requisite for understanding SMEs' central role in achieving national and regional climate goals. This is because ASEAN is experiencing rapid economic growth, diversifying the energy mix, and commitment to environmental sustainability. As nations transition from fossil fuel to renewable energy, SMEs will inevitably be a key player (Gennari, 2023). It is important to note that the ASEAN Economic Community Blueprint 2025 and national green growth strategies emphasize the importance of sustainable practices. However, the inclusion of SMEs in these frameworks remains limited. This apparent gap presents the urgent need for targeted research and actionable solutions tailored to ASEAN and its unique socioeconomic and environmental dynamics (Agrawal *et al.*, 2024).

This chapter makes several key contributions to the literature. While existing research predominantly emphasizes the role of large industries, this study focuses on the significant contribution of SMEs to GHG emissions. The chapter first provides a deeper understanding of SMEs' impact on CO_2 emissions by focusing on theoretical and empirical analysis. Second, the chapter explores the relationship between SMEs and CO_2 emissions through a theoretical mathematical model, offering insights into how SME activities influence environmental outcomes. This approach contributes to a more nuanced interpretation of the role of SMEs in environmental sustainability. Third, the econometric modeling employed in this study integrates variables such as industrial growth, globalization, and the green economy index. This comprehensive approach allows for evaluating the implications of industrialization, globalization, and green economic revival policies within the context of ASEAN countries, enabling a critical assessment of these strategies for sustainable development.

The rest of the chapter is structured as follows: Section 2 discusses the current literature, Section 3 represents the theoretical background, Section 4 introduces the variables and the experimental model, Section 5 presents the main findings, and Section 6 presents the key points of the research and discusses the proposed practical policies.

2. Literature Review

2.1. *Environmental impact of SMEs*

SMEs are vital to global economic development but pose significant environmental challenges (Naradda *et al.*, 2020). The Organisation for Economic Cooperation and Development (OECD, 2018) estimates that SMEs contribute to 60–70% of industrial pollution in Europe, while in Southeast Asia, their carbon emissions are equally significant (Taghizadeh-Hesary *et al.*, 2023). This environmental footprint stems from outdated production technologies, inefficient energy use, and insufficient integration into environmental policies (Fawcett and Hampton, 2020).

Research highlights SMEs' dual role as contributors to and potential mitigators of environmental pollution. Lopes de Sousa Jabbour *et al.* (2020) found that manufacturing SMEs disproportionately contribute to air pollution, while Meng *et al.* (2018) identified SMEs in China's power and heat sectors as significant sources of CO_2 emissions. Conversely, Samargandi and Sohag (2022) showed that SMEs in Saudi Arabia, under supportive frameworks, effectively promote green energy adoption. Similarly, Zhang and Fang (2022) reported that EU government initiatives during the COVID-19 pandemic spurred the emergence of eco-friendly SMEs, illustrating how targeted policies can redirect SME activities toward sustainability.

2.2. *Barriers to green transformation*

Despite their potential to contribute to sustainability, SMEs face substantial barriers to adopting environmentally friendly practices (Wang *et al.*, 2023). Financial constraints are among the most significant challenges. Purwandani and Michaud (2021) highlighted the high costs of adopting green technologies and limited access to green financing as critical obstacles. In developing economies, Alam *et al.* (2022) found that while high-profit SMEs have greater capacity for environmental initiatives, smaller enterprises often lack the resources and expertise needed for green transitions.

The adoption of advanced technologies presents another hurdle. Jamwal *et al.* (2023) emphasized the difficulties SMEs face in implementing Industry 4.0 technologies, such as smart manufacturing, which can enhance energy efficiency and reduce emissions. These challenges are compounded by insufficient technical expertise and institutional support. Moreover, regulatory gaps hinder SMEs' alignment with sustainability goals. Choudhary *et al.* (2022) noted that many SMEs remain reluctant to adopt eco-friendly practices in the post-pandemic era due to the lack of clear policy guidance and financial incentives. Similarly, Shihata *et al.* (2022) stressed the need for governments to define financial incentives and regulatory frameworks tailored to SMEs, ensuring their inclusion in broader sustainability initiatives.

2.3. *Policy and technological interventions for sustainability*

Targeted policy interventions and technological advancements are essential to unlocking SMEs' environmental potential. The OECD (2021) recommends combining regulatory measures, financial support, and capacity-building initiatives to facilitate SMEs' green transformation. These include green loans, subsidies, and technical assistance programs to reduce energy intensity and promote resource efficiency.

Regional collaboration and technological transfer can further enhance SMEs' sustainability efforts. Shahzad *et al.* (2022) emphasized the importance of partnerships between SMEs and larger enterprises to accelerate the adoption of green technologies. In ASEAN, the ASEAN Economic Community Blueprint 2025 highlights the need to integrate SMEs into national sustainability frameworks, leveraging regional cooperation to share innovations and best practices (Taghizadeh-Hesary *et al.*, 2023). The role of corporate social responsibility (CSR) is also critical. Le (2022) found that CSR-driven initiatives can foster green innovation among SMEs, enabling them to align their activities with sustainable development goals. Furthermore, Alraja *et al.* (2022) demonstrated how targeted programs during the COVID-19 pandemic facilitated eco-friendly practices among SMEs, offering valuable lessons for ASEAN economies.

The literature underscores the complex relationship between SMEs and environmental sustainability. While SMEs significantly contribute to CO_2 emissions, they also hold immense potential for driving green growth under appropriate policy and institutional frameworks. This study builds on these insights to examine SMEs' roles in achieving ASEAN's sustainability goals, focusing on their contributions to CO_2 emissions and the implications for green economic policies.

3. Theoretical Background

It is widely acknowledged that SMEs face significant challenges in accessing environmental information. Compared to larger corporations, SMEs often have lower technological expertise and lack the financial resources required to address environmental concerns. This creates a stark contrast between SMEs and their larger counterparts. While large firms can raise capital through stock issuance to fund sustainability initiatives, SMEs typically rely on bank loans, which rarely prioritize environmental objectives. As a result, SMEs are under considerably less pressure to address environmental issues or implement improvements in this area.

Businesses' production functions vary depending on their size. The first function applies to large corporations (Eq. (1)), while the second is specific to SMEs (Eq. (2)):

$$G^L(Y_L, \mathrm{CO_2}^{\mathrm{L}}) = F^L(K, N, E) \tag{1}$$

$$G^{\mathrm{SME}}(Y_{\mathrm{SME}}, \mathrm{CO_2}^{\mathrm{SME}}) = F^{\mathrm{SME}}(K, N, E) \tag{2}$$

In the production functions, the outputs and associated CO_2 emissions are determined by three primary inputs: capital (K), the labor force (N), and energy (E). For SMEs, this relationship (Eq. (2)) can be further refined and expressed in the form of a Cobb–Douglas production function, as shown in Eq. (3):

$$G^{\mathrm{SME}}(Y_{\mathrm{SME}}, \mathrm{CO_2}^{\mathrm{SME}}) = K^{\alpha}.N^{\beta}.E^{\gamma} \tag{3}$$

where α, β, and γ are the capital, labor force, and energy elasticities, respectively.

SMEs try to maximize their profits through output and budget constraints, as shown in Eq. (4):

$$\pi^{\mathrm{SME}} = Y^{\mathrm{SME}} - P_E.E - r.K - w.N \tag{4}$$

The maximization can be run with regard to the three inputs of capital, labor, and energy as in Eqs. (5–7):

$$\begin{aligned} \frac{\partial \pi^{\mathrm{SME}}}{\partial E} &= \frac{\partial Y_{\mathrm{SME}}}{\partial E} - P_E = 0 \\ &= \gamma \frac{Y_{\mathrm{SME}}}{E} - P_E = 0 \\ E &= \frac{\gamma . Y_{\mathrm{SME}}}{P_E} \end{aligned} \tag{5}$$

$$\begin{aligned} \frac{\partial \pi^{\mathrm{SME}}}{\partial K} &= \frac{\partial Y_{\mathrm{SME}}}{\partial K} - r = 0 \\ &= \alpha \frac{Y_{\mathrm{SME}}}{K} - r = 0 \\ K &= \frac{\alpha . Y_{\mathrm{SME}}}{r} \end{aligned} \tag{6}$$

$$\frac{\partial \pi^{\text{SME}}}{\partial N} = \frac{\partial Y_{\text{SME}}}{\partial N} - w = 0$$
$$= \beta \frac{Y_{\text{SME}}}{N} - w = 0 \qquad (7)$$
$$N = \frac{\beta . Y_{\text{SME}}}{w}$$

Banks can allocate loans to SMEs 1 and 2, where the respective capital levels are denoted as $K1$ and $K2$ based on the previously discussed production function. This relationship is outlined in Eq. (8):

$$K = \frac{\alpha . Y_{\text{SME}}}{r} \xrightarrow{\text{yields}} K^1 = \frac{\alpha^1 . Y^1{}_{\text{SME}}}{r}, \quad K^2 = \frac{\alpha^2 . Y^2{}_{\text{SME}}}{r} \qquad (8)$$

Typically, banks allocate loans to SMEs by evaluating their marginal capital productivity, which is the conventional approach to loan distribution. However, this method overlooks environmental considerations, such as the CO_2 emissions associated with SME activities.

The left side of Figure 1 illustrates the output maximization for SMEs 1 and 2. Point a represents the maximum output level and reflects the typical allocation of loans by banks to these SMEs. However, in the context of CO_2 emissions, the optimal loan allocation is represented by Point b. If banks prioritize only output and profitability, they would choose Point a, whereas incorporating environmental considerations makes Point b the preferable choice.

In the second quadrant, output (Y1+Y2) is represented, while CO_2 emissions from SMEs 1 and 2 are shown in the fourth quadrant. By combining these two factors, the first quadrant can be used to analyze the relationship between output and CO_2

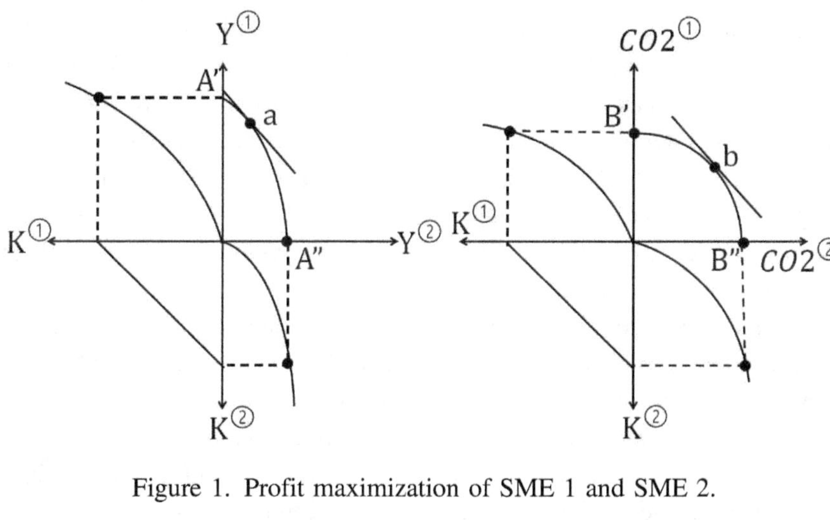

Figure 1. Profit maximization of SME 1 and SME 2.

Source: Authors' depiction.

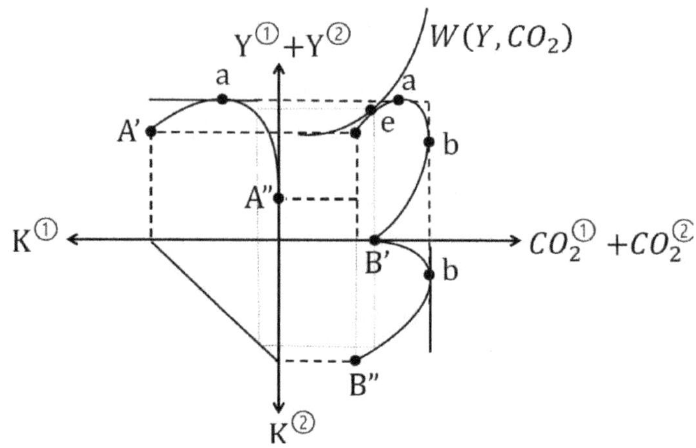

Figure 2. Profit maximization of SME 1 and SME 2 (mixed approach).

Source: Authors' depiction.

emissions. Traditionally, Point a represents maximum output and Point b indicates the peak CO_2 emissions. However, when environmental considerations are included, the optimal balance shifts to Point e in the first quadrant, where profit and emissions are jointly evaluated.

Banks should adopt a dual-criteria approach to guiding SMEs toward selecting Point e over Points a or b. This approach integrates output and CO_2 emissions into loan allocation models. By incentivizing green activities, such as cleaner production methods and energy-efficient practices, banks can promote environmentally responsible behavior among SMEs. This approach aligns financial and environmental objectives and motivates SMEs to adopt sustainable practices.

Another critical aspect of this issue is how SMEs can enhance their focus on reducing CO_2 emissions. The size of a company significantly influences its approach to environmental protection. While large corporations face pressure from investors to adopt sustainable practices, SMEs often lack such external scrutiny. If governments enforce carbon taxes across all companies, SMEs may encounter challenges due to limited resources. As illustrated in Eqs. (9) and (10), incorporating a carbon tax (t) into the profit optimization framework reduces profitability for SMEs. This underscores the need for carefully designed policies that balance environmental goals with the economic viability of smaller enterprises.

The coefficient θ also represents technological advancements that influence output and CO_2 emissions. SMEs must adopt improved technologies to enhance energy efficiency and lower carbon intensity. However, this transition often requires external support. Governments play a crucial role in facilitating this by implementing targeted policies and initiatives, such as subsidies, tax incentives, and grants, to encourage SMEs to invest in cleaner and more efficient technologies.

$$\frac{\partial \pi^{\text{SME}}}{\partial E^s} = \theta \frac{Y^{\text{SME}}}{E^s} - P_E - t \frac{\partial \text{CO}_2{}^s}{\partial E^s} \tag{9}$$

$$\pi^s = Y^s - P_E E^s - rK^s - w^{as} - t\text{CO}_2{}^2 \tag{10}$$

Mathematically, when an SME incorporates both output and CO_2 emissions into its operational considerations, its production output can be expressed through Eqs. (11) and (12):

$$G(Y^s, \text{CO}_2{}^s) = (K^s)^\alpha (N^s)^\beta (E^s)^\theta \tag{11}$$

$$(Y^s)^a (\text{CO}_2{}^s)^b = (K^s)^\alpha (N^s)^\beta (E^s)^\theta \tag{12}$$

Equation (12) can be transformed into logarithmic form as Eq. (13):

$$a \log Y^s + b \log (\text{CO}_2{}^s) = \alpha \log K^s + \beta \log N^s + \theta \log E^s \tag{13}$$

The derivations of Eq. (13) regarding energy are Eq. (14) as follows:

$$\frac{\partial \log \text{CO}_2{}^s}{\partial \log E^s} = \frac{\theta}{b} \tag{14}$$

Equation (14) can be reorganized as Eq. (15):

$$\frac{\partial \text{CO}_2{}^s}{\partial E^s} \cdot \frac{\bar{E}^s}{\bar{\text{CO}}_2{}^s} = \frac{\theta}{b} \tag{15}$$

Or

$$\frac{\partial \text{CO}_2{}^s}{\partial E^s} = \frac{\theta}{b} * \frac{\overline{\text{CO}_2^s}}{\bar{E}^s} \tag{16}$$

The derivation of profit regarding energy is calculated as Eq. (17):

$$\frac{\partial \pi^s}{\partial E^s} = \theta \frac{Y^s}{E^s} - P_E - t * \frac{\theta}{b} * \frac{\overline{\text{CO}_2^s}}{\bar{E}^s} \tag{17}$$

Based on the proportion of output to energy, Eq. (18) can be calculated:

$$\theta \frac{Y^s}{E^s} = P_E + t * \frac{\theta}{b} * \frac{\overline{\text{CO}_2^s}}{\bar{E}^s} \tag{18}$$

Finally, the optimized amount of energy consumption for an SME can be reached through Eq. (19):

$$E^s = \frac{\theta * Y^s}{P_E + t * \frac{\theta}{b} * \frac{\overline{\text{CO}_2^s}}{\bar{E}^s}} \tag{19}$$

If b represents the level of CO_2 emissions and θ denotes energy intensity, implementing appropriate government policies can aid SMEs in reducing both b and θ. Under such a framework, Eq. (13) can be reformulated as Eq. (20):

$$a \log Y^s + b' \log (\text{CO}_2^s) = \alpha \log K^s + \beta \log N^s + \theta \log E^s \tag{20}$$

Where

$$b' = g(\text{tech}'), \quad \theta = t(\text{tech}') \tag{21}$$

Technological advancements transferred from large companies to SMEs present an effective solution for reducing CO_2 emissions and decreasing energy intensity. By leveraging innovations developed by larger firms, SMEs can adopt more efficient practices and contribute significantly to environmental sustainability.

Providing financial incentives for SMEs effectively encourages them toward environmentally friendly activities.

Another effective approach to encourage environmentally friendly activities among SMEs is to provide direct financial incentives. Governments can offer subsidies or green loans to support SMEs in reducing their CO_2 emissions using their technologies. Without such support, many SMEs struggle to secure the capital needed to implement effective environmental protection measures.

In addition to carbon taxation for large enterprises and SMEs, which can be politically sensitive due to widespread support for smaller businesses, three alternative policy measures are recommended:

1. **Technology Transfer from Large Companies to SMEs**

Governments encourage large corporations to innovate by reducing energy consumption (input side) and lowering CO_2 emissions in their production processes (output side). When such technological progress results in patents for energy and carbon efficiency, governments could purchase or co-invest in these patents and facilitate their transfer to SMEs for implementation. This approach not only aids smaller enterprises but could also generate additional revenue by selling these patents to foreign firms.

2. **Encouraging Technological Progress Among SMEs**

SMEs should also be incentivized to develop technologies that enhance energy efficiency and reduce carbon emissions. These innovations could be registered as patents, and governments could provide funding or purchase them to enable widespread adoption across the SME sector.

3. **Integrating CO_2 Emissions Disclosure into Bank Lending Practices**

Currently, most bank loans do not account for the carbon emissions of SMEs. For instance, 90% of SMEs in the UK are unaware of their CO_2 emission levels, a situation mirrored in other economies. Governments should build capacity to help SMEs measure and disclose their emissions. Innovative methods, such as satellite-sensed GHG data, could enable accurate assessments and facilitate the implementation of GHG taxes. This approach would align financial incentives with environmental accountability, encouraging SMEs to adopt greener practices (ul-Haq *et al.*, 2015; Huo *et al.*, 2022a).

4. Empirical Modelling and Results

4.1. *Data description*

Examining the environmental impact of SME activities is vital in the post-COVID-19 era, as efforts toward economic recovery and sustainable economic growth through SME development mark this period. This study addresses this critical issue within the context of ASEAN economies, where GDP growth and sustainable recovery have been central to economic planning over recent decades. In this analysis, CO_2 emissions are used as a proxy for environmental pollution. At the same time, the proportion of the labor force employed in SMEs relative to the total labor force (SMEEM) serves as the explanatory variable representing SME activity.

To explore the long-term relationship between CO_2 emissions and SMEEM, four additional control variables — economic growth, globalization, industrialization, and green economic promotion — are incorporated into the econometric model. The relevance of these control variables in influencing CO_2 emissions has been established in prior research. For example, globalization's impact on emissions has been studied by Farooq *et al.* (2022), Huo *et al.* (2022b), and Liu *et al.* (2020), while the relationship between industrialization and CO_2 emissions has been analyzed by Mahmood *et al.* (2020) and Aslam *et al.* (2021). Similarly, economic growth and emissions have been linked in studies by Espoir *et al.* (2022) and Karaaslan and Çamkaya (2022), and the role of green economic promotion in reducing emissions has been explored by Dong *et al.* (2022) and Hao *et al.* (2021). This research contributes to understanding how SME activities in ASEAN economies interact with broader environmental and economic factors, offering insights into achieving a sustainable balance between development and environmental protection.

The selected variables for data were collected through various databases that cover the period 2010 to 2020. The starting year, 2010, was chosen because this study utilizes the Global Green Economy Index (GGEI) as a proxy for green development introduced that year. Additionally, data for certain variables were not available for 2021 and 2022. Hence, to ensure a balanced data panel for the 10 ASEAN member countries, 2020 was set as the endpoint.

The primary information of selected variables is presented in Table 1.

4.2. *Econometric equation strategy*

According to the selected variables, the initial econometric equation can be written as shown in Eq. (9):

$$\begin{aligned} \mathrm{CO}_{i,t} = \alpha_0 + \alpha_1.\mathrm{SMEEM}_{i,t} + \alpha_2.\mathrm{KOF}_{i,t} + \alpha_3.\mathrm{INDUS}_{i,t} + \alpha_4.\mathrm{GGEI}_{i,t} \\ + \alpha_5.\mathrm{ECOGR}_{i,t} + \varepsilon_{i,t} \end{aligned} \tag{22}$$

Table 1. Variables' information.

Variable	Symbol	Unit	Source
CO_2 emissions	CO	Kilo tons	World Bank, BP
Employees in SMEs/Total labor force * 100 (ratio)	SMEEM	%	World Bank, ADB, and official websites of ASEAN countries
Globalization index	KOF	—	KOF Swiss Economic Institute
Industry, value added (% growth)	INDUS	%	World Bank
Global Green Economic Index	GGEI	—	Knoema
Economic growth	ECOGR	%	World Bank, official websites of ASEAN countries

Source: Authors' calculations.

To identify the most suitable estimation method, it is essential to analyze the characteristics and properties of the selected variables. The initial step is to conduct a unit root test to assess the stationarity of the variables. This involves employing two widely recognized panel unit root tests: the augmented Dickey–Fuller (ADF) and Phillips–Perron (PP) tests. If the variables are stationary at their first difference, it suggests the potential for a long-run relationship among them. To confirm this, the Johansen co-integration test is subsequently performed. Once co-integration is verified, the study employs the FMOLS method to estimate the model parameters. FMOLS, introduced by Phillips and Hansen (1990), is designed to handle small sample sizes while addressing potential endogeneity and serial correlation issues, ensuring accurate and reliable estimates (Faruque *et al.*, 2022).

4.3. *Estimation results*

This study's panel unit root tests provide essential insights into the variables' stationarity. Table 2 presents the results, demonstrating that all variables achieve stationarity after their first differences. This suggests the potential for long-run relationships among the variables, which justifies proceeding with further co-integration analysis.

The Johansen co-integration test confirms the presence of long-term relationships. Before conducting the test, the optimal lag length must be identified, which is determined using the Akaike Information Criterion (AIC) and the Bayesian Information Criterion (BIC). Table 3 summarizes the outcomes of the Johansen co-integration test, which reveals a single co-integration vector using the trace approach.

These results confirm the existence of a long-term equilibrium relationship between the dependent and explanatory variables.

The Westerlund co-integration test is applied as an additional validation method to ensure robustness. As shown in Table 4, the results corroborate the findings of the Johansen co-integration test, further affirming the long-run relationship among the variables under study.

Table 2. Panel unit root tests.

		CO	SMEEM	KOF	INDUS	GGEI	ECOGR
ADF test	Level	1	1	1	1	1	1
	1st difference	0.002	0.007	0.001	0.004	0.006	0.003
PP test	Level	1	1	1	1	1	1
	1st difference	0.002	0.009	0.001	0.001	0.004	0.006
KPSS test	Level	1.239	−0.032	0.024	0.047	1.202	−0.029
	1st difference	9.392	−2.304	6.172	7.183	10.489	−3.956

Note: CO, SMEEM, KOF, INDUS, GGEI, and ECOGR stand for CO_2 emissions, SME employees to total labor force, globalization index, industry value added, global green economy index, and economic growth, respectively.
Source: Authors' calculations.

Table 3. Johansen co-integration test.

Trace			
Hypothesized no of CE(s)	Eigenvalue	Trace stat.	*p*-value
None*	0.48443	45.1173	0.0060
At most 1	0.30130	14.2912	0.0732
At most 2	0.02192	2.00179	0.1403
Maximum eigenvalue			
Hypothesized no of CE(s)	Eigenvalue	Max-Eigen	*p*-value
None*	0.48443	22.6038	0.0153
At most 1	0.30130	11.3829	0.0948
At most 2	0.02192	2.00179	0.1143

Source: Authors' calculations.

Table 4. Robustness check of co-integration test.

Statistic	Value
Gt	−1.702**
Ga	−2.283
Pt	−4.392**
Pa	−1.293***

Source: Authors' calculations.

Table 5. FMOLS estimation results.

Variable	Coefficient	p-value
Employees in SMEs/Total labor force*100 (ratio)	3.452	0.011
Globalization index	−1.387	0.885
Industry, value added (% growth)	1.101	0.000
Global Green Economic Index	−0.738	0.0567
Economic growth	3.989	0.003

Source: Authors' calculations.

The FMOLS method is then used to estimate the coefficients of the explanatory variables. The results, reported in Table 5, provide critical insights into the dynamics of SME activity and environmental outcomes in ASEAN economies.

The findings indicate that an increase in the proportion of employees in SMEs contributes positively to CO_2 emissions, highlighting that SME development in these countries currently needs to be aligned with sustainable development objectives. This relationship suggests that higher labor involvement in SMEs results in increased production and activity, which ultimately leads to more significant environmental degradation. These findings are consistent with studies by Efobi *et al.* (2019), Jabbour *et al.* (2022), Yin *et al.* (2022), and Yan *et al.* (2022). However, they contrast with research by Samargandi and Sohag (2022) and Xiang *et al.* (2022), emphasizing the potential for SMEs to play a positive role in reducing environmental pollution.

This outcome underscores the need for ASEAN economies to adopt targeted reforms that align SME growth with green initiatives. Strategies to manage the relationship between SME development and CO_2 emissions should focus on promoting environmentally sustainable practices in small and medium enterprises.

The analysis finds a negative but statistically insignificant coefficient regarding the globalization index, suggesting no significant long-term relationship between globalization and CO_2 emissions in ASEAN countries. While globalization has the potential to facilitate sustainable development through technology transfer and the exchange of innovative ideas, its impact on emissions reduction in ASEAN remains limited. This aligns with findings by Farooq *et al.* (2022), Huo *et al.* (2022b), and Liu *et al.* (2020). To harness the benefits of globalization, ASEAN nations must adopt "green globalization" strategies, as suggested by Zhang *et al.* (2022), which could promote economic, social, and political integration while advancing green energy development.

Industrialization shows a positive and statistically significant relationship with CO_2 emissions, with a 1% increase in industrial value-added growth, leading to approximately a 1.1% rise in emissions. This relationship reflects the reliance of ASEAN industries on outdated technologies, high energy intensity, and non-renewable energy sources. While industrialization has driven economic progress in the region, these limitations hinder its sustainability. Policymakers must focus on transitioning industries toward cleaner, more energy-efficient practices to align industrial growth with environmental goals.

The green economic indicator negatively and significantly impacts CO_2 emissions, indicating that efforts to promote green policies in ASEAN over the past decade have been effective. These findings suggest that ASEAN nations should continue developing innovative financing instruments and incentive programs to support green economic recovery. Such initiatives include increasing energy efficiency, expanding the use of renewable energy, and strengthening commitments to environmental standards.

Finally, the results reveal a strong positive relationship between economic growth and CO_2 emissions in ASEAN member states, with a coefficient of approximately 3.9 — the highest among all explanatory variables. This indicates that GDP growth in the region is not currently aligned with green growth principles. The findings highlight the critical need for ASEAN economies to adopt strategies that decouple economic expansion from environmental degradation, especially as the post-COVID-19 era emphasizes rapid recovery and growth. Failure to address this issue will exacerbate global climate change and undermine long-term sustainability objectives.

4.4. *Robustness check*

Two additional checks are performed to ensure the robustness and validity of the empirical estimations. First, the dynamic ordinary least squares (DOLS) estimator is employed as an alternative to the FMOLS method. Pedroni (2001) proposed the group-mean DOLS estimation approach to address the homogenous slope coefficients inherent in the DOLS technique. The results of this robustness check are presented in Table 6.

The results confirm that the coefficients for the ratio of employees in SMEs remain positive and statistically significant. This is consistent with the results obtained through FMOLS in Table 5, which validates the reliability of the initial empirical analysis.

The second robustness check involves modifying and replacing the control variables in the model. The inflation rate and urbanization are substitutes for economic growth and the globalization index, respectively. The results of this alternative estimation are summarized in Table 7.

Table 6. Group-mean DOLS estimation results (1st robustness check).

Variable	Coefficient	*p*-value
Employees in SMEs/Total labor force*100 (ratio)	0.043	0.002
Globalization index	−0.493	0.319
Industry, value added (% growth)	0.002	0.024
Global Green Economic Index	−0.101	0.000
Economic growth	1.203	0.014

Source: Authors' calculations.

Table 7. FMOLS estimation with new control variables (2nd robustness check).

Variable	Coefficient	*p*-value
Employees in SMEs/Total labor force*100 (ratio)	0.011	0.015
Urbanization	0.024	0.004
Industry, value added (% growth)	0.192	0.131
Global Green Economic Index	−0.039	0.000
Inflation rate	0.004	0.001

Source: Authors' calculations.

Despite replacing control variables, the coefficient for the ratio of employees in SMEs remains positive and significant. This outcome reinforces the reliability of the primary findings presented in Table 5. This confirms the robustness of the empirical analysis and its conclusions.

5. Conclusions and Practical Policy Implications

5.1. *Concluding remarks*

This study explored the relationship between SMEs and CO_2 emissions in ASEAN countries from 2010 to 2020, focusing on their role in achieving carbon neutrality. While SMEs are critical drivers of economic development in the region, the findings highlight their significant contribution to CO_2 emissions, underscoring a misalignment between SME growth and sustainability goals. The analysis reveals that current SME development pathways are incompatible with environmental protection objectives, creating a pressing need for targeted reforms. Achieving carbon neutrality requires revisiting existing sustainability policies to integrate SMEs into the broader framework of green growth. This includes implementing targeted green financing mechanisms, revising environmental regulations to encompass SME operations, and restructuring bank lending practices to incentivize sustainable business models. Additionally, governments must prioritize policies that promote green technologies and low-carbon industrial practices within the SME sector. By addressing these gaps, ASEAN countries can align SME development with their sustainability objectives, fostering a balanced approach to economic growth and environmental protection.

5.2. *Policy implications*

Based on the study's findings and recent research trends, the following policy recommendations are proposed to align SME development in ASEAN with carbon neutrality and sustainable growth:

1. **Enhance Access to Green Financing**

Governments and financial institutions should develop and expand green financial products tailored to SMEs, such as concessional loans, grants, and green bonds. These instruments can support SMEs in adopting energy-efficient technologies and implementing low-carbon business practices. Non-financial support, including advisory services, can enhance SMEs' capacity to navigate sustainability transitions. A study by Saydaliev and Chin (2023) emphasizes the importance of financial incentives in promoting low-carbon practices within supply chains, highlighting the role of cost-sharing and preferential financing mechanisms in encouraging SMEs to adopt sustainable practices.

2. **Implement Carbon Pricing Mechanisms**

Introducing carbon taxes or cap-and-trade systems can incentivize SMEs to reduce emissions by integrating carbon costs into their operational decisions. Revenues generated from these mechanisms can be reinvested into SME-targeted programs, such as subsidies for renewable energy adoption or technology modernization. Ohlendorf *et al.* (2021) discuss the effectiveness of carbon pricing in bridging the gap between policy ambitions and actual emission reductions, suggesting that well-designed carbon pricing mechanisms can drive SMEs toward greener practices.

3. **Facilitate Technology Transfer and Regional Collaboration**

Establishing partnerships between SMEs and larger corporations or research institutions can accelerate the transfer of green technologies. Regional cooperation within ASEAN can facilitate the dissemination of innovations and best practices, enabling SMEs to modernize production processes and adopt sustainable practices more effectively. Schaper (2022) highlights the critical role of substantial investments in green and low-carbon initiatives to address climate change effectively and promote sustainable economic growth, underscoring the importance of collaborative efforts in technology transfer.

4. **Support Renewable Energy Adoption**

Governments should provide subsidies or tax incentives for SMEs to integrate renewable energy sources into their operations. Policies such as feed-in tariffs for small-scale renewable energy projects can promote the transition from fossil fuels, reducing SMEs' carbon footprints while enhancing energy security. A study by Taghizadeh-Hesary and Phoumin (2023) examines how internal carbon pricing impacts carbon reduction, indicating that such measures can facilitate SMEs' adoption of renewable energy.

5. **Mandate Corporate Sustainability Reporting**

Introducing policies that encourage or require SMEs to disclose their environmental performance, including GHG emissions and energy consumption, can drive improvements in sustainability practices and attract environmentally conscious investors and customers. Taghizadeh-Hesary *et al.* (2020) provide a meta-analysis of the distributional impacts of carbon pricing, suggesting that transparency in environmental performance can enhance the effectiveness of such policies and promote equitable outcomes.

These policy recommendations highlight practical strategies for enabling ASEAN SMEs to align their operations with carbon-neutral objectives. By prioritizing access to green financing, renewable energy adoption, and technology transfer, ASEAN governments can create a supportive environment for SMEs to contribute to sustainable growth and environmental protection.

5.3. *Limitations and recommendations for future research*

This study significantly contributes to the literature by examining the relationship between SMEs and carbon emissions in ASEAN countries. However, several limitations warrant further exploration. First, the study uses data from 2010 to 2020 due to more recent and comprehensive dataset limitations. Incorporating up-to-date data could enhance the robustness of the findings, especially as the landscape of green economic recovery continues to evolve. Second, a panel data approach limits the ability to capture country-specific dynamics within ASEAN. While this approach provides a broad overview, it may overlook individual member states' unique socioeconomic and policy environments. Third, the econometric model employed is suitable for the study's objectives; however, it does not account for nonlinear relationships or interactions that may influence the relationship between SMEs and environmental outcomes.

Future research should explore deeper country-specific analyses within ASEAN to account for individual member states' unique socioeconomic and policy environments, providing more tailored insights and recommendations. Employing advanced econometric techniques, such as machine learning and artificial neural networks, could uncover complex nonlinear relationships and improve predictions of SME impacts on environmental outcomes. Additionally, examining SMEs' adoption of green technologies, including barriers and the effectiveness of policy incentives, would offer valuable insights for promoting energy-efficient and low-carbon innovations. Studies could also explore the transition of SMEs to circular economy models, emphasizing resource efficiency and waste reduction across micro (firm-level), meso (industry-level), and macro (policy-level) dimensions. Furthermore, sector-specific research could identify the environmental challenges and opportunities unique to industries such as manufacturing, agriculture, and services, enabling targeted strategies for green growth. Finally, future studies should assess the long-term effectiveness of green financing initiatives and regulatory frameworks, comparing ASEAN policies with those of other regions to derive actionable lessons for aligning SME activities with sustainable and carbon-neutral objectives.

References

Agrawal, R, S Agrawal, A Samadhiya, A Kumar, S Luthra and V Jain (2024). Adoption of green finance and green innovation for achieving circularity: An exploratory review and future directions. *Geoscience Frontiers*, 15(4), 101669.

Alam, A, AM Du, M Rahman, H Yazdifar and K Abbasi (2022). SMEs respond to climate change: Evidence from developing countries. *Technological Forecasting and Social Change*, 185, 122087, doi: 10.1016/j.techfore.2022.122087.

Alava, JJ and GG Singh (2022). Changing air pollution and CO_2 emissions during the COVID-19 pandemic: Lessons learned and future equity concerns of post-COVID recovery. *Environmental Science and Policy*, 130, 1–8, doi: 10.1016/j.envsci.2022.01.006.

Alraja, MN, R Imran, BM Khashab and M Shah (2022). Technological innovation, sustainable green practices, and SMEs sustainable performance in times of crisis (COVID-19 pandemic). *Information Systems Frontiers*, 24(4), 1081–1105.

ASEAN Secretariat (2015). *ASEAN Economic Community Blueprint 2025*. ASEAN Secretariat.

Aslam, B, J Hu, S Shahab, A Ahmad, M Saleem, SSA Shah and M Hassan (2021). The nexus of industrialization, GDP per capita, and CO2 emission in China. *Environmental Technology and Innovation*, 23, 101674, doi: 10.1016/j.eti.2021.101674.

Chien, F, QT Ngo, CC Hsu, KY Chau and R Iram (2021). Assessing the mechanism of barriers towards green finance and public spending in small and medium enterprises from developed countries. *Environmental Science and Pollution Research*, 28(43), 60495–60510.

Choudhary, P, NK Kumar Jain and A Panda (2022). Making SMEs circular economy compliant by reducing single-use plastic. *Journal of Business Research*, 149, 448–462, doi: 10.1016/j.jbusres.2022.05.038.

Dai, R, H Feng, J Hu, Q Jin, H Li, R Wang and X Zhang (2021). The impact of COVID-19 on small and medium-sized enterprises (SMEs): Evidence from two-wave phone surveys in China. *China Economic Review*, 67, 101607, doi: 10.1016/j.chieco.2021.101607.

Dong, K, B Wang, J Zhao and F Taghizadeh-Hesary (2022). Mitigating carbon emissions by accelerating green growth in China. *Economic Analysis and Policy*, 75, 226–243, doi: 10.1016/j.eap.2022.05.011.

Efobi, U, T Belmondo, E Orkoh, SN Atata, O Akinyemi and I Beecroft (2019). Environmental pollution policy of small businesses in Nigeria and Ghana: Extent and impact. *Environmental Science and Pollution Research International*, 26(3), 2882–2897, doi: 10.1007/s11356-018-3817.

Espoir, DK, B Mudiangombe Mudiangombe, F Bannor, R Sunge and JM Tshitaka (2022). CO_2 emissions and economic growth: Assessing the heterogeneous effects across African climate regimes. *Science of the Total Environment*, 804, 150089, doi: 10.1016/j.scitotenv.2021.150089.

Farooq, S, I Ozturk, MT Majeed and R Akram (2022). Globalisation and CO_2 emissions: A global panel analysis. *Gondwana Research*, 106, 367–378, doi: 10.1016/j.gr.2022.02.002.

Faruque, MO, MAJ Rabby, MA Hossain, MR Islam, MMU Rashid and SM Muyeen (2022). A comparative analysis to forecast carbon dioxide emissions. *Energy Reports*, 8, 8046–8060, doi: 10.1016/j.egyr.2022.06.025.

Fawcett, T and S Hampton (2020). Why and how energy efficiency policy should address SMEs. *Energy Policy*, 140, 111337, doi: 10.1016/j.enpol.2020.111337.

Gennari, F (2023). The transition towards a circular economy. A framework for SMEs. *Journal of Management and Governance*, 27(4), 1423–1457.

Gherghina, ŞC, MA Botezatu, A Hosszu and LN Simionescu (2020). Small and medium-sized enterprises (SMEs): The engine of economic growth through investments and innovation. *Sustainability*, 12(1), 347.

Hao, LN, M Umar, Z Khan and W Ali (2021). Green growth and low carbon emission in G7 countries: How critical the network of environmental taxes, renewable energy, and human capital is? *Science of the Total Environment*, 752, 141853, doi: 10.1016/j.scitotenv.2020.141853.

Huo, C, J Hameed, A Sharif and NU Baig (2022b). Nexus of globalisation to CO_2 emissions. *Environmental Research*, 212(A), 113067, doi: 10.1016/j.envres.2022.113067.

Huo, C, J Hameed, A Sharif, G Albasher, O Alamri, N Alsultan and NU Baig (2022a). Recent scenario and nexus of globalisation to CO_2 emissions: Evidence from wavelet and Quantile on Quantile Regression approach. *Environmental Research*, 212(A), 113067, doi: 10.1016/j.envres.2022.113067.

Jabbour, ABLS, NO Ndubisi and BM Roman Pais Seles (2022). Sustainable development in Asian manufacturing SMEs: Progress and directions. *Journal of Cleaner Production*, 355, 131781, doi: 10.1016/j.jclepro.2022.131781.

Jamwal, A, R Agrawal and M Sharma (2023). Challenges and opportunities for SMEs in adopting Industry 4.0 technologies. *Operations Management Research*, doi: 10.1007/s12063-023-00428-2.

Karaaslan, A and S Çamkaya (2022). The relationship between CO_2 emissions, economic growth, health expenditure, and renewable and non-renewable energy consumption: Empirical evidence from Turkey. *Renewable Energy*, 190, 457–466, doi: 10.1016/j.renene.2022.03.139.

Koçyiğit, Y and B Akkaya (2020). The role of organizational flexibility in organizational agility: A research on SMEs. *Business Management and Strategy*, 11(1), 110–123.

Le, TT (2022). How do corporate social responsibility and green innovation transform corporate green strategy into sustainable firm performance? *Journal of Cleaner Production*, 362, 132228, doi: 10.1016/j.jclepro.2022.132228.

Li, R and S Li (2021). Carbon emission post-coronavirus: Continual decline or rebound? *Structural Change and Economic Dynamics*, 57, 57–67, doi: 10.1016/j.strueco.2021.01.008.

Liu, L, J Zhang, J Xu and Y Wang (2022). Intellectual capital and financial performance of Chinese manufacturing SMEs: An analysis from the perspective of different industry types. *Sustainability*, 14(17), 10657.

Liu, M, X Ren, C Cheng and Z Wang (2020). Globalisation and CO_2 emissions in G7. *Science of the Total Environment*, 718, 137379, doi: 10.1016/j.scitotenv.2020.137379.

Liu, Z, P Ciais, Z Deng, R Lei, SJ Davis, S Feng and HJ Schellnhuber (2020). Near-real-time monitoring of global CO_2 emissions reveals the effects of the COVID-19 pandemic. *Nature Communications*, 11(1), 5172.

Lopes de Sousa Jabbour, AB, NO Ndubisi and BM Roman Pais Seles (2020). Sustainable development in Asian manufacturing SMEs: Progress and directions. *International Journal of Production Economics*, 225, 107567, doi: 10.1016/j.ijpe.2019.107567.

Mahmood, H, TTY Alkhateeb and M Furqan (2020). Industrialisation, urbanisation and CO_2 emissions in Saudi Arabia: Asymmetry analysis. *Energy Reports*, 6, 1553–1560, doi: 10.1016/j.egyr.2020.06.004.

Meng, B, Y Liu, R Andrew, M Zhou, K Hubacek and Y Gao (2018). More than half of China's CO_2 emissions are from micro, small, and medium-sized enterprises. *Applied Energy*, 230, 712–725, doi: 10.1016/j.apenergy.2018.08.107.

Naradda Gamage, SK, EMS Ekanayake, GAKN Abeyrathne, RPIR Prasanna, JMSB Jayasundara and PSK Rajapakshe (2020). A review of global challenges and survival strategies of small and medium enterprises (SMEs). *Economies*, 8(4), 79.

Ohlendorf, N, M Jakob, JC Minx, C Schröder and JC Steckel (2021). Distributional impacts of carbon pricing: A meta-analysis. *Environmental and Resource Economics*, 78(1), 1–42. https://doi.org/10.1007/s10640-020-00521-1.

Oliinyk, O, Y Bilan, H Mishchuk, O Akimov and L Vasa (2021). The impact of migration of highly skilled workers on the country's competitiveness and economic growth. *Montenegrin Journal of Economics*.

OECD (2018). *SME Policy Index: Environmental Policies and SMEs*. OECD iLibrary.

OECD (2021). *Facilitating the Green Transition for SMEs*. OECD iLibrary.

OECD (2023). *SMEs: Key Drivers of Green and Inclusive Growth*. OECD iLibrary.

Ozanne, LK, M Chowdhury, G Prayag and DA Mollenkopf (2022). SMEs navigating COVID-19: The influence of social capital and dynamic capabilities on organisational resilience. *Industrial Marketing Management*, 104, 116–135, doi: 10.1016/j.indmarman.2022.04.009.

Pedroni, P (2001). Purchasing power parity tests in cointegrated panels. *Review of Economics and Statistics*, 83(4), 727–731, doi: 10.1162/003465301753237803.

Phillips, PCB and BE Hansen (1990). Statistical inference in instrumental variables regression with I(1) processes. *Review of Economic Studies*, 57(1), 99–125, doi: 10.2307/2297545.

Purwandani, D and G Michaud (2021). What are the drivers and barriers for green business practices? *Environment Systems and Decisions*, 41(1), 135–149, doi: 10.1007/s10669-021-09821-3.

Ruggerio, CA (2021). Sustainability and sustainable development: A review of principles and definitions. *Science of the Total Environment*, 786, 147481.

Sage (2023). U.S. SMEs struggle with sustainability more than global peers. Sage Report.

Samargandi, N and K Sohag (2022). The interaction of finance and innovation for a low-carbon economy: Evidence from Saudi Arabia. *Energy Strategy Reviews*, 41, 100847, doi: 10.1016/j.esr.2022.100847.

Saydaliev, HB and L Chin (2023). Role of green financing and financial inclusion to develop the cleaner environment for macroeconomic stability: Inter-temporal analysis of ASEAN economies. *Economic Change and Restructuring*, 56(4), 3839–3859. https://doi.org/10.1007/s10644-022-09419-y.

Schaper, MT (2022). SME responses to climate change in Southeast Asia. *ISEAS–Yusof Ishak Institute, Trends in Southeast Asia*, 2022(2), 1–37.

Schaper, MT and RYY Wong (2021). Calculating the carbon footprint and minimum greenhouse gas production of SMEs in Southeast Asia. *ISEAS Perspective*, 2021(169), 1–13.

Shahzad, M, Y Qu, SU Rehman and AU Zafar (2022). Adoption of green innovation technology to accelerate sustainable development among manufacturing industry. *Journal of Innovation & Knowledge*, 7(4), 100231.

Shihata, LA, AA Ghaly and J Kiefer (2022). Energy efficiency improvement in manufacturing SMEs. *Procedia CIRP*, 107, 729–733, doi: 10.1016/j.procir.2022.05.053.

Sikarwar, VS, A Reichert, M Jeremias and V Manovic (2021). COVID-19 pandemic and global carbon dioxide emissions: A first assessment. *Science of the Total Environment*, 794, 148770, doi: 10.1016/j.scitotenv.2021.148770.

Singh, AK (2022). A study on the growth and role of SMES in Indian economy. *International Journal of Financial Management and Economics*, 5(2), 114–117.

Statista (2023). Leading ESG implementation challenges for SMEs in Asia Pacific. Statista Report.

Taghizadeh-Hesary, F and H Phoumin (2023). *Green Finance and Renewable Energy in ASEAN and East Asia*. Economic Research Institute for ASEAN and East Asia.

Taghizadeh-Hesary, F, H Phoumin and E Rasoulinezhad (2023). SMEs and carbon neutrality in ASEAN: The need to revisit sustainability policies. *Economic Research-Ekonomska Istraživanja*, 36(1), 1234–1250. https://doi.org/10.1080/1331677X.2023.2177180.

ul-Haq, Z, AD Rana, M Ali, K Mahmood, S Tariq and Z Qayyum (2015). Carbon monoxide (CO) emissions and its tropospheric variability over Pakistan using satellite-sensed data. *Advances in Space Research*, 56(4), 583–595, doi: 10.1016/j.asr.2015.04.026.

Wang, D, R Si and S Fahad (2023). Evaluating the small and medium sized enterprises motivating factors and influencing barriers about adoption of green practices. *Environment, Development and Sustainability*, 25(4), 3029–3041.

World Economic Forum (2023a). *Data Unleashed: Empowering Small and Medium Enterprises (SMEs) for Innovation and Success*. World Economic Forum.

World Economic Forum (2023b). *Why SMEs are Key to a More Sustainable and Inclusive World*. World Economic Forum.

Xiang, D, T Zhao and N Zhang (2022). How can government environmental policy affect the performance of SMEs: Chinese evidence. *Journal of Cleaner Production*, 336, 130308, doi: 10.1016/j.jclepro.2021.130308.

Yan, Y, Y Chen and J Miao (2022). Eco-innovation in SMEs: A scientometric review. *Environmental Science and Pollution Research International*, 29(32), 48105–48125, doi: 10.1007/s11356-022-20657-5.

Yin, C, MP Salmador, D Li and MB Lloria (2022). Green entrepreneurship and SME performance: The moderating effect of firm age. *International Entrepreneurship and Management Journal*, 18(1), 255–275, doi: 10.1007/s11365-021-00757-3.

Zhang, D and Y Fang (2022). Are environmentally friendly firms more vulnerable during the COVID-19 pandemic? *Journal of Cleaner Production*, 355, 131781, doi: 10.1016/j.jclepro.2022.131781.

https://doi.org/10.1142/9789819812783_0002

ACHIEVING GREENHOUSE GAS MITIGATION THROUGH CLIMATE CHANGE CONTROL WITH THE ROLE OF FINANCIAL DEVELOPMENT: INSIGHTS FROM BRICS[††]

ZHEN LIU[*,§], JIALI TIAN[*,¶], LEILING WANG[†,||] and RUBAB GUL[‡,**]

[*]*School of Business, Nanjing Normal University, P. R. China*

[†]*School of Business, Zhengzhou University, Zhengzhou 450001, P. R. China*

[‡]*School of Business, NUML University, Islamabad, Pakistan*

[§]*zhenliu_cn@yahoo.com*

[¶]*tianjiali_1999@163.com*

[||]*wangleiling@zzu.edu.cn*

[**]*rubabgul414@gmail.com*

The study inquired the role of financial development (FD) on climate change control in COVID-19 period to identify the ways useful to achieve greenhouse gas mitigation in BRICS economies. BRICS countries are included because of their high energy-environment dependence and their need for climate financing through FD promoting greenhouse gas emission. The projected role of FD activity on climate change mitigation is inferred using the generalized methods of moments (GMM). The study results indicated that five out of the six climate change mitigation indicators have a long-term correlation with BRICS's CO_2 emissions. On the other side, there is no evidence of integration between variables in Russia. Moreover, the findings revealed that there 18% rise in FD is estimated, this raised the probability of effective climate change mitigation by 39% in the post-COVID-period, and it reduces greenhouse gas mitigations by 24.7%. The results also highlighted that there is a one-way correlation between energy use and climate drifts. On these findings, policymakers and environmental regulators in BRICS could take inspiration from our study to plan and revisit greenhouse gas mitigation through proper environmental legislation. Additionally, it also encourages other countries and economies to perform comparable assessments and select the best course of action. Hence, this study provides detailed and viable recommendations for key stakeholders for consideration and application to achieve the intended objectives.

Keywords: Financial development; climate change mitigation; greenhouse gas mitigation; COVID-19 period; BRICS economies.

[§]Corresponding author.

[††]This chapter was originally published in Climate Change Economics, Vol. 13, No. 3, April 2022, published by World Scientific Publishing, Singapore. Reprinted with permission.

1. Introduction

Countless tragic catastrophes have marred the start of the 21st century, affecting institutions throughout the world (Alemzero *et al.*, 2021). Fuel price upheavals arising out of global financial crises and now the COVID-19 epidemic (Iqbal and Bilal, 2021a; Li *et al.*, 2021a), which has killed many people and disrupted businesses, have questioned the basis of ecologically friendly electricity (Iqbal *et al.*, 2021a). Non-inexhaustible petroleum product energy is often used to make the majority of like-ability and electricity shippers; nonetheless, these transporters suffer from the hotness misfortune (Li *et al.*, 2021b). Higher variable sustainable power sources have an impact on the system's adaptability and its ability to sustain its stability (Anh Tu *et al.*, 2021). Despite this, the recent influenza and global economic slump have significantly weakened the global market for green activities, which might increase the risk to environmental goals (Iqbal *et al.*, 2021b).

A country's financial structure has an important role to play in the growth of both the economy and the environment because of its deterministic relevance (Ahmad *et al.*, 2021). People, climate, and the economy benefit from a sustainable monetary framework, rather than simply those who benefit from the system itself. On the other hand, the phrase "green money" encompasses not just environmental finance (Iqbal and Bilal, 2021b)), but also other natural aims such as sustainable development, and a safe ecosystem monetary framework that includes green loans, green securities, and green home equity lines of credit (Alemzero *et al.*, 2021).

To put it simply, funding is a major roadblock to the growth of environmentally friendly electricity (Creutzig *et al.*, 2015a). The bulk of world energy speculations began in 2018 with coal and oil as the primary sources of carbon emissions (Zhang *et al.*, 2021). About 39% of energy-related investments were made in environmentally friendly energy, compared to only 19% in the overall energy sector, for example. Because of the COVID-19 event and the wider financial crisis, interest in sustainable power, energy productivity, and other green projects decreased significantly in 2019–2021 (Schwanen *et al.*, 2011). Just like financial crises, the COVID-19 occurrence produced a massive reduction in oil and gas prices. Sustainable power initiatives, such as solar, wind, and other renewable power sources, are less prudent as compared to conventional power sources because of lower petroleum derivative prices. The Paris Climate Agreement and several Sustainable Development Goals (SDGs) are in jeopardy as a result of this decrease in financial supporters' premium on endless advances.

Green finance or green framework funding is still a major concern for many organizations. Because of their capital-intensive nature, these jobs need hefty borrowings. It's very uncommon for green initiatives to be associated with "greater risk and poorer returns all through the early stages of creative work" (Mi *et al.*, 2019). In Asia, where the monetary system is restricted by banks and banks are the primary sources of funding, access to capital for green activities is particularly difficult because of this. Financial speculators are rare in China, but they are more inclined to support green initiatives, since banks often see green projects as risky (Shan *et al.*, 2018). Despite the fact that China proclaimed its motivator bundles to fight the COVID-19 emergencies, these impetuses don't speed up the energy change, or some other Chinese new green arrangement has been recognized, but interest in the petroleum product over the spotless or sustainable power has been pushed.

While a wide range of work is available that examines the economic, monetary, and environmental aspects of sustainable electricity, there is still a need for more research. When it comes to strategy makers who are concerned with sustainable economic growth and climate, green money is the area of income that has yet to be explored as much as carbon dioxide (CO_2) and environmental change in the last several years. When it comes to economic growth, green money and several other elements play an important role (Sharp *et al.*, 2011). Generally speaking, there aren't a lot of questions that need an in-depth investigation in this study. First is the concern whether or not green money increases speculative interest in green power. "Green money" refers to the interest in monetary vehicles that are linked to renewable energy and other green businesses. The green money market is a reference to the resources, safeguards, and assets linked with renewable energy and other environmentally friendly efforts (Iqbal and Bilal, 2021a).

Solid green money markets are now seen as essential for the advancement of new sustainable innovation initiatives, especially in recent times (Ivanova *et al.*, 2020). Second, there is also the question of whether or not financial growth contributes to power speculation (He *et al.*, 2019). There is a strong correlation between economic growth and the development of environmentally sustainable power alternatives, according to most research (Anser *et al.*, 2020). Increased financial growth propels the nation to shift from nonecologically friendly to environmentally safe sources of electricity. As a result, more money in the bank means more people are interested in renewable energy initiatives. Third, is there any link between environmentally friendly power ventures and sustainable power output and private backing in energy speculation? Environmentally friendly electricity is becoming more popular as a result of economic growth and green money. While unlimited power output is a component of absolute sustainable power, these requirements might also be linked to sustainable power speculation (Claessens and Laeven, 2003). There is a growing need for renewable energy sources that can provide an infinite supply of electricity. Economic growth leads to a shift from nonrenewables to renewables, which in turn increases the investment of private financial supporters.

As a result of the questions posed, the present evaluation is planned to investigate the interest in CO_2 and other financial, financial, and energy-related indicators (Meltzer, 2016). At the outset, this study looks at the connection between carbon dioxide emissions and green money. Because green money is seen as a regulator of ecological sustainability, which promotes the use of renewable energy, the causative role of green finance in CO_2 is broken down (Shahbaz *et al.*, 2013). Flow studies also disentangle the causal relationship between CO_2 emissions and increases in the production of renewable electricity. In this manner, the growth of sustainable power might be essential for environmentally friendly power endeavors since inexhaustible power is one of the variables that addresses environmentally friendly power. In the third section of our study, we examine the connection between CO_2 emissions and financial progress (Chen *et al.*, 2019).

As stated in the literature, the more money spent, the more likely it is that we will make progress toward a future powered by renewable energy sources (Tamazian *et al.*, 2009). In the same way, China is a developing economic power and maintains its position as the world's second-largest economy and the leader in the importation of energy, thus its contribution to GDP is important to consider (Li *et al.*, 2021c). Finally, there are large-scale sustainable power-CO_2 initiatives despite the fact that the great majority of financial backers continue to place their resources in the petroleum product energy sector in search of higher yields. According to the present global and specifically Chinese focus on the controllable course of events, financial supporters might play a crucial role in determining the long-term viability of sustainable electricity initiatives. So, the review's last step is to investigate the link between private investment in energy and carbon dioxide emissions. The present review used GMM power range and GMM intelligence to achieve both short-term and long-term causal relationships between the components of interest (Paramati *et al.*, 2021).

The aims of the study are multifold: first, it examines the role of FD on climate change mitigation in the context of BRICS economies. Second, the study extends to investigate how greenhouses gases can be mitigated through climate change mitigation and FD. Third, what is the role of climate investment, carbon emission and greenhouse gas mitigation in these empirical nexuses? By this, the study contributes both theoretically and practically. The study extends the body of knowledge by testing the study variables and investigating the recent topicality. This is the theoretical contribution of recent research. The findings of study not only shed light on the partnership between environmental policy and financial recommendations for climate change mitigation, but also yield critical knowledge regarding greenhouses gases mitigation and economic recovery in BRICS economies. This is the practical contribution of the research. These findings, which make use of a smart approach for GMM technique, are crucial since they provide essential and innovative strategy experiences for policy makers, lead representatives and scientists. This endeavor may lead to environmentally friendly economic recovery promotion that might be positively affected by the unpredictability of these circumstances. Hence, the study presents the significant role of FD during the COVID-19 period on climate change and greenhouse gas mitigation in BRICS countries.

This study consists of five sections — introduction, literature review, methodology, results and discussion, and conclusions and policy recommendations.

2. Literature Review

Before the COVID-19 epidemic, there was a lot of writing about green money, but now, there is a lot of writing about green money that is considered insufficient

(Feng *et al.*, 2017). Only a few studies have focused on green money and venture capital in conjunction with other financial, ecological, and energy aspects (Green *et al.*, 2006). China's justifiable development and production-based CO_2 emissions from 1998 to 2017 were examined that focused on the role of green speculation (Liu *et al.*, 2019). The review used an autoregressive dispersed slacks integration technique and found that long-term CO_2 outflows and their drivers are linked to creation. Results reveal that green investments and ecologically responsible electricity consumption significantly reduce CO_2 emissions, but transparent exchanges increase them. These final two characteristics are essential for Chinese growth to be controllable. As much as green enterprise is associated with sustainable development, COVID-19 is a test for every sector (Xu and Li, 2020).

Green securities markets are examined in this regard in order to examine their role in the post-COVID-19 phase of green money facilitation (Wilson *et al.*, 1998). For the Asia and Pacific regions, the review used a pooled OLS and totaled the least squares assessment of least squares. According to the results of the experiments, the increased risk and heterogeneity associated with green bonds led to a higher yield (Muganyi *et al.*, 2021). In addition, the focus claimed that 60% of the green security market was influenced by the banking sector (Yuan *et al.*, 2021). However, the returns on the green bonds issued by the banking sector were lower than expected (Wang *et al.*, 2021).

However, it is argued that the financial sector had a worse capacity for absorption of unexpected hazards (Zaman *et al.*, 2016). COVID-19's financial institutions and markets require immediate assistance because of this component. A need for carbon-free and eco-friendly ecological arrangements was thus established in order to meet realistic natural goals, according to the assessment. However, green money, such as green inclines, green securities, and greenhouse loans, may be a realistic option for achieving natural maintainability. The SDGs and the Paris Agreement on Climate Change are also linked to environmental sustainability (Opp *et al.*, 2014). As a result, the COVID-19 pandemic's optimum SDG portfolio selection was the focus of attention. The model for the best allocation of resources in the SDGs was constructed in a hypothetical manner. According to the findings, the present allocation of financial supporters to SDGs depends on several counseling groups, resulting in the mutilation of the venture portfolio. As an alternative method, environmental pollution and waste disposal may be used to create an optimal portfolio (Powlson *et al.*, 2014).

It was concluded by earlier studies that preparing for green production and carbon assessment might be beneficial in dealing with ecological difficulties such as energy reuse, CO_2 emissions, and garbage recycling. China's 2020 energy plan was evaluated and it was found that the adoption of most current innovations like heat syphoning, heat-and-power storage and demand response fundamentally increases energy production while reducing fuel consumption and annual costs. As a result, enthusiasm in green projects has decreased environmental risks and increased the amount of renewable energy in the overall power mix (Creutzig *et al.*, 2015b). However, following the invention of COVID-19, the circumstances for each monetary movement changed. COVID-19 pandemic's influence on the techniques for appropriate energy in both present and future conditions was examined in this way. COVID-19's influence on sustainable power advancement methods necessitates the identification of short-term demands, according to the authors.

In the same way, both mid- and long-term operational methods should be designed to achieve environmentally friendly power goals in the most effective and sustainable manner possible (Rogelj *et al.*, 2013). The researchers looked at the BRICS countries from 2005 to 2019 and used the differentiation in differences (DID) approach to examine the green money and environmental change alleviation nexus (Klenert *et al.*, 2020). Results of this review showed that the use of environmentally friendly power sources and populations of fossil fuel byproducts (FDI), expansion, FDI, specialized participation award, innovative work (R&D), and speculation with the private sector primarily contribute to green financing and environmental change moderation in districts (Condon *et al.*, 2009). Furthermore, the examination looked into how the new pandemic, COVID-19, might be managed and progressed.

According to the evaluation, progress toward the SDGs was lacking prior to the epidemic, and funding for their achievement may be reduced as a result (Nielsen *et al.*, 2020). That being said, the evaluation acknowledges that a shift in the allocation of petroleum derivatives for sustainable power and energy distribution, as well as a carbon tax that promotes environmental arrangements, might more easily contribute to SDGs achievement in the COVID-19 pandemic time period (Peeters and Dubois, 2010). In addition to the final alternative study, researchers are exploring the accepted procedures and channels for the green financial recuperation and expanding practical and thorough ventures, as well as examining the accepted processes and channels for the green financial recovery (Paltsev and Capros, 2013).

The COVID-19 epidemic has also been linked to a substantial drop in energy demand, which lowers the cost of energy, which has also slowed down the spread of ecologically beneficial power plants (Warren *et al.*, 2013). It is also claimed here that clean energy ventures may be based on ecologically friendly power generation, particularly in power generation. COVID-19's influence on the global energy market was also discussed, as well as the methods for generating sustainable energy by the designers (Huang *et al.*, 2021). An analysis conducted by Kong *et al.* (2021) shows that investing in metropolitan formative projects, such as high-speed rail lines, significantly boosts green money and increases green efficiency. These speculations, however, have a favorable influence on the economy in the beginning and then gradually decrease. Additionally, there are studies that focus on the central idea of green money, such as an analysis of public expenditure and green FD in the BRICS region from 2008 to 2018, which examines the role of green money in that time period.

It has been shown that public investment in human resources and efficient power energy innovation R&D boosts the green and practical economy by using the GMM evaluation approach (Miao *et al.*, 2022; Wang and Luo, 2022). Because of their high per-capita GDP, countries' results vary widely. Green money's influence on China's natural quality and economic development is examined in this study. Green money's impact on environmental quality is still certain, but it depends on the economic development of the region, according to the results of the study (Xu *et al.*, 2022). To put it another way, green money creates a mutually beneficial situation in terms of both environmental quality and the financial market. The Chinese economy may require a large amount of private speculation in order to maintain a stable monetary system (Wu *et al.*, 2022; Guo *et al.*, 2019). However, according to the authors, the G20 needs to encourage the development of the green business sector and increase the transparency of data in order to increase green interest in the region (Liu *et al.*, 2022).

The second argument asserts that incentives placed a damper on greenhouse gas emission. Climate change mitigation support through FD is given largely not to those who require them but to those who otherwise cannot finance it (Riti *et al.*, 2017). In this way, government incentives slow down the mechanism of efficiency. Although conventional literature might overestimate the effect of FD by 30–50% for climate change mitigation, they argue that they may really be just responsible for that in less than 10% of the total sales (Tran, 2021; Cruz *et al.*, 2019). In order to enhance scientists' and engineers' efficiency, governments can finance or subsidize research and development activities. It releases more money for expenditure into R&D, which decreases corporate creativity. Sun *et al.* (2020) focus on small companies in the US as their research interest, and illustrate that subsidies to R&D contribute to crowding out Ireland's industrial industry which serves as a benchmark for testing their practical variability for greenhouse gas emission reduction. The studies come to the conclusion that at the national level, government-funded projects can crowd out research and development (Khosravi *et al.*, 2019; Le *et al.*, 2021). Hence, on the basis of the above-discussed review of the literature, the study proposes the hypothesis that:

- H1: *There is a significant role of FD on climate change mitigation during COVID-19 period in BRICS countries.*
- H2: *There is a significant role of FD on greenhouse gas mitigation during COVID-19 period in BRICS economies.*
- H3: *The climate change mitigation significantly reduces the greenhouse gasses during COVID-19 period and promotes green economic recovery in BRICS economies.*

3. Methodology

3.1. *Theoretical framework of study*

There has been much study on how climate change mitigation is linked to growth and the nexus between energy and growth, there has been no clear evidence to back this up (Anh Tu *et al.*, 2021; Iqbal and Bilal, 2021a). Both short- and long-term correlations between FD and CO_2 emissions in Malaysia have been validated by studies, whereas financial growth in India has been shown to contribute to climate change mitigation (Mi *et al.*, 2019); Creutzig *et al.*, 2015c; Schwanen *et al.*, 2011). However, notwithstanding these results, empirical evidence suggests that financial growth does not have a negative impact on climate change mitigation in 12 MENA (Middle East and North Africa) nations. Researchers concluded that financial growth is critical to reducing climate change mitigation in small and developing nations. It has been discovered that Pakistan's environmental quality is being harmed by the country's financial prosperity (Shan *et al.*, 2018). The UAE indicated that all Gulf Cooperation Council (GCC) nations save the United Arab Emirates had substantial greenhouse gas mitigation as a result of financial growth (UAE). There has been a one-way link between economic growth and climate change mitigation in the countries of the southern Mediterranean.

When it comes to the connection between trade and environmental deterioration, there are two opposing schools of thought. FD can improve the planet by increasing funding for renewables and mobilizing the resource ability to invest in ecologically friendly facilities and assure its lengthy sustainability. The application of sophisticated technology for environmentally friendly and clean manufacturing, which in turn enhances BRICS and international ecological responsibility, is also facilitated by wealth generation. The opposite is also true: a greater level of FD may have a negative impact on the environment. "Financial deepening makes it simpler for people to get low-cost loans to start a new company or grow an existing one," says Acheampong (2019). This results in an increase in energy usage, which has a negative impact on the environment. Using Shan *et al.* (2018) and Nasir *et al.* (2021), researchers constructed the following model to test the FD-footprint linkage.

$$\mathrm{FD}_t = \beta_0 + \alpha_1\mathrm{CCM}_t + \alpha_2\mathrm{REC}_t + \alpha_2\mathrm{CO}_{2t} + \alpha_4\mathrm{CI}_t + \alpha_5\mathrm{GHG}_t + £_t. \tag{1}$$

Equation (1) introduces the variables of the studies, where FD is at t time period, and this is the dependent variable of the study. Moreover, CCM is climate change mitigation, REC is renewable energy consumption, CO_2 measures carbon emission, CI is the climate investment, and GHG is abbreviated as greenhouse gas mitigation.

3.2. *Study data and context*

The BRICS economies are chosen because of their megaproject, and the data from 2001 to 2019 are gathered from the World Development Indicators (WDI) and the Economic Intelligence Unit (EIU). Using citations from the research, the financial indicators used in this research are connected to economic growth, and this study focuses on investigating the possible environmental barriers offered by Turkey and Indonesia. There has been a dramatic increase in industrial activity in this area since the 2015s, as seen by the chosen time period. Since BRICS's entry in 2015, the five-year data post-arrival are sufficient to predict future developments. Coherence was ensured by using logarithms for each and every one of the inputs.

Calculating energy efficiency is done by dividing the energy received by the energy inputs required for energy outputs, while the kg of oil equivalent per capita assesses the mitigation of climate change and CO_2 optimization. Gross domestic product (GDP) per capita (current US dollars) is used as a proxy for economic growth, domestic credit to the private sector (FD) is given as a percentage of GDP, and the percentage of the urban population in the total population is used as a proxy for urbanization to measure trade openness. As an alternative, the total amount of CO_2 emissions per person is calculated based on greenhouse gas emissions. This is followed by normalization of the data of the variables in order to solve the issue of unit measurement disparities.

3.3. *Data analysis techniques*

General nonlinear regression models with a restricted information structure do not typically retain the numerical equivalency result. For example, in probit regression models with endogenous regressors, RWE differs quantitatively from the pretty much constant focused GMM estimate. When instances are processed about variance decomposition components, the arithmetic comparability may be extended to a class of limited-information nonlinear regression models. The sequence manner is considered as a possible two-step linearized GMM with decreased type loading for the traditional thresh-holding estimate. Moreover, stationary test, threshold tests, OLS test and sensitivity analysis for robustness check were used.

To estimate the empirical findings, suppose

$E[m_i(\gamma_o)] = 0$ exactly identifies γ_o where $\gamma_0 = \gamma(\theta_0) : \mathbb{R}^P \rightarrow \mathbb{R}^8$ with $p < g$. Let γ be the solution to $\sum_i m_i(\gamma) = 0$.

Denote the linear expansion of $m_i(\gamma(\theta))$ around γ_o as $m_i^L(\theta, \gamma_o) = m_i(\gamma_o) + \frac{\partial m_i(\gamma_0)}{\partial y}(\gamma(\theta) - \gamma_0)$.

So the possible linearized GMM approximation difficulty is as

$$\min_\theta \left(\sum m_i^L(\theta, \hat{\gamma})\right)' \hat{W}_1 \left(\sum m_i^L(\theta, \hat{\gamma})\right), \tag{2}$$

where $\hat{W}_1$ is a positive semi-definite matrix. Then, the following hold: (a) The solution to (23) is numerically equivalent to the classical minimum distance estimator (MDE) that solves

$$\min_\theta (\gamma(\theta) - \hat{\gamma})' \hat{w}_2 (\gamma(\theta) - \hat{\gamma}), \tag{3}$$

where

$$\hat{W}_2 = \widehat{J}(\hat{\gamma})' \hat{W}_1 \widehat{J}(\hat{\gamma}) \quad \text{and} \quad \widehat{J}(\hat{\gamma}) = \sum \frac{\partial m_i(\hat{\gamma})}{\partial \gamma_0'}. \tag{4}$$

In the linear simultaneous model with

$$\min_{\theta_1} \left(\sum m_{i1}^{\text{LCM}}(\theta_1)\right)' \left(\sum m_{i1}^{\text{LC}}(\theta_1) m_{i1}^{\text{LC}}(\theta_1)'\right)^{-1} \left(\sum m_{i1}^{\text{LCM}}(\theta_1)\right), \tag{5}$$

Table 1. Descriptive estimates.

Parameter	Renewable energy consumption	Carbon investment	Carbon emission	Climate change	Greenhouse gasses
Minimum	0.4814	0.0337	0.0399	0.0276	0.0415
Maximum	0.9696	0.0213	0.6612	0.2676	0.8893
Kurtosis	0.8332	0.5105	0.0304	0.1804	0.0219
SD	0.8197	0.1873	0.0305	0.0791	0.0875
Mean	0.1135	0.0487	0.1236	0.0345	0.0477
Variance	0.6186	0.0428	0.8145	0.0724	0.0261

where

$$\begin{aligned} m_{i1}^{\mathrm{LCM}}(\theta_1) &= m_{i1}(\hat{\gamma}) + \frac{\partial m_{i1}(\hat{\gamma})}{\partial \gamma_1}(\gamma_1(\theta_1, \hat{\gamma}_2) - \hat{\gamma}_1) \quad \text{and} \quad m_{i1}^{\mathrm{LC}}(\theta_1) \\ &= m_{i1}(\hat{\gamma}) - \left[\sum \frac{\partial m_{i1}(\hat{\gamma})}{\partial \gamma_2'} + \sum \frac{\partial m_{i1}(\hat{\gamma})}{\partial \gamma_1'} \frac{\partial \gamma_1(\theta_1, \hat{\gamma}_2)}{\partial \theta_2'}\right] \\ &\quad \times \left(\sum \frac{\partial m_{i2}(\hat{\gamma}_2)}{\partial \gamma_2'}\right)^{-1} m_{i2}(\hat{\gamma}_2). \end{aligned} \tag{6}$$

Hence, the notations are similar to the ones used in this section, except that the moment functions and parameters have additional subscript t. So estimating the GMM following Eq. (6) is operationalized to predict the nexus between constructs and discuss the findings (Table 1).

4. Results and Discussion

4.1. *Study results and interpretations*

Most environmental and economic time series feature nonfixed metrics. Recurrent symptoms are common, although their severity and frequency might fluctuate over time. GMM soundness is used to study the relationship between CO_2 and other parameters, such as GDP, REEO, and IEPP, using the GMM method. We can uncover both the short-term and long-term connections between unsustainable energy undertakings and green money and monetary execution in the COVID-19 epidemic because the GMM rationality procedure integrates time and repetition space-based causality methodologies. Using GMM analysis, you may track the degree of co-development through time and across variable frequency. In comparison to other newly suggested causality theories, the GMM approach stands out because of these features. Nevertheless, the primary goal of this investigation is to create faster models based on a GMM process in order to fill in a gap in the writing. Both CO_2's GMM power range and CO_2's GMM awareness are evaluated in this section, as well as the elements that might affect their performance (Fig. 1).

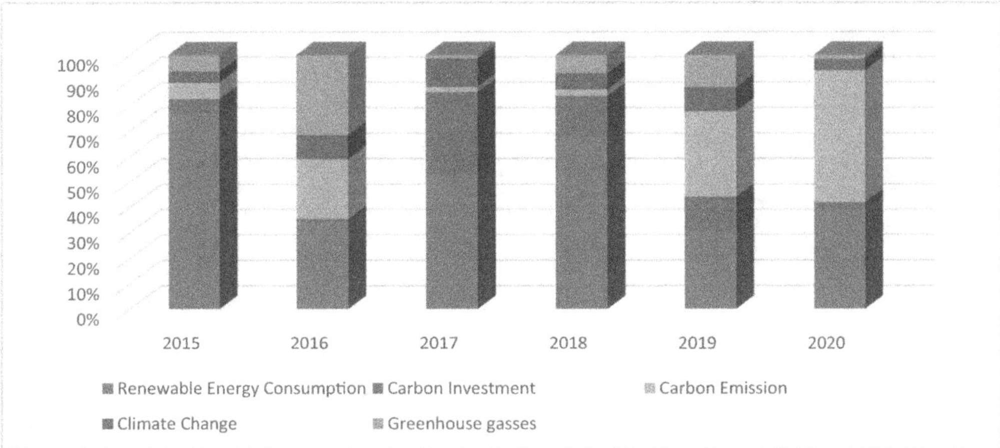

Figure 1. Study constructs sensitivity (as per sample time).

At the 5% level in GMM strength, Monte Carlo simulations are used to provide significance test findings. The thick dark lines represent this range. A shade from blue to red is used to cover the whole spectrum of strength. From 2015 to 2020, GMM power rangers detect volatility in renewable electricity predictions. Despite this, the highest levels of CO_2 volatility have only been seen during two time intervals. There is a particularly high level of uncertainty in the 2002 to 2006 timeframe, as well as midway between 2015 and 2018. Between 2002 and 2006, China's economy becomes increasingly focused on renewable energy and reducing its dependence on traditional oil products as a result of the global value rise from 2018 to 2020.

As a result, the price of power rose from $60 in 2015 to $147.30 in 2016 due to an increase in energy and petroleum demand in emerging nations. As a result, there is a larger degree of uncertainty in the market for ecologically friendly electricity. As a result of the global economic crises of 2007–2009, petroleum product energy prices have become increasingly vulnerable, which, in turn, contributes to the expansion of green energy projects. Since then, CO_2 has undergone a greater degree of fluctuation and volatility. In addition, there has been no distinct uncertainty around these two instability periods seen in the figure's chilly gaps. Figure 2 shows that the sustainable power yield as a level of the absolute power yield is the most unstable of all the criteria that might be considered. From 2015 to 2020, the GMM power range captures the volatility. Moreover, the unit root results are also explained (*see* Table 4). Due to a rise in oil prices, there has been an increase in the amount of renewable electricity generated (Table 2).

This is due to rising energy prices, which has led to a rise in the number of people interested in environmentally friendly power sources in China in the long term. According to paragraphs 3 and 4, there is no significant difference between the GDP and the price for individual investment. As oil and energy prices rose, China's GDP

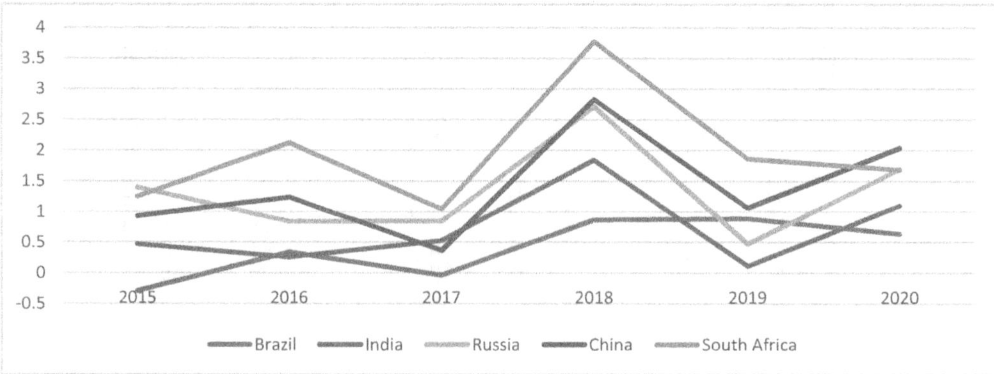

Figure 2. BRICS financing matrix for green FD to mitigate greenhouse gas.

Table 2. FD score of BRICS economies.

BRICS economies	Before COVID-19	During COVID-19
Brazil	−0.123	0.829
India	0.173	0.717
Russia	0.931	0.969
China	0.646	0.994
South Africa	0.847	0.013

began to display a subtler flightiness in the period between 2004 and 2009, which is very definitely linked to this. Regardless, the colored space in Fig. 3 reveals that China's GDP is not shaky at all. Figure 2 further shows that the economic objectives of the private sector fluctuate. In the context of everything, there is nothing out of the ordinary. Aside from the 2005 oil price spike and 2007–2009 global financial crisis, it can be observed that the changes do occur but are far less fundamental. Private entity in financial power theories did not indicate any fundamental fragile nature in the coloredspace.

The GMM influence range in China receives the fragile nature of the emerald yuan. During the selected time period, the GMM influence range identified just two periods with the most significant instability or caprice in the green currency. Precocity in green currency was greater between 2017 and 2020, according to this chart. The oil shock, such as the Nigerian oil crises, might have an impact to blame for this instability. It's also apparent from this figure's brighter yellow tone that this unusualness is less significant than the previous one. According to everyone, the rise in energy expenses between 2015 and 2019 may be attributed to the rise in quirkiness (Table 3).

The study explained that the stationary of the study indicator is established as tabulated in Table 4. These results are obtained by using augmented Dicky fuller

Table 3. Unit root outputs.

Measures	LLC test adjusted t-value	P value	Stationary
Financial development	5.972*	0.001 (< 0.05)	Established
Climate change mitigation	4.701	0.009 (< 0.05)	Established
Greenhouse gas mitigation	2.643*	0.016 (< 0.05)	Established
Carbon emission	5.781*	0.028 (< 0.05)	Established
Carbon investment	1.994*	0.010 (< 0.05)	Established
Renewable energy consumption	3.114*	0.031 (< 0.05)	Established

Note: *Means p value < 0.05 level of significance.

(ADF) test of stationary. Extending to it, the results of GMM analysis further elaborated the study estimates using two dependent variables such as climate change mitigation and greenhouse gas emission. Both variables were already hypothesized in Sec. 2. The GMM judiciousness approach works best when the data are noisy, non-fixed, and have varying following conditions must be met motions and important fractures. The study variables are used at the level of the GMM-created models. There is a strong correlation between red (smoking) and blue (nonsmoking) districts, although there is no correlation between these two colors in the linked figures. In the model fit analysis, the technique of large causation is shown by arrows enclosed by a

Table 4. GMM estimation with climate change mitigation as dependent variable.

	One-step (I)	Two-step (II)	One-step (III)	Two-step (IV)
Financial development	0.677	0.701	0.779	0.784
	(0.001)	(0.569)	(0.732)	(0.003)
Renewable energy consumption	0.284	0.425	0.024	0.595
	0.000	0.368	0.869	0.157
Carbon investment	0.000	0.484	0.817	0.085
	0.491	0.268	0.215	0.383
Carbon emission	0.318	0.117	0.659	0.516
	0.449	0.021	0.934	0.823
Climate change	0.244	0.254	0.666	0.767
	0.757	0.591	0.492	0.864
Greenhouse gasses	0.739	0.206	0.019	0.023
	0.561	0.463	0.861	0.751
Adjusted R^2	0.884		0.857	
Arellano-bond AR (1)	2.295		3.602	
	[0.000]		[0.000]	
Arellano-bond AR (2)	0.444		0.497	
	[0.501]		[0.592]	
Sargan test	131.17		139.21	
	[0.770]		[0.795]	

Note: *Means p value < 0.05 level of significance.

thick dull line. Right-provoking bolts foster a solid relationship, whereas left-provoking bolts foster negative ones.

However, Table 5 results show that FD is found significant with climate change mitigation at 66.7%, and carbon investment is also as significant with 0.285%. Likewise, carbon emission is significantly affected by the FD with 0.318. With such effects, climate change mitigation shows 0.666% change due to FD and 0.244 due to carbon investment. While, greenhouse gas mitigation is altered statistically with 0.739 by the FD and 0.236 by the carbon investment. Table 5 shows adjusted *R*-square as 0.884 and 0.857, respectively.

Extending to it, the findings of the study revealed that FD has a significant role on climate change mitigation with 57.8% and on greenhouse mitigation with 67.9% in BRICS economies under COVID-19. Carbon investment and climate change mitigation are found significantly connected at 58.9% with climate change mitigation, and at 67.4% with greenhouse gasses mitigation. The role of FD on carbon emission (i.e., CO_2 emission) is also found significant with 0.573 (p value < 0.05). While, the climate change mitigation is significantly influenced as 0.467 and 0.349, and the greenhouse gasses are estimated at 0.876 and 0.893. The adjusted square values are found as 0.762 and 0.555 on the role of FD on climate change mitigation in BRICS countries. These results are tabulated in Table 6.

Table 5. GMM estimation: greenhouse gasses mitigation as dependent variable.

	One-step (I)	Two-step (II)	One-step (III)	Two-step (IV)
Financial development	0.578	0.679	0.202	0.591
	(0.000)	(0.333)	(0.032)	(0.503)
Renewable energy consumption	0.332	0.409	0.414	0.344
	0.006	0.572	0.784	0.007
Carbon investment	0.598	0.376	0.674	0.573
	0.541	0.000	0.321	0.008
Carbon emission	0.573	0.236	0.147	0.479
	0.009	0.037	0.244	0.707
Climate change	0.467	0.349	0.809	0.656
	0.593	0.667	0.372	0.571
Greenhouse gasses	0.876	0.893	0.082	0.234
	0.444	0.309	0.764	0.657
Adjusted R^2	0.762		0.555	
Arellano-bond AR (1)	1.150		2.751	
	[0.001]		[0.008]	
Arellano-bond AR (2)	0.409		0.511	
	[0.618]		[0.599]	
Sargan test	315.78		341.99	
	[0.758]		[0.767]	

Note: *Means p-value < 0.05 level of significance.

Table 6. Threshold effect outcomes.

				Critical estimates		
Variable	Design	Significance	F-value	10%	5%	1%
CCM	1 Threshold	0.000*	11.93*	23.14	15.43	10.64
	2 Threshold	0.349	5.18	25.09	28.77	17.81
	3 Threshold	0.672	6.95	29.29	26.01	29.71
GHG	1 Threshold	0.078	7.73	5.63	3.01	2.17
	2 Threshold	0.572	4.16	3.91	2.97	2.25
	3 Threshold	0.004*	18.89*	12.08	11.71	10.01
Model		Threshold		Threshold estimator		0.2784
95% level of CI		[0.1349, 0.1461]				

Note: Significance means p value < 0.05 level of significance shown with *sign, CI stands for confidence interval.

In addition, bolts pointing directly, up straight, or opted to leave indicate that the influence cursor is responsible for the first, but bolts pointing down, discussion figure, it is assumed that both the bidirectional causal associations are found in the time spans that are clearly defined in the conversation start figuring. However, this audit supports Hoang *et al.* (2021a) the COVID-19 pandemic abatement by massive energy interests according to an exact perspective. A clean energy theory may theoretically be used here, but it's possible to make it safe for ecology. The GMM impartiality technique was used to examine the relationship between the TRE and GDP, and the findings. The graphic shows the direction in which the bolts are moving in the dark construction, as evidenced by the results of the evaluation. This suggests that a change in GDP will result in changes in CO_2 emissions. This short-term causal link between CO_2 emissions and GDP, as shown by the graph, only extends from 2003 to 2007, a span of time of just five years. The study findings revealed that FD has a significant role in climate change mitigation in the COVID-19 era in the context of BRICS countries.

To robust the study findings, we used threshold estimation techniques to estimate the temporal differences and similarities among the study constructs (*see* Table 7). An integrated model makes it possible to make valid statistical and economic inferences about the underlying variables. The study period estimator to choose remains an open-ended topic. Ordinary Least Squares (OLS) is one of the most often used estimators in the econometric literature.

The findings of the study are reported in Table 8. To verify the threshold level, we must confirm the findings of Tables 5–7. The results revealed that climate change mitigation and greenhouse gas mitigation are increasing faster due to FD and carbon investment to finance climate control in the COVID-19 period. By this, the findings of the study are aligned with the results of various previous studies (Anh Tu *et al.*, 2021; Iqbal *et al.*, 2021b; Li *et al.*, 2021a; Iqbal and Bilal, 2021b).

Table 7. Regression output about threshold estimation.

Estimates	Coefficients	T-value	$P > \|t\|$
CCM (FDs $\leq$ 0.684)	0.0451*	2.78	0.003*
GHS (FDs > 0.684)	0.0579*	2.19	0.000*
Carbon emission	0.3456	0.67	0.561
Carbon Investment	0.5140	0.36	0.432
Renewable Energy Consumption	0.6731	0.21	0.562*
Constant	0.5678	0.34	0.008*

Note: *Means p value < 0.05 level of significance.

Table 8. Sensitivity analysis score (country-wise).

	2015	2016	2017	2018	2019	2020
Brazil	−0.113*	−0.394*	−0.226*	−0.148*	−0.334	−0.086*
India	0.469*	−0.857*	−0.692*	−0.092*	−0.182*	0.257*
Russia	−0.378*	−0.018*	0.968*	0.157*	0.913	0.684*
China	0.265*	0.543*	0.301*	−0.397	−0.556*	0.166*
South Africa	0.186*	0.983**	0.328*	0.319*	−0.259*	−0.143*

Note: *Means p value < 0.05 level of significance.

4.2. *Robustness analysis*

Financial progress in OPEC countries is compatible with this audit, which provides proof that economic advancement is not harmful to ecological authority. According to the standard Kuznets twist (EKC) theory, a rise in compensation increases the use of unmanageable sources of power in the primary stage, which might have a comparable negative impact on the environment. Directly after attaining the breaking point level of pay, the economy begins shifting toward renewable energy that is not harmful to the environment, but this shift in the business also has a major effect on the financial sector.

Figures 1 and 2 depict how GMM prudence revealed the link between study constructs. Both short-and long-term causations have been identified in the double cross edges of these variables in this unique causal link between the components (see Table 3).

To reduce monetary, natural, and monetary vulnerabilities, these measures are widely acknowledged to be effective (Sun *et al.*, 2022; Iqbal *et al.*, 2021b). There is a specific focus on the monetary, natural, and ecologically friendly power accounts of China in this exploratory research. However, this research might be extended to many countries and regions throughout the world. It was possible to establish a link between the pursuit of renewable energy, climate investment, and climate change mitigation through FD using this time series analysis (Table 10).

Table 10. Robust connection of FD with climate change and greenhouse gasses.

	Before COVID-19 outbreak			During COVID-19 outbreak		
	FD	Climate change mitigation	Greenhouse gasses mitigation	FD	Climate change mitigation	Greenhouse gasses mitigation
Financial development$_{t-1}$	0.567	0.594	0.683	4.139	4.415	5.5763
Wald test	0.34*	0.27*	0.53	2.39*	4.36**	4.19**
Significance	(0.19)	(0.25)	(0.51)	(0.02)	(0.01)	(0.03)
Climate change mitigation $_{t-1}$	2.89	2.01	2.75	4.17	4.195	5.555
Wald test	2.11	2.29	2.88	2.85*	2.18**	2.89**
Significance	(0.00)	(0.31)	(0.28)	(0.04)	(0.02)	(0.01)
Greenhouse gasses mitigation$_{t-1}$	3.11	3.09	2.10	2.16	2.77	2.17
Wald test	2.73	2.56	2.03	2.27	2.31	2.54
Significance	(0.01)	(0.07)	(0.02)	(0.01)	(0.01)	(0.00)

Note: *Means p value < 0.05 level of significance.

The study has been done on the topic of sustainable power, as well as other monetary, financial and energy-related indicators. As a general rule, the essay will investigate the impact of COVID-19 on various ecological, economical, and monetary elements. However, this evaluation acknowledges that there is a void in the literature about the causal link between the interests in environmentally friendly power, green money, monetary development, limitless power yield, and the energy venture with private speculation following the COVID-19 surge. For this purpose, the present review used an evaluation method that was different from the one used in normal exams. The study data were analyzed in this study, which focused on China as the most affected economy. This investigation used the GMM power range and the GMM cognizant approach for precise examination. Since it allows for both short-term and long-term causal relationships, this technique is effective.

4.3. *Discussion*

The first thing to notice is that the bolts are hurling toward the left, which is a plausible assumption given a wide range of factors. As a result, the causal effect reveals that between 2019 and 2020, CO_2 and FDi had a unidirectional causality. When it comes to the second season's causation, it seems that the bolts are moving in the same direction from 2018 to 2019 as they did in the previous era. Similarly, this shows that there is a unidirectional causal connection flowing from CO_2 to Fdi. Because of this, China's green cash would be adversely affected by any shift in CO_2 production techniques.

Secondly, it is thought that the recurrence of the succeeding time period causal impact is more evident than the first time period causality. Keeping an eye on CO_2 emissions or using green money is critical in both time periods, it is thought, since premiums on products that have no negative impact on the environment are taken into account in both cases. The latest facts are in line with previous discoveries.

The study estimates the high predictability, according to the results of the GMM power range. Even though REEO and FDi were both unstable in one and two time frames, they were both unstable in the same time period. In contrast, the variables, such as GDP and IEPP, showed no signs of fluctuation across the time period studied. Both the unidirectional and bidirectional causal relationships between the components have been identified. At different time frames, a bidirectional causal connection has been discovered between CO_2 and REEO. A unidirectional causal link between GDP and CO_2 has been found, but only in the near term.

Additional causal links between CO_2 and FDi may be found in both the short and long terms, as well (Mohsin *et al.*, 2021). This suggests that CO_2 is an important component of the FDi. Private speculation cannot be an effective strategy measure for CO_2 since there is no causal relationship between IEPP and CO_2. Aside from revealing unpredictability at different time intervals, all of the evaluated findings reveal causality. In any event, the experimental study of CO_2 and control parameters, including REEO, GDP, IEPP, and FDi, in the chosen time period, yielded no unexpected or causative correlations. Based on observations, the present evaluation recommends several feasible strategy recommendations that need CO_2 moment considerations and implementation. The precise findings reveal the unstable conduct of sustainable power speculation, green money, and endless power yield right away.

Due to these aspects' unpredictability, plans should be devised to tackle them either by establishing set percentages of the financial plan or by establishing real checks and balances in these areas. Furthermore, it hass been observed that interest in sustainable power fundamentally increases green money, and so, the environmentally friendly power venture should be improved, which may also contribute to other natural management elements. Like other ecologically beneficial developments, the Green Money Upgrade just contributes to this effort. Strategies should thus address green money improvement in order to stimulate environmentally friendly power speculation and the sustainable power era. For green money, additional consideration should be given to techniques that focus on limitless rather than petroleum-derived power, since this will have a greater impact on the sustainable power venture.

To reduce monetary, natural, and monetary vulnerabilities, these measures are widely acknowledged to be effective. There is a specific focus on the monetary, natural, and ecologically friendly power accounts of China in this exploratory research. However, this research might be extended to many countries and regions throughout the world. It was possible to establish a link between the pursuit of renewable energy, green currency, and an infinite supply of resources using this time series analysis.

5. Conclusion and Policy Recommendations

The study aims to test the role of FD on climate change mitigation and greenhouse gas mitigation in BRICS countries during COVID-19. The study presents the pre-and-post COVID-19 findings. To draw the inference among the constructs, ADF test, GMM test, panel threshold test, regression test and sensitivity analysis tests were applied. The study findings have been done on the topic of environmental finance policy and other related indicators such as carbon emission and climate investment. As a general rule, this paper has investigated the impact of COVID-19 on various ecological, economical, and monetary elements. However, this evaluation acknowledges that there is a void in the literature about the causal link between the interests in environmentally friendly power, green money, monetary development, limitless power yield, and the energy venture with private speculation following the COVID-19 surge. For this purpose, the present review used an evaluation method that was different from the one used in normal exams. Time-series data from 2015 to 2020 were analyzed in this study, which focused on China as the most affected economy. This investigation used the GMM power range and the GMM cognizant approach for precise examination. Since it allows for both short-term and long-term causal relationships, this technique is effective.

Due to these aspects' unpredictability, plans should be devised to tackle them either by establishing set percentages of the financial plan or by establishing real checks and balances in these areas. Furthermore, it has been observed that interest in sustainable power fundamentally increases green money, and so, the environmentally friendly power venture should be improved, which may also contribute to other natural management elements. Like other ecologically beneficial developments, the Green Money Upgrade just contributes to this effort. Strategies should thus address green money improvement in order to stimulate environmentally friendly power speculation and the sustainable power era. For green money, additional consideration should be given to techniques that focus on limitless rather than petroleum-derived power, since this will have a greater impact on the sustainable power venture.

Additional causal links between climate change mitigation through FD may be found in both the short- and long-term, as well. This suggests that climate change mitigation is an important component of the FD. Private speculation cannot be an effective strategy measure for climate change mitigation since there is no causal relationship between IEPP and CO_2. Aside from revealing unpredictability at different time intervals, all of the evaluated findings reveal causality. Based on observations, the present evaluation recommends several feasible strategy recommendations that need CO_2 moment considerations and implementation. The precise findings reveal the unstable conduct of sustainable power speculation, green money, and endless power yield right away. For green economic recovery in the post-COVID-19 period the study suggests the following policy recommendations;

- Screening and first assessment of potential green stimulus measures connected with climate change and greenhouse gas mitigation activities.
- Initiating the dissemination of the lists of measures and feedback of stakeholders.
- Participation of working group of national climate pollution emitting industries federation.
- Enrich the list of climate change stimulus measures sent to the finance ministries to promote FD.
- Modeling greenhouse gas emission reduction pathways through FD.
- Assignment of sustainability scores based on impact assessment to reduce greenhouse gas emission.
- Prioritization of financial measures for climate change mitigation and greenhouse gas reduction from already available budgets.

For the COVID-19 era, we believe that implementing the suggested policy changes properly might help manage climate change and reduce greenhouse gas emissions. Such policies aimed at boosting investments in renewable energy technologies should be implemented in order to reduce emissions and combat climate change. It is necessary to build strong financial sectors to support research institutions' efforts to produce less carbon or carbon-free energy. Future research studies should be warranted on such themes to expand the body of knowledge and present the implications for key stakeholders.

Acknowledgments

This paper is supported by the National Natural Science Foundation of the people's Republic of China with the approval No. 71873069 and is sponsored by the Humanities and Social Sciences Youth Fund of the Ministry of Education of the People's Republic of China with the approval No. 17YJC790202.

References

Ahmad, B, S Iqbal, M Hai and S Latif (2021). The interplay of personal values, relational mobile usage and organizational citizenship behavior. In *Interactive Technology and Smart Education*. Bingley: Emerald Publishing Limited.

Alemzero, DA, N Iqbal, S Iqbal, M Mohsin, NJ Chukwuma and BA Shah (2021). Assessing the perceived impact of exploration and production of hydrocarbons on households' perspective of environmental regulation in Ghana. *Environmental Science and Pollution Research*, 28(5), 5359–5371.

Anh Tu, C, F Chien, MA Hussein, MM Ramli, Y Psi, MSS Iqbal and AR Bilal (2021). Estimating role of Green Financing on Energy Security, Economic and Environmental Integration of BRI member countries. *The Singapore Economic Review*, doi: 10.1142/S0217590821500193.

Anser, MK, MA Khan, K Zaman, AA Nassani, SE Askar, MMQ Abro and A Kabbani (2020). Determination of resource curse hypothesis in mediation of financia development and clean energy sources: go-for-green resource policies. *Resources Policy*, 66, 101640.

Chen, L, X Zhang, F He and R Yuan (2019). Regional green development level and its spatial relationship under the constraints of haze in China. *Journal of Cleaner Production*, 210, 376–387.

Claessens, S and L Laeven (2003). Financial development, property rights, and growth. *The Journal of Finance*, 58(6), 2401–2436.

Condon, PM, D Cavens and N Miller (2009). *Urban Planning Tools for Climate Change Mitigation*. Cambridge, MA: Lincoln Institute of Land Policy.

Creutzig, F, P Jochem, OY Edelenbosch, L Mattauch, DP van Vuuren, D McCollum and J Minx, (2015a). Transport: A roadblock to climate change mitigation? *Science*, 350(6263), 911–912.

Creutzig, F, P Jochem, OY Edelenbosch, L Mattauch, DP van Vuuren, D McCollum and J Minx, (2015b). Transport: A roadblock to climate change mitigation? *Science*, 350(6263), 911–912.

Creutzig, F, NH Ravindranath, G Berndes, S Bolwig, R Bright, F Cherubini, H Chum, E Corbera, M Delucchi, A Faaij, J Fargione, H Haberl, G Heath, O Lucon, R Plevin, A Popp, C Robledo-Abad, S Rose, P Smith, A Stromman, S Suh, O Maserasera (2015c). Bioenergy and climate change mitigation: An assessment. *Gcb Bioenergy*, 7(5), 916–944.

Cruz, L, D Imori, JP Ferreira, JJ Guilhoto, E Barata and P Ramos (2019). Energy–economy–environment interactions: A comparative analysis of Lisbon and Sao Paulo metropolitan areas. *Journal of Environmental Assessment Policy and Management*, 21(1), 1950002.

Feng, C, M Wang, GC Liu and JB Huang (2017). Green development performance and its influencing factors: A global perspective. *Journal of Cleaner Production*, 144, 323–333.

Green, CJ, CH Kirkpatrick and V Murinde (2006). Finance for small enterprise growth and poverty reduction in developing countries. *Journal of International Development: The Journal of the Development Studies Association*, 18(7), 1017–1030.

Guo, M, Y Hu and J Yu (2019). The role of financial development in the process of climate change: Evidence from different panel models in China. *Atmospheric Pollution Research*, 10(5), 1375–1382.

He, L, R Liu, Z Zhong, D Wang and Y Xia (2019). Can green financial development promote renewable energy investment efficiency? A consideration of bank credit. *Renewable Energy*, 143, 974–984.

Huang, J, X Wang, H Liu and S Iqbal (2021). Financial consideration of energy and environmental nexus with energy poverty: Promoting financial development in G7 economies. *Frontiers in Energy Research*, 9, 666.

Iqbal, S and AR Bilal (2021a). Energy financing in COVID-19: How public supports can benefit? *China Finance Review International*.

Iqbal, S and AR Bilal (2021b). Investment performance: Emotional beasts are dragging into the darkness of the castle. *Global Business Review*, 09721509211044309.

Iqbal, S, AR Bilal, M Nurunnabi, W Iqbal, Y Alfakhri and N Iqbal (2021a). It is time to control the worst: testing COVID-19 outbreak, energy consumption and CO_2 emission. *Environmental Science and Pollution Research*, 28(15), 19008–19020.

Iqbal, S, F Taghizadeh-Hesary, M Mohsin and W Iqbal (2021b). Assessing the role of the green finance index in environmental pollution reduction. *Estudios de economía aplicada*, 39(3), 12.

Ivanova, D, J Barrett, D Wiedenhofer, B Macura, M Callaghan and F Creutzig (2020). Quantifying the potential for climate change mitigation of consumption options. *Environmental Research Letters*, 15(9), 093001.

Khosravi, F, TB Fischer and U Jha-Thakur (2019). Multi-criteria analysis for rapid strategic environmental assessment in tourism planning. *Journal of Environmental Assessment Policy and Management*, 21(4), 1950013.

Le, TH, HC Le and F Taghizadeh-Hesary (2020). Does financial inclusion impact CO_2 emissions? Evidence from Asia. *Finance Research Letters*, 34, 101451.

Li, W, F Chien, CC Hsu, Y Zhang, MA Nawaz, S Iqbal and M Mohsin (2021a). Nexus between energy poverty and energy efficiency: Estimating the long-run dynamics. *Resources Policy*, 72, 102063.

Li, W, F Chien, QT Ngo, TD Nguyen, S Iqbal and AR Bilal (2021b). Vertical financial disparity, energy prices and emission reduction: Empirical insights from Pakistan. *Journal of Environmental Management*, 294, 112946.

Li, ZZ, RYM Li, MY Malik, M Murshed, Z Khan and M Umar (2021c). Determinants of carbon emission in China: How good is green investment? *Sustainable Production and Consumption*, 27, 392–401.

Liu, H, Y Wang, Q Li, N Yang, Z Wang and Q Wang (2022). Research on the evolution characteristics of oxygen-containing functional groups during the combustion process of the torrefied corn stalk. *Biomass and Bioenergy*, 158. doi: 10.1016/j.biombioe.2022.106343.

Liu, X, E Wang and D Cai (2019). Green credit policy, property rights and debt financing: Quasi-natural experimental evidence from China. *Finance Research Letters*, 29, 129–135.

Meltzer, JP (2016). Financing low carbon, climate resilient infrastructure: the role of climate finance and green financial systems. In *Climate Resilient Infrastructure: The Role of Climate Finance and Green Financial Systems* (September 21, 2016).

Mi, Z, D Guan, Z Liu, J Liu, V Viguié, N Fromer and Y Wang (2019). Cities: The core of climate change mitigation. *Journal of Cleaner Production*, 207, 582–589.

Miao, R, Y Liu, L Wu, D Wang, Y Liu, Y Miao, J Ma (2022). Effects of long-term grazing exclusion on plant and soil properties vary with position in dune systems in the Horqin Sandy Land. *CATENA*, 209. doi: 10.1016/j.catena.2021.105860.

Mohsin, M, H Ullah, N Iqbal, W Iqbal and F Taghizadeh-Hesary (2021). How external debt led to economic growth in South Asia: A policy perspective analysis from quantile regression. *Economic Analysis and Policy*, 72, 423–437.

Muganyi, T, L Yan and HP Sun (2021). Green finance, fintech and environmental protection: Evidence from China. *Environmental Science and Ecotechnology*, 7, 100107.

Nielsen, KS, PC Stern, T Dietz, JM Gilligan, DP van Vuuren, MJ Figueroa, C Folke, W Gwozdz, D Ivanova, LA Reisch, MP Vandenbergh, KS Wolske and R Wood (2020). Improving climate change mitigation analysis: a framework for examining feasibility. *One Earth*, 3(3), 325–336.

Paltsev, S and P Capros (2013). Cost concepts for climate change mitigation. *Climate Change Economics*, 4(supp01), 1340003.

Paramati, SR, D Mo and R Huang (2021). The role of financial deepening and green technology on carbon emissions: evidence from major OECD economies. *Finance Research Letters*, 41, 101794.

Peeters, P and G Dubois (2010). Tourism travel under climate change mitigation constraints. *Journal of Transport Geography*, 18(3), 447–457.

Popp, A, F Humpenöder, I Weindl, BL Bodirsky, M Bonsch, H Lotze-Campen, C Müller, A Biewald, S Rolinski, M Stevanovic, J Ph and JP Dietrich (2014). Land-use protection for climate change mitigation. *Nature Climate Change*, 4(12), 1095–1098.

Powlson, DS, CM Stirling, ML Jat, BG Gerard, CA Palm, PA Sanchez and KG Cassman (2014). Limited potential of no-till agriculture for climate change mitigation. *Nature Climate Change*, 4(8), 678–683.

Riti, JS, Y Shu, D Song and M Kamah (2017). The contribution of energy use and financial development by source in climate change mitigation process: A global empirical perspective. *Journal of Cleaner Production*, 148, 882–894.

Rogelj, J, DL McCollum, A Reisinger, M Meinshausen and K Riahi (2013). Probabilistic cost estimates for climate change mitigation. *Nature*, 493(7430), 79–83.

Schwanen, T, D Banister and J Anable (2011). Scientific research about climate change mitigation in transport: A critical review. *Transportation Research Part A: Policy and Practice*, 45(10), 993–1006.

Shahbaz, M, QMA Hye, AK Tiwari and NC Leitão (2013). Economic growth, energy consumption, financial development, international trade and CO_2 emissions in Indonesia. *Renewable and Sustainable Energy Reviews*, 25, 109–121.

Shan, Y, D Guan, K Hubacek, B Zheng, SJ Davis, L Jia, & HJ Schellnhuber (2018). City-level climate change mitigation in China. *Science Advances*, 4(6), eaaq0390.

Sharp, EB, DM Daley and MS Lynch (2011). Understanding local adoption and implementation of climate change mitigation policy. *Urban Affairs Review*, 47(3), 433–457.

Sun, H, CA Samuel, JCK Amissah, F Taghizadeh-Hesary and IA Mensah (2020). Nonlinear nexus between CO_2 emissions and economic growth: A comparison of OECD and B&R countries. *Energy*, 212, 118637.

Sun, L, S Fang, S Iqbal and AR Bilal (2022). Financial stability role on climate risks, and climate change mitigation: Implications for green economic recovery. *Environmental Science and Pollution Research*, 1–12. doi: 10.1007/s11356-021-17439-w.

Tamazian, A, JP Chousa and KC Vadlamannati (2009). Does higher economic and financial development lead to environmental degradation: evidence from BRIC countries. *Energy Policy*, 37(1), 246–253.

Tran, QH (2021). The impact of green finance, economic growth and energy usage on CO_2 emission in Vietnam: A multivariate time series analysis. *China Finance Review International*. doi: 10.1016/j.frl.2020.101520.

Wang, H and Q Luo (2022). Can a colonial legacy explain the pollution haven hypothesis? A city-level panel analysis. *Structural Change and Economic Dynamics*, 60, 482–495. doi: 10.1016/j.strueco.2022.01.004.

Wang, J, W Wang, Q Ran, M Irfan, S Ren, X Yang, H Wu, M. Ahmad (2021). Analysis of the mechanism of the impact of internet development on green economic growth: Evidence from 269 prefecture cities in China. *Environmental Science and Pollution Research*, 1–15. doi: 10.1007/s11356-021-16381-1.

Warren, R, J VanDerWal, J Price, JA Welbergen, I Atkinson, J Ramirez-Villegas, TJ Osborn, A Jarvis, J Lowe (2013). Quantifying the benefit of early climate change mitigation in avoiding biodiversity loss. *Nature Climate Change*, 3(7), 678–682.

Wilson, A, JL Uncapher, L McManigal, WD Browning, LH Lovins and M Cureton (1998). *Green Development: Integrating Ecology and Real Estate* (Vol. 9). New York: John Wiley & Sons.

Wu, B, H Liang and S Chan (2022). Political connections, industry entry choice and performance volatility: Evidence from China. *Emerging Markets Finance & Trade*, 58(1), 290–299. doi: 10.1080/1540496X.2021.1904878.

Xu, X and J Li (2020). Asymmetric impacts of the policy and development of green credit on the debt financing cost and maturity of different types of enterprises in China. *Journal of Cleaner Production*, 264, 121574.

Xu, X, C Wang and P Zhou (2021). GVRP considered oil-gas recovery in refined oil distribution: From an environmental perspective. *International Journal of Production Economics*, 235, 108078. doi: 10.1016/j.ijpe.2021.108078.

Yuan, G, Q Ye and Y Sun (2021). Financial innovation, information screening and industries' green innovation — Industry-level evidence from the OECD. *Technological Forecasting and Social Change*, 171, 120998.

Zaman, K, A bin Abdullah, A Khan, MR bin Mohd Nasir, TAAT Hamzah and S Hussain (2016). Dynamic linkages among energy consumption, environment, health and wealth in BRICS countries: green growth key to sustainable development. *Renewable and Sustainable Energy Reviews*, 56, 1263–1271.

Zhang, L, F Huang, L Lu, X Ni and S Iqbal (2021). Energy financing for energy retrofit in COVID-19: recommendations for green bond financing. *Environmental Science and Pollution Research*, 1–12. doi: 10.1007/s11356-021-17440-3.

https://doi.org/10.1142/9789819812783_0003

BEHAVIORAL DETERMINANTS OF PRIVATE INVESTMENT IN RENEWABLE ENERGY

AMIR RAHMANI[*,§,¶], ALI BONYADI NAEINI[*,||], FARHAD TAGHIZADEH-HESARY[†,**] and ROOHALLAH ABOOJAFARI[‡,††]

[*]*School of Management, Economics and Progress Engineering*
Iran University of Science & Technology (IUST), Narmak, Tehran, Iran

[†]*Tokai Research Institute for Environment and Sustainability*
Tokai University, Tokyo, Japan

[‡]*Knowledge-Based Economy Department*
Technology Study Institute, Iran
[§]*amir_rahmani@pgre.iust.ac.ir*
[¶]*rahmani.amir2021@gmail.com*
[||]*bonyadi@iust.ac.ir*
[**]*farhad@tsc.u-tokai.ac.jp*
[††]*aboojafari@tsi.ir*

Green finance and renewable energy (RE) investments are crucial for addressing climate change and achieving the United Nations' Sustainable Development Goals (SDGs). The private sector has significant potential to boost investment in green projects; however, decisions to invest in RE are often influenced by various risks that are rooted in psychological factors. This chapter employs a quantitative research approach to examine the key determinants influencing investment intentions in RE projects. The study reveals that attitudes, subjective norms, and perceived behavioral control positively and significantly affect individuals' willingness to invest in RE projects. In contrast, perceived risk has a notable negative impact on investment intentions. These findings contribute to theoretical discussions and provide empirical insights for policymakers and environmental advocates aiming to encourage individual investments in RE projects.

Keywords: Green finance; renewable energy; sustainability; behavioral insights; investment intention.

1. Introduction

Energy plays a fundamental role in driving social and economic progress, facilitating improved living standards and technological advancements. Yet, the global energy landscape faces a growing crisis due to escalating population levels and unsustainable energy consumption patterns (Chofreh *et al.*, 2021; Masukujjaman *et al.*, 2021). Approximately 80% of the world's energy demand is met by burning fossil fuels, contributing significantly to harmful emissions and accelerating climate change (Abbasi *et al.*, 2022). The pace at which Earth's climate is changing is unprecedented, with regions such as South Asia experiencing annual greenhouse gas (GHG) emission growth rates of 3.6%, followed by the Middle East and East Asia (Lamb *et al.*, 2021). These alarming trends underscore the urgent need to transition toward cleaner energy sources.

In this context, renewable energy presents a viable solution, offering multiple benefits, including enhanced public health, expanded access to clean energy, environmental protection, and reduced GHG emissions (Rahmani *et al.*, 2024c). However, the development and scaling of RE projects are highly dependent on sufficient financing (Taghizadeh-Hesary and Yoshino, 2019; Yoshino *et al.*, 2019). The concept of *green finance*, which channels funds from public, private, and non-profit sectors into sustainable projects, has emerged as a critical mechanism for addressing climate challenges. Despite the potential of green finance, recent disruptions in the global marketplace, exacerbated by the COVID-19 pandemic, have raised concerns about meeting climate targets due to underinvestment in RE projects (Taghizadeh-Hesary *et al.*, 2021a). In 2021, global RE investments reached USD 366 billion, with the bulk of this investment concentrated in China, Europe, and the United States. However, regions like the Middle East accounted for less than 2% of this total, reflecting significant disparities in green finance across the globe (IRENA, 2021).

The Middle East, a region heavily reliant on fossil fuels, presents challenges and opportunities in transitioning to RE (Aien and Mahdavi, 2020). Iran, one of the largest global oil and gas producers, derives 99% of its energy from fossil fuels, placing it among the top ten CO_2-emitting countries. Tehran, the capital, suffers from severe air pollution, with only 30 clean air days annually, contributing to thousands of deaths and severe health impacts. Nevertheless, Iran has significant potential for RE development, particularly in solar and wind power (Tavana *et al.*, 2019). Despite this potential, inadequate financial resources and the lack of effective policies have hindered the country's progress toward achieving its RE goals.

The private sector, comprising utilities, corporations, developers, individuals, and households, is a crucial contributor to the financing of RE projects. Between 2013 and 2018, private investors accounted for 85% of global RE investment, but since 2019, their participation has significantly declined. Securing private investment, especially from individuals, remains one of the key challenges in advancing RE initiatives. Individuals and households, in particular, have the potential to play a pivotal role in contributing to RE development and supporting the achievement of Sustainable Development Goals (SDGs) (IRENA, 2020).

While financial returns are important, psychological factors significantly shape individuals' investment decisions in RE projects (Bauer and Menrad, 2019). In recent years, researchers have become increasingly interested in investigating the psychological aspects of individuals' behavior regarding climate change and GHG emissions (Zahedi *et al.*, 2019).

Although behavioral intentions influence investing in RE projects, knowledge and understanding in this field are lacking (Gamel *et al.*, 2022; Yee *et al.*, 2022).

Researchers (Copur and Gutter, 2019; Gamel *et al.*, 2022; Yee *et al.*, 2022) recently proposed several theories and models to investigate the behavioral intentions of individuals. They found that the theory of planned behavior (TPB), with the constructs of "attitude," "subjective norms," and "perceived behavior control," is an appropriate model that can be used to explain investment intention (INI) (Bin-Nashwan and Muneeza, 2023; Gamel *et al.*, 2022; Kastner *et al.*, 2021; Lai, 2019; Yee *et al.*, 2022). Among the other factors, perceived risk has emerged as an essential determinant of INI, particularly in green finance. Perceived risk refers to the subjective assessment of potential negative consequences, such as financial loss, technological failure, or policy uncertainty, that individuals associate with investing in RE projects. This variable has gained increasing attention in behavioral research, influencing the intention to invest and the attitudes toward RE investments. By incorporating perceived risk, this extended TPB model offers a more comprehensive understanding of the psychological determinants influencing individuals' investment decisions. Individuals often weigh the potential risks associated with RE investments against their perceived benefits, and this risk assessment can significantly impact their overall intention to invest.

To test the extended model, a study conducted a survey of individuals in Tehran, employing structural equation modeling (SEM) to validate the hypotheses and assess the relationships between variables. SEM is a powerful method for estimating complex relationships among multiple dependent and independent variables while accounting for measurement errors. This method ensures a more accurate understanding of the theoretical constructs under investigation.

The findings from this study underscore the importance of psychological factors, particularly perceived risk, in shaping individuals' intentions to invest in RE projects. The extended TPB model, including perceived risk, offers a more robust framework for understanding investment behaviors. These insights provide valuable contributions to both academic literature and practical policymaking. Policymakers, especially in fossil fuel-dependent regions, can use these findings to design better policies and create favorable conditions for green financing, ultimately encouraging individuals to engage in RE investments.

The chapter is organized as follows: Section 2 offers an in-depth review of the literature and the theoretical framework. Section 3 outlines the materials and methods employed in the study. Section 4 presents the statistical results, while Section 5 discusses the findings and concludes with policy recommendations to encourage individual investment in RE projects.

2. Literature Review and Model Development

2.1. *Green finance and investment in renewable energy*

The growing concern over climate change and the global push for sustainability have significantly emphasized the need for RE investments. This focus gained momentum through international agreements, particularly the 2015 Paris Agreement, where member nations committed to reducing GHG emissions and increasing the utilization of RE sources (Qadir *et al.*, 2021). The success of RE projects and other large-scale infrastructure developments is fundamentally tied to adequate financing. Energy finance can be categorized into six primary sectors: energy and financial markets, pricing mechanisms, corporate finance for energy companies, green finance and investment, energy derivatives markets, and risk management strategies (Sachs *et al.*, 2019).

Green finance has emerged as a crucial instrument for advancing sustainability and achieving the United Nations' SDGs. However, the financing of green projects continues to be a substantial challenge. Establishing a comprehensive and effective financial framework is essential to scale up investments in projects that benefit the environment and society (Qadir *et al.*, 2021). Various innovative financial tools and policies have been developed in response to this need, commonly called green finance mechanisms. These include green bonds, green banks, carbon market instruments, fiscal policies incentivizing sustainability, green central banking practices, financial technologies (fintech), and community-based green funds (Sachs *et al.*, 2019). These instruments aim to mitigate financial risks, facilitate investments in RE, and drive the transition toward a low-carbon economy (Taghizadeh-Hesary *et al.*, 2021a; Taghizadeh-Hesary and Yoshino, 2019).

Green finance has far-reaching implications beyond the economic sphere. It significantly impacts public health, environmental protection, and national security (Chen and Zhao, 2022). By supporting investments in sustainable energy solutions, green finance not only promotes the reduction of GHG emissions but also contributes to economic growth and resilience, fostering safer, healthier living conditions for individuals (Taghizadeh-Hesary *et al.*, 2021a; Taghizadeh-Hesary and Yoshino, 2019). In this context, various forms of finance, such as *sustainable finance, environmental finance, carbon finance*, and *climate finance*, all operate within the broader scope of green finance (Taghizadeh-Hesary *et al.*, 2021a). While each area focuses on different aspects of environmental sustainability, they collectively emphasize the importance of mobilizing resources to address climate change and achieve SDGs.

The literature on green finance consistently shows a strong correlation between funding for environmentally sustainable projects and progress in combating climate change. Several studies highlight the importance of green finance in influencing energy policy, reducing GHG emissions, and driving investments in RE projects (Rahmani *et al.*, 2023). As investments in green financing, climate finance, and low-carbon technologies grow, they have the potential to directly and indirectly support the realization of multiple SDGs (Rahmani *et al.*, 2023; Taghizadeh-Hesary *et al.*, 2021a; Taghizadeh-Hesary and Yoshino, 2019).

One of the major obstacles to expanding green finance is the limited participation of both the private and public sectors. The literature suggests that increasing the involvement of these sectors is critical to addressing the global climate crisis (Taghizadeh-Hesary *et al.*, 2021b). The private sector, in particular, holds immense potential to significantly contribute to green financing efforts by increasing investments in RE projects. This increased investment can reduce environmental risks and accelerate the transition to RE sources (Qadir *et al.*, 2021; Taghizadeh-Hesary *et al.*, 2021b; Taghizadeh-Hesary and Yoshino, 2019). Reforms in financial policies, coupled with clear regulations and strategies aimed at supporting green finance, can further enhance investment levels. Additionally, the introduction of public green financing tools can help to alleviate the perceived risks associated with green investments, making them more attractive to both public and private investors (Taghizadeh-Hesary *et al.*, 2021b).

Substantial investment in RE is required to meet the targets established in the Paris Agreement, specifically maintaining the global temperature increase below the 2°C threshold. Approximately $1.1 trillion per year will need to be invested in RE projects between 2021 and 2030. This level of investment is essential for ensuring that the necessary infrastructure is developed and that countries can transition toward cleaner, more sustainable energy systems. Achieving these goals will require a concerted effort from both governments and the private sector and innovative financing strategies that make green projects more accessible and less risky for investors (IRENA, 2021).

The International Renewable Energy Agency (IRENA) report (IRENA, 2020) reveals that the private sector has been the dominant force behind investments in RE projects, contributing approximately 85% of the total funding. In contrast, government investment in these projects has been relatively modest. Despite the significant role of private sector involvement, individuals, households, and corporate investors have constituted a smaller proportion of the total private investment pool, and their contributions experienced a notable decline between 2013 and 2018. For instance, while the overall investment in RE projects in 2019 reached USD 311 billion (Taghizadeh-Hesary *et al.*, 2021b), investment from individuals and corporations saw a steep reduction during that period. Although this investment level remained relatively unchanged in 2020, the global investment in RE increased to USD 366 billion in 2021. However, this figure still falls short of the projected targets necessary for meeting climate change goals and achieving sustainable development objectives (IRENA, 2021; Mathis, 2022).

Another cause for concern is the decrease in private sector investment in RE projects to below 70% after 2019, highlighting a significant challenge in mobilizing the necessary capital to combat climate change and meet the goals set by international frameworks such as the Paris Agreement (Rahmani *et al.*, 2023). This downward trend in private sector participation threatens the global ambition of transitioning to a sustainable energy future. It underscores the importance of government intervention and policy reform to encourage more consistent and substantial investment in RE (Rahmani *et al.*, 2023).

To address the shortfall in RE investment, policymakers and researchers have increasingly focused on the critical need to develop and refine financing mechanisms and regulatory frameworks that can support the growth of green finance and encourage greater participation from both the public and private sectors. Financing RE projects has become one of the central challenges in achieving SDGs, as access to capital plays a decisive role in determining the success of large-scale RE initiatives. Governments must actively create a conducive environment for investment by establishing comprehensive frameworks that reduce perceived risks, incentivize private sector participation, and mobilize capital from various stakeholders (Yee *et al.*, 2022).

A key component of this effort is ensuring that government policies are aligned with long-term sustainability goals, particularly in the energy sector. Clear and supportive regulations can help mitigate the uncertainties that often deter potential investors from engaging in RE projects. When individuals and corporations perceive investment risks as manageable, they are more likely to commit their financial resources to these initiatives. In particular, small-scale investors can be a vital source of capital for RE projects, provided that the right incentives and protections are in place (Li *et al.*, 2022).

Japan offers a prime example of how innovative financing models and regulatory frameworks can stimulate investment in RE. In Japan, solar and wind energy projects have been partly financed through the Hometown Investment Trust (HIT) model, which provides a unique form of crowdfunding that allows individuals to invest in RE projects online by selecting projects that align with their personal interests (Yoshino *et al.*, 2019). Unlike traditional investment models, HIT enables individuals to support RE initiatives not for financial profits but to receive goods or services generated by the projects. This model has proven to be highly effective in making RE investments more accessible to a broader segment of the population, including small investors who might otherwise be excluded from such opportunities.

The HIT crowdfunding model exemplifies the potential for alternative financing schemes to drive significant investment in RE. By reducing the reliance on large institutional investors and allowing ordinary citizens to participate directly, HIT fosters greater community involvement and ensures that the benefits of RE projects are more widely distributed. Additionally, the social aspect of HIT, where investors can feel a sense of ownership and contribution to sustainable energy efforts, can further motivate participation (Rahmani *et al.*, 2023).

In a study conducted by Yoshino *et al.* (2019), a financing model was proposed that integrates HIT funds with spillover tax payments to make RE projects more attractive to individual investors. The spillover tax component of the model is designed to enhance the financial viability of RE projects, incentivizing small-scale investors by reducing their tax liabilities and offering more favorable returns on investment. This dual approach, combining the accessibility of crowdfunding with the financial incentives provided by tax breaks, presents a compelling case for how governments can play a proactive role in encouraging greater participation in RE investments.

Moreover, the spillover tax mechanism addresses one of the key barriers to investment in REs: perceived financial risk. Small-scale investors, particularly individuals, often perceive RE projects as too risky because of the long time horizons involved or the uncertainty surrounding policy and market conditions (Rahmani *et al.*, 2023; Yoshino *et al.*, 2019). By offering spillover tax benefits, governments can reduce these perceived risks and make RE projects more financially appealing to a wider range of investors. Such tax incentives can effectively lower the cost of entry into the RE market, thus democratizing access to green investment opportunities.

The success of RE investment efforts will depend on policy reform, financial innovation, and public engagement. Governments must adopt a multifaceted approach that includes regulatory support, tax incentives, and public outreach initiatives to create a thriving market for RE investments. In this context, models like HIT and spillover tax incentives offer valuable insights into how alternative financing schemes can be leveraged to increase investment in RE and help achieve the ambitious goals outlined in international agreements such as the Paris Accord.

In conclusion, while private sector investment has historically driven the development of RE, the recent decline in participation underscores the urgent need for stronger policy and regulatory support. Governments must lead in creating an environment where private sector actors, including small-scale investors, feel confident in contributing to the green energy transition.

2.2. *Theoretical model*

When individuals decide to invest, they deliberately choose to forgo their present financial resources in exchange for potential future returns. These returns may manifest as capital gains, income, or dividends. While expenditures on consumption goods provide immediate gratification and utility to individuals, investments aim to ensure long-term benefits and a higher standard of living in the future (Else and Curwen, 2006). From a traditional economic perspective, profit maximization is the primary objective of investment decisions. Investors accept varying degrees of risk, understanding that the possibility of losing some or all of their invested capital is inherent to the investment process. Several factors, including interest rates, savings levels, demand, availability of internal funds, and tax policies, are key influences on investment behavior. This rational model assumes that investors seek to optimize their financial outcomes (Else and Curwen, 2006).

However, an alternative strand of literature, particularly in behavioral economics and psychology, challenges the assumption that investment decisions are purely rational. These fields assert that human behavior is often shaped by a complex interplay of cognitive, emotional, cultural, ethical, and environmental factors, making it challenging to reduce investment behavior to a simple profit-maximizing formula (Frijns *et al.*, 2008; Thanki *et al.*, 2022). Behavioral economists argue that logical calculations of risk and return do not purely drive investment decisions but are influenced by biases, heuristics, and emotions that can often lead to seemingly irrational behaviors.

In the context of green finance and RE investments, understanding the motivations behind individuals' investment decisions requires a comprehensive analysis that goes beyond the traditional economic view. The complexity of RE investments, combined with the uncertainties associated with green technologies and long-term environmental outcomes, means that individuals may be influenced by a broader range of factors, including ethical concerns, environmental awareness, and social responsibility (Gamel *et al.*, 2022; Lundheim *et al.*, 2021; Yee *et al.*, 2022; Ziaei, 2022).

Investment theory provides a useful framework for examining how individuals allocate resources to available investment opportunities within individual and broader economic organizations (Merton, 1982). However, to develop a more holistic theory of investment behavior, it is necessary to start by identifying the various influences on individual decision-making. Maher and Braskamp (1987) (Baumgartel, 1987) introduced *Personal Investment Theory (PI)*, which provides a foundation for understanding individual investment behavior. PI posits that investment decisions are influenced by three core components:

(a) **Beliefs about oneself**: These include an individual's perceptual, psychological, and emotional characteristics that shape how they see themselves as investors. Self-perception is crucial in influencing an individual's confidence in making investment decisions, including their risk tolerance and perceived financial acumen.
(b) **Perception of goals**: This refers to an individual's goals in various contexts, whether financial, ethical, environmental, or social. For example, some individuals may prioritize financial returns, while others may value contributing to environmental sustainability through investments in RE projects. These goals help determine how individuals assess the attractiveness of different investment opportunities.
(c) **Perceived alternatives for pursuing goals**: This component involves the behavioral options that individuals consider appropriate and achievable. Individuals weigh the alternatives they perceive as accessible, including traditional financial products or more innovative and socially conscious investment opportunities, such as those in green finance or RE (Baumgartel, 1987; Spielberger, 2005).

Importantly, economic indicators and financial returns are not the only factors influencing individual investment decisions, especially in the case of RE projects. Non-financial factors, such as environmental sustainability, social responsibility, and personal ethics, play a significant role in individuals' decision-making processes. These factors often align with individuals' values and long-term objectives rather than immediate financial gain (Menyeh, 2021).

Psychological factors are particularly influential in shaping individuals' investment behavior. Studies have shown that attitudes, beliefs, and emotions strongly impact the willingness to invest, especially in areas with perceived risk, such as RE. Psychological factors become even more significant in green finance, where environmental consciousness and the desire to contribute to sustainable development can drive investment decisions (Park and Oh, 2022).

One of the most widely used frameworks for understanding investment behavior from a psychological perspective is the *Theory of Planned Behavior (TPB)*. The TPB was developed as an extension of the earlier *Theory of Reasoned Action (TRA)*, originally introduced by Ajzen (Ajzen, 2012). The TPB posits that three core constructs, namely attitude, subjective norms, and perceived behavioral control, collectively influence and predict an individual's behavioral intention (Ajzen, 2012; Gamel *et al.*, 2022):

(a) **Attitude** refers to an individual's positive or negative evaluation of a specific behavior, in this case investing in RE. It captures the beliefs and evaluations individuals hold regarding the benefits or drawbacks of engaging in RE investments. If individuals perceive that RE investments contribute positively to environmental protection and offer long-term financial returns, they are more likely to develop a favorable attitude toward the behavior (Gamel *et al.*, 2022; Rahmani and Naeini, 2023; Yee *et al.*, 2022).

(b) **Subjective norms** involve the perceived social pressures or expectations from others — such as family, friends, or professional networks — regarding the behavior. When individuals believe that important people in their lives expect them to engage in RE investments, they are more likely to form the intention to invest. Social influences play a vital role in shaping investment behavior, especially in communities or networks where sustainability and ethical investing are highly regarded (Gamel *et al.*, 2022; Rahmani *et al.*, 2024a; Yee *et al.*, 2022).

(c) **Perceived behavioral control** reflects an individual's perception of how easy or difficult it will be to perform the behavior based on their assessment of the resources, skills, and opportunities available. In the context of RE investments, perceived behavioral control refers to the extent to which individuals believe they have the financial resources, knowledge, or access to investment platforms to participate in RE projects. A higher sense of control is associated with a stronger intention to invest, as individuals feel more capable of managing the potential challenges associated with such investments (Gamel *et al.*, 2022; Rahmani *et al.*, 2024b; Yee *et al.*, 2022).

The TPB provides a robust theoretical model for analyzing how individuals form intentions to invest in RE projects. It accounts for both rational and non-rational influences on behavior. The model suggests that individuals do not make investment decisions in isolation but rather consider a variety of internal and external factors, including their own attitudes, the expectations of others, and their perceived ability to take meaningful action.

This chapter builds on an extended version of the TPB by incorporating additional psychological variables, such as perceived risk, to deepen the understanding of the decision-making process for RE investments. Perceived risk is particularly relevant in the context of RE investments, where uncertainties related to technology, policy changes, and long-term returns may deter potential investors. By including perceived risk in the TPB framework, this study aims to provide a more nuanced analysis of the psychological factors driving individuals' investment decisions in RE.

2.3. *Conceptual framework and Hypotheses development*

2.3.1. *TPB constructs: Attitude, subjective norms, and perceived behavioral control*

Empirical research has shown that attitude, subjective norms, and perceived behavioral control significantly impact investment decisions. In the context of RE, positive attitudes toward RE investments, favorable social pressures (subjective norms), and a sense of control over the investment process can strongly motivate individuals to take action. Several studies have highlighted how attitudes, subjective norms, and perceived behavioral control positively influence the intention to invest in RE projects (Daiyabu *et al.*, 2023; Gamel *et al.*, 2022; Proudlove *et al.*, 2020; Yee *et al.*, 2022). For instance, individuals who view RE investments as both financially rewarding and environmentally responsible are more likely to engage in such investments if they feel encouraged by their social networks and have confidence in their ability to manage the investment process.

One study (Thanki *et al.*, 2022), which applied the TPB model to socially responsible investments (SRIs), demonstrated that these constructs influence general investment behaviors and are crucial in guiding decisions toward ethical and sustainable investments. The results revealed that the TPB constructs significantly and positively impacted individuals' intentions to invest in socially responsible ventures, such as RE projects. This finding suggests that attitudes toward sustainability, social reinforcement, and a perception of control play a vital role in driving investment decisions in RE.

Raut's (2020) study further illustrates the importance of psychological factors in the decision-making process of individual investors. In his research, attitudes, subjective norms, and perceived behavioral control emerged as significant determinants of investment behavior. This reinforces the idea that psychological influences are central to understanding why individuals invest in RE, particularly when they perceive these investments as aligned with their financial interests and environmental values. For example, individuals who hold positive attitudes toward green investments are more likely to see RE projects as viable and impactful, especially when they perceive encouragement from others and feel capable of successfully investing.

Research consistently supports the effectiveness of TPB in predicting INIs, especially when dealing with complex, long-term investments like those in RE. TPB has been used to analyze investment behaviors in various domains, and its constructs have consistently been found to positively influence individuals' intentions. Studies (Bin-Nashwan and Muneeza, 2023; Conradie *et al.*, 2021; Daiyabu *et al.*, 2023; Gamel *et al.*, 2022; Kastner *et al.*, 2021; Lai, 2019; Proudlove *et al.*, 2020; Yee *et al.*, 2022) have shown that individuals with favorable attitudes toward RE investments, supportive social environments, and a high sense of control over their ability to invest are significantly more likely to follow through on their intentions.

A study conducted in Malaysia explored the added constructs of *evaluation of the regulatory framework* and *risk aversion* and found that attitudes, subjective norms, the regulatory environment, and perceptions of behavioral control all significantly influenced INIs in RE projects. This emphasizes the importance of favorable regulations in encouraging investments and reducing perceived risks (Yee *et al.*, 2022).

In Germany, research on wind energy investments revealed that factors such as individuals' consumption profiles and prior *investment experience* positively influenced INIs, in addition to the traditional TPB constructs. This finding highlights the importance of experience and personal energy consumption habits in shaping investment behaviors, particularly in technologically advanced markets like wind energy (Gamel *et al.*, 2022).

An Australian study (Proudlove *et al.*, 2020) used multiple linear regression to analyze INIs in RE. It confirmed that attitudes, subjective norms, and perceived behavioral control were significant predictors of INIs. This study further supports the general applicability of the TPB model across different regional contexts, even with smaller sample sizes.

In Nigeria, a study incorporated *tax incentives* as an additional construct and demonstrated that attitudes and subjective norms were positively associated with INIs. This finding highlights the crucial role that government policies, particularly tax incentives, play in encouraging investment in RE in emerging markets (Daiyabu *et al.*, 2023).

By leveraging the TPB framework, this study aims to extend existing research on individuals' investment decisions in RE. Specifically, it examines how attitudes, subjective norms, and perceived behavioral control influence individuals' intentions to invest in RE projects, with a particular focus on how psychological factors mediate these decisions. Drawing on prior studies, the following hypotheses have been formulated to guide the analysis:

H1: Attitude toward investment positively affects the intention to invest in RE projects. This hypothesis builds on the assumption that individuals who hold favorable attitudes toward RE projects, particularly in terms of their financial, ethical, and environmental benefits, are more likely to develop strong intentions to invest.

H2: Subjective norms positively affect the intention to invest in RE projects. This hypothesis suggests that individuals who perceive positive social pressure from significant others, including family, friends, and professional networks, are more likely to form intentions to invest in RE projects. When individuals feel that their investment aligns with the values and expectations of those around them, they are more motivated to act.

H3: Perceived behavioral control positively influences the intention to invest in RE projects. This hypothesis posits that individuals who feel confident in their ability to invest, based on their financial resources, knowledge of RE projects, and access to investment platforms, will be more likely to translate their intentions into action.

2.3.2. *Perceived risk of investment*

In traditional and green finance, risk is an ever-present factor influencing investment decisions. While green finance offers new opportunities for sustainable growth and environmental preservation, it is not immune to the uncertainties and risks inherent in financial markets. Investment risk remains one of investors' most significant factors before committing to RE projects. Numerous studies (Hussain *et al.*, 2021; Ilbahar *et al.*, 2022; Qadir *et al.*, 2021; Taghizadeh-Hesary and Yoshino, 2020; Yoshino *et al.*, 2019) have thoroughly examined how these risks affect investor behavior and decision-making, highlighting that the development of green energy projects is often fraught with uncertainty and complexity due to a variety of risks (Taghizadeh-Hesary and Yoshino, 2020).

Perceived risk is particularly influential in shaping decisions related to RE investments because these projects are often viewed as novel, technologically advanced, and less predictable than traditional energy projects. The literature identifies a range of risks that can hinder future investment in RE, such as technology risk, feasibility risk, political risk, operational risk, state support, and demand risk (Taghizadeh-Hesary *et al.*, 2021b). These risks can emerge from the inherent uncertainty surrounding new technologies, volatile market conditions, regulatory frameworks, and political instability. As a result, private sector investment in RE is frequently constrained by these concerns. Investors, especially those unfamiliar with RE technologies or markets, are often reluctant to commit their resources due to the potential for project failure or financial loss (Yoshino *et al.*, 2019).

Various risks influencing investor participation in RE projects have been extensively studied (Hussain *et al.*, 2021; Ilbahar *et al.*, 2022). One key finding is that investors perceive RE projects as riskier than traditional energy investments, which explains why many hesitate to engage in green finance. For instance, investors may perceive technology risk as particularly high in the RE sector, given the evolving nature of green technologies such as solar panels, wind turbines, or energy storage systems. These technologies are often in their early stages of development, making their long-term reliability and profitability uncertain. Feasibility risk, which encompasses the technical and economic viability of RE projects, is another critical factor, as investors may doubt whether these projects can deliver the promised returns over time (Taghizadeh-Hesary and Yoshino, 2020).

Additionally, political and regulatory risks play a significant role in shaping investor behavior. Changes in government policies, shifts in energy subsidies, or uncertainty surrounding carbon taxes can all create an unpredictable environment for RE investments. For instance, some governments may provide generous subsidies for RE projects only to withdraw them later due to changing political priorities. This creates instability in the market and increases perceived risk for investors, leading to a reluctance to invest without clear, long-term policy commitments. Similarly, operational risks, including issues related to the day-to-day functioning of RE projects, can deter investors who worry about potential breakdowns, maintenance challenges, or inefficiencies in energy production.

One of the most critical aspects of perceived risk is how investors evaluate the likelihood and severity of negative outcomes. Research suggests that individuals' behavior is significantly shaped by their perception of risk, how likely they believe a threat is, and how severe they perceive the consequences to be (Zobeidi *et al.*, 2022). This perception can include financial risks and environmental, social, and health risks that could affect the broader community or the investor personally. For instance, an investor might be concerned about the environmental consequences of a failed renewable energy project or how changes in societal energy consumption could influence future demand for renewable energy.

Because perceived risk involves uncertainty and the potential for negative outcomes, it profoundly impacts decision-making processes. Studies have shown that individuals with high levels of perceived risk are less likely to invest in RE projects (Nur Aini and Lutfi, 2019). For instance, one study found that risk perception negatively affects investment decision-making, leading investors to avoid high-risk opportunities in favor of safer, more predictable investments. This aligns with another study (Singh and Bhattacharjee, 2019), which revealed that investors with a lower perception of risk are more likely to invest in high-risk stocks than those who prefer low-risk, stable options like deposits. These findings highlight how the perception of risk directly influences the investments individuals are willing to make.

In the context of RE investments, reducing perceived risk is crucial for encouraging greater participation from both individual and institutional investors. Given that RE projects often have longer time horizons and may require significant upfront capital, perceived risk becomes a barrier to entry for many potential investors. Green financing mechanisms, such as government-backed guarantees, tax incentives, or long-term contracts like Power Purchase Agreements (PPAs), can help mitigate these risks by offering financial security and stability. By reducing the financial uncertainties associated with RE investments, these mechanisms can foster greater investor confidence and make RE projects more attractive to a wider range of investors.

In conclusion, perceived risk remains critical in shaping investment decisions within the RE sector. While the potential for high returns and the promise of sustainability make RE projects appealing, various risks, such as technological, political, and operational uncertainties, can deter investment. Therefore, mitigating these risks through policy reforms, financial instruments, and increased transparency is essential to fostering greater investor participation. By addressing these concerns, governments and financial institutions can help create a more stable and supportive environment for green finance, ultimately promoting the growth and development of RE projects.

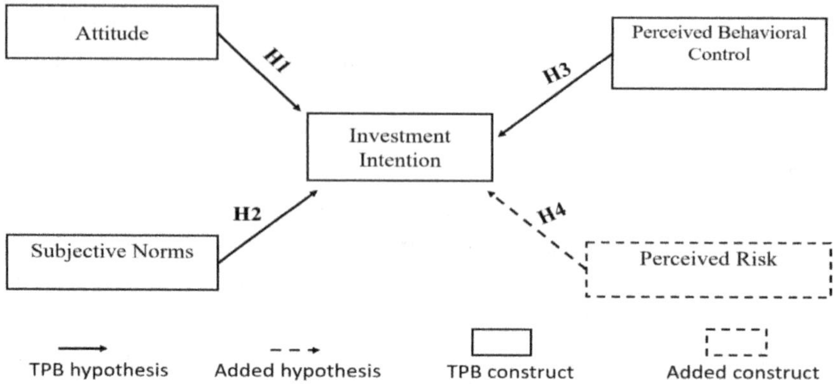

Figure 1. Proposed model for predicting individuals' *INI*s in RE projects.

This extended section reflects the importance of perceived risk in RE investments and how it impacts investor behavior. Based on previous research findings, the current study proposes to test other hypotheses:

H4: Perceived risk of investment negatively influences INI.

According to the theoretical basis and literature discussed previously, the proposed model of study, including variables, hypotheses, and the relationships between them, is illustrated in Figure 1.

3. Materials and Methods

3.1. *Measurement scales*

The measurement scales for the constructs in this study were adapted from previous research to ensure validity and reliability. In particular, four items to measure attitude were sourced from the study by (Lai, 2019), while three items for perceived behavioral control were taken from the work of Raut (2020). For INI, four items were extracted from the study by Irfan *et al.* (2021). Perceived risk was measured using four items based on the work of Angowski *et al.* (2021), and subjective norms were evaluated using three items from Raut (2020).

The structured questionnaire utilized a 5-point Likert scale where 1 = strongly disagree, 2 = disagree, 3 = neither agree nor disagree, 4 = agree, and 5 = strongly agree. Twelve experts reviewed the questionnaire to ensure its content validity. The content validity index (CVI) for each item exceeded 0.80 and the content validity ratio (CVR) was greater than 0.56, confirming the questionnaire's validity.

3.2. *Data collection*

For this study, a cross-sectional survey was designed to gather data from 205 randomly selected individuals in Tehran. The data were collected over two months using a combination of structured questionnaires and face-to-face interviews. Each participant was given clear instructions to ensure accurate responses, and the questionnaire took approximately 45 to 60 minutes to complete.

The demographic characteristics of the final sample are as follows: Most respondents were male (86%), and most were between the ages of 40 and 50 (35%). A significant portion of respondents (51%) held a university or college degree, and 61% of participants reported having a low level of financial knowledge, while only 11% claimed to have high financial literacy. Most respondents (70%) had no prior experience investing in financial markets.

3.3. *SEM and data analysis*

To empirically test the proposed research model and its hypotheses, we employed SEM. SEM is a comprehensive statistical technique for evaluating complex relationships between observed and latent variables. Unlike traditional first-generation statistical methods, such as multiple regression or logistic regression, SEM allows for the simultaneous examination of multiple constructs and their relationships, taking into account measurement errors and unobserved variables [39]. This makes SEM particularly well suited for analyzing the intricate relationships between psychological constructs.

The data analysis began with a confirmatory factor analysis (CFA) to evaluate the validity and reliability of the measurement model. CFA assesses the relationship between latent and observed variables and is critical for ensuring that the scales used in the study accurately measure the intended constructs. The CFA results were evaluated using the following criteria for reliability and validity: Cronbach's alpha (α), McDonald's omega (ω), and composite reliability (CR), all of which needed to be greater than 0.7 to confirm the reliability of the constructs. Additionally, maximal reliability (MaxR(H)) was computed, which also required a value above 0.7 to confirm the reliability of the measurement scales.

We also assessed the convergent validity of the constructs using factor loadings, CR, and the average variance extracted (AVE). The acceptable thresholds for factor loadings were greater than 0.5 (with p-values < 0.05), and CR values needed to be higher than AVE. Divergent validity was tested by ensuring that AVE values exceeded the maximum shared variance (MSV) and the average shared variance (ASV). Additional tests for divergent validity included the Fornell–Larcker criterion and the Heterotrait-Monotrait Ratio (HTMT), all of which confirmed the robustness of the constructs.

The structural model's overall fit was assessed using several key indices, including the root mean square error of approximation (RMSEA), comparative fit index (CFI), and the standardized root mean square residual (SRMR). Additional goodness-of-fit indices, such as the NFI, were also calculated to provide a comprehensive evaluation of the model's fit to the data.

Following the confirmation of the model's reliability, validity, and goodness of fit, we tested the research hypotheses. The coefficients of determination (R^2) were computed to evaluate how much variance in the dependent variable (INI) could be explained by the independent variables (attitude, subjective norms, perceived behavioral control, and perceived risk).

4. Results

The results from the analysis confirm the validity and reliability of the proposed model and its constructs. Several statistical tests were performed, including the Kaiser–Meyer–Olkin (KMO) measure of sampling adequacy and Bartlett's test of sphericity. The KMO value of 0.887 indicates that the sample size was highly adequate for factor analysis, as values above 0.8 demonstrate good adequacy. Bartlett's test of sphericity yielded a highly significant result (chi-square = 2617.370, df = 153, $p < 0.001$), suggesting that the correlations between the variables were sufficient to justify factor analysis and SEM.

4.1. *Factor loadings and reliability*

The internal consistency and reliability of the measurement model were evaluated using Cronbach's alpha (α) and McDonald's omega (ω) for each latent variable, as shown in Table 1.

The results indicated high reliability across all constructs, as all values exceeded the acceptable threshold of 0.7. Specifically, attitude (ATT) had an α of 0.907 and McDonald's omega of 0.914, indicating very high internal consistency. Perceived behavioral control (PBC) also exhibited strong reliability with $\alpha = 0.884$ and McDonald's omega = 0.887. INI showed an α of 0.895 and McDonald's omega of 0.900, further confirming reliability. Perceived risk (PRI) was the highest with $\alpha = 0.944$ and McDonald's omega = 0.951, and subjective norms (SUN) had an α of 0.846 and McDonald's omega of 0.858.

The factor loadings for each of the items were significant and ranged between 0.738 and 0.904, indicating strong correlations between the observed variables and their respective latent constructs. The highest-ranked factor loadings were observed in the perceived risk variable, with items like "Components may generate less electricity over time than expected" (pr4) having a loading of 0.902.

4.2. *Validity assessment*

The validity indices are presented in Table 2. The CR for all variables exceeded the threshold of 0.7, with attitude having a CR of 0.908, PBC a CR of 0.885, and INI a CR of 0.897. These results confirm the high reliability of the constructs. The AVE for all constructs was also greater than 0.5, confirming convergent validity, with the highest AVE observed for perceived risk (PRI) at 0.808.

Table 1. Statements for measuring the latent variables.

Latent and observed Variables	Factor loading (r)	p-values	Rank
Attitude (ATT) (Lai, 2019) ($\boldsymbol{\alpha = 0.907}$, **McDonald's omega** ($\boldsymbol{\omega}$) $\boldsymbol{= 0.914}$)			
• I think that investment in RE projects is an intelligent choice. (at1)	0.893	0.000	1
• I think that investing in RE projects is a good idea. (at2)	0.825	0.000	2
• In my opinion, investing in RE projects is valuable. (at3)	0.815	0.000	4
• I think that investment in RE projects is enjoyable. (at4)	0.842	0.000	3
Perceived Behavior Control (PBC) (Raut, 2020) ($\boldsymbol{\alpha = 0.884}$, **McDonald's omega** ($\boldsymbol{\omega}$) $\boldsymbol{= 0.887}$)			
• I am able to identify which projects to invest in. (pb1)	0.872	0.000	1
• I have the necessary knowledge to invest in RE projects. (pb2)	0.828	0.000	2
• I can invest in favorable projects conveniently. (pb3)	0.843	0.000	3
Investment Intention (INI) (Irfan *et al.*, 2021) ($\boldsymbol{\alpha = 0.895}$, **McDonald's omega** ($\boldsymbol{\omega}$) $\boldsymbol{= 0.900}$)			
• I intend to invest in RE projects. (in1)	0.895	0.000	1
• The attitude of consuming fewer fossil fuels makes me invest in RE projects. (in2)	0.808	0.000	2
• I intend to invest in green projects soon. (in3)	0.799	0.000	3
• I intend to encourage others to invest in RE projects. (in4)	0.804	0.000	4
Perceived Risk (PRI) (Angowski *et al.*, 2021) ($\boldsymbol{\alpha = 0.944}$, **McDonald's omega** ($\boldsymbol{\omega}$) $\boldsymbol{= 0.951}$)			
• Investing in RE projects cannot meet the electricity demand. (pr1)	0.901	0.000	2
• I perceive the investment in RE projects as risky. (pr2)	0.888	0.000	4
• I am concerned that investing in RE projects will harm the environment. (pr3)	0.904	0.000	3
• Components may generate less electricity over time than expected. (pr4)	0.902	0.000	1
Subjective Norms (SUN) (Raut, 2020) ($\boldsymbol{\alpha = 0.846}$, **McDonald's omega** ($\boldsymbol{\omega}$) $\boldsymbol{= 0.858}$)			
• My colleagues and friends like to invest in RE projects. (sn1)	0.804	0.000	2
• Those who have an important influence on me think that I should invest in RE projects. (sn2)	0.874	0.000	1
• People whose opinions I value would prefer that I should invest in RE projects. (sn3)	0.738	0.000	3

Regarding discriminant validity, the MSV for each variable was lower than the AVE, further confirming the distinctiveness of the constructs. For example, the AVE for attitude was 0.713, higher than its MSV of 0.385, satisfying the discriminant validity criterion. The maximal reliability (MaxR(H)) values were all above 0.7, with perceived risk (PRI) showing the highest MaxR(H) at 0.944.

The HTMT analysis, as seen in Table 3, revealed that all correlations between the constructs were within acceptable limits. The highest correlation was observed between ATT and INI with an HTMT ratio of 0.632, followed by ATT and SUN at 0.482. None of the HTMT values exceeded 0.85, indicating strong discriminant validity between the constructs.

Table 2. Validity indices.

Variables	Model Validity Measures (CR)	(AVE)	(MSV)	MaxR(H)
ATT	0.908	0.713	0.385	0.913
PBC	0.885	0.719	0.118	0.887
INI	0.897	0.685	0.385	0.905
PRI	0.944	0.808	0.221	0.944
SUN	0.848	0.651	0.241	0.862

Note: $*p < 0.050$; $**p < 0.010$; $***p < 0.001$.

Table 3. Heterotrait-Monotrait Ratio of Correlations (HTMT).

	ATT	PBC	INI	PRI	SUN
ATT					
PBC	0.207				
INI	0.632	0.333			
PRI	0.436	0.197	0.474		
SUN	0.482	0.115	0.473	0.250	

Table 4. Model fit indices.

	CFI	SRMR	RMSEA	P-Close	PNFI	NFI
Estimate	0.990	0.072	0.005	0.999	0.780	0.955
Threshold	>0.95	<0.08	<0.06	>0.05	>0.5	>0.9
Interpretation	***	***	***	***	***	***

4.3. *Model fit indices*

The goodness-of-fit indices, presented in Table 4, demonstrate that the model fits the data well.

The CFI was 0.990, well above the acceptable threshold of 0.95, indicating an excellent fit. The RMSEA was 0.005, below the recommended cut-off of 0.06, and the ** SRMR was 0.072, slightly above the recommended cut-off of 0.08 but still within an acceptable range. The P-close value was 0.999, showing strong evidence that the model fits the population data well.

Other indices, including the NFI of 0.955 and the parsimony normed fit index (PNFI) of 0.780, further confirm the adequacy of the model's fit. These results collectively suggest that the model adequately represents the relationships among the observed and latent variables and supports the hypothesized structure of the extended TPB model.

4.4. *Structural model and hypothesis testing results*

The results from the structural model provide valuable insights into the factors that influence individuals' intentions to invest in RE projects. Each path coefficient (β) illustrates how changes in psychological and social factors affect INI. The analysis of these results highlights the practical implications of each variable and its corresponding impact on investment behaviors. The structural model presented in Figure 2 was developed to examine the relationships between the key variables.

The model was evaluated using standardized regression coefficients, and the hypotheses were tested based on these paths. The results from the structural model are summarized in Table 5. The standardized path coefficient for the relationship between attitude and INI is $\beta = 0.385$, with a p-value of 0.000. This finding demonstrates a positive and significant relationship between attitude and the intention to invest in REs.

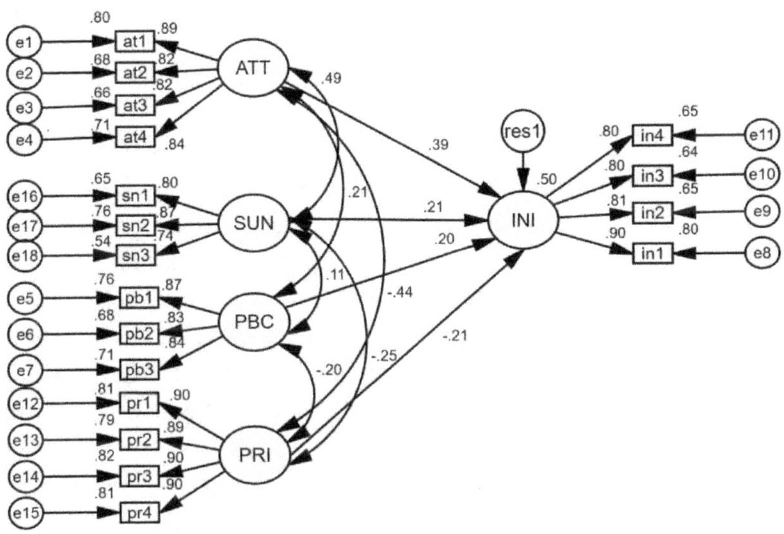

Figure 2. Standardized structural model.

Table 5. Regression path estimates.

Hypotheses	Structural paths	β	p-value	Conclusion
H1	ATT → INI	0.385	0.000	Supported
H2	SUN → INI	0.208	0.004	Supported
H3	PBC → INI	0.199	0.001	Supported
H4	PRI → INI	−0.210	0.002	Supported

A 0.385 increase in β suggests that for every unit increase in positive attitude toward RE investments, the intention to invest rises by 38.5%.

The relationship between subjective norms and INIis captured by a path coefficient of $\beta = 0.208$, with a p-value of 0.004. This coefficient indicates that for each unit increase in the social influence or pressure perceived by an individual, the intention to invest in RE projects increases by 20.8%.

The standardized path coefficient for perceived behavioral control and INIis $\beta = 0.199$, with a *p*-value of 0.001. This coefficient reflects a positive relationship, suggesting that as individuals' perceived control over their ability to invest increases, their intention to invest in RE projects also increases by 19.9%.

In contrast to the other variables, perceived risk has a negative relationship with INI, with a path coefficient of $\beta = -0.210$ and a *p*-value of 0.002. This indicates that as perceived risk increases by one unit, the intention to invest in RE projects decreases by 21%.

The R^2 value of 0.505 for the INI indicates that the model explains approximately 50.5% of the variance in individuals' intentions to invest in RE. This suggests that the combination of attitude, subjective norms, perceived behavioral control, and perceived risk provides a strong explanatory framework for understanding investment behaviors in the RE sector.

5. Discussion and Conclusion

The study's findings have profound implications for understanding the key psychological and social factors influencing individuals' INIs in RE projects. This is particularly relevant within the context of developing economies like Iran, where green finance is in its nascent stages, and the transition from fossil fuels to RE is essential for achieving sustainable growth. The results highlight how variables like attitude, subjective norms, perceived behavioral control, and perceived risk shape investment behaviors and how these insights can be translated into effective policy measures to foster green finance and RE development.

The attitude of individuals toward investing in RE projects plays a critical role in shaping investment decisions. As the study reveals, a positive attitude toward RE investments significantly increases the likelihood of participation. The strong correlation between attitude and INI is consistent with several previous studies (Daiyabu *et al.*, 2023; Proudlove *et al.*, 2020; Yee *et al.*, 2022). Individuals are more likely to invest in RE projects when they perceive them as beneficial, intelligent choices. These findings align with studies that emphasize the importance of a general evaluation of behavior, as noted in Ajzen's TPB framework [52]. In this study, attitudes were found to explain 32% of the variance in INI, further supporting the hypothesis that attitude is one of the most influential predictors of investment behaviors in RE. This result implies that individuals who perceive RE investments as beneficial, intelligent, and valuable are likelier to commit to these projects. For instance, if investors view RE as an environmentally responsible choice and financially rewarding, their motivation to invest strengthens. The positive impact of attitude on INI underscores the importance of promoting the value and advantages of RE through educational campaigns, financial literacy programs, and real-world success stories of RE investments. A well-formed, positive perception of RE investments is critical to enhancing individuals' willingness to participate in green financing initiatives.

The positive relationship between attitude and INI has significant policy implications. Governments and institutions must foster positive attitudes toward RE investments by addressing misconceptions and highlighting the long-term financial and environmental benefits. The following policy measures can be considered:

(a) **Public awareness campaigns**: Governments should initiate extensive awareness campaigns that promote the economic benefits and environmental impact of investing in RE. This can help shape more positive attitudes and boost participation in green finance.
(b) **Sustainability education programs**: Introducing sustainability and financial literacy programs in schools and universities will help cultivate a generation of investors with a favorable attitude toward RE investments.
(c) **Tax credits and incentives**: Offering financial incentives, such as tax credits for individuals investing in RE, can enhance positive attitudes toward green finance, reinforcing the perception that it is a wise financial decision.
(d) **Public–private partnerships**: Collaborating with financial institutions and private entities to develop RE projects can increase public trust and generate more favorable attitudes toward these investments.
(e) **Corporate social responsibility initiatives**: Encouraging businesses to promote RE investments among employees and customers can create a positive ripple effect, boosting public attitudes toward green finance.

The data also strongly supported the role of subjective norms in influencing INI. This indicates that when individuals perceive that significant people, such as family, friends, or colleagues, encourage or expect them to invest in RE, they are more likely to do so. For example, if someone's social circle places a high value on sustainability or green investments, they are more likely to align their actions with those expectations. The findings show that social pressure, or the influence of key individuals such as family and peers, plays a crucial role in shaping investment behaviors. This result is consistent with previous studies (Daiyabu *et al.*, 2023; Gamel *et al.*, 2022; Proudlove *et al.*, 2020; Yee *et al.*, 2022) in the field of RE investments, which indicate that individuals are more likely to invest when they perceive social approval. The significance of subjective norms in this study further reveals the power of social influence in driving sustainable investment behaviors. In practical terms, this finding emphasizes the need for social campaigns and peer-driven initiatives to promote RE investments, as individuals are more likely to act when they feel that others in their close circles expect them to do so.

Given the importance of subjective norms, policymakers can implement the following strategies that leverage social dynamics to boost green finance participation:

(a) **Community-led investment projects**: Establishing cooperative or community-based RE projects where individuals invest collectively can promote social approval for green finance and foster stronger subjective norms favoring RE investments.
(b) **Social media campaigns**: Promoting RE investments using platforms like Instagram, Twitter, and YouTube can mobilize younger generations, who are influenced by social media trends.
(c) **Peer investment initiatives**: Creating programs where friends or family members can invest together in RE projects can reinforce positive subjective norms and increase the social desirability of green investments.
(d) **Recognition programs**: Governments and local authorities can recognize individuals or communities that actively participate in RE projects, providing social incentives for others to follow suit.
(e) **Engagement with community leaders**: Collaborating with local influencers, religious leaders, and community activists can enhance the visibility and social credibility of green finance initiatives, helping to strengthen subjective norms.

The study also found that perceived behavioral control positively influences INIs, though this influence is somewhat weaker than attitude and subjective norms. Individuals who feel confident in navigating financial platforms, understanding investment risks, and choosing the right RE projects are likelier to make actual investments. This result highlights the importance of providing investors with easy access to information, user-friendly investment platforms, and support tools. Policymakers and financial institutions can significantly improve participation rates in RE projects by simplifying the investment process and enhancing potential investors' knowledge. Previous studies (Gamel *et al.*, 2022; Yee *et al.*, 2022) support this conclusion, highlighting that perceived control is a significant driver of INI.

To enhance perceived behavioral control, the following policy measures can be considered:

(a) **Simplifying investment platforms**: Developing user-friendly platforms that allow individuals to easily invest in RE projects can help improve their sense of control over their investments.
(b) **Financial literacy programs**: Offering workshops and online resources that educate potential investors on how to navigate green finance options and manage risks can increase their perceived control.
(c) **Government-backed green investment products**: Providing low-risk, government-guaranteed RE investment products can empower individuals to invest with confidence, knowing that their investments are secure.

(d) **Improved access to green finance tools**: Creating more accessible green bonds, green credits, and RE investment funds can help individuals feel more in control of their financial decisions.
(e) **Personalized financial advisory services**: Offering tailored advisory services that guide individuals through investing in RE projects can help increase perceived behavioral control, especially for first-time investors.

One of the more striking findings from the study is the negative impact of perceived risk on INI, with a β of -0.210. This indicates that as individuals' perceptions of risk increase, their likelihood of investing in RE projects decreases. Perceived risk, which encompasses uncertainties related to technological failure, market volatility, and unstable policy environments, is a major barrier to green finance participation. Perceived risk encompasses various uncertainties related to technology, market conditions, and policy environments, which can make investors hesitant. For instance, an investor who believes that RE projects have a high risk of failure or low financial returns will be dissuaded from participating, regardless of the potential environmental benefits. These findings are consistent with previous research (Lodhi, 2014; Nur Aini and Lutfi, 2019; Singh and Bhattacharjee, 2019; Zobeidi *et al.*, 2022) that suggests risk aversion is a significant deterrent for individuals considering sustainable investments.

To mitigate perceived risk, governments and financial institutions must develop strategies that address these uncertainties and reassure investors of the security of their investments. The following policy recommendations can be drawn from these findings:

(a) **Government-backed guarantees**: Offering guarantees on RE investments, especially for first-time investors, can reduce perceived financial risk and increase participation in green finance.
(b) **Tax incentives for green investments**: Tax credits or deductions for investments in RE projects can offset perceived financial risks and encourage more significant investment.
(c) **Long-term RE policies**: Establishing stable, long-term energy policies that are resistant to political changes can help reduce investors' uncertainty and create a more secure investment environment.
(d) **Green bonds and subsidies**: Expanding the availability of green bonds and government subsidies for RE projects can reduce market risk and provide investors with more predictable returns.
(e) **Risk-sharing mechanisms**: Governments and private financial institutions can collaborate to share the risks of RE investments, ensuring that individuals are not solely responsible for potential losses.

In conclusion, policymakers, financial institutions, and environmental advocates can leverage these findings to design interventions encouraging broader participation in green finance. By addressing investment barriers and promoting the benefits of RE, stakeholders can accelerate the transition to sustainable energy.

The policy implications outlined provide a comprehensive roadmap for fostering greater individual engagement in RE projects, thereby contributing to global sustainability and climate goals. Implementing government-backed guarantees, tax incentives, long-term policies, green bonds, and risk-sharing mechanisms can create a more secure and attractive environment for investors.

Furthermore, enhancing public awareness and education about the benefits and opportunities of RE investments is crucial. By building investor confidence and demonstrating the viability and profitability of RE projects, private capital can be mobilized toward sustainable initiatives.

Collaboration between the public and private sectors is essential to develop innovative financial instruments and supportive policies that reduce perceived risks and enhance returns on RE investments. Such partnerships can drive the large-scale deployment of renewable energy technologies, contributing significantly to achieving the United Nations' SDGs.

In summary, a concerted effort from all stakeholders, underpinned by supportive policies and risk mitigation strategies, is vital to mobilize individual investments in renewable energy and advance global sustainability objectives.

References

Abbasi, KR, M Shahbaz, J Zhang, M Irfan and R Alvarado (2022). Analyze the environmental sustainability factors of China: The role of fossil fuel energy and renewable energy. *Renewable Energy*, 187, 390–402. https://doi.org/10.1016/j.renene.2022.01.066.

Aien, M and O Mahdavi (2020). On the way of policy making to reduce the reliance of fossil fuels: Case study of Iran. *Sustainability*, 12, 1–28. https://doi.org/10.3390/su122410606.

Ajzen, I (2012). The theory of planned behavior. *Handbook of Theories of Social Psychology*, 50, 438–459. https://doi.org/10.4135/9781446249215.n22.

Angowski, M, T Kijek, M Lipowski and I Bondos (2021). Factors affecting the adoption of photovoltaic systems in rural areas of Poland. *Energies*, 14, 5272. https://doi.org/10.3390/en14175272.

Bauer, A and K Menrad (2019). Standing up for the Paris Agreement: Do global climate targets influence individuals' greenhouse gas emissions? *Environmental Science and Policy*, 99, 72–79. https://doi.org/10.1016/j.envsci.2019.05.015.

Baumgartel, HJ (1987). *The Motivation Factor — A Theory of Personal Investment*. Lexington Books/DC Heath and Com.

Bin-Nashwan, SA and A Muneeza (2023). Investment decisions in digital sukuk in the time of COVID-19: Do tax incentives matter? *Journal of Sustainable Finance and Investment*, 13, 589–613. https://doi.org/10.1080/20430795.2021.1978918.

Chen, H and X Zhao (2022). Use intention of green financial security intelligence service based on UTAUT. *Environmental Development and Sustainability*. https://doi.org/10.1007/s10668-022-02501-5.

Chofreh, AG, FA Goni, JJ Klemeš, SM Seyed Moosavi, M Davoudi and M Zeinalnezhad (2021). Covid-19 shock: Development of strategic management framework for global energy. *Renewable and Sustainable Energy Reviews*, 139. https://doi.org/10.1016/j.rser.2020.110643.

Conradie, PD, O De Ruyck, J Saldien and K Ponnet (2021). Who wants to join a renewable energy community in Flanders? Applying an extended model of theory of planned behaviour to understand intent to participate. *Energy Policy*, 151, 112121. https://doi.org/10.1016/j.enpol.2020.112121.

Copur, Z and MS Gutter (2019). Economic, sociological, and psychological factors of the saving behavior: Turkey Case. *Journal of Family and Economic Issues*, 40, 305–322. https://doi.org/10.1007/s10834-018-09606-y.

Daiyabu, YA, NAA Manaf and H Mohamad Hsbollah (2023). Extending the theory of planned behaviour with application to renewable energy investment: The moderating effect of tax incentives. *International Journal of Energy Sector Management*, 17, 333–351. https://doi.org/10.1108/IJESM-11-2021-0011.

Else, P and P Curwen (2006). *Principles of Microeconomics*. Cengage Learning Asia Pte Limited. https://doi.org/10.4324/9780203018002.

Frijns, B, E Koellen and T Lehnert (2008). On the determinants of portfolio choice. *Journal of Economic Behavior and Organization*, 66, 373–386. https://doi.org/10.1016/j.jebo.2006.04.004.

Gamel, J, A Bauer, T Decker and K Menrad (2022). Financing wind energy projects: An extended theory of planned behavior approach to explain private households' wind energy investment intentions in Germany. *Renewable Energy*, 182, 592–601. https://doi.org/10.1016/j.renene.2021.09.108.

Hussain, J, K Zhou, F Muhammad, D Khan, A Khan, N Ali and R Akhtar (2021). Renewable energy investment and governance in countries along the belt & Road Initiative: Does trade openness matter? *Renewable Energy*, 180, 1278–1289. https://doi.org/10.1016/j.renene.2021.09.020.

Ilbahar, E, C Kahraman and S Cebi (2022). Risk assessment of renewable energy investments: A modified failure mode and effect analysis based on prospect theory and intuitionistic fuzzy AHP. *Energy*, 239. https://doi.org/10.1016/j.energy.2021.121907.

IRENA (2021). *World Energy Transitions Outlook: 1.5°C Pathway*. International Renewable Energy Agency.

IRENA (2020). *Global Landscape of Renewable Energy Finance 2020*. International Renewable Energy Agency, Abu Dhabi.

Irfan, M, Y Hao, M Ikram, H Wu, R Akram and A Rauf (2021). Assessment of the public acceptance and utilization of renewable energy in Pakistan. *Sustainable Production and Consumption*, 27, 312–324. https://doi.org/10.1016/j.spc.2020.10.031.

Kastner, I, A Becker, S Bobeth and E Matthies (2021). Are professionals rationals? How organizations and households make e-car investments. *Sustainability*, 13, 1–19. https://doi.org/10.3390/su13052496.

Lai, CP (2019). Personality traits and stock investment of individuals. *Sustainability*, 11. https://doi.org/10.3390/su11195474.

Lamb, WF, T Wiedmann, J Pongratz, R andrew, M Crippa, JGJ Olivier, D Wiedenhofer, G Mattioli, A Al Khourdajie, J House, S Pachauri, M Figueroa, Y Saheb, R Slade, K Hubacek, L Sun, SK Ribeiro, S Khennas, S De La Rue Du Can, L Chapungu, SJ Davis, I Bashmakov, H Dai, S Dhakal, X Tan, Y Geng, B Gu and J Minx (2021). A review of trends and drivers of greenhouse gas emissions by sector from 1990 to 2018. *Environmental Research Letters*, 16. https://doi.org/10.1088/1748-9326/abee4e.

Li, Z, TH Kuo, W Siao-Yun and L The Vinh (2022). Role of green finance, volatility and risk in promoting the investments in Renewable Energy Resources in the post-covid-19. *Resources Policy*, 76. https://doi.org/10.1016/j.resourpol.2022.102563.

Lodhi, S (2014). Factors influencing individual investor behavior: An empirical study of city Karachi. *IOSR Journal of Business and Management*, 16, 68–76. https://doi.org/10.9790/487x-16236876.

Lundheim, SH, S Vesely, A Nayum and CA Klöckner (2021). From vague interest to strong intentions to install solar panels on private homes in the North — An analysis of psychological drivers. *Renewable Energy*, 165, 455–463. https://doi.org/10.1016/j.renene.2020.11.034.

Masukujjaman, M, SS Alam, C Siwar and SA Halim (2021). Purchase intention of renewable energy technology in rural areas in Bangladesh: Empirical evidence. *Renewable Energy*, 170, 639–651. https://doi.org/10.1016/j.renene.2021.01.125.

Mathis, W (2022). Energy Transition Drew Record $755 Billion of Investment in 2021. Bloomberg.com.

Menyeh, BO (2021). Financing electricity access in Africa: A choice experiment study of household investor preferences for renewable energy investments in Ghana. *Renewable and Sustainable Energy Reviews*, 146. https://doi.org/10.1016/j.rser.2021.111132.

Merton, RC (1982). On the microeconomic theory of investment under uncertainty. *Handbook of Mathematical Economics*, 2, 601–669. https://doi.org/10.1016/S1573-4382(82)02008-6.

Nur Aini, NS and L Lutfi (2019). The influence of risk perception, risk tolerance, overconfidence, and loss aversion towards investment decision making. *Journal of Economics Business and Accounting Ventura*, 21, 401. https://doi.org/10.14414/jebav.v21i3.1663.

Park, SR and KS Oh (2022). Integration of ESG Information into Individual Investors' Corporate Investment Decisions: Utilizing the UTAUT Framework. *Frontiers in Psychology*, 13. https://doi.org/10.3389/fpsyg.2022.899480.

Proudlove, R, S Finch and S Thomas (2020). Factors influencing intention to invest in a community owned renewable energy initiative in Queensland, Australia. *Energy Policy*, 140, 111441. https://doi.org/10.1016/j.enpol.2020.111441.

Qadir, SA, H Al-Motairi, F Tahir and L Al-Fagih (2021). Incentives and strategies for financing the renewable energy transition: A review. *Energy Reports*, 7, 3590–3606. https://doi.org/10.1016/j.egyr.2021.06.041.

Rahmani, A, R Aboojafari, AB Naeini and J Mashayekh (2024a). Adoption of digital innovation for resource efficiency and sustainability in the metal industry. *Resources Policy*, 90, 104719. https://doi.org/10.1016/j.resourpol.2024.104719.

Rahmani, A, R Aboojafari, F Taghizadeh-Hesary, AB Naeini and J Mashayekh (2024b). Consumers' behavioral economics in renewable energy. In *A Modern Guide to Energy Economics*. Edward Elgar Publishing, 28–55.

Rahmani, A and AB Naeini (2023). Predicting intention in applying solar energy technologies in agriculture industry: A moderated and mediated model. *Cleaner and Responsible Consumption*, 8, 100102. https://doi.org/10.1016/j.clrc.2023.100102.

Rahmani, A, AB Naeini, J Mashayekh, R Aboojafari, T Daim and H Yalcin (2024c). Green innovation for a greener future: A meta-analysis of the impact on environmental performance. *Journal of Cleaner Production*, 460, 142547. https://doi.org/10.1016/j.jclepro.2024.142547.

Rahmani, A, J Mashayekh, R Aboojafari and AB Naeini (2023). Determinants of households' intention for investment in renewable energy projects. *Renewable Energy*, 205, 823–837. https://doi.org/10.1016/j.renene.2023.01.096.

Raut, RK (2020). Past behaviour, financial literacy and investment decision-making process of individual investors. *International Journal of Emerging Markets*, 15, 1243–1263. https://doi.org/10.1108/IJOEM-07-2018-0379.

Sachs, JD, WT Woo, N Yoshino and F Taghizadeh-Hesary (2019). Why is green finance important? *SSRN Electronic Journal*. https://doi.org/10.2139/ssrn.3327149.

Singh, R and J Bhattacharjee (2019). Measuring equity share related risk perception of investors in economically backward regions. *Risks*, 7, 12. https://doi.org/10.3390/risks7010012.

Spielberger, C (2005). *Encyclopedia of Applied Psychology*. Academic press. https://doi.org/10.5860/choice.42-3796.

Taghizadeh-Hesary, F and N Yoshino (2020). Sustainable solutions for green financing and investment in renewable energy projects. *Energies*, 13. https://doi.org/10.3390/en13040788.

Taghizadeh-Hesary, F and N Yoshino (2019). The way to induce private participation in green finance and investment. *Financial Research Letters*, 31, 98–103. https://doi.org/10.1016/j.frl.2019.04.016.

Taghizadeh-Hesary, F, N Yoshino and H Phoumin (2021a). Analyzing the characteristics of green bond markets to facilitate green finance in the post-covid-19 world. *Sustainability*, 13. https://doi.org/10.3390/su13105719.

Taghizadeh-Hesary, F, N Yoshino, E Rasoulinezhad and C Rimaud (2021b). Power purchase agreements with incremental tariffs in local currency: An innovative green finance tool. *Global Finance Journal*, 50, 100666. https://doi.org/10.1016/j.gfj.2021.100666.

Tavana, A, A Emami Javid, E Houshfar, A Mahmoudzadeh Andwari, M Ashjaee, S Shoaee, A Maghmoomi and F Marashi (2019). Toward renewable and sustainable energies perspective in Iran. *Renewable Energy*, 139, 1194–1216. https://doi.org/10.1016/j.renene.2019.03.022.

Thanki, H, S Shah, HS Rathod, AD Oza and DD Burduhos-Nergis (2022). I am ready to invest in socially responsible investments (SRI) options only if the returns are not compromised: Individual investors' intentions toward SRI. *Sustainability*, 14, 11377. https://doi.org/10.3390/su141811377.

Yee, CH, U Al-Mulali and GM Ling (2022). Intention towards renewable energy investments in Malaysia: Extending theory of planned behaviour. *Environmental Science and Pollution Research*, 29, 1021–1036. https://doi.org/10.1007/s11356-021-15737-x.

Yoshino, N, F Taghizadeh-Hesary and M Nakahigashi (2019). Modelling the social funding and spill-over tax for addressing the green energy financing gap. *Economic Modelling*, 77, 34–41. https://doi.org/10.1016/j.econmod.2018.11.018.

Zahedi, S, JM Batista-Foguet and L van Wunnik (2019). Exploring the public's willingness to reduce air pollution and greenhouse gas emissions from private road transport in Catalonia. *Science of the Total Environment*, 646, 850–861. https://doi.org/10.1016/j.scitotenv.2018.07.361.

Ziaei, SM (2022). The impacts of household social benefits, public expenditure on labour markets, and household financial assets on the renewable energy sector. *Renewable Energy*, 181, 51–58. https://doi.org/10.1016/j.renene.2021.09.017.

Zobeidi, T, N Komendantova and M Yazdanpanah (2022). Social media as a driver of the use of renewable energy: The perceptions of instagram users in Iran. *Energy Policy*, 161, 112721. https://doi.org/10.1016/j.enpol.2021.112721.

https://doi.org/10.1142/9789819812783_0004

ANALYSIS OF THE CARBON ALLOWANCE ALLOCATION AND SECTORAL COVERAGE IN THE CARBON MARKET UNDER THE NEW CLIMATE AMBITION: A CASE STUDY OF CHINA[†]

SI CHENG

Center of Hubei Cooperative Innovation for Emissions Trading System, Hubei University of Economics, Wuhan 430205, P. R. China

School of Low Carbon Economics, Hubei University of Economics, Wuhan 430205, P. R. China

JIHONG ZHANG[*]

Institution of Quality Development Strategy, Wuhan University, Wuhan 430072, P. R. China

whu_jhzhang@whu.edu.cn

SHAOZHOU QI

Climate Change and Energy Economics Study Center, Economics and Management School, Wuhan University, Wuhan 430072, P. R. China

Reasonable allocation of carbon allowances and determination of coverage in the carbon market are essential to the realization of the emissions reduction goal. Using China as an example, we propose a multi-criteria allocation scheme based on the principle of equity, efficiency and feasibility, considering carbon abatement costs and carbon leakage risks. An improved zero-sum gains-data envelopment analysis model in accordance with China's new carbon intensity target in climate ambition is used for allowance allocation. Subsequently, the sectoral coverage choice of the carbon market is proposed. We obtain an optimal reallocation scheme after five iterations. The results show that the allocation method in this study can better promote the carbon market to reduce emissions at a lower cost while preventing carbon leakage to a certain extent. Based on the contribution to the overall emission reduction, the emission reduction costs and carbon leakage risks, we further classify the sectors into three categories. With China as an example, these findings lay a scientific basis for China to achieve its climate ambition through the carbon market, and also have global implications in regard to developing a more scientific allocation scheme, especially for carbon markets in emerging and developing countries.

Keywords: Carbon allowances; carbon market; multi-criteria allocation; climate ambition; sectoral coverage; zero sum gains-data envelopment analysis (ZSG-DEA).

[*]Corresponding author.

[†]This chapter was originally published in Climate Change Economics, Vol. 13, No. 3, April 2022, published by World Scientific Publishing, Singapore. Reprinted with permission.

1. Introduction

The Paris Agreement has encouraged countries around the world to restrain climate change (An *et al.*, 2022). As part of carbon pricing policies, i.e., carbon tax (Mortha *et al.*, 2021), the carbon market has become an important tool for global countries to achieve their emission reduction commitments. In the post-COVID-19 era, well-designed carbon markets are a key strategy to achieving green recovery goals around the world. The 26th UN Climate Change Conference of the Parties (COP26) negotiators also finalized the rules that govern international cooperation and carbon markets. As of 2020, 46 national and 32 subnational jurisdictions have implemented or planned to adopt carbon pricing as a tool to achieve emission reduction commitments, including many developing countries and emerging economies. There are now 61 carbon pricing initiatives in place or scheduled for implementation, making up 31 carbon markets (World Bank, 2020b).

At this stage, China is under unprecedented pressure of carbon mitigation. In order to alleviate heavy pressure on mitigating climate change, China has integrated the target of carbon reduction into national economic plans (Shi *et al.*, 2021a). Carbon market has become one of the core policy instruments to achieve the goal of carbon peak and carbon neutrality (Wang *et al.*, 2022). Eight carbon trading pilots have been successively put into effect since 2013, and the national carbon market was officially launched in December 2017. China has expanded its commitments to climate pact with a commitment to reach an emission peak around 2030 and achieve carbon neutrality by 2060 (Shi *et al.*, 2021b). At the Climate Ambition Summit 2020, China announced further commitments for 2030 that it would lower its carbon emissions per unit of GDP by over 65% from the 2005 level. Compared with the targets, China announced in 2015 to lower carbon intensity by 60–65% by 2030, China has scaled up its nationally determined contributions. In this context, China has published a framework for carbon peaking and neutrality, confirming plans to strengthen and expand the national carbon market. It confirms the planned coverage expansion, the diversification of trading instruments, and the improvement of the allocation and management of allowances for the national national Emission Trading System (ETS).

Carbon allowance allocation and sectoral coverage are some of the most important concerns in the construction of a carbon market (Qian *et al.*, 2018). The allocation of carbon allowances may significantly affect the sharing of the emissions reduction burden (Stoerk *et al.*, 2019). The ETS scope defines the boundaries of the policy. It therefore has implications for the effort sharing between the covered sectors to meet economy-wide emission reduction targets. Based on the sharing of the emissions reduction burden of different sectors, the determination of sectoral coverage needs to fully consider the contribution to the overall emission reduction, emission reduction costs and carbon risks (World Bank, 2020a; Rannou *et al.*, 2021). In general, it is best to include a variety of economic sectors into the ETS if marginal abatement costs differ across sectors and added sectors offer low-cost abatement options. However, since the first batch of carbon trading pilots in 2013, the plan for sectoral coverage in the national carbon market has been reduced (Lin and Jia, 2020a). When the national carbon market was officially launched in December 2017, only the power generation industry was covered. China has indicated that it will gradually expand its coverage in the future, including industrial sectors, which are covered by most global carbon markets.

Assessing the scientific criterion of carbon allowance allocation among different industrial sectors based on the new climate ambition and the choice of sectoral coverage in the national carbon market would provide vital policy implications for deploying an effective and mature national carbon market in China. Moreover, there are an increasing number of emerging economies interested in including carbon trading into state plans, while the mechanism designs of carbon market in developed countries may be unsuitable for them. Emerging economies face a social-economic context unique from that of developed economies due to the uncertainty of their economic situation (Tran, 2021). Unlike developed countries, China's emissions reduction target is based on emissions intensity, instead of absolute emissions. China has to convert its emissions intensity target to an absolute emissions target (Qi and Cheng, 2018). Besides, as a major source of greenhouse gas emissions, China's industry has consumed more than 70% of its total energy, whereas its value added only accounted for about 40% of the total GDP (Zhang and Hao, 2017). These sectors are the cornerstone of the country, providing energy and raw materials, and it is difficult for the economy to survive and develop without. Thus, the allowance allocation and coverage of these sectors require an adequate balance between emission reduction responsibilities and emission reduction costs. Accordingly, evaluations and recommendations with respect to allowance allocation and sectoral coverage of the Chinese carbon market are also propitious to provide realistic reference and guidance for other emerging economies in establishing their own carbon markets and meeting their emission reduction commitments.

To explore the scientific criterion of carbon allowance allocation in the carbon market under the new climate ambition, this study adopted the principles of equity, efficiency and feasibility for carbon allowance allocation. An improved zero sum gains-data envelopment analysis (ZSG-DEA) model proposed by Fang *et al.* (2019) was used to allocate the carbon allowances from 2017 to 2030 for 27 industrial sectors. In order to clarify the responsibilities for emissions reduction, based on the contribution to the overall emission reduction, the emission reduction costs and carbon leakage risks, the sectors were further classified into three categories, labeled as "sectors that are prioritized and compulsorily included," "sectors that are encouraged to be included," and "sectors that are voluntarily included," respectively. Based on the above results, several policy implications were proposed in order to help the emerging and developing countries to optimize the carbon markets to meet their climate goals.

The main contributions of this paper are two-fold: First, a multi-criteria allocation scheme based on the principle of equity, efficiency and feasibility, considering carbon abatement costs and carbon leakage risks was proposed. Second, we integrated multi-criteria allocation principles and indicators into an improved ZSG-DEA model, which promotes the transparency and scientific robustness of carbon allowance allocation.

The remainder of this paper is structured as follows. Section 2 reviews the related literature. Section 3 introduces the methodology and data. Section 4 presents the research results. Section 5 discusses carbon allowance allocation under different indicators and compares them with the literature. The conclusion and policy recommendation are presented in Sec. 6.

2. Literature Review

2.1. *Criterion of carbon allowances allocation among sectors*

Several scholars have investigated the allocation of carbon allowances for China's industrial sectors based on the emission intensity reduction target in 2020 (Zhang and Hao, 2017; Zhou *et al.*, 2019; Chen *et al.*, 2018; Dong *et al.*, 2018). More specifically, some scholars further conducted studies on certain sectors such as in the building materials industry (Zhao *et al.*, 2018), the power industry (Ji *et al.*, 2017; Li and Wang, 2019) and high-energy-consuming industries (Wu *et al.*, 2020).

Allocation criteria play an important role in carbon allowance allocation (Zhou *et al.*, 2019). Equity, efficiency and feasibility are recognized as the most important principles. The equity principle refers to universal rights to development, high living standards and the right to produce some CO_2 emissions (Zhang and Hao, 2017; Dong *et al.*, 2018; Zhou *et al.*, 2019).The efficiency principle refers to the decomposition of the total control needs to reflect the same emission reduction efforts, which reflects the emission control technology and emission reduction potential (Yi *et al.*, 2011; Zhang and Hao, 2017; Wu *et al.*, 2020; Wang *et al.*, 2022). The feasibility principle refers to the realization of emission reduction goals to consider emission reduction costs and economic development (Fang *et al.*, 2018). Zhou *et al.* (2019) defined the carbon marginal abatement cost imitated by data envelopment analysis (DEA) as an index of the feasibility principle. Fang *et al.* (2019) used the elasticity coefficient of energy consumption to measure feasibility from the perspective of an economic pillar.

2.2. *Method for allocating carbon allowances*

Regarding allocation methods, many scholars have used the single-criterion approach to investigate carbon allowances allocation at the industrial level due to its simplicity (Zhou and Wang, 2016). However, multi-criteria allocation, which integrates different allocation principles, can produce fewer differences between the smallest and the largest targets for different entities and enables more consensus-based entitlements. Thus, the multi-criteria allocation approach is receiving increasing attention. Various approaches to allocating emissions allowance have been proposed and were summarized and divided into four categories by Zhou and Wang (2016): the indicator approach, the optimization method, the game theoretic approach and the hybrid approach. The optimization method, aimed at improving the technical efficiency of the whole system, namely DEA, has emerged as another common method for allocating carbon allowances (An *et al.*, 2021).

In the traditional DEA, the inputs and outputs of each decision-making unit (DMU) are completely independent. However, when the total amount of input (output) is constant, this assumption is obviously unfounded (Zeng *et al.*, 2016). To overcome this weakness, a revised DEA model, namely ZSG-DEA, was proposed by Lins *et al.* (2003) The rationale of ZSG-DEA for allocating carbon allowances is that when a DMU decreases its carbon allowances to yield greater DEA efficiency, the allowances entitled to any other DMUs must be increased by the same amount to maintain the overall allowances (Fang *et al.*, 2019). At the industrial level, Zhang and Hao (2017) employed the input-oriented ZSG-DEA model to examine the efficiency of allocation solutions among industrial sectors in China. Chen *et al.* (2018) used the ZSG-DEA model to optimize carbon emission quotas and establish a reasonable distribution plan.

2.3. *Sectoral coverage choices in the carbon market*

Sectoral coverage has been studied by many scholars (Lin and Jia, 2020b); Qian *et al.*, 2018; Lin and Jia, 2017; Qi and Cheng, 2018), several of whom have adopted the Computable General Equilibrium (CGE) model. Lin and Jia (2020b)) used the dynamic recursive CGE model and found that when more industries are covered in the carbon market, it will lead to a higher GDP performance and lower carbon prices. In addition, based on the CGE model, Lin and Jia (2020a) suggested that covering only three enterprises — cement, chemical and electric power — is sufficient for emissions reduction. While Qian *et al.* (2018) concluded that the coverage of sectors with high emissions and emission intensities would lead to the highest emission reduction effects.

Another group of studies classified the sectors into different types based on the results of carbon allowance allocation. Based on the public emission reduction pledge of a specific product or service according to carbon emission calculations, the sectors were classified into four categories: sectors for compulsory reduction, sectors for emission reduction, sectors for encouraging reduction and voluntary reduction (Zhao *et al.*, 2017). Zhou *et al.* (2019) classified the industrial sectors according to their carbon abatement responsibilities and carbon reduction capacities.

In summary, the literature offers an important foundation for this study, but leaves room for improvement. First, from the perspective of allocation criteria and the choice of sectoral coverage of the carbon market, few studies have considered sectors' carbon abatement costs and carbon leakage risks, which are unique elements that must be analyzed in allowance allocation under the context of the carbon market. Second, when it comes to running a ZSG-DEA model, the boundary between input and output variables often seems ambiguous. To promote the transparency, scientific robustness and policy relevance of allocation, Fang *et al.* (2019) introduced an improved ZSG-DEA model for the allocation of provincial Carbon emission allowance (CEA) in accordance to China's Intended Nationally Determined Contributions (INDCs), which can also be used for allowance allocation at the sectoral level. Further, the existing literature primarily focuses on ways to achieve China's 2020 goals instead of its new target in climate ambition.

Therefore, based on the principle of equity, efficiency and feasibility, in this study, we employ the indicators of carbon abatement costs and carbon leakage risks to integrate the carbon market into the criteria for carbon allowance allocation. The research method employed in this study integrates multi-criteria allocation principles and indicators into an improved ZSG-DEA model in accordance with China's climate ambition proposed by Fang *et al.* (2019), which promotes the transparency and scientific robustness of carbon allowance allocation.

3. Methodology and Data

Figure 1 depicts the research framework for this study. First, the multi-criteria allocation scheme is used as the output variable of the ZSG-DEA model to reflect the principles of equity, efficiency and feasibility. Second, we estimate industries' initial carbon allowance allocation based on their historical carbon emissions, and then reallocate the initial carbon allowances given their DEA efficiency obtained from the ZSG-DEA model. We then continue the process of reallocation until all industries have reached a DEA efficiency of 100%. Finally, based on abatement costs and carbon leakage risks, we propose an inclusion order for industrial sectors covered by the national carbon market.

3.1. *Multi-criteria allocation scheme*

The principles of equity, efficiency and feasibility are adopted in this study for carbon allowance allocation. Thus, carbon emissions in all industrial sectors are measured from the perspectives of the responsibility, potential, capacity, cost and risk for reducing emissions. Based on the representativeness of indicators and a comprehensive review of the literature, Table 1 presents the suite of indicators used to capture these principles.

The labor input and historical carbon emissions of sectors are used to measure their carbon reduction responsibilities (Dong *et al.*, 2018; Zhao *et al.*, 2017). Energy intensity, the proportion of coal consumption and the R&D investment intensity of sectors are used to represent their carbon reduction potential and carbon reduction capacity, respectively (Zhang and Hao, 2017; Zhou *et al.*, 2019; Dong *et al.*, 2018).

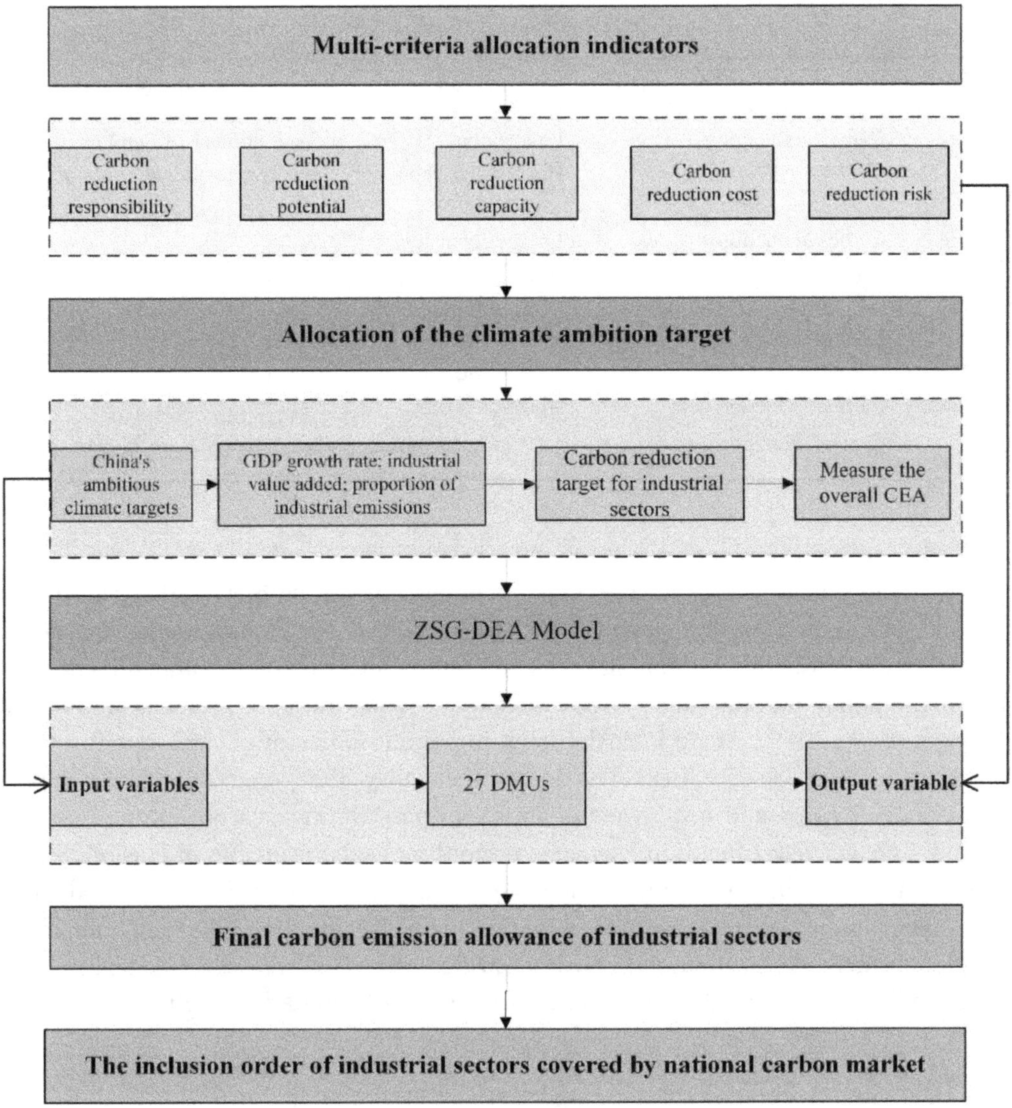

Figure 1. Research framework.

Carbon emission reduction cost refers to the ratio of direct and indirect costs incurred by an industry due to carbon emissions in the production and operation of the industry's value added. According to the feasibility principle, the higher the carbon emission reduction costs, the smaller the emission reduction responsibility that the industry should bear (Zhou *et al.*, 2019). In the context of the carbon market, industrial carbon reduction cost is expressed as the ratio of industrial carbon emissions multiplied by the carbon price of the industry's value added (Sun *et al.*, 2019).

Table 1. Initial multi-criteria indicators for carbon allowances allocation.

Principle	Dimension	Symbol	Indicator	Description
Equity	Carbon reduction responsibility	x_1	Labor input	Average number of employees
		x_2	Historical carbon emissions	Cumulative historical emissions
Efficiency	Carbon reduction potential	x_3	Energy intensity	$\frac{\text{Energy consumption}}{\text{Industrial value added}}$
		x_4	Proportion of coal consumption	$\frac{\text{Final coal consumption}}{\text{Total energy end consumption}}$
	Carbon reduction capacity	x_5	R&D investment intensity	$\frac{\text{Industrial R\&D expenditures}}{\text{Industrial value added}}$
Feasibility	Carbon reduction cost	x_6	Abatement costs	$\frac{\text{(Carbon emissions} \times \text{carbon price)}}{\text{Industrial value added}}$
	Carbon reduction risk	x_7	Carbon leakage risk	$\frac{\text{Industry export volume+industry import volume}}{\text{Industry total output+industry import volume}}$

Carbon emission reduction risk refers to the industry's carbon leakage risk in the context of the carbon market. The implementation of the carbon market can cause carbon leakage through the competitive channel, that is, the carbon market increases the production costs of the industrial sectors, thereby affecting their competitiveness in the international market, and carbon leakage occurs through production transfer (Branger *et al.*, 2016). Trade intensity is an important indicator of the strength of the industry's carbon leakage risk. The larger the value, the greater the international competition it faces and the lower its ability to pass through carbon costs, thus incurring a greater risk of carbon leakages. According to the principle of feasibility, the greater the trade intensity, the smaller the industry's responsibility for reducing emissions (Sun *et al.*, 2019). In this study, we adopt the EU ETS trade intensity calculation method (Monjon and Quirion, 2011).

All indicators are standardized and the calculation formula is as follows:

$$P_{it} = \frac{x_{it} - \min_i}{\max_i - \min_i}, \tag{1}$$

where x_{it} and P_{it} refer to the quantified indicator i in year t before and after standardization, respectively, and $\min_i$ and $\max_i$ refer to the minimum and maximum value of indicator i in the period 2005–2014, respectively.

Unlike other indicators, a higher ranking of R&D investment intensity would lead to fewer shares of carbon allowances. Therefore, this indicator can be standardized with the following formula:

$$P_{it} = \frac{\max_i - x_{it}}{\max_i - \min_i}. \tag{2}$$

To enhance the objectivity and rationality of the multi-criteria allocation scheme, we conduct a correlation analysis between the annual carbon emissions by industry and seven indicators to ensure that the indicators are highly correlated with carbon emissions. The formulas are as follows:

$$\mathrm{CE}_t = \mathrm{a}x_i + b + \varepsilon, \tag{3}$$

$$x_i = a'x_j + b' + \varepsilon', \tag{4}$$

where CE_t refers to the carbon emission of the industry in year t; a and a' refer to the correlation coefficients; b and b' refer to the intercept term; ε and ε' refer to the residual term; and x_i and x_j refer to the indicators i and, j, respectively.

3.2. *Allocation of the climate ambition target*

China has set its carbon intensity target for 2030, which is a 65% reduction from the 2005 level, but has not set a separate carbon intensity reduction target for the industrial sectors. It is therefore necessary to transform the overall carbon intensity target into a reduction target for industrial sectors. The relationship of carbon emission intensity between China and industrial sectors can be expressed as follows:

$$\frac{\mathrm{CE}_{\mathrm{industry}_t}}{\mathrm{IVA}_t} = \frac{\mathrm{CE}_t}{\mathrm{GDP}_t} \times \frac{\mathrm{GDP}_t}{\mathrm{IVA}_t} \times \frac{\mathrm{CE}_{\mathrm{industry}_t}}{\mathrm{CE}_t}, \tag{5}$$

where CE_t and GDP_t denote the carbon emissions and GDP of China in year t, respectively, and $\mathrm{CE}_{\mathrm{industry}_t}$ denotes the industrial carbon emission in year t. The carbon emission intensity of industry sectors can be further expressed as follows:

$$I_t = I_t' \times \frac{\mathrm{CE}_{\mathrm{industry}_t}}{\mathrm{CE}_t} / \frac{\mathrm{IVA}_t}{\mathrm{GDP}_t}. \tag{6}$$

The carbon intensity of industrial sectors I_t in year t can be estimated by China's carbon intensity in year t, the proportion of industrial carbon emissions in total emissions and the ratio of industrial value added to GDP in year t.

China has been committed to emissions reduction since 2005 and has achieved its reduction goals earlier than expected. For instance, the CO_2 emissions intensity in 2017 had already dropped 46% from the 2005 level (Ministry of Ecology and Environment, 2018). Hence, China's 2030 carbon intensity needs to drop by 35.2% from its 2017 levels. Assuming that the proportion of industrial carbon emissions and industrial value added remain constant, China's carbon intensity target can be transformed into an intensity reduction target for industrial sectors using the following equation:

$$I_{2030} - I_{2017} = \frac{\mathrm{CE.industry}}{\mathrm{CE}} / \frac{\mathrm{IVA}_t}{\mathrm{GDP}_t} \left(I_{2030}' - I_{2017}'\right). \tag{7}$$

To realize the allocation of carbon allowances, the overall allowances must be measurable. Assuming that there will be a linear decline in carbon emission intensity, the annual GDP is assumed to grow at a constant rate. Hence, the overall carbon allowances can be expressed as

$$\mathrm{TCA}_t = \mathrm{IVA}_t \times I_{2017} \times (1-q)^{t-2017}, \tag{8}$$

$$q = 1 - \sqrt[14]{\frac{I_{2030}}{I_{2017}}}, \tag{9}$$

where TCA_t refers to the overall carbon allowances in year t; IVA_t refers to the industrial value added in year t; I_{2017} and I_{2030} refer to the industrial emission intensity in 2017 and 2030, respectively; and q refers to the rate of decline in industrial emission intensity in the next 14 years.

The initial carbon allowances by industry can be determined in accordance with the weights of historical carbon emissions for different industries, with the aim of causing as little derivation as possible.

$$\mathrm{ICEA}_p = \mathrm{TCA} \times \frac{\mathrm{CE}_p}{\sum \mathrm{CE}_p}, \tag{10}$$

where TCA refers to the overall carbon allowances from 2017 to 2030. ICEA_p refers to the initial carbon allowances of industry p, and CE_p refers to the historical carbon emissions of industry p. The resulting ICEA is adopted as an input variable that would be reallocated through the ZSG-DEA model afterward.

3.3. *ZSG-DEA model*

The classic DEA model assumes that the inputs or outputs of each DMU are independent; that is, the use of a certain input by a certain DMU will not affect the use of that input by other DMUs. However, if the total amount of an input or output indicator is constant, to improve efficiency and reduce factor input (increasing output), an inefficient DMU requires other DMUs to increase their input (decrease output). In this case, they are independent of each other. The assumption of the classic DEA model is clearly no longer available. In the process of allowance allocation, the fact that the overall carbon allowances are fixed will make the original DEA method for improving the efficiency of DMUs and adjusting the allocation results ineffective under the classic DEA model.

To maximize DEA efficiency while keeping constant the overall carbon allowances by 2030 as inputs, this study adopts an input-oriented ZSG-DEA model. One prominent merit of this model is that it allows for the optimization of all the DMUs to reach the DEA frontier without altering overall carbon allowances. For instance, provided that DMU_k ($k = 1, \ldots, 27$) with carbon allowances of X_k is an inefficient unit with its DEA efficiency θ, the carbon allowances of DMU_k must be reduced by $X_k(1-\theta)$ to reach the DEA frontier, and other DMUs would increase their allowances according to the weights expressed as $\frac{X_i}{\sum_{i \neq k} X_i} X_k(1-\theta)$. In principle, inefficient DMUs continue to be reallocated until they reach the DEA frontier. After several rounds of reallocation, the DEA efficiency of all DMUs will be equal to 1. The ZSG-DEA model is formulated as follows:

$$E_{\text{ZSG}} = \min\theta, \tag{11}$$

$$\text{s.t}\begin{cases} \sum_{i=1}^{27} \lambda_i \cdot y_i^{\text{responsibility}} \geq y_k^{\text{responsibility}}, \\ \sum_{i=1}^{27} \lambda_i \cdot y_i^{\text{potential}} \geq y_k^{\text{potential}}, \\ \sum_{i=1}^{27} \lambda_i \cdot y_i^{\text{capacity}} \geq y_k^{\text{capacity}}, \\ \sum_{i=1}^{27} \lambda_i \cdot y_i^{\text{cost}} \geq y_k^{\text{cost}}, \\ \sum_{i=1}^{27} \lambda_i \cdot y_i^{\text{risk}} \geq y_k^{\text{risk}}, \\ \sum_{i=1}^{27} \lambda_i \cdot X_i \left[1 + \frac{X_i}{\sum_{i \neq k} X_i} X_k(1-\theta)\right] \leq \theta \cdot X_k, \\ \sum_{i=1}^{27} \lambda_i = 1, \\ \lambda_i \geq 0, i = 1, \ldots, 27, \end{cases}$$

where θ refers to the DEA efficiency of DMUs, E_{ZSG} refers to the minimum DEA efficiency of DMU_k, λ_i refers to the weight of the DMU of i, X_i refers to the initial allowances as input and y_i refers to the quantified principles.

3.4. *Data sources and processing*

To calculatez the overall carbon allowances, the GDP growth must first be set. The report on the government's work delivered at the Second Session of the 13th National People's Congress of the People's Republic of China indicates that the expected growth rate of GDP is 6.0%. Thus, in this study, the rate of annual GDP growth is 6.0% on average.

Second, the industrial value added during the period 2020–2030 has not been announced. First, GDP can be predicted by 2020–2030 according to the assumed annual GDP growth rate of 6.0%. Then, based on the ratio of industrial value added to GDP in 2015–2019, the industrial value added in 2020–2030 can be calculated.

Table 2 presents the data source for the measurement of the overall carbon allowances, the initialization of industrial carbon allowances and the construction of the initial multi-criteria allocation index. We utilized MATLAB to predict the aforementioned indicators for the period 2017–2030 with the Grey Model (1,1). SPSS 16.0 was applied to investigate the correlation as well as the standardization process.

In this study, 27 two-digital industries in China's industrial sector were selected as the study sample (Table A1). There are 41 two-digital industries in the current national

Table 2. Initial indicators of the DEA-ZSG model and data sources.

Composition	Indicators	Data sources
Input variables	Carbon emissions by industry	China Energy Statistical Yearbook (2006–2017), Intergovernmental Panel on Climate Change (IPCC) Guidelines for National Greenhouse Gas Inventories 2006
Output variables	Cumulative historical emissions	
	Labor input	China Industry Statistical Yearbook (2006–2017)
	Abatement costs	
	Energy intensity	China Energy Statistical Yearbook (2006–2017)
	Proportion of coal consumption	
	R&D investment intensity	*China Statistical Yearbook on Science and Technology (2006–2017)*
	Carbon leakage risk	World Input-Output Database

industry classification. This classification has been revised and adjusted three times since its first publication in 1984. Since the data range of this study is from 2005 to 2016, the industry classification of the 2011 version (GB/T4547-2011) was used. Five industries — mining support activities, mining of other ores, other manufacturing, utilization of waste resources and repair services for metal product machinery and equipment — are excluded to maintain coherence and consistency in the data. The data for the manufacture of automobiles and manufacture of railway, ship, aerospace and other transportation equipment are added and combined as the transportation equipment manufacturing industry. In addition, industries that lack available statistical data were excluded.

4. Results

4.1. *Final multi-criteria allocation scheme*

To enhance the objectivity and rationality of the multi-criteria allocation scheme, we conduct a correlation analysis between the annual carbon emissions by industry and indicators. The results of the correlation analysis are shown in Table 3.

The indicators of labor (x_1) and coal consumption ratio (x_4) had no significant correlation with carbon emissions ($p > 0.05$); hence, they were eliminated. The final multi-criteria indicators for carbon allowance allocation are shown in Fig. 2.

4.2. *Ranking of industrial sectors based on multi-criteria indicators*

Figure 3 depicts the ranking of industrial sectors based on the indicators of responsibility, potential, capacity, cost and risk.

Table 3. Correlation between indicators and carbon emissions.

	CE	x_1	x_2	x_3	x_4	x_5	x_6	x_7
CE	1							
x_1	0.12	1						
x_2	0.92***	0.12	1					
x_3	0.36**	−0.06	0.27***	1				
x_4	0.03	0.04	−0.00	0.11	1			
x_5	0.17***	−0.38***	0.16***	0.25***	1			
x_6	0.94***	0.07	0.78***	0.46***	0.16***	0.22***	1	
x_7	−0.31***	0.24***	−0.27***	−0.29***	−0.40***	−0.38***	−0.32***	1

Notes: Standard errors are shown in parentheses; *, **, and *** denote $p < 0.1, p < 0.05$, and $p < 0.01$, respectively.

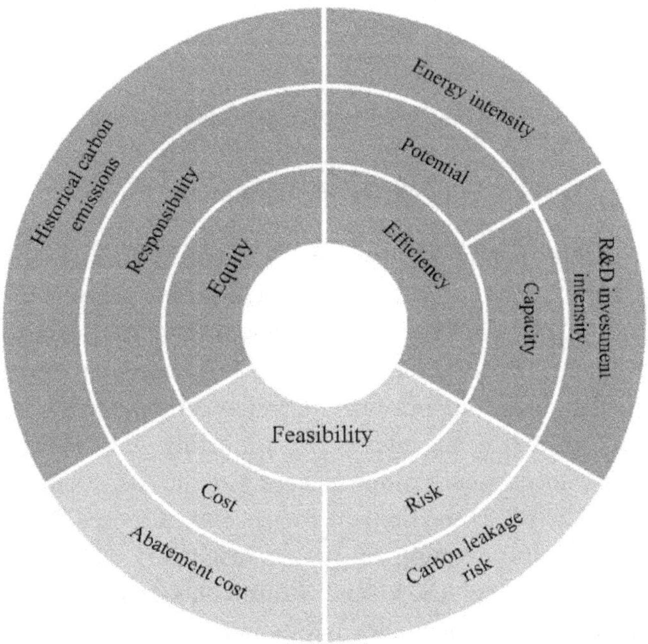

Figure 2. Final multi-criteria indicators for carbon allowance allocation.

As shown, the responsibility and cost indicators have gained prominence in three main sectors: raw chemical materials and chemical products (S14), smelting and pressing of ferrous metals (S18) and production and supply of electric power, steam and hot water sectors (S27). Such sectors have large emissions and high emission reduction costs, and the implementation of the carbon market has a greater impact on these sectors. Therefore, when allocating allowances, it is important to pay attention to the cost pressures of carbon price fluctuations in these sectors.

The potential indicator gained prominence in the sectors of petroleum processing and coking (S13), raw chemical materials and chemical products (S14), nonmetal

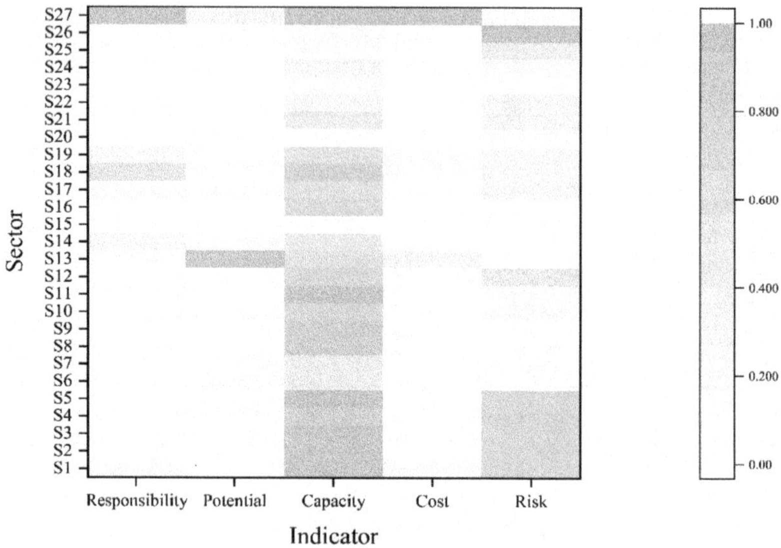

Note: The spectrum primarily shows the sectors' rankings within each indicator instead of quantifying the contributions of various indicators to a single sector.

Figure 3. Ranking of all sectors based on the five indicators.

mineral products (S17), melting and pressing of ferrous metals (S18), melting and pressing of nonferrous metals (S19) and production and supply of electric power, steam and hot water (S27). The energy intensities of these sectors are relatively large, indicating that at the current technological level, their emission reduction potential is relatively huge. We can, therefore, prioritize reducing carbon emissions in these sectors.

Twenty-one sectors have advantages in reflecting the indictors of capacity through carbon allowances reallocation, except for the six sectors of medical and pharmaceutical products (S15), equipment for special purposes (S22), transportation equipment (S23), electric equipment and machinery (S24), electronic and telecommunications equipment (S25) and instruments, meters, cultural and office machinery (S26). The capacity indicator is dominated by R&D investment intensity, which corresponds to an enhanced ability to control carbon emissions and, therefore, to less carbon allowances.

The risk indicator that reflects the carbon leakage risk of industrial sectors in the context of the carbon market had gained prominence in the sectors of coal mining and dressing (S1), petroleum and natural gas extraction (S2), ferrous metals mining and dressing (S3), nonferrous metals mining and dressing (S4), nonmetal minerals mining and dressing (S5), electronic and telecommunications equipment (S25) and instruments, metals, cultural and office machinery (S26). These sectors have larger trade intensity and greater international competition, and thus face higher carbon leakage risks in the implementation of the national carbon market. Therefore, such sectors should be placed under less pressure to reduce carbon emissions at the beginning of the carbon market.

4.3. *Final carbon allowances allocation and carbon emission reduction responsibility of industrial sectors*

4.3.1. *Carbon allowances allocation*

Figure 4 presents the DEA efficiency of the initial allocation and its reallocation. Seven out of the twenty-seven sectors have DEA efficiency that is higher than the average initial efficiency (0.38). Nonferrous metals mining and dressing (S4), tobacco processing (S9), petroleum processing and coking (13), smelting and pressing of nonferrous metals (S19) and instruments, meters, cultural and office machinery (S26) already reached the DEA frontier, where the DEA efficiency is equal to 1. The average DEA efficiency increases to 0.91 after the first reallocation, and the production and supply of electric power, steam and hot water (S27) reach the DEA frontier. The average DEA efficiency amounts to 0.99 as a result of the fourth reallocation, and the number of sectors with the DEA efficiency of 1 increases to 16. Ultimately, all sectors achieve a maximum DEA efficiency of 1 after the final reallocation.

Figure 5 depicts the carbon allowances of the 27 sectors in descending order and the estimated cumulative carbon emissions' share in 2017–2030. Most of the carbon allowances are concentrated in six sectors, that is, production and supply of electric power, steam and hot water (S27), smelting and pressing of ferrous metals (S18), raw

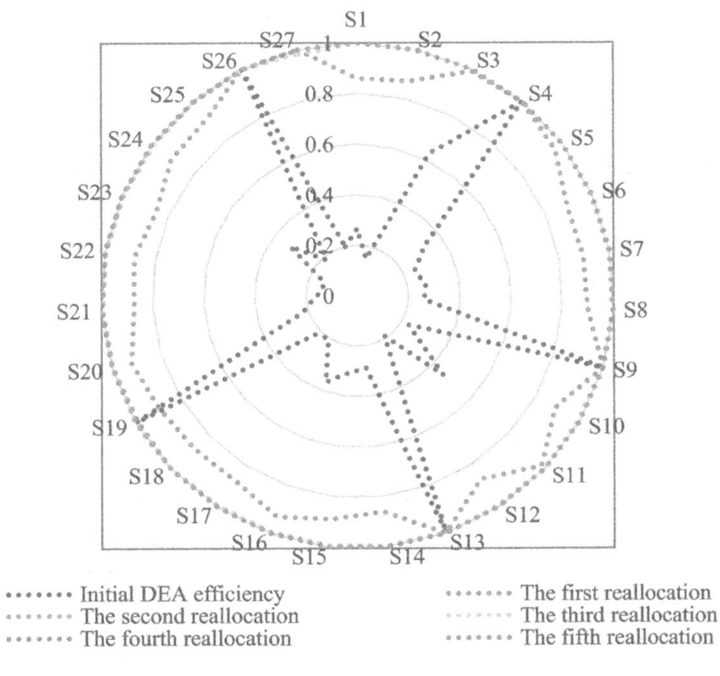

Figure 4. DEA efficiency of initial allocation and reallocation.

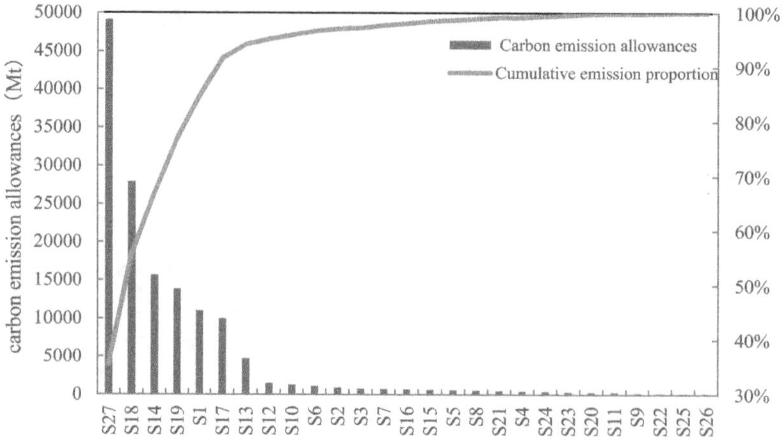

Figure 5. Carbon allowances of 27 industrial sectors in descending order.

chemical materials and chemical products (S14), smelting and pressing of nonferrous metals (S19), coal mining and dressing (S1) and nonmetal mineral products (S17), which obtained the major part of carbon allowances, accounting for 88.67% of all carbon allowances in 2017–2030. This result is essentially consistent with those reported by Zhou *et al.* (2019). These sectors are the cornerstone of the country, providing energy and raw materials, and it is difficult for the economy to survive and develop without them. Meanwhile, these sectors are characterized by high emissions, high energy intensity and large abatement costs, which means that they have great potential and should take more responsibility for emission reductions. Thus, the carbon market plays an important role in promoting low-cost emissions reduction in such sectors.

4.3.2. *Carbon emission reduction responsibility*

To investigate the carbon emission reduction distribution of the responsibility of 27 industrial sectors, this study further calculates the space for carbon emissions (SCE) of the sectors (Fang *et al.*, 2019).

Figure 6 illustrates different levels of ratios, from the highest to the lowest, representing SCE in carbon emissions of various industrial sectors. Negative SCE can be found in 16 sectors, that is, S27, S18, S14, S19, S1, S17, S12, S6, S15, S10, S13, S7, S23, S24 and S20, indicating that these sectors have major shares of the overall emission reduction. The SCE percentages, or the carbon reduction percentages of these sectors, range from 29% to 2%, and their annual average carbon reduction ranges from 1446.29 Mt of the production and supply of electric power, steam and hot water sector (S27) to 0.66 Mt of the ordinary machinery sector (S21). As analyzed in Sec. 4.2, sectors S27, S18, S14, S19, S17 and S13 have larger carbon reduction potential; thus, we can give priority to reducing carbon emissions in these sectors. Sectors S15, S23 and S24 have the advantage of carbon reduction capacity in terms of R&D investment, and thus have a stronger ability to control carbon emissions.

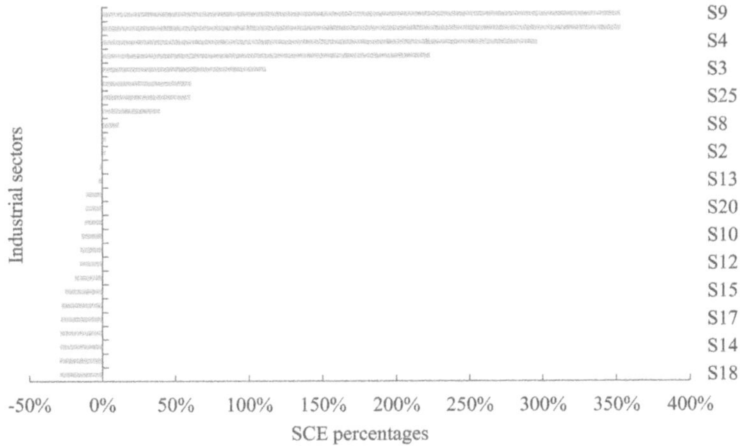

Figure 6. SCE percentages of 27 industrial sectors.

Positive SCE can be found in 11 sectors, that is, S16, S2, S25, S22, S8, S26, S9, S11, S5, S4 and S3, which means that these sectors are under relatively low levels of carbon emission reduction. The SCE percentages of these sectors range from 3% to 353%, and their annual average SCEs range from 1.32 Mt of the chemical fiber sector (S16) to 28.98 Mt of the ferrous metals mining and dressing sector (S3). Sectors S2, S3, S4, S5, S25 and S26 have a relatively high risk of carbon leakage; thus, these sectors should be given a certain amount of emission space.

4.4. *Abatement cost, carbon leakage and carbon emission reduction responsibility of industrial sectors*

Abatement costs and the risk of carbon leakage are unique elements that need to be considered in allowance allocation in the context of the carbon market. The greater the difference in emission reduction costs of the covered industrial sectors, the more emission reduction opportunities, and trading opportunities there will be, thereby minimizing the overall emission reduction costs. At the same time, we must also consider the industry's carbon leakage risk so as not to affect its international competitiveness.

Figure 7 depicts the abatement cost–carbon leakage risk–SCE relationship for sectors with negative SCE. The abatement costs of sectors with negative SCE vary widely, ranging from 0.003 to 1.0 after standardization. At the same time, the carbon leakage risks of these sectors are relatively low, mostly below 0.5 after standardization. This result shows that the allocation method in this study can better promote the carbon market to reduce emissions at a lower cost while preventing carbon leakage to a certain extent.

4.5. *Inclusion order of industrial sectors covered by the national carbon market*

The national carbon market should cover multiple industries. The power industry was first included as a breakthrough in the construction of the national carbon market.

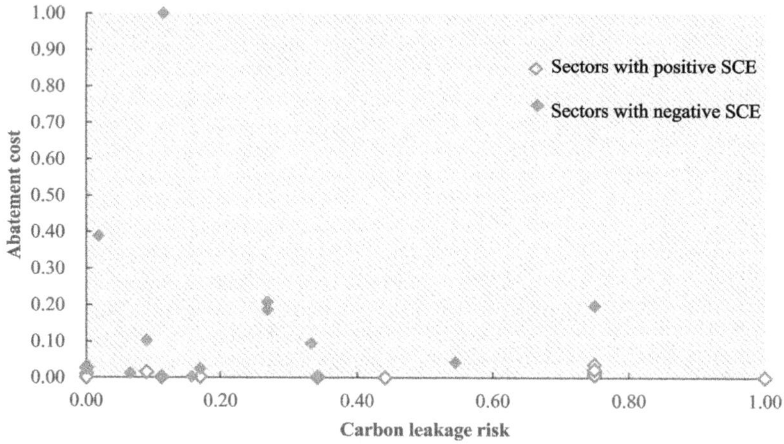

Figure 7. Abatement costs-carbon leakage risk–SCE relationship plot for different industrial sectors.

Several key emission industries will gradually be included in the future. In order to monitor the emission reductions of different industrial sectors more effectively, and provide a reference for the choice of sectors covered by the national carbon market in the meantime, in this study, we further classify the sectors with negative SCE based on the abatement costs and carbon leakage risks.

In Fig. 8, 16 industrial sectors with negative SCE by carbon leakage risks are plotted on the horizontal axis and abatement costs are plotted on the vertical axis. It is evident from Fig. 8 that the regions are divided into four clusters according to carbon leakage risks and abatement costs. The average value of carbon leakage risks of these

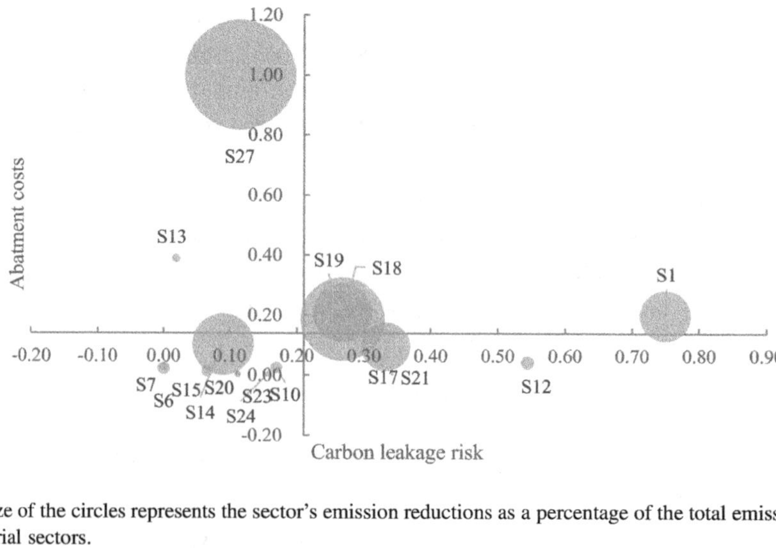

Note: The size of the circles represents the sector's emission reductions as a percentage of the total emission reductions of all industrial sectors.

Figure 8. Classification of industrial sectors based on abatement costs and carbon leakage risks.

sectors is set as the boundary of high risk and low risk, as represented by a dotted horizontal line. Similarly, the average value of abatement costs is set as the boundary of high cost and low cost, as represented by a dotted vertical line. Divided by these two reference lines, 16 sectors are clustered into four zones.

Based on the contribution to the overall emission reduction, the emission reduction costs and carbon leakage risks, all the sectors are classified into three categories. Sectors that contribute more to the overall emission reduction should be included as a priority to ensure the completion of emission reduction targets of the carbon market (Zhao *et al.*, 2017). These sectors are classified as sectors that are prioritized and compulsorily included in the national carbon market. Sectors that have less shares of overall emission reduction but with lower emission reduction costs and carbon leakage risks are categorized as sectors that are encouraged to be included in the national carbon market. Covering different and diverse sectors can provide greater emissions reduction potential and lower abatement costs (Qi and Cheng, 2018).The remaining sectors characterized by higher abatement costs and higher carbon leakage risks are classified as sectors voluntarily included in the national carbon market.

(1) Sectors that are prioritized and compulsorily included in the national carbon market, which include coal mining and dressing (S1), nonmetal mineral products (S17), raw chemical materials and chemical products (S14), melting and pressing of ferrous metals (S18), melting and pressing of nonferrous metals (S19) and production and supply of electric power, steam and hot water (27). As shown in Fig. 8, these five sectors have major shares of overall emission reduction, accounting for about 97% of the total emission reduction of all industrial sectors. In order to give full play to the role of the carbon market in reducing emissions and promoting the achievement of the 2030 target, these sectors should be the first to be considered in the system. Compared with S14 and S27, S1, S18 and S19 have relatively higher abatement costs and carbon leakage risks above the average level. Thus, when designing the allocation plan, these sectors should be given a greater percentage of free allowances.

(2) Sectors that are encouraged to be included in the national carbon market. These sectors are in the third zone, including food processing (S6), food production (S7), textile industry (S10), medical and pharmaceutical products (S15), transportation equipment (S23) and electric equipment and machinery (S24), which have relatively lower abatement costs and low carbon leakage risks, and in the meantime have fewer shares of overall emission reduction, thus having fewer effects on the target of carbon emission reduction. Therefore, these sectors can be selectively and voluntarily included in the national carbon market to activate the market and provide more opportunities for low-cost emission reduction. Because of their relatively lower abatement costs and carbon leakage risks, the proportion of allowances obtained by auctions in such sectors can be appropriately increased.

(3) Sectors that are voluntarily included in the national carbon market. These sectors are in the second and fourth zones, including papermaking and paper products (S12), petroleum processing and coking, (S13) and ordinary machinery (S21). Compared

with sectors in the third zone, although these sectors also have fewer shares of the overall emission reduction, their abatement costs or carbon leakage risks are relatively high; thus, these sectors can voluntarily join the carbon market.

5. Discussion

5.1. *Carbon allowances allocation under different schemes*

To further explore how changes in indicators affect carbon allowances, we compared two allocation schemes: (1) the allocation of carbon allowances under the multi-criteria scheme proposed in this study and (2) ignoring the abatement costs and carbon leakage risks. The results show the carbon allowance allocation in each of the schemes, and the changes in carbon allowances allocation in Scheme 1 compared with those in Scheme 2 are shown in Fig. 9.

Although the results of the two allocation schemes are quite similar, differences are present. Scheme 1 allocates more allowances than Scheme 2 for some sectors, especially in the coal mining and dressing sector (S1) with higher carbon leakage risk, and the production and supply of electric power, steam and hot water sector (S27) with higher abatement costs. Scheme 1 allocates less allowances than Scheme 2 for some sectors with lower carbon leakage risks or lower abatement costs such as the petroleum processing and coking sector (S13) and the nonmetal mineral products sector (S17).

5.2. *Carbon allowances allocation comparison with literature*

Figure 10 presents a comparison of Zhang and Hao (2017) analysis of the carbon allowance allocation for industrial sectors with ours. Zhang and Hao (2017) used the

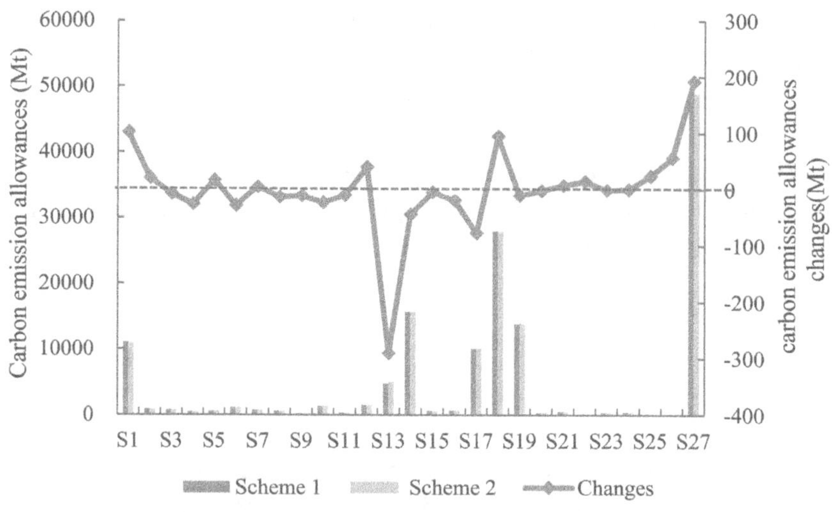

Figure 9. Comparison of different allocation schemes.

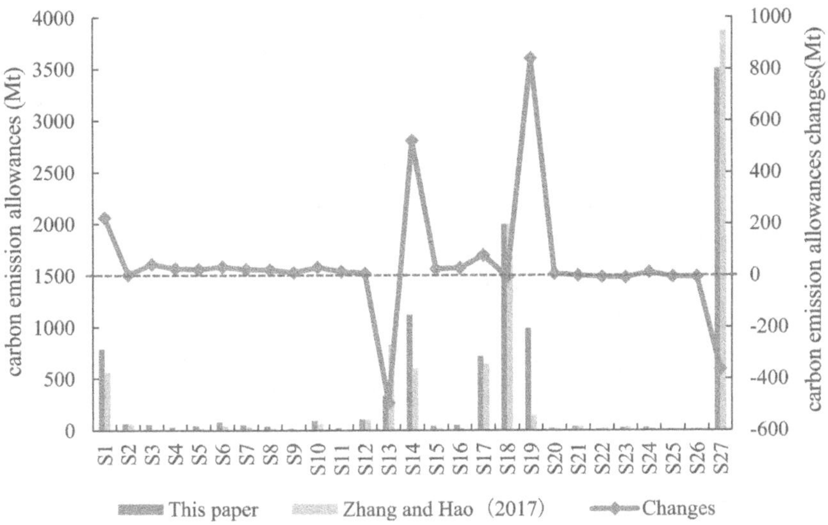

Note: All the results have been converted into annual average carbon allowances.

Figure 10. Comparison of the allocation of China's carbon allowance derived from the literature.

per-capita output value of industrial sectors, accumulated emissions and energy intensity to measure carbon emission reduction capacity, responsibility and potential, respectively. The results of this comparison show that we allocate more allowances for sectors of S1 with higher carbon leakage risk, raw chemical materials and chemical products (S14), and smelting and pressing of nonferrous metals (S19) due to their relatively lower capacity for carbon emission reduction and their lower R&D investment intensity, and allocate less allowances for sectors of S13 because of their lower abatement costs and S27 for their relatively higher capacity for carbon emission reduction.

6. Conclusion and Policy Recommendation

Based on China's carbon intensity target in climate ambition, in this study, we first establish a new multi-criteria allocation scheme based on the principles of equity, efficiency and feasibility, and integrate the abatement cost and carbon leakage risk indicators in the context of the carbon market. Subsequently, China's 2030 carbon intensity target under climate ambition is transformed into a reduction target for industrial sectors. Finally, a ZSG-DEA model is used to allocate the carbon allowances from 2017 to 2030 for 27 industrial sectors.

The main finding is that all sectors achieve a maximum DEA efficiency of 1 after the final reallocation and most of the carbon allowances are concentrated in six sectors. Negative SCE appears in 16 sectors, indicating that these sectors have major shares of the overall emission reduction. We further analyze the abatement cost–carbon leakage risk–SCE relationship for sectors with negative SCE, and find that the abatement costs of these sectors vary widely, while their carbon leakage risks are relatively low. This result indicates that the allocation method in this study can better help the carbon market reduce emissions at a lower cost, while preventing carbon leakage to a certain extent. Based on the above results, we propose that the order of inclusion of industrial sectors covered by the national carbon market be related to their shares of the overall emission reduction, abatement costs and carbon leakage risks. The sectors are classified into three categories.

Based on the above results, several policy implications can be proposed. First, our results identify that most of the carbon allowances are concentrated in six sectors which are characterized by high emissions, high energy intensity and large abatement costs. Policy makers should make full use of carbon market to promote low-cost emissions reduction in such sectors. Second, when allocating initial carbon allowances, policy makers should consider emissions reduction responsibility, potential, capacity, cost and risk. For those sectors with larger carbon reduction potential, stronger carbon reduction capacity may be considered sharing the greatest emissions' reduction burdens. While those sectors with higher risk of carbon leakage should be given a certain amount of emission space. Besides, policy makers should gradually expand the coverage of carbon market by taking shares of the overall emission reduction, abatement costs and carbon leakage risks of sectors into account. Diverse sectors facilitate low-cost abatement and price discovery, and C better responds to the global carbon market framework and rules proposed by cop26. Sectors that contribute more to the overall emission reduction should be included as a priority to ensure the completion of emission reduction targets of the carbon market, while sectors characterized by higher abatement costs and higher carbon leakage risks should be voluntarily included in the carbon market.

Nevertheless, this study has a few limitations that require further investigation. First, due to the limitations of the data, this study uses industrial R&D expenditures to measure carbon reduction capacity. This could be improved using data that are more relevant to emissions reduction investments. Second, future research could consider the allocation plan under the 2°C and 1.5°C IPCC targets.

Acknowledgments

This work was supported by the Humanity and Social Science Youth Foundation of the Ministry of Education in China [grant number 19YJC790017]; National Natural Science Foundation of China (NSFC): Carbon market and power market system reduction mechanism under dual carbon target [grant number 72174151]; National education foundation of China social science planning fund: Environmental and energy trading market coupled carbon emission reduction mechanism under the dual carbon target [grant number 21YJZH113].

Appendix A

Table A1. Industrial sectors included in the calculation.

Sector	Name
S1	Coal Mining and Dressing
S2	Petroleum and Natural Gas Extraction
S3	Ferrous Metals Mining and Dressing
S4	Nonferrous Metals Mining and Dressing
S5	Nonmetal Minerals Mining and Dressing
S6	Food Processing
S7	Food Production
S8	Beverage Production
S9	Tobacco Processing
S10	Textile Industry
S11	Garments and Other Fiber Products
S12	Papermaking and Paper Products
S13	Petroleum Processing and Coking
S14	Raw Chemical Materials and Chemical Products
S15	Medical and Pharmaceutical Products
S16	Chemical Fiber
S17	Nonmetal Mineral Products
S18	Smelting and Pressing of Ferrous Metals
S19	Smelting and Pressing of Nonferrous Metals
S20	Metal Products
S21	Ordinary Machinery
S22	Equipment for Special Purposes
S23	Transportation Equipment
S24	Electric Equipment and Machinery
S25	Electronic and Telecommunications Equipment
S26	Instruments, Meters, Cultural and Office Machinery
S27	Production and Supply of Electric Power, Steam, and Hot Water

References

An, Y, D Zhou, Q Wang, X Shi and F Taghizadeh-Hesary (2022). Mitigating size bias for carbon pricing in small Asia-Pacific countries: Increasing block carbon tax. *Energy Policy*, 161(5), 112771.

An, Y, D Zhou, J Yu, X Shi and Q Wang (2021). Carbon emission reduction characteristics for China's manufacturing firms: Implications for formulating carbon policies. *Journal of Environmental Management*, 284(4), 112055.

Branger, F, P Quirion and J Chevallier (2016). Carbon leakage and competitiveness of cement and steel industries under the EU ETS: Much ado about nothing. *Energy Journal*, 37(3), 109–135.

Chen, L, F He and J Wang (2018). Allocative efficiency of carbon emission allowances among sectors in China. *Polish Journal of Environmental Studies*, 27(2), 557–564.

Dong, F, Y Han, Y Dai, R Long and B Yu (2018). How carbon emission quotas can be allocated fairly and efficiently among different industrial sectors: The case of Chinese industry. *Polish Journal of Environmental Studies*, 27(6), 2883–2891.

Fang, G, M Liu, L Tian, M Fu and Y Zhang (2018). Optimization analysis of carbon emission rights allocation based on energy justice—The case of China. *Journal of Cleaner Production*, 202, 748–758.

Fang, K, Q Zhang, Y Long, Y Yoshida, L Sun, H Zhang, Y Dou and S Li (2019). How can China achieve its intended nationally determined contributions by 2030? A multi-criteria allocation of China's carbon emission allowance. *Applied Energy*, 241, 380–389.

Ji, X, G Li and Z Wang (2017). Allocation of emission permits for China's power plants: A systemic Pareto optimal method. *Applied Energy*, 204, 607–619.

Li, M and P Wang (2019). Research on carbon emission quota allocation in power industry. In *IOP Conference Series: Earth and Environmental Science*, Vol. 300, Institute of Physics Publishing.

Lin, B and Z Jia (2017). The impact of Emission Trading Scheme (ETS) and the choice of coverage industry in ETS: A case study in China. *Applied Energy*, 205, 1512–1527.

Lin, B and Z Jia (2020a). Why do we suggest small sectoral coverage in China's carbon trading market? *Journal of Cleaner Production*, 257, 120557.

Lin, B and Z Jia (2020b). Does the different sectoral coverage matter? An analysis of China's carbon trading market. *Energy Policy*, 137, 111164.

Lins, MPE, EG Gomes, JCCB Soares de Mello and AJR Soares de Mello (2003). Olympic ranking based on a zero-sum gains DEA model. *European Journal of Operational Research*, 148(2), 312–322.

Ministry of Ecological and Environment (2018). Annual Report on China's Policies and Actions on Climate Change 2018. Ministry of Ecological and Environment.

Monjon, S and P Quirion (2011). Addressing leakage in the EU ETS: Border adjustment or output-based allocation?*Ecological Economics*, 70(11), 1957–1971.

Mortha, A, F Taghizadeh-Hesary and XV Vo (2021). The impact of a carbon tax implementation on non-CO_2 gas emissions: The case of Japan. *Australasian Journal of Environmental Management*, 28(4), 355–372.

Qi, S and S Cheng (2018). China's national emissions trading scheme: Integrating cap, coverage and allocation. *Climate Policy*, 18(sup1), 45–59.

Qian, H, Y Zhou and L Wu (2018). Evaluating various choices of sector coverage in China's national emissions trading system (ETS). *Climate Policy*, 18(sup1), 7–26.

Rannou, Y, MA Boutabba and P Barneto (2021). Are Green Bond and Carbon Markets in Europe complements or substitutes? Insights from the activity of power firms. *Energy Economics*, 104(4), 105651.

Shi, X, TS Cheong, J Yu and X Liu (2021a). Quality of life and relative household energy consumption in China. *China and World Economy*, 29(5), 127–147.

Shi, X, Y Sun and Y Shen (2021b). China's ambitious energy transition plans. *Science*, 373, 170.

Stoerk, T, DJ Dudek and J Yang (2019). China's national carbon emissions trading scheme: Lessons from the pilot emission trading schemes, academic literature, and known policy details. *Climate Policy*, 19(4), 472–486.

Sun, YP, JJ Xue, XP Shi, KY Wang, SZ Qi, L Wang and C Wang (2019). A dynamic and continuous allowances allocation methodology for the prevention of carbon leakage: Emission control coefficients. *Applied Energy*, 236, 220–230.

Tran, QH (2021). The impact of green finance, economic growth and energy usage on CO_2 emission in Vietnam – A multivariate time series analysis. *China Finance Review International*, ahead-of-print(ahead-of-print).

Wang, X-Q, C-W Su, O-R Lobonţ, H Li and M Nicoleta-Claudia (2022). Is China's carbon trading market efficient? Evidence from emissions trading scheme pilots. *Energy*, 245, 123240.

World Bank (2020a). *Emissions Trading in Practice: A Handbook on Design and Implementation*. World Bank.

World Bank (2020b). *State and Trends of Carbon Pricing 2020*. World Bank.

Wu, F, N Huang, F Zhang, L Niu and Y Zhang (2020). Analysis of the carbon emission reduction potential of China's key industries under the IPCC 2°C and 1.5°C limits. *Technological Forecasting and Social Change*, 159, 120198.

Yi, W-J, L-L Zou, J Guo, K Wang and Y-M Wei (2011). How can China reach its CO_2 intensity reduction targets by 2020? A regional allocation based on equity and development. *Energy Policy*, 39(5), 2407–2415.

Zeng, S, Y Xu, L Wang, J Chen and Q Li (2016). Forecasting the allocative efficiency of carbon emission allowance financial assets in China at the provincial level in 2020. *Energies*, 9(5), 329.

Zhang, YJ and JF Hao (2017). Carbon emission quota allocation among China's industrial sectors based on the equity and efficiency principles. *Annals of Operations Research*, 255, 117–140.

Zhao, R, N Min, Y Geng and Y He (2017). Allocation of carbon emissions among industries/sectors: An emissions intensity reduction constrained approach. *Journal of Cleaner Production*, 142, 3083–3094.

Zhao, S, Y Shi and J Xu (2018). Carbon emissions quota allocation based equilibrium strategy toward carbon reduction and economic benefits in China's building materials industry. *Journal of Cleaner Production*, 189, 307–325.

Zhou, J, Y Li, X Huo and X Xu (2019). How to allocate carbon emission permits among China's industrial sectors under the constraint of carbon intensity? *Sustainability*, 11(3), 914.

Zhou, P and M Wang (2016). Carbon dioxide emissions allocation: A review. *Ecological Economics*, 125, 47–59.

https://doi.org/10.1142/9789819812783_0005

NEXUS OF CLIMATE CONDITIONS WITH ENERGY-ENVIRONMENTAL GROWTH INTEGRATION: HOW DO ECONOMIC INDICATORS MATTER?[†]

YANLIANG ZHU

School of Economics and Management
Guangdong University of Petrochemical Technology
Maoming, P. R. China
jxzyl436@163.com

KAIFENG WANG*

Guangdong Academy of Social Sciences
Guangzhou, P. R. China

Jingdezhen University, Jingdezhen, P. R. China
2015010027@m.scnu.edu.cn

ROBINA IRAM

School of Finance and Economics
Institute of Industrial Economics
Jiangsu University, Zhenjiang 212013, P. R. China
robinamohsin22@yahoo.com

There has been a change in economic research from focusing on economic growth to focusing on sustainable development when it comes to economic development. This research aims to examine the link between China's socioeconomic progress and the degradation of the environment. Between 1995 and 2018, the information in this study was collected. We looked at factors including the percentage of tourism in total exports, total and renewable energy consumption and GDP per capita when calculating the emissions they have on the environment. CO_2 emission shows long-term causation, but the feedback causality hypothesis holds in the short term between the variables of concern. There is a one-way correlation between GDP, CO_2 emissions and the use of renewable energy; access to better water, sanitation and electricity; access to renewable energy; and access to improved water, sanitation and electricity to CO_2 emissions. It was shown that CO_2 emissions, GDP and energy usage had a positive long-term correlation. In contrast, tourism, renewable energy and access to better water and sanitation all had a negative long-term correlation. GDP's contribution to future CO_2 emission fluctuations ranges from 7% to 25%, with energy use at 7%–15%, renewable energy use at 1%–4.5% and tourism at 5.8%–10%. Meanwhile, access to better water, sanitation and electricity is at 9%, 1.13% and 3%, respectively, according to the variance decomposition analysis. Sustainable

*Corresponding author.

[†]This chapter was originally published in Climate Change Economics, Vol. 13, No. 3, May 2022, published by World Scientific Publishing, Singapore. Reprinted with permission.

development in China necessitates a strong policy to adopt renewable energy sources, sustainable tourism growth and improved access to safe drinking water, sanitary facilities and power.

Keywords: Environmental concerns; growth basis; economic development; climate change; carbon emission; China.

1. Introduction

Economic development has been there till the last quarter of the previous century. Still, since then, the focus of economic research has been shifted to analyze the concept of sustainable development (Alemzero *et al.*, 2021). This concept demands a balanced environment, society and economy (Li *et al.*, 2021c). Sustainable development also requires studying the linkage between socioeconomic developments and resulting environmental pressure (Iqbal *et al.*, 2021). Since socioeconomic development and environmental indicators show regional disparities, ecological degradation is interconnected to socioeconomic development that needs to be investigated, especially in developing countries where it has become a severe issue (Li *et al.*, 2021b).

The emissions of CO_2 from different sources have almost 78% contribution toward the total greenhouse gas (GHG) emissions during the time 1970–2010 (Anh Tu *et al.*, 2021) and has been considered a hurdle in the achievement of sustainable development (Iqbal *et al.*, 2021). China launched Environmental Policy in 2005 for environmental protection and sustainable economic growth (Ahmad *et al.*, 2021). However, per capita GHG emissions in China have increased by 29% from 1990 to 2014, even though the population has also increased by 72% over the same period (World Bank, 2018). Transforming Our World: the 2030 Agenda for Sustainable Development by the United Nations provides a plan of action for prosperity — fulfilling the lives of human beings by socioeconomic progress and protecting the planet from degradation to fulfill the needs of present and future generations (Iqbal and Bilal, 2021). This agenda demands that countries attain socioeconomic development but not at the cost of environmental degradation (Liu *et al.*, 2021a). Although a balanced link between economy, society and environment is fundamental for sustainable development, economic development is often preferred over the environment in policy formulation (Schwalm *et al.*, 2013). How different forces affect the association between the socioeconomic and environmental aspects of the development is needed for detailed analysis to understand the complex link between socioeconomic and environmental indicators (Iqbal and Bilal, 2021).

The selection of suitable indicators for analysis is a crucial point toward analyzing the status of sustainable development. Zhang *et al.* (2021) described various indicators that can provide the best analysis for analyzing the interconnectedness of socioeconomic development and environmental problems. A mix of socioeconomic indicators is selected to explore the possible impact of development on environmental damage in China (Chen *et al.*, 2021). We have selected population access to safe drinking water, sanitation, and electricity and share of tourism in total export as critical variables in addition to commonly used variables such as total energy consumption, renewable energy consumption and GDP to check their impacts on CO_2 emission (Chen *et al.*, 2019). The selection of socioeconomic and environmental indicators is justified by extant literature. The selected key variables have a critical role in economic prosperity and ecological sustainability (Goodland, 1995; McKinnon, 2010; Morelli, 2011; Sutton, 2004; Ones and Dilchert, 2012; Moldan *et al.*, 2012; Yoshino *et al.*, 2021; Ward, 2012; Ko, 2020). Since energy use and economic growth are positively correlated to CO_2 emission (Jiang *et al.*, 2019; Taghizadeh-Hesary *et al.*, 2021; Xing and Fuest, 2018; Tiep *et al.*, 2021), hence, ignoring their possible impact is not justified.

Renewable energy use not only affects sustained economic development but CO_2 emission reduction as well is also inevitable to include in the selection of variables for analysis (Yousaf *et al.*, 2020; Winner, 2012; Ren *et al.*, 2020; Sun *et al.*, 2016). Tourism is also positively associated with CO_2 emission (Tehreem *et al.*, 2020) and its economic importance (10.5% share in GDP by 2018) justifies its inclusion in the analysis. Furthermore, the minimal literature on investigating the tourism-environment nexus and its long-run positive interaction with CO_2 in the case of China (Sharif *et al.*, 2017) further justifies its inclusion in the analysis (Karatas *et al.*, 2018).

The methodology selected for the energy-growth-environment nexus is mostly criticized in the existing literature. The socioeconomic development and environmental indicators are endogenously integrated (Zhu *et al.*, 2020), so a proper methodology and selection of the data type are essential for robust results. Panel estimation techniques fail to overcome the problem (Rasheed and Anser, 2017). So, country-level analysis using a time series data set seems a better option to avoid biased results (Miao *et al.*, 2022). We opted for a nonparametric regression technique — Fully Modified Ordinary Least Square (FMOLS) to control endogeneity, serial correlation and consistent results. Moreover, we applied the Canonical Cointegration Regression (CCR) model based on data transformation does not affect cointegration; the correlation between the error term and repressor to have asymptotically efficient estimators.

The current study has the following specific contributions to existing literature. This is the first study evaluating the possible long-run dynamics of socioeconomic development on environmental degradation in China. However, the one-panel data-based study of Shen *et al.* (2021) exists for China. Such studies flop to give in-depth analysis at the country level and might be misleading to formulate local strategies for the desired outcome. This research will be exceptional and exclusively on China and will serve as a benchmark to investigate how the developments have affected the environment. This will help develop strategies to achieve the UN's agenda for 2030. Second, it will give guidelines to achieve human well-being through socioeconomic development strategies ensuring sustainability at the same time.

This paper is arranged as follows. The second part briefly discusses the available literature. The third part provides a descriptive analysis. The fourth part explains the econometric procedures. The fifth part discusses the empirical findings. Finally, the sixth part comprises conclusions and gives research implications of the study.

2. Literature Review

Nexus among energy use, economic growth and environment has been the focus of the most recent research (Zameer *et al.*, 2020; Halliru *et al.*, 2021; Amar, 2021; Liu *et al.*, 2021b; Abdollahi, 2020; Ahmed *et al.*, 2020; Nguyen *et al.*, 2020; Nathaniel, 2020). But some studies have also analyzed the environmental benefits of renewable energy use (Murshed, 2020; Sharif *et al.*, 2020; Zafar *et al.*, 2020; Khan *et al.*, 2020), tourism (Muresan *et al.*, 2021; Arrobas *et al.*, 2020; Saarinen *et al.*, 2020; Bhat and Mishra, 2021; Nugroho and Numata, 2020) in energy, economy and environment nexus (Chai *et al.*, 2020; Khan *et al.*, 2020; Shakib *et al.*, 2021; Pandey *et al.*, 2020; Mehmood, 2021). However, little research has investigated the interaction between socioeconomic development and environmental damage despite its critical importance on ecological sustainability and economic prosperity. Table 1 gives a brief literature review related to the current study.

3. Methodology

3.1. *Models specification*

The economic growth and energy use nexus have been empirically investigated since 1970. Energy utilization is a complementary input and labor and capital in the economic growth models of neo-classical and endogenous growth theory. Keeping in view the importance of renewable and nonrenewable energy use in the energy-growth nexus by Ozturk (2016), tourism's contribution in economic, social and infrastructural development and toward CO_2 emissions, the role of access to improved water and sanitation toward economic growth and environmental well-being (Takala, 2017) and a strong emphasis on improving their access globally under the Sustainable Development Goals agenda (Zhou *et al.*, 2018), we develop the following functional form of econometric model:

$$\mathrm{CE}_t = f(\mathrm{GDP}_t, \mathrm{EN}_t, \mathrm{REN}_t, \mathrm{TOU}_t, \mathrm{WAT}_t, \mathrm{SAN}_t, \mathrm{EL}_t), \tag{1}$$

where CE, GDP, EN, REN, TOU, WAT, SAN and EL represents CO_2 emission, economic growth, energy use, renewable energy use (% of total energy), the share of tourism (%) in exports, access to improved water, sanitation and electricity, respectively.

3.2. *Models specification*

Following Hossain (2012), we developed the following three models:

$$\mathrm{CE}_t = A_0 \mathrm{GDP}_t^{\alpha_1} \mathrm{EN}_t^{\alpha_2} \mathrm{REN}_t^{\alpha_3} \mathrm{TOU}_t^{\alpha_4} \mathrm{WAT}_t^{\alpha_5} \epsilon^{\varepsilon_t}, \tag{2}$$

Table 1. An overview of the selected literature.

Author(s)	Variables	Method	Countries	Time period	Findings
Jebli *et al.* (2014)	CO_2, tourism, economic growth, trade openness and renewable energy	ARDL, DOLS, FMOLS	Central and South America	1995–2010	(1) Renewable energy → CO_2 & trade; Tourism → Trade; Economic growth → Trade & tourism (2) CO_2 ↔ Renewableenergy ↔ Tourism ↔ CO_2 (3) CO_2 is inversely related to tourism and renewable energy.
Solarin (2014)	CO_2, energy use, real GDP, urbanization, tourism and financial development	VECM, ARDL	Malaysia	1972–2010	(1) Tourism → CO_2 (2) Economic growth and tourism do not show a causal association.
Zaman *et al.* (2016)	Tourism, CO_2, FDI, trade, energy use, urbanization and economic growth	Panel-fixed effect regression and Dumitrescu Hurlin causality test	11 Transition Economies	1995–2013	(1) The results showed the direct association between income per capita and CO_2. (2) International tourism receipts and expenditures increase both CO_2 and income. (3) Results showed the energy-led emissions, income-led energy demand and income-led emissions.
Chakamera and Alagidede (2017)	Infrastructure stock (access to water, sanitation) and economic growth	PCA, GMM	Sub Saharan Africa	2000–2014	(1) The positive association between infrastructural development and the economy. (2) Long-run results are more evident than the short run.

Table 1. (*Continued*)

Author(s)	Variables	Method	Countries	Time period	Findings
Dogan and Aslan (2017)	Real income, energy use, tourism and CO_2	FMOLS, DOLS	European countries	1995–2011	(1) CO_2 increases due to energy use and decreases due to actual income and tourism. (2) Real income $\leftrightarrow CO_2 \leftrightarrow$ Energy use (3) Tourism $\rightarrow CO_2$
Gamage *et al.* (2017)	Income, energy use, CO_2 and tourism	ECM, DOLS, VECM	Sri Lanka	1974–2013	(1) The EKC hypothesis does not exist. (2) The environmental damage due to energy use. (3) Tourism and renewable effect were found beneficial for the environment.
Işik *et al.* (2017)	CO_2, trade openness, economic growth, tourism and financial development	ARDL, VECM	Greece	1970–2014	(1) The CO_2 increases due to economic growth, trade, financial development and tourism.
Jebli and Youssef (2017)	CO_2, agricultural value-addition, renewable energy and real GDP	VECM, OLS, FMOLS, DOLS	5 North African countries	1980–2011	(1) CO_2 emissions $\leftrightarrow$ Agriculture; Agriculture $\rightarrow$ GDP; GDP $\rightarrow$ Renewable energy; Renewable energy $\rightarrow$ Agriculture. (2) CO_2 emission increases due to economic growth. (3) The CO_2 decreases due to agricultural value addition.
Jiang and Bai (2017)	Energy use and economic growth	EMD method	China	1953–2015	(1) Energy use $\leftrightarrow$ Economic growth (short run) (2) Economic growth $\rightarrow$ Energy utilization (long run)

Table 1. (*Continued*)

Author(s)	Variables	Method	Countries	Time period	Findings
Khan *et al.* (2017)	GHGs, urbanization, energy use, financial development, trade openness and renewable energy	GMM, FMOLS, VECM	34 countries	2001–2014	(1) GHG $\leftrightarrow$ Urbanization (America); GHG $\leftrightarrow$ Trade (Europe); Financial development $\leftrightarrow$ Trade (Asia); Urbanization $\leftrightarrow$ Trade (Africa) (2) The GHG decreases are due to increased trade, urbanization, financial development and renewable energy.
Ohlan (2017)	Economic growth, tourism and financial development	VECM, ARDL	India	1960–2014	(1) Tourism $\rightarrow$ Economic growth
Sharif *et al.* (2017)	Economic growth, CO_2 and tourism	ARDL bounds test, FMOLS, DOLS	China	1972–2013	(1) Tourism $\rightarrow$ CO_2.
Sherafatian-Jahromi *et al.* (2017)	Tourism and CO_2	Panel cointegration and PMG techniques	5 Southeast Asian countries	1979–2010	(1) The cointegration between CO_2 and tourism exists. (2) The inverted U-shaped link established for tourism and CO_2. (3) CO_2 rises due to energy use and economic growth.
Stamatiou and Dritsakis (2017)	Economic growth, CO_2 and energy use	VECM	Italy	1960–2011	(1) Economic growth $\rightarrow$ Energy use & CO_2 (2) Energy consumption $\leftrightarrow$ CO_2
Zoundi (2017)	CO_2, renewable energy, income per capita, primary energy and population	GMM, DOLS	25 African countries	1980–2012	(1) The direct relationship was observed between CO_2 and income per capita. (2) Renewable energy and CO_2 emissions are negatively associated.

Table 1. (*Continued*)

Author(s)	Variables	Method	Countries	Time period	Findings
Khan *et al.* (2018a)	GHG, agriculture value-added, vegetable area, forest area, renewable energy, hydroelectricity and coal electricity	The Toda and Yamamoto approach, CCR, FMOLS	China	1981–2015	(1) Renewable energy → GHGs; Forest area → GHGs & coal electricity; Vegetable area → Forest area; Hydroelectricity → Forest area. (2) GHG emission decreases due to renewable energy, vegetable and forest area and agriculture value-added.
Khan *et al.* (2018b)	GHG, forest area, trade, financial development, sanitation, renewable energy and urbanization	Toda and Yamamoto approach, GMM, FMOLS	24 lower-middle-income countries	1990–2015	(1) GHG ↔ Urbanization (Asia); Energy ↔ Renewable energy (Asia); Financial development ↔ Forest area(Asia); Renewable energy ↔ Forest (Asia) (2) GHG reduced due to trade, forest area, sanitation, financial development, urbanization and renewable energy.

$$\mathrm{CE}_t = B_0 \mathrm{GDP}_t^{\beta_1} \mathrm{EN}_t^{\beta_2} \mathrm{REN}_t^{\beta_3} \mathrm{TOU}_t^{\beta_4} \mathrm{SAN}_t^{\beta_5} \epsilon^{\varepsilon_t}, \tag{3}$$

$$\mathrm{CE}_t = C_0 \mathrm{GDP}_t^{\gamma_1} \mathrm{EN}_t^{\gamma_2} \mathrm{REN}_t^{\gamma_3} \mathrm{TOU}_t^{\gamma_4} \mathrm{EL}_t^{\gamma_5} \epsilon^{\varepsilon_t}. \tag{4}$$

The natural logarithm is taken to minimize the heteroscedasticity, and Eqs. (2)–(4) turns into

$$\begin{aligned} \ln(\mathrm{CE}_t) = {} & \alpha_0 + \alpha_1 \ln(\mathrm{GDP}_t) + \alpha_2 \ln(\mathrm{EN}_t) + \alpha_3 \ln(\mathrm{REN}_t) \\ & + \alpha_4 \ln(\mathrm{TOU}_t) + \alpha_4 \ln(\mathrm{WAT}_t) + \varepsilon_t, \end{aligned} \tag{5}$$

where $\alpha_0 = \ln(A_0)$, t denotes the time, and α_1, α_2, α_3, α_4 and α_5 are coefficient.

$$\begin{aligned} \ln(\mathrm{CE}_t) = {} & \beta_0 + \beta_1 \ln(\mathrm{GDP}_t) + \beta_2 \ln(\mathrm{EN}_t) + \beta_3 \ln(\mathrm{REN}_t) + \beta_4 \ln(\mathrm{TOU}_t) \\ & + \beta_4 \ln(\mathrm{SAN}_t) + \varepsilon_t, \end{aligned} \tag{6}$$

where $\beta_0 = \ln(B_0)$, t denotes the time period, and β_1, β_2, β_3, β_4, and β_5 show the elasticity of CE concerning selected variables.

$$\begin{aligned} \ln(\mathrm{CE}_t) = {} & \gamma_0 + \gamma_1 \ln(\mathrm{GDP}_t) + \gamma_2 \ln(\mathrm{EN}_t) + \gamma_3 \ln(\mathrm{REN}_t) + \gamma_4 \ln(\mathrm{TOU}_t) \\ & + \gamma_4 \ln(\mathrm{EL}_t) + \varepsilon_t, \end{aligned} \tag{7}$$

where $\gamma_0 = \ln(C_0)$, t denotes the time period, and γ_1, γ_2, γ_3, γ_4, and γ_5 show the elasticity of CE concerning selected variables.

3.3. *Econometric procedure*

3.3.1. *Unit root tests*

First, the integration order for each variable series was explored by using three conventional tests (ADF) (Dickey and Fuller, 1979).

$$\Delta x_t = \rho \Delta x_{t-1} + \sum_{j=2}^{p} \varphi_j \Delta x_{t-j+1} + \varepsilon_1, \tag{8}$$

$$\Delta x_t = \rho \Delta x_{t-1} + c + \sum_{j=2}^{p} \varphi_j \Delta x_{t-j+1} + \varepsilon_1, \tag{9}$$

$$\Delta x_t = \rho \Delta x_{t-1} + c + bt + \sum_{j=2}^{p} \varphi_j \Delta x_{t-j+1} + \varepsilon_1 (\text{with } \sim> \varepsilon_t \sim> \mathrm{BB}(0, \sigma_\epsilon^2)). \tag{10}$$

These models employed the null hypothesis that the series has nonconstant variance, mean and auto-covariance. Verifying the null hypothesis implies the nonstationary variable series in any model (Pan and Chen, 2021). These models are employed in the Phillips–Perron test (Belaid and Abderrahmani, 2013).

3.3.2. *Co-integration test*

Variables show the order of cointegration (1,1) if the variables are nonstationary individually at the first difference, but a linear combination of variables must be stationary at level. The presence of cointegration ensures the existence of Granger causality (Khan *et al.*, 2017a). We applied the Johansen (1988, 1991) cointegration test explained in the below model:

$$\Delta y_t = \mu + \sum_{i=1}^{k} \Gamma_i \Delta y_{t-1} + \Pi y_{t-1} + \varepsilon_t, \tag{11}$$

where y_t shows a 6×1 vector of the selected variables (CO_2, GDP, energy use, renewable energy, tourism, access to improved water, sanitation and electricity); the parameters Γ and Π stand for 6×6 coefficient matrix; μ is a 6×1 vector of constant terms; ε is a 6×1 vector of white noise error terms. It relies upon the maximum likelihood estimation and the trace statistics (λ_{trace}), where the λ_{trace} the statistic shows the null hypothesis of no cointegration ($r = 0$), and the alternative hypothesis shows the cointegration ($r > 0$) (Rawat *et al.*, 2020).

3.3.3. *Granger causality test*

The presence of cointegration implies the Granger causality between the variables, which was tested by Engle and Granger test, described below. In addition, this study used the augmented causality test by the inclusion of ECM in a multivariate pth order of vector error correction model (VECM) (Hossain, 2011) for three cases such as the model with improved water access [Eq. (12)], the model with improved sanitation access [Eq. (13)] and model with electricity access [Eq. (14)], which are expressed as

$$\begin{bmatrix} \Delta\ln\text{CE}_t \\ \Delta\ln\text{GDP}_t \\ \Delta\ln\text{EN}_t \\ \Delta\ln\text{REN}_t \\ \Delta\ln\text{TOU}_t \\ \Delta\ln\text{WAT}_t \end{bmatrix} = \begin{bmatrix} C_1 \\ C_2 \\ C_3 \\ C_4 \\ C_5 \\ C_6 \end{bmatrix} + \sum_{k-1}^{p} \begin{bmatrix} \beta_{11k} & \beta_{12k} & \beta_{13k} & \beta_{14k} & \beta_{15k} & \beta_{16k} \\ \beta_{21k} & \beta_{22k} & \beta_{23k} & \beta_{24k} & \beta_{25k} & \beta_{26k} \\ \beta_{31k} & \beta_{32k} & \beta_{33k} & \beta_{34k} & \beta_{35k} & \beta_{36k} \\ \beta_{41k} & \beta_{42k} & \beta_{43k} & \beta_{44k} & \beta_{45k} & \beta_{46k} \\ \beta_{51k} & \beta_{52k} & \beta_{53k} & \beta_{54k} & \beta_{55k} & \beta_{56k} \\ \beta_{61k} & \beta_{62k} & \beta_{63k} & \beta_{64k} & \beta_{65k} & \beta_{66k} \end{bmatrix} \begin{bmatrix} \Delta\ln\text{CE}_{t-k} \\ \Delta\ln\text{GDP}_{t-k} \\ \Delta\ln\text{EN}_{t-k} \\ \Delta\ln\text{REN}_{t-k} \\ \Delta\ln\text{TOU}_{t-k} \\ \Delta\ln\text{WAT}_{t-k} \end{bmatrix}$$

$$+ \begin{bmatrix} \lambda_1 \\ \lambda_2 \\ \lambda_3 \\ \lambda_4 \\ \lambda_5 \\ \lambda_5 \\ \lambda_6 \end{bmatrix} \text{ECM}_{it-1} + \begin{bmatrix} \varepsilon_{1it} \\ \varepsilon_{2it} \\ \varepsilon_{3it} \\ \varepsilon_{4it} \\ \varepsilon_{5it} \\ \varepsilon_{6it} \end{bmatrix}, \tag{12}$$

$$\begin{bmatrix} \Delta \mathrm{lnCE}_t \\ \Delta \mathrm{lnGDP}_t \\ \Delta \mathrm{lnEN}_t \\ \Delta \mathrm{lnREN}_t \\ \Delta \mathrm{lnTOU}_t \\ \Delta \mathrm{lnSAN}_t \end{bmatrix} = \begin{bmatrix} C_1 \\ C_2 \\ C_3 \\ C_4 \\ C_5 \\ C_6 \end{bmatrix} + \sum_{k-1}^{p} \begin{bmatrix} \beta_{11k} & \beta_{12k} & \beta_{13k} & \beta_{14k} & \beta_{15k} & \beta_{16k} \\ \beta_{21k} & \beta_{22k} & \beta_{23k} & \beta_{24k} & \beta_{25k} & \beta_{26k} \\ \beta_{31k} & \beta_{32k} & \beta_{33k} & \beta_{34k} & \beta_{35k} & \beta_{36k} \\ \beta_{41k} & \beta_{42k} & \beta_{43k} & \beta_{44k} & \beta_{45k} & \beta_{46k} \\ \beta_{51k} & \beta_{52k} & \beta_{53k} & \beta_{54k} & \beta_{55k} & \beta_{56k} \\ \beta_{61k} & \beta_{62k} & \beta_{63k} & \beta_{64k} & \beta_{65k} & \beta_{66k} \end{bmatrix} \begin{bmatrix} \Delta \mathrm{lnCE}_{t-k} \\ \Delta \mathrm{lnGDP}_{t-k} \\ \Delta \mathrm{lnEN}_{t-k} \\ \Delta \mathrm{lnREN}_{t-k} \\ \Delta \mathrm{lnTOU}_{t-k} \\ \Delta \mathrm{lnSAN}_{t-k} \end{bmatrix}$$

$$+ \begin{bmatrix} \lambda_1 \\ \lambda_2 \\ \lambda_3 \\ \lambda_4 \\ \lambda_5 \\ \lambda_5 \\ \lambda_6 \end{bmatrix} \mathrm{ECM}_{it-1} + \begin{bmatrix} \varepsilon_{1it} \\ \varepsilon_{2it} \\ \varepsilon_{3it} \\ \varepsilon_{4it} \\ \varepsilon_{5it} \\ \varepsilon_{6it} \end{bmatrix}, \tag{13}$$

$$\begin{bmatrix} \Delta \mathrm{lnCE}_t \\ \Delta \mathrm{lnGDP}_t \\ \Delta \mathrm{lnEN}_t \\ \Delta \mathrm{lnREN}_t \\ \Delta \mathrm{lnTOU}_t \\ \Delta \mathrm{lnEL}_t \end{bmatrix} = \begin{bmatrix} C_1 \\ C_2 \\ C_3 \\ C_4 \\ C_5 \\ C_6 \end{bmatrix} + \sum_{k-1}^{p} \begin{bmatrix} \beta_{11k} & \beta_{12k} & \beta_{13k} & \beta_{14k} & \beta_{15k} & \beta_{16k} \\ \beta_{21k} & \beta_{22k} & \beta_{23k} & \beta_{24k} & \beta_{25k} & \beta_{26k} \\ \beta_{31k} & \beta_{32k} & \beta_{33k} & \beta_{34k} & \beta_{35k} & \beta_{36k} \\ \beta_{41k} & \beta_{42k} & \beta_{43k} & \beta_{44k} & \beta_{45k} & \beta_{46k} \\ \beta_{51k} & \beta_{52k} & \beta_{53k} & \beta_{54k} & \beta_{55k} & \beta_{56k} \\ \beta_{61k} & \beta_{62k} & \beta_{63k} & \beta_{64k} & \beta_{65k} & \beta_{66k} \end{bmatrix} \begin{bmatrix} \Delta \mathrm{lnCE}_{t-k} \\ \Delta \mathrm{lnGDP}_{t-k} \\ \Delta \mathrm{lnEN}_{t-k} \\ \Delta \mathrm{lnREN}_{t-k} \\ \Delta \mathrm{lnTOU}_{t-k} \\ \Delta \mathrm{lnEL}_{t-k} \end{bmatrix}$$

$$+ \begin{bmatrix} \lambda_1 \\ \lambda_2 \\ \lambda_3 \\ \lambda_4 \\ \lambda_5 \\ \lambda_5 \\ \lambda_6 \end{bmatrix} \mathrm{ECM}_{it-1} + \begin{bmatrix} \varepsilon_{1it} \\ \varepsilon_{2it} \\ \varepsilon_{3it} \\ \varepsilon_{4it} \\ \varepsilon_{5it} \\ \varepsilon_{6it} \end{bmatrix}, \tag{14}$$

where $t = p+1, p+2, p+3, \ldots, T$. C_i, β_i and λ_i shows the estimated parameters, Δ is the first difference, ECM_{it-1} is the one-period lag of error-term and ε_{it} shows serially independent error terms with zero mean. The elasticity coefficients (CEs) with respect to GDP, energy use, renewable energy, share tourism in exports, population access to improved water, improved sanitation and electricity were estimated using FMOLS and

CCR methods (Li *et al.*, 2021a). The FMOLS can control the endogeneity and serial correlation. It was constructed as (Bilgili *et al.*, 2016):

$$\hat{\beta}^*_{\text{GFM}} = N^{-1} \sum_{i=1}^{N} \hat{\beta}^*_{\text{FM},i}, \tag{15}$$

where $\hat{\beta}^*_{\text{FM},i}$ is the traditional FMOLS estimator. The value of t-statistic is found as

$$t_{\hat{\beta}^*_{\text{GFM}}} = N^{-1/2} \sum_{i=1}^{N} t_{\hat{\beta}^*_{\text{FM},i}}. \tag{16}$$

Han (1996) mentioned the first time use of CCR procedure by Park (1992). This transformation is responsible for the absence of correlation between the error term of the cointegrating model and repressors. Therefore, the CCR provides asymptotically efficient estimators.

4. Results and Discussion

4.1. *Data and descriptive statistics*

The data period for the current study is from 1995 to 2018 taken from World Development Indicators. Table 2 reports the descriptive statistics. On average, per capita, CO_2 was 0.81 metric tons, which were the maximum (0.99 metric tons) in 2007 and the minimum (0.62 metric tons) in 1991. The GDP per capita was 921.25 constant 2010 USD on average, which was the maximum (1140.21 constant 2010 USD) in 2015 and minimum (741.80 constant 2010 USD) in 1990. The EN consumption was 465.45 kg of oil equivalent per capita on average, with a maximum in 2007 and a minimum in 1991. Out of total energy use, the share of renewable energy was 49.70% on average, which was more (58.09%) in 1991 and less (43.95%) in 2007. The exports are vital for any developing country, and the share of tourism in exports was 4.80% in total exports, which shows a gradual decline from 1990 to 2015. The population access to improved water was 88.95%, followed by electricity (79.07%) and improved sanitation (41.66%). Unfortunately, the mean value of access to improved sanitation was less than 50%. Table 1 also explores the normality of variables using kurtosis, skewness and Jarque–Bera statistics. All the selected variables series showed normality which is a good sign for the empirical analysis.

4.2. *Unit root test result*

Table 3 shows the outcome of unit root tests. In case 1, all results reject the stationary and confirm the unit roots in all the selected variables at the 1% and 5% significance levels. However, all tests confirmed the stationary in all variables at the first difference, which reveals that the integration order was 1, i.e., I(1) for all variables. Table 4 describes the empirical findings of the Johansen cointegration test. The existence of cointegration is required for the Granger causality and long-run elasticity. This test

Table 2. Descriptive statistics (1990–2015).

Descriptive indicators	Variables					Control variables		
	CE	GDP	EN	REN	TOU	SAN	WAT	EL
Unit	Metric tons per capita	Constant 2010 USD per capita	kg of oil equivalent per capita	% of total EN	% of total exports	% of population		
Mean	0.81	921.25	465.45	49.70	4.80	41.66	88.95	79.07
Median	0.80	866.97	464.23	49.42	4.70	41.40	89.00	79.12
Maximum	0.99	1140.21	523.76	58.09	6.38	63.50	91.40	99.15
Minimum	0.62	741.80	397.27	43.95	3.12	23.70	86.30	58.74
Std. Dev.	0.12	124.27	34.97	3.96	1.11	13.16	1.58	12.33
Skewness	−0.13	0.26	−0.41	0.61	−0.11	0.09	−0.08	−0.06
Kurtosis	1.67	1.56	2.21	2.35	1.61	1.70	1.81	1.78
Jarque–Bera	2.00	2.54	1.42	2.05	2.16	1.86	1.57	1.64
Probability	0.37	0.28	0.49	0.36	0.34	0.39	0.46	0.44

Table 3. Results of unit root tests.

Variables	Case 1: At level [intercept and trend]			Case 2: First difference [intercept only]			Case 3: First difference [intercept and trend]			Integration order
	ADF	DF GLS	PP	ADF	DF GLS	PP	ADF	DF GLS	PP	
lnCE	−3.120	−2.105	−0.949	−5.203*	−4.573*	−5.180*	−5.907*	−5.489*	−5.812*	I (1)
lnGDP	−3.391***	−2.595	−1.881	−3.340**	−3.290*	−3.065**	−3.432***	−3.502**	−3.010	I (1)
lnEN	−0.895	−1.091	−0.895	−3.740*	−3.734*	−3.740*	−4.499*	−4.431*	−4.498*	I (1)
lnREN	−1.164	−1.389	−1.030	−4.839*	−4.664*	−4.839*	−5.670*	−5.468*	−5.716*	I (1)
lnTOU	−3.169	−3.195***	−3.099	−7.363*	−7.485*	−7.415*	−7.289*	−7.603*	−7.518*	I (1)
lnSAN	−0.486	−2.212	−1.139	−2.725***	−1.889**	−2.744***	−3.645**	−3.109***	−5.346*	I (1)
lnWAT	−0.427	−0.940	1.292	−3.503**	−3.505*	−3.503**	−5.068*	−5.207*	−5.758*	I (1)
lnEL	−1.832	−1.545	−2.269	−9.108*	−8.946*	−8.570*	−10.348*	−10.417*	−10.667*	I (1)
Critical values 1%	−4.468	−3.770	−4.374	−3.738	−2.665	−3.738	−4.394	−3.770	−4.394	—
5%	−3.645	−3.190	−3.603	−2.992	−1.956	−2.992	−3.612	−3.190	−3.612	
10%	−3.261	−2.890	−3.238	−2.636	−1.609	−2.636	−3.243	−2.890	−3.243	

Notes: *Significance level: 1%, **Significance level: 5%, ***Significance level: 10%.

Table 4. Results of the Johansen cointegration test.

		Trace		Max-eigenvalues	
Hypothesis	Eigenvalues	Statistics	*p*-values	Statistics	*p*-values
H_0	The model with access to improved water access (model 1)				
None*	0.916	151.222	95.754	0.000	0.916
At most 1*	0.803	91.916	69.819	0.000	0.803
At most 2*	0.708	52.943	47.856	0.015	0.708
At most 3	0.457	23.415	29.797	0.226	0.457
At most 4	0.211	8.778	15.495	0.386	0.211
At most 5	0.121	3.093	3.841	0.079	0.121
H_0	The model with access to improved sanitation (model 2)				
None*	0.977	181.385	95.754	0.000	0.977
At most 1*	0.775	90.686	69.819	0.001	0.775
At most 2*	0.674	54.862	47.856	0.010	0.674
At most 3	0.502	27.955	29.797	0.080	0.502
At most 4	0.373	11.225	15.495	0.198	0.373
At most 5	0.000	0.008	3.841	0.930	0.000
H_0	The model with access to electricity (model 3)				
None*	0.910	154.134	95.754	0.000	0.910
At most 1*	0.835	96.248	69.819	0.000	0.835
At most 2*	0.729	52.957	47.856	0.015	0.729
At most 3	0.447	21.631	29.797	0.320	0.447
At most 4	0.209	7.413	15.495	0.530	0.209
At most 5	0.072	1.798	3.841	0.180	0.072

Note: *Shows hypothesis rejection at a 5% significance level.

provides two indicators like trace statistics and max-eigenvalues statistics. In the current study, both trace and max-eigenvalues tests indicate two cointegration (s) associations in China. The presence of cointegration among these variables allowed us to explore the Granger causality. Table 5 examines the VECM result for the causality between carbon dioxide emission, GDP, energy use, renewable energy, tourism share in exports, access to improved water, sanitation and electricity in the short and long run. A negative and significant ECM coefficient is required to establish the long-run causality of a specific variable with all other variables. The Granger causality analysis was performed by treating the variables (access to improved water, sanitation and electricity) as control variables.

The long-run causality of CO_2 was found in China in all three models. It showed that the selected variables have a causal impact on CO_2 in the long run. The third case explored the long-run causality for renewable energy consumption. According to short-run causality results, the feedback hypothesis was established between CO_2 and GDP (models 1 and 3); tourism and renewable energy consumption (all models); tourism and improved water (model 1); tourism and enhanced sanitation (model 2);

Table 5. VECM Granger F-test results.

Variables	Case 1: Model with access to improved water access						
	ΔlnCE	ΔlnGDP	ΔlnEN	ΔlnREN	ΔlnTOU	ΔlnWAT	ECM
ΔlnCE		6.02** (0.049)	14.09* (0.001)	5.94*** (0.051)	4.62*** (0.099)	0.88 (0.645)	−0.336* (0.010)
ΔlnGDP	4.61*** (0.099)		0.32 (0.853)	0.45 (0.797)	7.03** (0.030)	13.40* (0.001)	−0.010 (0.716)
ΔlnEN	0.88 (0.645)	4.81*** (0.091)		4.94 (0.140)	10.65* (0.005)	14.09* (0.001)	−0.292 (0.670)
ΔlnREN	0.26 (0.878)	1.47 (0.480)	2.20 (0.333)		8.72** (0.013)	16.71* (0.001)	−0.606 (0.342)
ΔlnTOU	2.41 (0.30)	0.56 (0.756)	0.39 (0.824)	6.973** (0.031)		12.879* (0.002)	−0.068 (0.675)
ΔlnWAT	0.74 (0.692)	2.67 (0.264)	0.408 (0.816)	18.12 (0.001)	17.01* (0.001)		0.006 (0.517)
Variables	Case 2: Model with access to improved sanitation						
	ΔlnCE	ΔlnGDP	ΔlnEN	ΔlnREN	ΔlnTOU	ΔlnSAN	ECM
ΔlnCE		8.53** (0.014)	10.18* (0.006)	1.335 (0.513)	2.92 (0.233)	3.38 (0.185)	−0.454** (0.013)
ΔlnGDP	3.38 (0.185)		0.07 (0.965)	0.03 (0.988)	7.07** (0.029)	8.53** (0.014)	−0.004 (0.939)
ΔlnEN	0.54 (0.765)	1.78 (0.410)		0.27 (0.873)	6.56** (0.038)	9.49* (0.009)	−0.526 (0.498)
ΔlnREN	0.13 (0.937)	1.00 (0.606)	0.03 (0.986)		6.48** (0.039)	11.71* (0.003)	−0.133 (0.777)
ΔlnTOU	1.52 (0.469)	0.36 (0.837)	0.45 (0.798)	7.00** (0.030)		9.14* (0.010)	−0.142 (0.575)
ΔlnSAN	11.06* (0.004)	19.74* (0.001)	1.44 (0.486)	31.02* (0.001)	11.60* (0.003)		−0.028 (0.124)
Variables	Case 3: Model with access to electricity						
	ΔlnCE	ΔlnGDP	ΔlnEN	ΔlnREN	ΔlnTOU	ΔlnEL	ECM
ΔlnCE		12.35* (0.002)	17.79* (0.001)	1.96 (0.376)	3.65 (0.162)	5.35*** (0.069)	−0.290** (0.012)
ΔlnGDP	5.356*** (0.069)		0.86 (0.651)	2.17 (0.338)	11.17* (0.004)	12.35* (0.002)	−0.013 (0.631)
ΔlnEN	0.94 (0.625)	1.63 (0.442)		2.37 (0.305)	8.13** (0.017)	13.24* (0.001)	−0.026 (0.970)
ΔlnREN	2.26 (0.323)	0.34 (0.845)	5.10*** (0.078)		11.51* (0.003)	17.49* (0.001)	−1.146*** (0.070)
ΔlnTOU	3.54 (0.171)	0.91 (0.636)	1.42 (0.493)	7.18** (0.028)		12.64* (0.002)	−0.025 (0.739)
ΔlnEL	15.13 (0.001)	1.02 (0.600)	1.76 (0.416)	4.57* (0.001)	12.70* (0.002)		−0.004 (0.639)

Notes: *p*-values are reported in the parentheses.
*Significance level: 1%, **significance level: 5%, ***significance level: 10%.

tourism and electricity access (model 3). The feedback hypothesis revealed that the said variables placed a causal impact on each other. In addition, a one-way short-run causal association was observed from energy use to CO_2 (all models); tourism to GDP per capita (all models); REN to CO_2 emission (model 1); tourism to CO_2 emission (model 1); electricity access to CO_2 emission (model 3); GDP to CO_2 emission (model 2); improved water to GDP per capita (model 1); improved sanitation to GDP per capita (model 2); electricity access to GDP per capita (model 3); GDP to energy use (model 1); tourism to EN use (all models); improved water to renewable energy consumption (model 1); improved water to EN (model 1); improved sanitation to REN consumption (model 2); improved sanitation to EN (model 2); CO_2 emission to improved sanitation (model 2); GDP per capita to improved sanitation (model 2); REN to improved sanitation (model 2); EN use to REN (model 3); renewable energy to electricity access (model 3); electricity access to energy consumption (model 3); and electricity access to renewable energy (model 3).

The results of the Granger causality analysis justify the selection of these variables in this research. Moreover, the population access to improved water, sanitation and electricity also showed a substantial role in the energy-growth-environment nexus. The access to enhanced water placed a causal impact on GDP, EN, REN and tourism. It highlighted the importance of population access to improved water in the country. Similarly, access to improved sanitation placed a causal impact on GDP, energy use, renewable energy and tourism. In the same way, access to electricity has a causal effect on CO_2 emission, GDP, energy use, renewable energy and tourism. The causality results stressed the importance of renewable energy, tourism and access to improved water, sanitation and electricity in the environment-growth nexus.

4.3. *The long-run elasticity of* CE_t

Table 6 explores the long-run elasticity coefficients of CO_2 emission. The long-run elasticity estimation was performed in three cases using access to improved water, sanitation and electricity as control variables. According to FMOLS results, the increase in per capita CO_2 was 0.231% (case 1) and 0.196% (case 3) due to 1% rise in per capita GDP. The increase in CO_2 emission was 1.196% (case 1), 0.612% (case 2) and 0.726% (case 3) due to 1% rise in the use of energy. The fall in per capita CO_2 was 0.113% (case 1) and 0.156% (case 3) due to 1% increase in the tourism share in exports. The decrease in per capita CO_2 emission was 1.117% (case 2) and 1.093% (case 3) for 1% increase in renewable energy. The fall in per capita CO_2 emission was 1.664% and 0.334% due to 1% increase in the population access to improved water and electricity, respectively. According to CCR results, the decrease in per capita CO_2 was 0.267% (case 2) and 0.402% (case 3) due to 1% rise in per capita GDP. The rise in per capita CO_2 was 1.765% (case 1), 1.160% (case 2) and 1.230% (case 3) due to 1% increase in energy use. The decrease in per capita CO_2 emission was 0.300% (case 1), 0.331% (case 2) and 0.382% (case 3) due to 1% increase in the tourism

Table 6. Long-run elasticity of CE_t.

Variables	Co-integration regression tests							
	FMOLS				CCR			
	Coef.	Std. error	t-Stat.	Prob.	Coef.	Std. error	t-Stat.	Prob.
	Model [access to improved water]							
LnGDP	0.231**	0.110	2.088	0.050	−0.177	0.115	−1.543	0.139
lnEN	1.196*	0.281	4.257	0.000	1.765*	0.364	4.856	0.000
lnREN	−0.383	0.246	−1.553	0.136	0.102	0.317	0.321	0.752
lnTOU	−0.113**	0.049	−2.281	0.034	−0.300*	0.064	−4.675	0.000
lnWAT	−1.664**	0.611	−2.725	0.013	−2.174*	0.750	−2.898	0.009
Diagnostic tests	test Stat.	Prob.	Decision		test Stat.	Prob.	Decision	
JB test for normality of error	0.520	0.771	Normality exist		0.116	0.944	Normality exist	
	Model [access to improved sanitation]							
lnGDP	0.132	0.124	1.066	0.299	−0.402*	0.140	−2.874	0.009
lnEN	0.612*	0.145	4.238	0.000	1.160*	0.192	6.049	0.000
lnREN	−1.117*	0.083	−13.438	0.000	−0.900*	0.079	−11.392	0.000
lnTOU	−0.118	0.069	−1.698	0.105	−0.331*	0.091	−3.638	0.002
lnSAN	−0.091	0.062	−1.478	0.155	−0.149***	0.075	−1.994	0.060
Diagnostic tests	test Stat.	Prob.	Decision		test Stat.	Prob.	Decision	
JB test for normality of error	2.869	0.238	Normality exist		0.489	0.783	Normality exist	

Table 6. (*Continued*)

Variables	Co-integration regression tests							
	FMOLS				CCR			
	Coef.	Std. error	t-Stat.	Prob.	Coef.	Std. error	t-Stat.	Prob.
	Model [access to electricity]							
lnGDP	0.196***	0.103	1.901	0.072	−0.267**	0.111	−2.413	0.026
lnEN	0.726*	0.134	5.411	0.000	1.230*	0.192	6.396	0.000
lnREN	−1.093*	0.059	−18.657	0.000	−0.823*	0.056	−14.723	0.000
lnTOU	−0.156**	0.057	−2.727	0.013	−0.382*	0.080	−4.742	0.000
lnEL	−0.344**	0.126	−2.743	0.013	−0.487*	0.161	−3.020	0.007
Diagnostic tests	test Stat.	Prob.	Decision		test Stat.	Prob.	Decision	
JB test for normality of error	2.015	0.365	Normality exist		0.087	0.958	Normality exist	

Notes: ln denotes natural logarithms, CE denotes CO_2 emissions, GDP denotes gross domestic product, EN denotes energy use, REN denotes renewable energy consumption, TOU denotes tourism, SAN is access to improved sanitation, WAT is access to improved water and EL denotes access to electricity.

*Significance level: 1%, **Significance level: 5%, ***Significance level: 10%.

share in exports. The decrease in per capita CO_2 emission was 0.900% (case 2) and 0.823% (case 3) due to 1% increase in the use of renewable energy. The decrease in per capita CO_2 was 2.174%, 0.149% and 0.487% due to 1% increase in the population access to improved water, sanitation and electricity, respectively. It is cleared from the regression coefficients that renewable energy consumption, tourism, population access to improved water, sanitation and electricity can easily offset the increase in the per capita CO_2 emission resulted due to increasing per capita energy use and per capita GDP.

4.4. *Variance decomposition analysis of selected variables*

This analysis was performed using the Cholesky technique to explore the future relative contribution of selected dependent variables toward CO_2 emission in China within a 10-year time horizon. The methodology examined the percentage of every standard deviation shock in CO_2 emission due to GDP, energy use, renewable energy, tourism, access to improved water, sanitation, and electricity. Table 7 reports results; in case 1, the contribution of GDP, energy use, renewable energy, tourism and improved water access is 25.63%, 7.52%, 1.75%, 9.93% and 9.025%, respectively. In case 2, the contribution of GDP, energy use, renewable energy, tourism and improved sanitation access is 13.98%, 11.09%, 1.80%, 5.78% and 1.13%, respectively. While in case 3, the contribution of GDP, energy use, renewable energy, tourism and electricity access is 7.34%, 14.51%, 4.50%, 6.20% and 3.02 in the 10th year in China.

4.5. *Discussion*

With a population of almost 200 million, China has the third-highest CO_2 intensity rate among the studied countries at 4.6% (Fazal *et al.*, 2021). Similarly, Mexico and Brazil face an economic burden due to the COVID-19 crises, with a dismal economic performance due to the pandemic's impact on sustainable environmental performance (Meo *et al.*, 2021). Financial funds availability and pooling in funds in the E7 economies have fallen from nearly pre-COVID levels of 34% per barrel at the start of the year to 30% in March. The country is primarily reliant on oil and gas revenues. China's real GDP is expected to contract by between 4.4% and 7.2% due to the pandemic's persistence and severity (Aftab *et al.*, 2021). This will reverse the considerable gains made during the economy's three consecutive years of growth from 2016 (Bano *et al.*, 2021).

Urban access to electricity is approximately 100%, but rural access is about 32%. Renewable energy accounts for 92.2% of final consumption. Brazil intends to increase this to nearly 100% by 2030 (Abid *et al.*, 2021). China has the lowest rate of access to clean fuels and cooking technology among the studied nations, at 3.51%. Inadequate access to clean technology explains why the country cooks with more harmful fuels. In Brazil, air pollution is the most prevalent risk factor for premature deaths (Anwar *et al.*, 2021). Additionally, about 65,000 early deaths and 3.1 million disability-adjusted life

Table 7. Results of sensitivity analysis.

Cholesky ordering lnCE lnGDP lnEN lnREN lnTOU lnWAT							
Variance decomposition of lnCE							
Period	S.E.	lnCE	lnGDP	lnEN	lnREN	lnTOU	lnWAT
1	0.019	100.000	0.000	0.000	0.000	0.000	0.000
2	0.032	63.212	0.072	0.336	1.268	19.254	15.859
3	0.046	62.446	0.043	8.239	2.386	12.590	14.296
4	0.060	52.083	7.584	6.298	1.456	16.942	15.637
5	0.075	50.148	13.144	7.660	1.096	16.010	11.941
10	0.112	46.152	25.632	7.515	1.751	9.934	9.016
Cholesky ordering lnCE lnGDP lnEN lnREN lnTOU lnSAN							
Variance decomposition of lnCE							
Period	S.E.	lnCE	lnGDP	lnEN	lnREN	lnTOU	lnSAN
1	0.022	100.000	0.000	0.000	0.000	0.000	0.000
2	0.034	89.109	2.181	0.003	0.517	7.021	1.170
3	0.046	77.528	7.399	7.373	2.100	4.957	0.643
4	0.051	76.094	6.530	7.369	1.855	7.042	1.110
5	0.058	72.267	5.855	10.903	1.524	8.566	0.885
10	0.076	66.222	13.981	11.086	1.799	5.781	1.132
Cholesky ordering lnCE lnGDP lnEN lnREN lnTOU lnEL							
Variance decomposition of lnCE							
1	0.024	100.000	0.000	0.000	0.000	0.000	0.000
2	0.036	81.287	7.820	4.271	0.191	4.994	1.437
3	0.050	80.355	10.542	3.293	2.344	2.700	0.767
4	0.055	78.742	8.915	2.854	3.751	4.611	1.127
5	0.059	78.017	7.825	3.077	3.844	6.262	0.974
10	0.067	64.434	7.341	14.506	4.502	6.200	3.018

years per year occur in China due to home pollution caused by cooking with solid fuels (Abbas *et al.*, 2020).

Additionally, the details show the amount spent on the total use of the Illinois Bureau of Tourism (IBT) and drive by truckers (DBT) framework. Under IBT, helpless families will be hotter, with 3.9% of their revenue, and the poorest families will be 3.1% hotter. Surprisingly, the wealthiest families could also spend the same low rate of 4.6% compared to other disadvantaged families (Damian Felladam Tangonyire, 2019). This is because the monthly payments to affluent families are very high, with a low family budget. Under the DBT paradigm, the poorest households will pay more than the threshold for sustainable environmental performance indicators, while the wealthiest households pay at least 1.9% (Sohail *et al.*, 2021).

According to the statistics, a 1% significance level suggests that rising vertical fiscal imbalance decreases the amount of government environmental control, which is consistent with the expectations of decision makers (Mahmood *et al.*, 2020). A significant positive association has been shown between environmental regulation and CO_2. This implies that increasing environmental regulation by 1% leads to a 0.206% reduction in CO_2. In column 4, the correlation coefficient of the mediator has greater importance. Each percent increase in Financial Inclusion (FI) results in an extra 0.86 percent increase in CO_2 emissions (Ullah *et al.*, 2020). As such, it is conceivable for FI to emit CO_2 directly. Therefore, it is feasible for government and environmental policy to play a supporting role in achieving environmental fairness. The raised environmental performance also increased carbon emissions by affecting environmental control, resulting in an additional 0.14% of CO_2 being released (Nawaz *et al.*, 2020). The variance decomposition analysis results show that in case 1, the contribution of GDP, energy use, renewable energy, tourism and improved water access toward CO_2 emission is 25.63%,7.52%, 1.75%, 9.93% and 9.025%, respectively. In case 2, the contribution of GDP, energy use, renewable energy, tourism and improved sanitation access toward CO_2 emission is 13.98%, 11.09%, 1.80%, 5.78% and 1.13%, respectively. While in case 3, the contribution of GDP, energy use, renewable energy, tourism and electricity access toward CO_2 emission is 7.34%, 14.51%, 4.50%, 6.20% and 3.02%, respectively, in China.

Indeed, the fifth through seventh columns of Table 1 provide the regression findings for the industrial structure mediator. Column 5 asserts that FI has a sizable and beneficial effect on the industrial structure, contributing to industry structure following H2b expectations (Ali *et al.*, 2021). A 1% increase in column 6's industrial structure results in an 11.14% increase in carbon emissions. Environmental sustainability for South Asia is a significant concern as it is the hub of the world's most severe external factors, including climate change and water and food poverty. The World Bank anticipates that the temperature in the area will increase by 6°C by 2100, which is staggering. Therefore, the phrase sustainability indicators should be referred to as environmental sustainability indicators (Haseeb and Azam, 2021). They were chosen based on several parameters, for example, CO_2 emissions per capita, energy generation CO_2, forest ratio, the percentage of financial inclusion funds through penetration dimensions, availability dimensions, usage dimensions and CH_4 emissions (Abbasi *et al.*, 2020; Sajid, 2021).

Furthermore, our findings indicate that per capita energy consumption may be used as a metric for measuring environmental performance. This is mainly substantiated by the fact that energy consumption varies per capita among countries in different stages of development (Achille Dargaud Fofack and Enow Asu Derick, 2020). According to the study's results, energy consumption per capita is a cumulative intensity measure for evaluating economic performance. Power consumption per person may also be used as a proxy for measuring the quality of life (Mahmood *et al.*, 2019). According to recent studies, a high degree of reliance on carbon-based energy imports is harmful to the environment (Barua *et al.*, 2020; Hashmi *et al.*, 2020). Countries that rely on energy for economic development due to high-tech demands yet lack green energy sources are regarded as having poor environmental performance (Shakib *et al.*, 2021; Tanveer *et al.*, 2021).

5. Conclusions and Policy Implications

The sustainable developments goals (2030 Agenda) focus on reducing the existing gap between socioeconomic developments and ensuring environmental sustainability globally. The sustainable development paradigm requires investigating the linkages between socioeconomic development and its accompanying ecological pressure but unabated ecological degradation is still a severe issue in the majority of the developing countries. Before the empirical analysis, the correct integration order was specified using three-unit root tests. The results of VECM showed the long-run causality of CO_2 in the country, while the short-run effects established the feedback hypothesis between CO_2 and selected repressors. The feedback hypothesis indicates that the said variables placed a causal impact on each other. For example, the access to improved water placed a causal impact on GDP, EN, REN and tourism. It highlighted the importance of population access to enhanced water in the country. Similarly, access to improved sanitation placed a causal impact on GDP, energy consumption, renewable energy and tourism.

In the same way, access to electricity placed a causal impact on CO_2, GDP, EN, REN and tourism. The causality results stressed the importance of renewable energy, tourism, and access to improved water, sanitation and electricity in the environment-growth nexus. The decrease in per capita CO_2 was 0.113% (case 1) and 0.156% (case 3) due to 1% increase in the tourism share in exports. The decrease in per capita CO_2 emission was 1.117% (case 2) and 1.093% (case 3) due to 1% rise in renewable energy. The decrease in per capita CO_2 was 1.664% and 0.334% due to 1% increase in the population access to improved water and electricity, respectively. It is clear from the long-run elasticity coefficients that renewable energy consumption, tourism, population access to improved water, sanitation and electricity can easily offset the increase in the per capita CO_2 emission resulting due to increasing energy use and GDP.

- These results from variance decomposition analysis have substantial policy implications for the Government of China. First, it is evident that energy use contribution toward CO_2 emission is expected to increase over time while renewable energy consumption's contribution rises modestly.
- This needs urgent attention to the current pattern of energy consumption use and the strong adoption of improved and cleaner technologies for renewable energy resources. Similarly, the contribution of tourism is alarming though expected to fall in the future.

- An urgent measure for sustainable and environmentally friendly tourism is needed to achieve sustainable development. Access to water resources still shows higher future contribution toward CO_2 emission, strongly demanding to improve the population access to improved water resources.
- Lastly, creating awareness on environmental protection and improving the adoption and implementation of climate change and ecological degradation strategies are recommended at the national level to have sustainable development in the future.

Acknowledgment

This study is supported by the Natural Science Foundation of Guangdong Province, China (2020A1515010772).

References

Abbas, S, LHC Hsieh, K Techato and J Taweekun (2020). Sustainable production using a resource–energy–water nexus for the Pakistani textile industry. *Journal of Cleaner Production*, 271, 122633.

Abbasi, K, Z Jiao, M Shahbaz and A Khan (2020). Asymmetric impact of renewable and non-renewable energy on economic growth in China: New evidence from a nonlinear analysis. *Energy Exploration and Exploitation*, 38(5), 1946–1967.

Abdollahi, H (2020). Investigating energy use, environment pollution, and economic growth in developing countries. *Environmental and Climate Technologies*, 24(1), 275–293.

Abid, N, M Ikram, J Wu and M Ferasso (2021). Towards environmental sustainability: Exploring the nexus among ISO 14001, governance indicators and green economy in China. *Sustainable Production and Consumption*, 27, 653–666.

Achille Dargaud Fofack and Enow Asu Derick (2020). Evaluating the bidirectional nexus between climate change and agriculture from a global perspective. *Malaysian Journal of Sustainable Agriculture*, 4(1), 40–43.

Aftab, S, A Ahmed, AA Chandio, BA Korankye, A Ali and W Fang (2021). Modeling the nexus between carbon emissions, energy consumption, and economic progress in China: Evidence from cointegration and causality analysis. *Energy Reports*, 7, 4642–4658.

Ahmad, B, S Iqbal, M Hai and S Latif (2021). The interplay of personal values, relational mobile usage and organizational citizenship behavior. *Interactive Technology and Smart Education*. DOI: 10.1108/ITSE-01-2021-0016.

Ahmed, Z, MM Asghar, MN Malik and K Nawaz (2020). Moving towards a sustainable environment: The dynamic linkage between natural resources, human capital, urbanization, economic growth, and ecological footprint in China. *Resources Policy*, 67, 101677.

Alemzero, DA, N Iqbal, S Iqbal, M Mohsin, NJ Chukwuma and BA Shah (2021). Assessing the perceived impact of exploration and production of hydrocarbons on households perspective of environmental regulation in Ghana. *Environmental Science and Pollution Research*, 28(5), 5359–5371.

Ali, S, L Ying, R Anjum, A Nazir, A Shalmani, T Shah and F Shah (2021). Analysis on the nexus of CO_2 emissions, energy use, net domestic credit, and GDP in China: An ARDL bound testing analysis. *Environmental Science and Pollution Research*, 28(4), 4594–4614.

Amar, AB (2021). Economic growth and environment in the United Kingdom: Robust evidence using more than 250 years data. *Environmental Economics and Policy Studies*, 23, 667–681. https://doi.org/10.1007/s10018-020-00300-8.

Anh Tu, C, F Chien, MA Hussein, MMY Ramli, MSS PsiMMSIqbal and AR Bilal (2021). Estimating role of green financing on energy security, economic and environmental integration of BRI member countries. *The Singapore Economic Review.*

Anwar, A, M Siddique, E Dogan and A Sharif (2021). The moderating role of renewable and non-renewable energy in environment-income nexus for ASEAN countries: Evidence from method of moments quantile regression. *Renewable Energy*, 164, 956–967.

Arrobas, F, J Ferreira, E Brito-Henriques and A Fernandes (2020). Measuring tourism and environmental sciences students' attitudes towards sustainable tourism. *Journal of Hospitality, Leisure, Sport and Tourism Education*, 27, 100273.

Bano, S, M Alam, A Khan *et al.* (2021). The nexus of tourism, renewable energy, income, and environmental quality: An empirical analysis of Pakistan. *Environment, Development and Sustainability*, 23, 14854–14877, https://doi.org/10.1007/s10668-021-01275-6.

Barua, P, SH Rahman, S Barua and IMM Rahman (2020). Climate change vulnerability and responses of fisherfolk communities in the South-Eastern coast of Bangladesh. *Water Conservation and Management*, 4(1), 20–31.

Bhat, AA and RK Mishra (2021). Demographic characteristics and residents' attitude towards tourism development: A case of Kashmir region. *Journal of Public Affairs*, 21(2), e2179.

Bilgili, F, E Koçak and Ü Bulut (2016). The dynamic impact of renewable energy consumption on CO_2 emissions: A revisited Environmental Kuznets Curve approach. *Renewable and Sustainable Energy Reviews*, 54, 838–845.

Chakamera, C and P Alagidede (2017). The Nexus between Infrastructure (Quantity and Quality) and Economic Growth (No. 673).

Chakamera, C and P Alagidede (2018). The nexus between infrastructure (quantity and quality) and economic growth in Sub Saharan Africa. *International Review of Applied Economics*, 32(5), 641–672.

Chai, J, H Shi, Q Lu and Y Hu (2020). Quantifying and predicting the water-energy-food-economy-society-environment nexus based on Bayesian networks-A case study of China. *Journal of Cleaner Production*, 256, 120266.

Chen, X, Q Quan, K Zhang and J Wei (2021). Spatiotemporal characteristics and attribution of dry/wet conditions in the Weihe River Basin within a typical monsoon transition zone of East Asia over the recent 547 years. *Environmental Modelling and Software: With Environment Data News*, 143, 105116.

Chen, Y, Z Wang and Z Zhong (2019). CO_2 emissions, economic growth, renewable and non-renewable energy production and foreign trade in China. *Renewable Energy*, 131, 208–216.

Damian Felladam Tangonyire (2019). Impact of climate change on farmers in the Talensi district of the Upper East Region of Ghana. *Malaysian Journal of Sustainable Agriculture*, 3(2), 35–45.

Dogan, E and A Aslan (2017). Exploring the relationship among CO_2 emissions, real GDP, energy consumption and tourism in the EU and candidate countries: Evidence from panel models robust to heterogeneity and cross-sectional dependence. *Renewable and Sustainable Energy Reviews*, 77, 239–245.

Fazal, R, SAU Rehman, AU Rehman, MI Bhatti and A Hussain (2021). Energy-environment-economy causal nexus in China: A graph theoretic approach. *Energy*, 214, 118934.

Gamage, A. (2014). CO2 Emission of Hotel Sector in Sri Lanka: A Case study & Scenario Analysis.

Goodland, R (1995). The concept of environmental sustainability. *Annual Review of Ecology and Systematics*, 26(1), 1–24.

Halliru, AM, N Loganathan and AA Golam Hassan (2021). Does FDI and economic growth harm environment? Evidence from selected West African countries. *Transnational Corporations Review*, 13(2), 237–251.

Han, HL (1996). Small sample properties of canonical cointegrating regressions. *Empirical Economics*, 21(2), 235–253.

Haseeb, M and M Azam (2021). Dynamic nexus among tourism, corruption, democracy and environmental degradation: A panel data investigation. *Environment, Development and Sustainability*, 23(4), 5557–5575.

Hashmi, SH, H Fan, Z Fareed and R Bannya (2020). Testing non-linear nexus between service sector and CO_2 emissions in China. *Energies*, 13(3), 526.

Iqbal, S and AR Bilal (2021a). Energy financing in COVID-19: How public supports can benefit?*China Finance Review International*.

Iqbal, S and AR Bilal (2021b). Investment performance: Emotional beasts are dragging into the darkness of the castle. *Global Business Review*.

Iqbal, S, AR Bilal, M Nurunnabi, W Iqbal, Y Alfakhri and N Iqbal (2021). It is time to control the worst: Testing COVID-19 outbreak, energy consumption and CO_2 emission. *Environmental Science and Pollution Research*, 28(15), 19008–19020.

Iqbal, S, F Taghizadeh-Hesary, M Mohsin and W Iqbal (2021). Assessing the role of the green finance index in environmental pollution reduction. *Studies of Applied Economics*, 39(3), 12.

Işik, C, E Kasımatı and S Ongan (2017). Analyzing the causalities between economic growth, financial development, international trade, tourism expenditure and/on the CO_2 emissions in Greece. *Energy Sources, Part B: Economics, Planning, and Policy*, 12(7), 665–673.

Jebli, MB and SB Youssef (2017). The role of renewable energy and agriculture in reducing CO_2 emissions: Evidence for North Africa countries. *Ecological Indicators*, 74, 295–301.

Jiang, Y, J Zhang, D Asante and Y Yang (2019). Dynamic evaluation of low-carbon competitiveness (LCC) based on improved Technique for Order Preference by similarity to an Ideal Solution (TOPSIS) method: A case study of Chinese steelworks. *Journal of Cleaner Production*, 217, 484–492.

Jiang, L and L Bai (2017). Revisiting the Granger causality relationship between energy consumption and economic growth in China: A multi-timescale decomposition approach. *Sustainability*, 9(12), 2299.

Karatas, M, E Sulukan and I Karacan (2018). Assessment of Turkey's energy management performance via a hybrid multi-criteria decision-making methodology. *Energy*, 153, 890–912.

Khan, A, F Muhammad, Y Chenggang, J Hussain, S Bano and MA Khan (2020). The impression of technological innovations and natural resources in energy-growth-environment nexus: A new look into BRICS economies. *Science of the Total Environment*, 727, 138265.

Khan, MTI, Q Ali and M Ashfaq (2018). The nexus between greenhouse gas emission, electricity production, renewable energy and agriculture in Pakistan. *Renewable Energy*, 118, 437–451.

Khan, MTI, MR Yaseen and Q Ali (2017). Dynamic relationship between financial development, energy consumption, trade and greenhouse gas: comparison of upper middle income countries from Asia, Europe, Africa and America. *Journal of Cleaner Production*, 161, 567–580.

Khan, SAR, Y Zhang, A Kumar, E Zavadskas and D Streimikiene (2020). Measuring the impact of renewable energy, public health expenditure, logistics, and environmental performance on sustainable economic growth. *Sustainable Development*, 28(4), 833–843.

Ko, H (2020). Measuring fiscal sustainability in the welfare state: Fiscal space as fiscal sustainability. *International Economics and Economic Policy*, 17(2), 531–554.

Li, W, F Chien, CC Hsu, Y Zhang, MA Nawaz, S Iqbal and M Mohsin (2021a). Nexus between energy poverty and energy efficiency: Estimating the long-run dynamics. *Resources Policy*, 72, 102063.

Li, W, F Chien, QT Ngo, TD Nguyen, S Iqbal and AR Bilal (2021b). Vertical financial disparity, energy prices and emission reduction: Empirical insights from China. *Journal of Environmental Management*, 294, 112946.

Li, Z, J Wang and S Che (2021c). Synergistic effect of carbon trading scheme on carbon dioxide and atmospheric pollutants. *Sustainability (Basel, Switzerland)*, 13(10), 5403.

Liu, H, P Yao, S Latif, S Aslam and N Iqbal (2021a). Impact of Green financing, FinTech, and financial inclusion on energy efficiency. *Environmental Science and Pollution Research*, 1–12.

Liu, X, H Kong and S Zhang (2021b). Can urbanization, renewable energy, and economic growth make environment more eco-friendly in Northeast Asia?*Renewable Energy*, 169, 23–33.

Mahmood, GG, H Rashid, S Anwar and A Nasir (2019). Evaluation of climate change impacts on rainfall patterns in Pothohar Region of Pakistan. *Water Conservation and Management*, 3(1), 1–6.

Mahmood, N, Z Wang and B Zhang (2020). The role of nuclear energy in the correction of environmental pollution: Evidence from China. *Nuclear Engineering and Technology*, 52(6), 1327–1333.

McKinnon, A, M Browne, A Whiteing and M Piecyk (Eds.) (2010). Green logistics: Improving the environmental sustainability of logistics. Kogan Page Publishers.

Mehmood, U (2021). Renewable-nonrenewable energy: Institutional quality and environment nexus in South Asian countries. *Environmental Science and Pollution Research*, 28(21), 26529–26536.

Meo, M, S Nathaniel, G Shaikh and A Kumar (2021). Energy consumption, institutional quality and tourist arrival in China: Is the nexus (a)symmetric amidst structural breaks? *Journal of Public Affairs*, 21(2), e2213.

Miao, R, Y Liu, L Wu, D Wang, Y Liu, Y Miao, Z Yang, M Guo, J Ma (2022). Effects of long-term grazing exclusion on plant and soil properties vary with position in dune systems in the Horqin Sandy Land. *CATENA*, 209, Part 2, 2022, 105860, ISSN 0341-8162, https://doi.org/10.1016/j.catena.2021.105860.

Moldan, B, S Janoušková and T Hák (2012). How to understand and measure environmental sustainability: Indicators and targets. *Ecological Indicators*, 17, 4–13.

Morelli, J (2011). Environmental sustainability: A definition for environmental professionals. *Journal of Environmental Sustainability*, 1(1), 2.

Muresan, IC, R Harun, FH Arion, AO Fatah and DE Dumitras (2021). Exploring residents' perceptions of the socio-cultural benefits of tourism development in the mountain area. *Societies*, 11(3), 83.

Murshed, M (2020). An empirical analysis of the non-linear impacts of ICT-trade openness on renewable energy transition, energy efficiency, clean cooking fuel access and environmental sustainability in South Asia. *Environmental Science and Pollution Research*, 27(29), 36254–36281.

Nathaniel, SP (2020). Modelling urbanization, trade flow, economic growth and energy consumption with regards to the environment in Nigeria. *GeoJournal*, 85(6), 1499–1513.

Nawaz, R, M Azam and H Zulfiqar (2020). Economic growth, energy and environmental degradation nexus: A case study in China. *Journal of Economic Impact*, 2(1), 13–23.

Nguyen, TT, TAT Pham and HTX Tram (2020). Role of information and communication technologies and innovation in driving carbon emissions and economic growth in selected G-20 countries. *Journal of Environmental Management*, 261, 110162.

Nugroho, P and S Numata (2020). Resident support of community-based tourism development: Evidence from Gunung Ciremai National Park, Indonesia. *Journal of Sustainable Tourism*, 1–16. DOI: 10.1080/09669582.2020.1755675.

Ohlan, R (2017). The relationship between tourism, financial development and economic growth in India. *Future Business Journal*, 3(1), 9–22.

Ones, DS and S Dilchert (2012). Environmental sustainability at work: A call to action. *Industrial and Organizational Psychology*, 5(4), 444–466.

Ozturk, I (2016). The relationships among tourism development, energy demand, and growth factors in developed and developing countries. *International Journal of Sustainable Development & World Ecology*, 23(2), 122–131.

Pan, D and H Chen (2021). Border pollution reduction in China: The role of livestock environmental regulations. *China Economic Review*, 69, 101681.

Pandey, S, E Dogan and D Taskin (2020). Production-based and consumption-based approaches for the energy-growth-environment nexus: Evidence from Asian countries. *Sustainable Production and Consumption*, 23, 274–281.

Park, JY (1992). Canonical cointegrating regressions. *Econometrica: Journal of the Econometric Society*, 119–143.

Rasheed, HMW and MK Anser (2017). Effect on brand loyalty in mobile phone purchasing (a case study in Bahawalpur, China). *Journal of Public Administration and Governance*, 7(1), 102–115.

Rawat, KS, R Kumar and SK Singh (2020). Distribution of nickel in different agro-climatic zones of Jharkhand, India. *Geology, Ecology, and Landscapes*, 4(1), 52–58.

Ren, FR, Z Tian, J Liu and YT Shen (2020). Analysis of CO_2 emission reduction contribution and efficiency of China's solar photovoltaic industry: Based on input-output perspective. *Energy*, 199, 117493.

Saarinen, J, N Moswete, JR Atlhopheng and WL Hambira (2020). Changing socio-ecologies of Kalahari: Local perceptions towards environmental change and tourism in Kgalagadi, Botswana. *Development Southern Africa*, 37(5), 855–870.

Sajid, MJ (2021). The nexus between environmental impact and agricultural sector linkages: A case study of China. *Atmosphere*, 12(9), 1200.

Schwalm, CR, DN Huntinzger, AM Michalak, JB Fisher, JS Kimball, B Mueller, Y Zhang (2013). Sensitivity of inferred climate model skill to evaluation decisions: A case study using CMIP5 evapotranspiration. *Environmental Research Letters*, 8(2), 24028.

Shakib, M, Y Hou, A Rauf, M Alam, M Murshed and H Mahmood (2021). Revisiting the energy-economy-environment relationships for attaining environmental sustainability: Evidence from belt and road initiative countries. *Environmental Science and Pollution Research*, 1–18.

Shakib, H Yumei, A Rauf *et al.* Revisiting the energy-economy-environment relationships for attaining environmental sustainability: Evidence from Belt and Road Initiative countries. *Environ Sci Pollut Res* 29, 3808–3825 (2022). https://doi.org/10.1007/s11356-021-15860-9.

Sharif, A, S Saha and N Loganathan (2017). Does tourism sustain economic growth? Wavelet-based evidence from the United States. *Tourism Analysis*, 22(4), 467–482.

Sharif, A, O Baris-Tuzemen, G Uzuner, I Ozturk and A Sinha (2020). Revisiting the role of renewable and non-renewable energy consumption on Turkey's ecological footprint: Evidence from quantile ARDL approach. *Sustainable Cities and Society*, 57, 102138.

Shen, H, SA Ali, M Alharthi, AS Shah, A Basit Khan and Q Abbas (2021). Carbon-free energy and sustainable environment: The role of human capital and technological revolutions in attaining SDGs. *Sustainability*, 13(5), 2636.

Sherafatian-Jahromi, R, MS Othman, SH Law and NW Ismail (2017). Tourism and CO_2 emissions nexus in Southeast Asia: new evidence from panel estimation. *Environment, Development and Sustainability*, 19(4), 1407–1423.

Sohail, MT, S Ullah, MT Majeed *et al.* (2021). Pakistan management of green transportation and environmental pollution: a nonlinear ARDL analysis. *Environmental Science and Pollution Research*, 28, 29046–29055 (2021), https://doi.org/10.1007/s11356-021-12654-x.

Solarin, SA (2014). Tourist arrivals and macroeconomic determinants of CO_2 emissions in Malaysia. *Anatolia*, 25(2), 228–241.

Stamatiou, P and N Dritsakis (2017). Dynamic modeling of causal relationship between energy consumption, and economic growth in Italy CO_2 Emissions. In *Advances in Applied Economic Research: Proceedings of the 2016 International Conference on Applied Economics (ICOAE)*. Springer, p. 99.

Sun, D, J Sun, X Zhang, Q Yan, Q Wei and Y Zhou (2016). Carbon markets in China: Development and challenges. *Emerging Markets Finance and Trade*, 52(6), 1361–1371.

Sutton, P (2004). A perspective on environmental sustainability. *Paper on the Victorian Commissioner for Environmental Sustainability*, 1–32.

Taghizadeh-Hesary, F, N Yoshino, Y Inagaki and PJ Morgan (2021). Analyzing the factors influencing the demand and supply of solar modules in Japan–Does financing matter. *International Review of Economics and Finance*, 74, 1–12.

Tanveer, A, H Song, M Faheem *et al.* (2021). Unveiling the asymmetric impact of energy consumption on environmental mitigation in the manufacturing sector of Pakistan. *Environmental Science and Pollution Research*, 28, 64586–64605 (2021). https://doi.org/10.1007/s11356-021-14955-7.

Tehreem, HS, MK Anser, AA Nassani, MMQ Abro and K Zaman (2020). Impact of average temperature, energy demand, sectoral value added, and population growth on water resource quality and mortality rate: It is time to stop waiting around. *Environmental Science and Pollution Research*, 27(30), 37626–37644.

Tiep, NC, M Wang, M Mohsin, HW Kamran and FA Yazdi (2021). An assessment of power sector reforms and utility performance to strengthen consumer self-confidence towards private investment. *Economic Analysis and Policy*, 69, 676–689.

Ullah, I, A Rehman, FU Khan, MH Shah and F Khan (2020). Nexus between trade, CO_2 emissions, renewable energy, and health expenditure in China. *The International Journal of Health Planning and Management*, 35(4), 818–831.

Ward, RB (2012). Achieving fiscal sustainability for state and local governments. In *The Oxford Handbook of State and Local Government Finance*. DOI: 10.1093/oxfordhb/9780199765362.013.0033.

Winner, H (2012). Fiscal competition and the composition of public expenditure: An empirical study. *Contemporary Economics*, 6(3), 38–54.

World Bank. (2018). Poverty and shared prosperity 2018: Piecing together the poverty puzzle.

Xing, J and C Fuest (2018). Central-local government fiscal relations and cyclicality of public spending: Evidence from China. *International Tax and Public Finance*, 25(4), 946–980.

Yoshino, N, T Schloesser and F Taghizadeh-Hesary (2021). Social funding of green financing: An application of distributed ledger technologies. *International Journal of Finance and Economics*, 26(4), 6060–6073.

Yousaf, S, MK Anser, M Tariq, SURS Jawad, S Naushad and Z Yousaf (2020). Does technology orientation predict firm performance through firm innovativeness?*World Journal of Entrepreneurship, Management and Sustainable Development*.

Zafar, MW, M Shahbaz, A Sinha, T Sengupta and Q Qin (2020). How renewable energy consumption contribute to environmental quality? The role of education in OECD countries. *Journal of Cleaner Production*, 268, 122149.

Zaman, K, M Shahbaz, N Loganathan and SA Raza (2016). Tourism development, energy consumption and Environmental Kuznets Curve: Trivariate analysis in the panel of developed and developing countries. *Tourism Management*, 54, 275–283.

Zameer, H, H Yasmeen, MW Zafar, A Waheed and A Sinha (2020). Analyzing the association between innovation, economic growth, and environment: Divulging the importance of FDI and trade openness in India. *Environmental Science and Pollution Research*, 27, 29539–29553.

Zhang, L, F Huang, L Lu *et al.* (2022). Energy financing for energy retrofit in COVID-19: Recommendations for green bond financing. *Environmental Science and Pollution Research*, 29, 23105–23116, https://doi.org/10.1007/s11356-021-17440-3.

Zhou, L, E Chan and H Song (2017). Social capital and entrepreneurial mobility in early-stage tourism development: A case from rural China. *Tourism Management*, 63, 338–350.

Zhu, D, SM Mortazavi, A Maleki, A Aslani and H Yousefi (2020). Analysis of the robustness of energy supply in Japan: Role of renewable energy. *Energy Reports*, 6, 378–391.

Zoundi, Z (2017). CO_2 emissions, renewable energy and the Environmental Kuznets Curve, a panel cointegration approach. *Renewable and Sustainable Energy Reviews*, 72, 1067–1075.

https://doi.org/10.1142/9789819812783_0006

CLIMATE FINANCE IN THE WAKE OF COVID-19: CONNECTEDNESS OF CLEAN ENERGY WITH CONVENTIONAL ENERGY AND REGIONAL STOCK MARKETS[‖‖]

SITARA KARIM[*,†,**], SHABEER KHAN[‡,††], NAWAZISH MIRZA[§,‡‡], SUHA M. ALAWI[¶,§§] and FARHAD TAGHIZADEH-HESARY[‖,¶¶]

[*]*School of Business, Faculty of Business, Design and Arts Swinburne University of Technology Sarawak Campus, Malaysia*

[†]*Department of Business Administration Faculty of Management Sciences ILMA University, Karachi, Pakistan*

[‡]*College of Business Al Yamamah University, Riyadh, Saudi Arabia*

[§]*Excelia Business School, La Rochelle, France*

[¶]*Department of Finance King Abdulaziz University, Saudi Arabia*

[‖]*Tokai University Research Institute for Environment and Sustainability Tokai University, Tokyo, Japan*

[**]*sitarakarim.malik@gmail.com*
[††]*sh_khan@yu.edu.sa*
[‡‡]*elahimn@excelia-group.com*
[§§]*salawi@kau.edu.sa*
[¶¶]*farhad@tsc.u-tokai.ac.jp*

Focusing on raising climate concerns and sustaining a clean ecosystem, the current study strives to examine the connectedness of clean energy markets with conventional energy markets and four regional stock markets of Asia, Pacific, Europe, and America for the period spanning January 1, 2004 to August 31, 2021. We employed the volatility connectedness methodology using dynamic conditional correlation (DCC-GARCH) estimates for analysis purposes. There is pronounced within class connectedness of all markets except conventional energy markets, which showed strong disconnection from the network. However, strong inter-class spillovers are reported between clean energy and regional stock markets. Time-varying analysis revealed that intense spillovers are shaped during the Global Financial Crisis, Shale Oil Crisis, and COVID-19 pandemic. Meanwhile, time-varying net connectedness estimates illuminate that world renewable energy and American stock markets are net transmitters, whereas leftover markets are net recipients of spillovers. Further analysis of sub-sample periods during GFC, SOR, and COVID-19 validate that intense spillovers are formed when markets experience unexpected financial, economic, and global health turmoil. We proposed significant implications for regional stock markets of Asia, Pacific, Europe and America to concentrate on the

[**]Corresponding author.

[‖‖]This chapter was originally published in Climate Change Economics, Vol. 13, No. 3, February 2022, published by World Scientific Publishing, Singapore. Reprinted with permission.

climate-friendly energy markets than conventional energy markets as they service the clean ecosystem motives more specifically.

Keywords: Clean energy markets; conventional energy markets; DCC-GARCH; regional markets; volatility analysis.

1. Introduction

Climate concerns accentuate the need to carefully assess the benefits of clean energy markets and conventional energy markets. Literature highlights that global climate changes are abrupt, uncertain, and sharply increasing with the continuous use of non-renewable energy sources such as the burning of fossil fuels and increasing the carbon footprints on the global ecosystem (Saeed *et al.*, 2021; Naeem *et al.*, 2021; Arif *et al.*, 2021; Karim, 2021a, 2021b; Elsayed *et al.*, 2020). Given these pronounced climate concerns, the International Energy Agency (2021) brings to the attention of policy-makers, regulatory bodies, governments, investors, and macro-prudential authorities of global markets to encourage the use of clean energy sources to overcome the environmental pressures. Therefore, clean energy markets carry significant features that support clean energy sources and reduce the use of conventional energy markets.

Since conventional energy markets (for example, crude oil) maintain their central position in the global economic system, this fact is undeniable that they originate from dirty sources of energy, which are the root causes of global warming, greenhouse gas emissions (GHGs), climate change, and inclined perils to the global environmental ecosystem. Conventional energy markets are mostly integrated into the financial system due to their deep-rooted history (Umar *et al.*, 2021; Elsayed *et al.*, 2020; Kang *et al.*, 2017). Thus, it is quite difficult to completely abolish conventional energy markets' usage and trading on foreign exchanges. The use of conventional energy sources is embarking on the need to adopt new government policies to smoothly shift from dirty energy sources to clean energy sources (Taghizadeh-Hesary *et al.*, 2021a,b). In this way, clean energy stocks are emerging as appealing investment streams for climate-friendly and socially responsible investors and market participants, leading the "future climate boom" through these investments.

Prior literature emphasized that distressed economic and financial events have adversely influenced the motives of clean energy versus conventional energy markets and investors to have to oscillate between these investment options. In addition, positioning the clean energy markets in optimal portfolios can also raise serious climate concerns, making it more difficult to choose between clean energy markets and conventional energy markets (Saeed *et al.*, 2021).

Given this background, it is high time to evaluate the current policies which move antagonistically to climate sustainability and are detrimental to the global ecosystem. Regional stock markets bear specific features (Naeem *et al.*, 2020) due to their geographical orientation and gross domestic products (GDPs), which also grab the attention of portfolio managers for risk mitigation and uncertainty avoidance

(Shahzad *et al.*, 2021; Saeed *et al.*, 2021; Abid *et al.*, 2020; Badaye and Narsoo, 2020). Thus, the contribution of the current research lies in the fact that it examines the connectedness of clean energy, conventional energy and regional stock markets returns by employing unique methodologies to stipulate significant ramifications for the policymakers, governments, investors, and strategists of global world.

Methodologically, the existing literature substantially lacks the volatility connectedness of clean energy markets with conventional energy markets and regional stock returns by employing the dynamic conditional correlation (DCC) GARCH analysis which stipulates useful information for the investors to choose among the investment streams. In the first step, a multivariate generalized autoregressive heteroskedasticity (GARCH) is applied to the dataset to obtain time-varying volatilities and then processed to get DCC estimates. Prior studies have employed the traditional Diebold and Yilmaz (2012) connectedness approach, but it suffers the disadvantage of window size and rolling window analysis in which loss of observations occurs. In addition, the volatility impulse response functions (VIRFs) are significant determinants of volatility connectedness without involving the rolling windows and loss of observations (Gabauer, 2020; Karim and Naeem, 2021).

In the light of the above discussion, the current study provides a novel contribution to the existing literature in the following ways. First, we examined the volatility connectedness of clean energy markets (Wilder Hill Clean Energy (WHCL), S&P Global Clean Energy (SPGC), and World Renewable Energy (RENX), with conventional energy markets (Crude Oil WTI (WTI), Heating Oil (HTO), and Natural Gas (NGS), and regional stock markets (MSCI Asia (ASIA), MSCI Europe (EURP), MSCI Pacific (PACF), and MSCI America (AMER)) for the period spanning January 1, 2004 to August 31, 2021. To the authors' best belief, this is the first study to include a blend of clean energy and conventional energy markets and regional stocks. Secondly, we employed the unique methodology of DCC-GARCH volatility connectedness to overcome window size problems and loss of observations during rolling window analysis. Third, the employed methodology provides evidence of time-varying attributes where significant economic events incurred during the sample period exhibit high volatility spillovers. Fourth, we also analyzed sub-samples of global financial crisis (2007–2009), shale oil revolution (2014–2015), and COVID-19 pandemic (2019–2020). Finally, we proposed significant implications for policymakers, regulation authorities, and investors to devise effective portfolio and risk management strategies.

Our findings regarding network connectedness for whole sample period manifest that renewable energy index (RENX) is the net transmitters of spillovers followed by American (AMER) stock market whereas moderate spillovers are transmitted from the markets of global clean energy (SPGC), Asia (ASIA), Europe (EURP) and Pacific (PACF). In return, Crude Oil (WTI), heating oil (HTO), natural gas (NGS), and WHCL are net recipients of spillovers. Strong disconnection of conventional energy markets emphasizes their less exposure to uncertainties and risks. Time-varying dynamics illustrate a sharp incline in spillovers during the aftermaths of Argentina's economic collapse (2001–2003), Global Financial Crisis (2007–2009), Europpean Debt Crisis (2010–2012), Shale oil crisis (2014–2015), Chinese market crash (2015–2016), Brexit referendum (2016–2017), US interest rate hike (2017–2018), and COVID-19 pandemic (2019–2020). Further, time-varying net connectedness reiterates that renewable energy and the American stock market are net transmitters of spillovers, whereas conventional energy markets are net recipients of spillovers. Overall, natural gas remained slightly connected with other markets, reflecting its strong integration among other financial markets and less susceptibility to shocks, which ultimately offers diversification to the remaining markets.

Our findings draw significant implications specifically for four regional stock markets and their respective policymakers, governments, regulators of regional markets, investors, and portfolio managers. Policymakers can relish the benefits of the study by encouraging governments to introduce financing in clean energy and renewable investments for climate-friendly initiatives. Moreover, policymakers and governments can lead clean and climate-oriented investments to reduce carbon emissions. By reassessing the current policies and devising updated strategies, regulatory bodies can also play their key role in introducing the clean and renewable energy markets for investment purposes as these avenues will facilitate developing a cleaner climate.

The rest of the study is arranged as follows: Section 2 presents the literature review; Sec. 3 explains the methodology of DCC-GARCH; Sec. 4 elaborates the empirical results; and finally, Sec. 5 concludes the study along with policy implications.

2. Literature Review

Literature examining the connectedness of clean energy markets with other financial markets is abundant. Similarly, literature also traces those studies that empirically examined the relationship between commodities and their interconnectedness with various asset classes to identify their potential features for these financial markets. In terms of clean energy markets, Saeed *et al.* (2021) examined the extreme quantile connectedness between clean/green assets and dirty energy stocks and found that the return connectedness of clean energy stocks, green bonds and energy ETFs are larger at both right and left tails. Moreover, there is time-varying dependence among the variables where less volatility is observed at the tails. Raghutla *et al.* (2021) elaborated on the benefits of financing in clean energy stocks. They reported an inverse relationship between clean energy consumption and CO_2 emissions and positive influence of economic growth, substantiating the advantages for policymakers to invest in the clean energy stocks to overcome the environmental hazards. Liu *et al.* (2020) examined the dynamic connectedness between green bonds and clean energy markets and positive time-varying tail dependence. In addition, extreme upward and downward movement of clean energy markets drawn spillover effect on green bonds.

Alkathery and Chaudhuri (2021) investigated the comovement between oil price, CO_2 emissions, renewable energy and energy equities among GCC stock markets. The authors reported the existence of volatility spillovers and comovement among global clean energy production, crude oil price, CO_2 emission price and GCC energy stocks. Interestingly, the authors narrated that conditional variances of all returns are influenced by the internal shocks coming from the markets themselves. Moreover, volatilities are persistent among the markets for long time horizons.

Uddin *et al.* (2019) studied the cross-quantile dependence of renewable energy stocks and reported two significant results: (1) the relationship between renewable energy stocks is not symmetric rather, it is asymmetric across quantiles and for longer lags, and (2) the positive impact of exchange rates on renewable energy stocks is only pronounced when markets are under extreme situations. Hammoudeh *et al.* (2020) investigated the nexus among green bonds, clean energy index, US conventional bonds, and CO2 emissions using the time-varying Granger causality test and narrated significant causality switching from US treasury bonds to green bonds. Naeem and Karim (2021) examined the tail-dependence between bitcoin and green financial assets and found a significant hedge facility of green markets for bitcoin, particularly clean energy index. Ji *et al.* (2020) examined the information spillovers and connectedness networks in the oil and gas markets using the ensemble empirical mode decomposition technique. The author found that the information transmits between oil and gas returns as their behavior varies across different time scales. Moreover, the total spillover connectedness is dynamic and carries volatile characteristics.

Using the network spillover methodology, Yoon *et al.* (2019) examined the network connectedness and spillovers between financial and commodity markets. The authors concluded that the US stock market is the top risk transmitter of spillovers, whereas precious metals and stock exchanges are net recipients of spillovers. In addition, adding different classes of commodities and stocks lessens the magnitude of total spillovers, which offer significant diversification benefits in a portfolio of stocks. Hernandez *et al.* (2019) investigated the hedge and diversification avenues of agriculture and precious metal commodities using the extreme quantile approach. The study found a positive impact of extreme lower quantiles of oil returns on the respective quantiles of gold, silver and rice returns. The authors also reported that these commodities do not offer hedge opportunities for oil market; hence, their diversification potential is substantiated to shield the investments from uncertainty and extreme risks. Ferrer *et al.* (2021) applied the methodology of time-frequency connectedness to examine the return and volatility connectedness between green and other asset classes. Findings uncover that connectedness is higher when market conditions are uneven and during shorter time periods.

Shaikh (2021) examined the impact of COVID-19 on the energy markets where data of multiple energy markets are employed such as energy stock indices, energy futures and exchange-traded funds, and implied volatility indices. The author found that energy ETFs and stock correlations are more pronounced and resilient with S&P

Table 1. Summarized literature review.

No.	Author(s)	Method(s)	Sample period	Findings
1.	Naeem *et al.* (2021a)	Cross-Quantilogram	2008–2019	There is an asymmetric relationship between green bonds and commodities and hedging and diversification benefits are highlighted.
2.	Saeed *et al.* (2021)	Quantile VAR	2012–2019	The return connectedness of clean energy, green bonds, crude oil, and energy stocks is mainly pronounced in the left and right tails.
3.	Pham (2021)	Cross-quantilogram framework		There is little connectedness between green bonds and green equity during normal circumstances whereas both markets are more connected during the extreme market movements.
4.	Shahzad *et al.* (2021)	Quantile generalized forecast error variance decomposition	2001–2020	The system-wide connectedness of different classes of assets shows varying behavior across multiple financial markets.
5.	Liu *et al.* (2021)	Conditional value-at-risk (CoVaR) and delta CoVaR	2011–2020	Green bonds and clean energy markets have positive time-varying average and tail dependence.
6.	Arif *et al.* (2021b)	Time-frequency analysis	2008–2020	There is low connectedness between green bonds and conventional financial markets. Connectedness is more pronounced during short-run as compared to long-run.
7.	Naeem *et al.* (2021b)	Time-frequency analysis; hedge ratios and hedge effectiveness	2013–2020	Green bonds reveal a significant weight in the overall network and are strongly connected with the USD and bond index. Green bonds can act as hedgers for some assets and can provide safe-haven features during tumbled periods.
8.	Wang *et al.* (2020)	Yield differential	2016–2019	Pricing premium of green bonds is most significant for investors with CSR orientation. Green bonds increase firm value in the long-run.
9.	Le *et al.* (2021)	Time-frequency analysis	2018–2020	There is very high connectedness among green bonds, fintech and cryptocurrencies. And volatility transmission is higher in the short-run than in the long-run.
10.	Naeem *et al.* (2021c)	Time-frequency analysis; spillover network	2008–2020	Green bonds and crude oil are strongly connected. Green bonds act as succor for risk transmission during crisis times.

500 energy stocks. The investor sentiments were highlighted and substantiated particularly during the pandemic and in the tails. Moreover, pessimistic investors switched towards put options and paid excess premiums from unparalleled risk in the energy stocks. Elsayed *et al.* (2020) examined the time-varying comovements between energy markets and global financial markets employing the technique of Diebold and Yilmaz (2012) where they found oil shocks are exogenous in nature. Meanwhile, the World energy index and World stock index are net transmitters of spillovers whereas clean energy is the net recipient of spillovers. Concurrently, the spillovers are time-dependent which highlights their intensity during the financial crisis period. Chuliá *et al.* (2019) examined the connectedness of energy markets using the DY[12] model for the period spanning 2008–2016 and found that volatility spillovers affected the energy markets significantly and the most integrated economy among European markets is Germany.

The above literature shows that studies strived to explain the relationship between clean energy and conventional energy markets but studies have not examined the connectedness of clean versus conventional energy markets along with four regional markets stock returns. Meanwhile, in terms of methodology, the current study supersedes prior studies by employing the volatility connectedness of the markets. Thus, the current study contributes to the existing literature gap by explicitly examining the connectedness of clean energy markets with conventional energy stocks and regional markets returns. Importantly, the studies employing the volatility connectedness using dynamic conditional correlation (DCC-GARCH) analysis for similar set of markets are also inexistent. Therefore, this study is novel in exploring the volatility connectedness of clean energy markets with conventional energy and regional stock markets such as Asia, Pacific, Europe, and America.

In addition, to clearly express the novelty of the study, Table 1 presents the summaries of earlier studies to identify the research gap.

3. Methodology

The current study examines the connectedness of clean energy markets with conventional energy markets and regional stocks of Asia, Pacific, Europe, and America. For analysis purpose, we applied the volatility connectedness approach (Dimpfl and Elshiaty, 2021), DCC-GARCH to measure the dynamic conditional correlational (DCC) among clean energy, conventional energy and regional stock markets.

3.1. *DCC-GARCH*

For examining the conditional volatility, we employed the two-step DCC-GARCH model following Engle (2002). The initial model can be written as

$$y_t = \mu_t + \epsilon_t, \quad \epsilon_t | F_{t-1} \sim N(0, H_t), \tag{1}$$

$$\epsilon = H_t^{1/2} u_t, \quad u_t \sim N(0, I), \tag{2}$$
$$H_t = D_t R_t D_t. \tag{3}$$

Here F_{t-1} exhibits the availability of the information up to $t-1$, whereas dimensional vectors y_t, μ_t, ϵ_t and u_t represent the estimated time series, conditional mean, error term, and standardized error term, respectively. Meanwhile, R_t, H_t, and $D_t = \text{diag}(h_{11t}^{\frac{1}{2}}, \ldots, h_{NNt}^{\frac{1}{2}})$ are $N \times N$ dimensional matrices which illustrate dynamic conditional correlations, time-varying conditional variance–covariance matrices, and the time-varying conditional variances in an orderly manner.

As a first step, D_t estimates GARCH model for each independent series following Bollerslev *et al.* (1988). In this way, one shock and one persistency parameter, based on Hansen and Lunde (2005), are assumed as follows:

$$h_{ii,t} = \omega + \alpha \epsilon_{i,t-1}^2 + \beta h_{ii,t-1}. \tag{4}$$

The second step involves computing the dynamic conditional correlations as follows:

$$R_t = \text{diag}(q_{iit}^{-\frac{1}{2}}, \ldots, q_{NNt}^{-\frac{1}{2}}) Q_t \, \text{diag}(q_{iit}^{-\frac{1}{2}}, \ldots, q_{NNt}^{-\frac{1}{2}}), \tag{5}$$
$$Q_t = (1 - a - b)\bar{Q} + a u_{t-1} u_{t-1}' + b Q_{t-1}. \tag{6}$$

Here conditional and unconditional standardized residual variance–covariance matrices are represented by Q_t and $\bar{Q}$ through $N \times N$ positive-definite dimensional matrices, respectively. In addition, $a(\alpha)$ and $b(\beta)$ represent non-negative shock and persistency parameters which fulfills the condition of $a + b < 1(\alpha + \beta \leq 1)$. Q_t and R_t exhibit time-varying characteristics as long as $a + b < 1$ is fulfilled otherwise, the model will be converted into CCC GARCH, where R_t is constant over time.

3.2. *Volatility impulse response function (VIRF)*

It is interesting to note that traditional connectedness approaches (Diebold and Yilmaz, 2012, 2014) and Hoffmann and Börner (2020) rely on the generalized impulse response function (GIRF) being independent of the orders of variables and measure the J-step-ahead of a shock for variable i on the variable j : $\text{GIRF}(J, \delta_{j,t} F_{t-1} = E(y_{t+j} | \epsilon_{j,t} = \delta_{j,t}, F_{t-1}) - E(y_{t+j} | \epsilon_{j,t} = 0, F_{t-1})$. In a similar way, the VIRF is the impact of a shock for a variable i on variable j's conditional volatilities, stated as

$$\Psi^g = \text{VIRF}(J, \delta_{j,t} F_{t-1} = E(H_{t+j} | \epsilon_{j,t} = \delta_{j,t}, F_{t-1}) - E(H_{t+j} | \epsilon_{j,t} = 0, F_{t-1}), \tag{7}$$

where $\delta_{j,t}$ is equal to one with a selection vector at jth position and zero otherwise.

For conditional variance–covariances by employing DCC-GARCH model of Engle and Sheppard (2001), the VIRF is accomplished in three steps. The first step involves the univariate GARCH (1,1) which forecasts the conditional volatilities $(D_{t+h} | F_t)$

in terms of

$$E(h_{ii,t+h}|F_t) = \omega + \alpha\delta_{1t}^2 + \beta h_{ii,t}h = 1, \tag{8}$$

$$E(h_{ii,t}|F_t) = \sum_{i=0}^{h-1} \omega(\alpha+\beta)^i + (\alpha+\beta)^{h-1}E(h_{ii,t+h-1}|F_t)h > 1. \tag{9}$$

In the second step, $E(Q_{t+h}|F_t)$ is predicted as

$$E(Q_{t+1}|F_t) = (1-a-b)\bar{Q} + au_t u_t' + bQ_t h = 1, \tag{10}$$

$$E(Q_{t+h}|F_t) = (1-a-b)\bar{Q} + aE(u_{t+h-1}u_{t+h-1}'|F_t) + bE(Q_{t+h-1}|F_t)h > 1, \tag{11}$$

where $E(u_{t+h-1}u_{t+h-1}'|F_t) \approx E(Q_{t+h-1}|F_t)$ which facilitates forecasting the dynamic conditional correlations.

In the final step, the conditional variance–covariances are measured as

$$\begin{aligned} E(R_{t+h}|F_t \approx \operatorname{diag}[E(q_{iit+h}^{-\frac{1}{2}}|F_t), \ldots, E(q_{NNt+h}^{-\frac{1}{2}}|F_t)] \\ \times E(Q_{t+h})\operatorname{diag}[E(q_{iit+h}^{-\frac{1}{2}}|F_t), \ldots, E(q_{NNt+h}^{-\frac{1}{2}}|F_t)], \end{aligned} \tag{12}$$

$$E(H_{t+h}|F_t) \approx E(D_{t+h}|F_t)E(R_{t+h}|F_t)E(D_{t+h}|F_t). \tag{13}$$

3.3. *Dynamic connectedness*

The generalized forecast error variance decomposition (GFEVD) is estimated based on VIRF which can be explained as the variance one variable casts on others (Diebold and Yilmaz, 2012). These are normalized variance shares which equal one after summing up. In other words, all variables collectively explain 100% of variable i's forecast error variance which is computed as follows:

$$\tilde{\O}_{ij,t}^{g}(J) = \frac{\sum_{t=1}^{j-1} \Psi_{ij,t}^{2,g}}{\sum_{j=1}^{N}\sum_{t=1}^{j-1} \Psi_{ij,t}^{2,g}}. \tag{14}$$

Here $\sum_{j=1}^{N} \tilde{\O}_{ij,t}^{g}(J) = 1$ and $\sum_{j=1}^{N} \tilde{\O}_{ij,t}^{g}(J) = N$. The aggregate effect is presented in the numerator of the ith shock whereas denominator is the cumulative sum of all the shocks. The total connectedness index (TCI) using the GFEVD is created as

$$C_t^g(J) = \sum_{i,j=1, i\neq j}^{N} \tilde{\O}_{ij,t}^{g}(J). \tag{15}$$

Similarly, the spillovers which variable i transmit to the variable j are known as total directional connectedness "TO" others and are known as

$$C_{i\to j,t}^{g}(J) = \frac{\sum_{i,j=1, i\neq j}^{N} \tilde{\O}_{ij,t}^{g}(J)}{\sum_{j=1}^{N} \tilde{\O}_{ij,t}^{g}(J)}. \tag{16}$$

On the other hand, the spillovers variable *i* receives from *j* variable are termed as total directional connectedness "FROM" other and are calculated as

$$C^{g}_{i\leftarrow j,t}(J) = \frac{\sum_{j=1,\,i\neq j}^{N} \tilde{\emptyset}^{g}_{ij,t}(J)}{\sum_{i=1}^{N} \tilde{\emptyset}^{g}_{ij,t}(J)}. \tag{17}$$

Subtracting the two equations from each other leads to the NET total directional connectedness which explains the influence of variables *i* on the network

$$C^{g}_{i,t} = C^{g}_{i\rightarrow j,t}(J) - C^{g}_{i\leftarrow j,t}(J). \tag{18}$$

Assuming that the variable *i* has positive (negative) NET total directional connectedness, then variable *i* is the net transmitter (receiver) of shocks explaining that variable *i* drives (driven by) the network connectedness.

4. Empirical Results

This section presents data and descriptive statistics along with empirical results of the main sample and sub-samples.

4.1. *Data and descriptive statistics*

This study investigates the connectedness of clean energy markets with conventional energy and regional stock markets. The clean energy markets included in the study are WHCL, SPGC, and RENX. Conventional energy markets are Crude Oil WTI (WTI), Heating Oil (HTO), and Natural Gas (NGS). Moreover, the data of four regional stock markets named as, MSCI Asia (ASIA), MSCI Europe (EURP), MSCI Pacific (PACF), and MSCI America (AMER) have been incorporated in the study. Mainly, data have been sourced from Datastream encompassing the period of January 1, 2004 to August 31, 2021.

Table 2 illustrates the summary statistics of clean energy, conventional energy and regional stock markets where among clean energy markets, the highest average return is exhibited by RENX followed by SPGC and WHCL. The conventional energy markets revealed comparable average results of WTI and HTO whereas NGS yields negative average return. Among regional markets, AMER exhibited the highest mean returns whereas ASIA and PACF yield parallel average returns. However, EURP showed the lowest average return out of all regional stock markets. Concurrently, highest variability in the returns of clean energy markets is revealed by RENX, succeeded by WHCL and SPGC. From conventional energy markets, NGS exhibited the highest whereas WTI and HTO manifested modest variability in returns. Among regional stock markets, almost all of the markets displayed comparable and modest variability in return series. Negative values of skewness for all clean energy, conventional energy, and regional stocks except NGS stress that these markets have experienced significant losses in their returns during the sample period. In addition,

Table 2. Descriptive statistics.

Group	Markets	Symbol	Mean	Max	Min	Std. Dev.	Skewness	Kurtosis	J-B
Clean Energy	Wilder Hill Clean Energy	WHCL	0.0043	14.5195	−16.2390	2.0863	−0.4535	9.1829	7496.058[a]
	S&P Global Clean Energy	SPGC	0.0075	18.0929	−14.9728	1.8082	−0.6102	16.4270	34893.17[a]
	World Renewable Energy	RENX	0.0294	42.2165	−41.6273	2.3154	−0.4433	82.8592	1224363[a]
Energy	Crude Oil WTI	WTI	0.0261	22.3940	−28.2206	2.5693	−0.1444	20.3324	57682.25[a]
	Heating Oil	HTO	0.0244	18.1962	−19.7284	2.1212	−0.0862	9.2753	7564.873[a]
	Natural Gas	NGS	−0.0083	26.7712	−18.0545	3.1564	0.6664	8.6719	6516.332[a]
Stocks	MSCI Asia	ASIA	0.0188	9.6881	−8.8394	1.1036	−0.3461	9.5002	8202.681[a]
	MSCI Europe	EURP	0.0129	10.7783	−14.0226	1.3281	−0.4687	14.0118	23445.35[a]
	MSCI Pacific	PACF	0.0181	9.2200	−9.2470	1.1168	−0.4271	9.7749	8950.834[a]
	MSCI America	AMER	0.0310	10.6258	−12.8460	1.1820	−0.6998	18.5647	46880.11[a]

Note: "a" indicates significance at 1%.

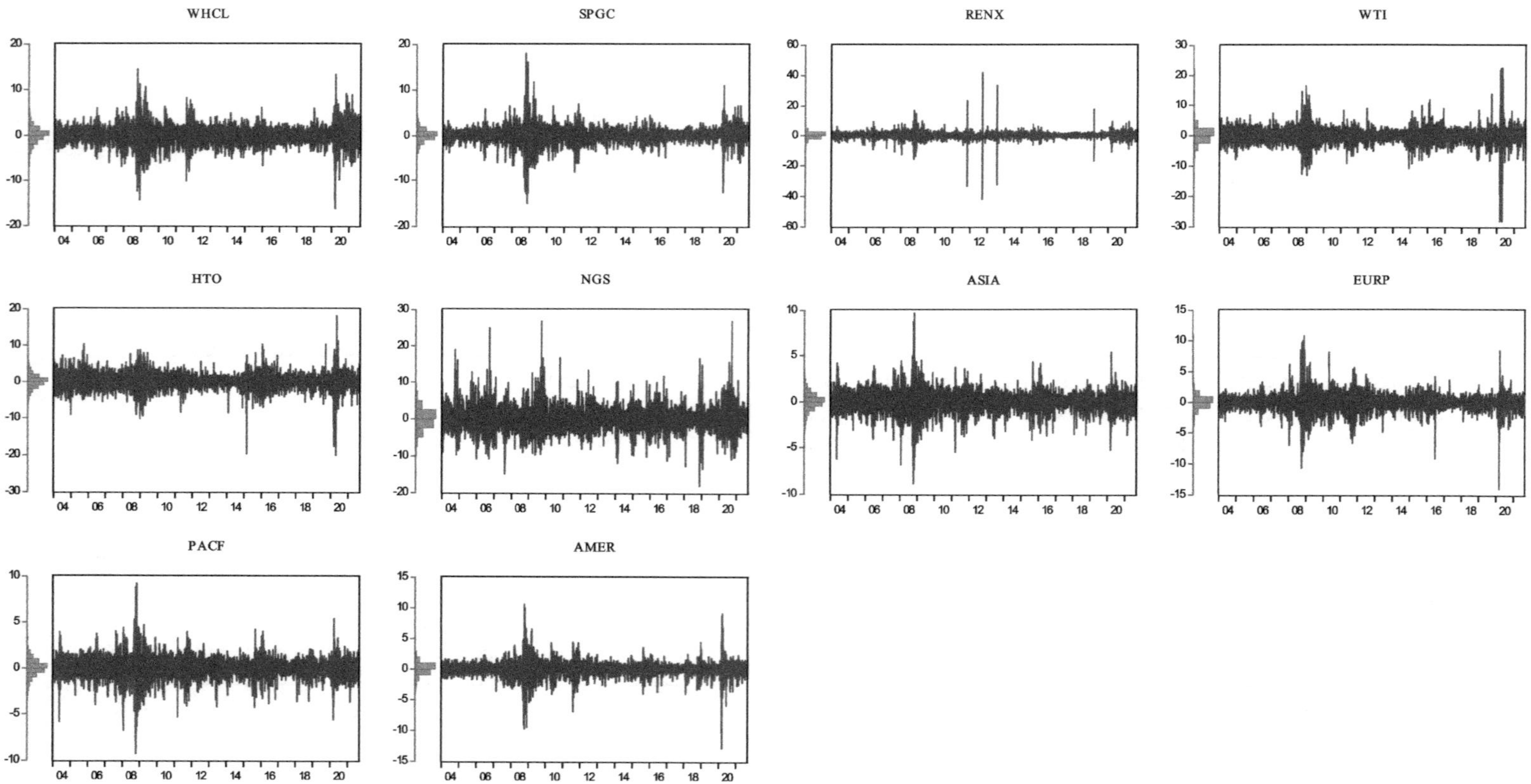

Note: This figure shows the time evolution of return series along with histogram on *y*-axis.

Figure 1. Time evolution of return series.

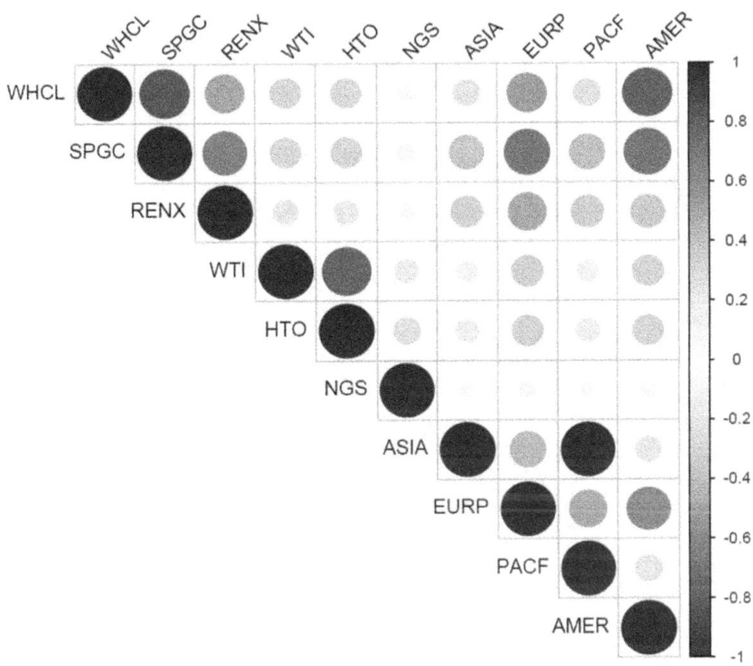

Figure 2. Correlation matrix.

Jarque–Bera normality test is indicative of abnormal values for all markets displaying that markets are not normally distributed.

Figure 1 displays the time evolution of return series for clean energy, conventional energy and regional stock markets where it is evident that markets undergo serious shocks particularly during global financial crisis, shale oil revolution and COVID-19 pandemic (Naeem *et al.*, 2021c; Karim *et al.*, 2021). WHCL, SPGC, NGS, ASIA, EURP, PACF, and AMER indicated susceptibility to larger shocks during GFC (2008-2010). RENX, HTO, NGS, EURP, and PACF revealed higher exposure to Shale oil crisis (2014–2015). Meanwhile, almost all markets showed comparable sensitivity to the global pandemic of COVID-19 with higher variation in the spillovers and return series.

Figure 2 demonstrates the correlation matrix of clean energy, conventional energy, and regional stock markets. The correlation heat-map illustrates the highest correlation between ASIA-PACF whereas high correlations are observed between the pairs of WHCL-SPGC, WHCL-AMER, SPGC-EURP, SPGC-AMER, and WTI-HTO. Further, moderate correlations are manifested by WHCL-RENX, WHCL-EURP, SPGC-RENX, and EURP-AMER. Overall, it is highlighted that clean energy markets are highly correlated with each other and moderately correlated with regional stock markets but there is a slight correlation with conventional energy markets. Conversely, conventional energy markets highlighted minimal correlations except WTI-HTO. Meanwhile, regional stock markets revealed the highest correlations between ASIA and PACF whereas moderate to slight correlations are observed among the rest of the markets.

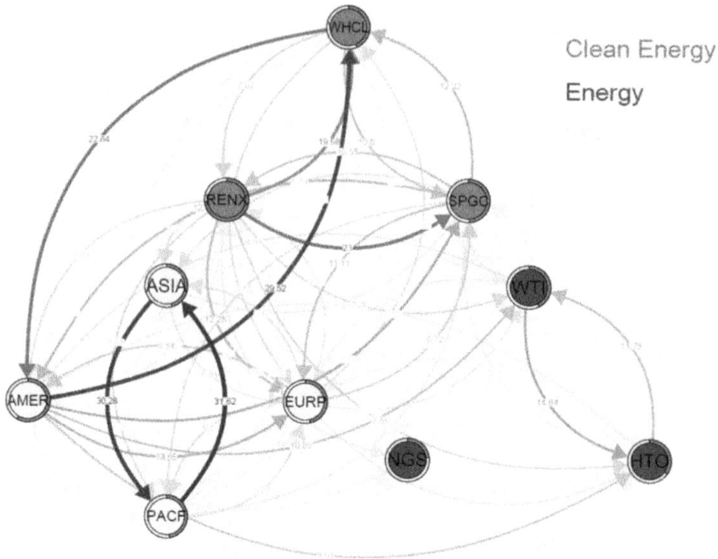

Notes: This figure shows the network connectedness among clean energy, energy, and regional stock markets using the DCC-GARCH connectedness framework. The red color in node represents the spillover from one market to all others in the system.

Figure 3. Network connectedness using DCC_GARCH model.

4.2. *Network connectedness using DCC-GARCH model*

Figure 3 displays network connectedness of clean energy, conventional energy, and regional stock markets. Evidently, it is presented in the figure that all three types of markets are clustered into three groups with strong intra-connectedness (Caporin *et al.*, 2021; Karim *et al.*, 2022a, 2022b) and pronounced inter-connectedness between clean energy and regional stock returns. However, conventional energy markets are disconnected from the network. Nodes on all types of markets denote net contribution (reception) of spillovers "TO" ("FROM") the network. While markets show strong intra-connectedness, spillovers between clean energy markets and regional stocks are also significantly transmitting (receiving) spillovers in a system-wide connectedness structure. Nodes of clean energy markets reveal that RENX is a net transmitter of spillovers followed by SPGC and WHCL. In line with Elsayed *et al.* (2020), a strong within-class interconnectedness of clean energy markets is due to their similar features whereas clean energy markets are less connected with other financial markets.

Among regional stock markets, AMER is the net transmitter of spillovers in line with Mensi *et al.* (2021) and Wang *et al.* (2020) who also reported that US stocks are net transmitters of spillovers among various asset classes. Conversely, ASIA, EURP, and PACF are shaping moderate spillovers. Interestingly, ASIA and PACF are strongly connected within the same class network which intuitively points toward their developing economies stressing that regions with comparable economic backgrounds, geographical tendencies, and growth opportunities tend to form strong spillovers within the same category of stocks. On the other hand, conventional energy markets, as illustrated from their nodes, are net recipients of spillovers from the overall system of markets where weak spillovers are formed between WTI and HTO and a stronger disconnection of these markets manifests their indifference to the external shocks. Since WTI, HTO, and NGS represent commodities markets, prior evidence validates that commodities, due to their inherent integration in the financial system (Kang *et al.*, 2017) tend to remain disconnected from the network indicating that they are less susceptible to external economic and financial shocks.

Correspondingly, inter-connectedness of clean energy markets and regional stock returns illustrate that AMER is transmitting strong spillovers to WHCL whereas receiving moderate spillovers from WHCL. Overall, it is highlighted that AMER and RENX are net transmitters of spillovers whereas SPGC, ASIA, PACF, EURP, and WHCL are transmitting moderate spillovers to other markets. Conventional energy markets mainly remained disconnected from the network which denotes their high risk-absorbance capacity when market circumstances are unfavourable. In this way, conventional energy markets can act as diversifiers for other financial markets due to their strong integration into the international financial system.

4.3. *Time-varying total connectedness*

Figure 4 displays total volatility connectedness using DCC-GARCH exhibiting time-varying properties of the network structure. The significant ups and downs in the graph

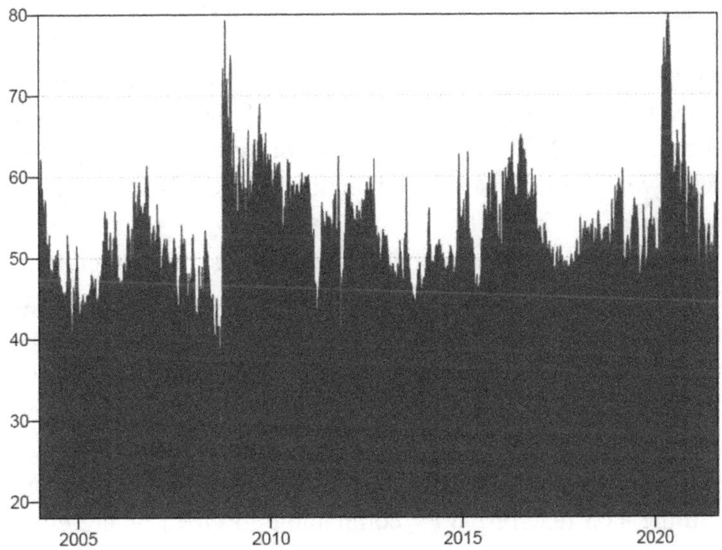

Note: This figure shows the total time-varying connectedness among clean energy, energy, and regional stock markets using the DCC-GARCH connectedness framework.

Figure 4. Time-varying total connectedness using DCC-GARCH model.

denote distressed economic events and recovery periods for each successive and intense volatility spillover. The first spike in the graph reflects aftermath of Argentina's economic default (2001–2003) where total connectedness index (TCI) reaches the level of 62% indicating that markets have undergone extreme economic distress period with intensified spillovers stressing investors' perplexity given the uncertainty of the business environment. Subsequently, the TCI declined gradually which indicates that markets started normalizing after the uncertainty of the markets is reduced. The successive jump in the graph reflects Global Financial Crisis (GFC) time (2007–2009) where global economy declined due to burst of US housing bubble[1] where gross domestic product (GDP) fall by 4.3% in December 2007 and unemployment inclined from 5% to 9.5% which again increased by 10% in October, 2009. Given this turmoil condition, financial markets also collapsed which resulted in intense spillovers where TCI touched the level of 80% in the graph. Literature (Nguyen *et al.*, 2020; Naeem *et al.*, 2021a,b; Kang *et al.*, 2021) highlight that financial contagion derived the connectedness of financial markets with strong spillovers when markets were highly prone to external shocks.

The next spike in the graph is indicative of European Debt Crisis (2010–2012), where balance sheet inaccuracies in the European Economy resulted in the high connectedness of global financial markets. The outbound resources were restricted from the central bank, ultimately intensifying the spillovers (Blundell-Wignall, 2012). In this financial turmoil period, the global financial markets show higher connectedness revealing varying attitudes of investors towards abrupt changes in the business cycles (Rufino, 2018). The consecutive jump in the graph (2014–2016) shows the occurrence of two major financial events, namely, Shale oil revolution and Chinese financial market crisis where the shale oil revolution is representative of volatility transmission among clean energy, conventional energy and regional stocks, and Chinese financial market crash symbolizes crash of the Chinese stock market in a single day (Womack, 2017). The higher connectedness during this period denotes that financial markets were forming stronger volatility spillovers due to abnormal market conditions (Nguyen *et al.*, 2020).

Similarly, the abrupt increase in the connectedness of financial markets during 2016–2017 represents Brexit referendum (Xiao *et al.*, 2019), where risk spillovers were intense due to the exit of UK from the European Union. Successively, 2017–2018 time period signals toward US interest rate hike. A sudden increase in interest rates shifted the financial markets into higher integration, reflecting uneven distressed economic conditions (Kang *et al.*, 2021; Elsayed *et al.*, 2020). Finally, a sheer rise in the system-wide connectedness during 2019–2020 shows the present global crisis of COVID-19 with the TCI reaching 80% comparable to GFC, where emergency health issues raised serious economic concerns for investors, regulators, and financial market participants (Adekoya and Oliyide, 2020). Concurrent with Bouri *et al.* (2021), the

[1]Please see: https://www.britannica.com/topic/great-recession.

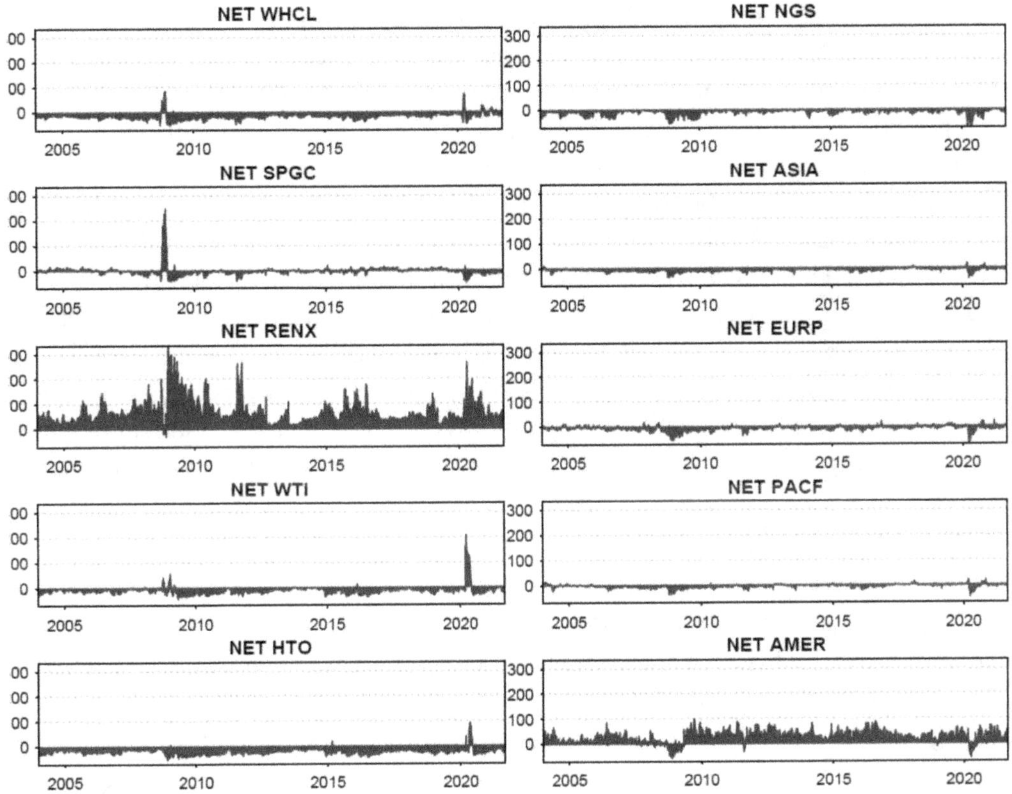

Note: This figure shows the time-varying Net connectedness among clean energy, energy, and regional stock markets using the DCC-GARCH connectedness framework.

Figure 5. Time-varying net connectedness using DCC-GARCH model.

financial contagion stimulates the financial markets towards higher connectedness. Overall, time-varying attributes in higher connectedness of clean energy, conventional energy, and regional stock markets reveal that global financial markets are sensitive to crisis periods, uncertain economic conditions, and market volatility is driven by stress periods. In this way, system-wide volatility connectedness becomes high during abnormal market conditions, and connectedness becomes lower when markets return to a new normal.

Figure 5 plots the graph of time-varying Net connectedness using DCC-GARCH model where the strength of spillovers determines their role as a net transmitter or net receiver of volatility spillovers. Parallel to the findings of Fig. 3, RENX is on the lead with transmitting maximum spillovers to other markets. Meanwhile, AMER transmits moderate volatility spillovers to the network. The net transmitting role of spillovers of RENX and AMER highlights the potential of clean energy markets to offset the risk and transmitting it to other financial markets under uneven economic conditions. Our findings corroborate Saeed *et al.* (2021), Elsayed *et al.* (2020), and Wang *et al.* (2020)

where clean energy markets and US stocks are net transmitters of spillovers. Contrarily, plots in the graph highlight that the rest of the clean energy, conventional energy and regional stock markets are maintaining near to zero spillovers necessitating their net recipient role. It also substantiates that conventional energy markets are mainly categorized under commodities and near to zero values of spillovers stresses that these markets are strongly integrated in the financial system therefore their exposure to external volatilities are minimal. These findings corroborate Yoon *et al.* (2019) where commodities receive spillovers from other financial markets. Moreover, time-varying net connectedness of individual markets illustrates that spillovers of RENX are intense during Global Financial Crisis, Shale Oil Crisis, and COVID-19 pandemic. Overall, WTI, HTO, and RENX showed intense spillovers during the global pandemic of COVID-19. In this way, spillovers show dynamic structure which depends on varying economic, financial, and global health conditions worldwide.

4.4. *Sub-sample analysis*

Figures 6–8 display the sub-sample analysis encompassing global financial crisis, shale oil crisis, and COVID-19 pandemic. Network connectedness of Fig. 6 illustrates high intra-connectedness of clean energy, conventional energy and regional stock markets. Nevertheless, strong inter-connectedness is observed between clean energy and regional markets. During GFC, the nodes on the markets highlight that SPGC,

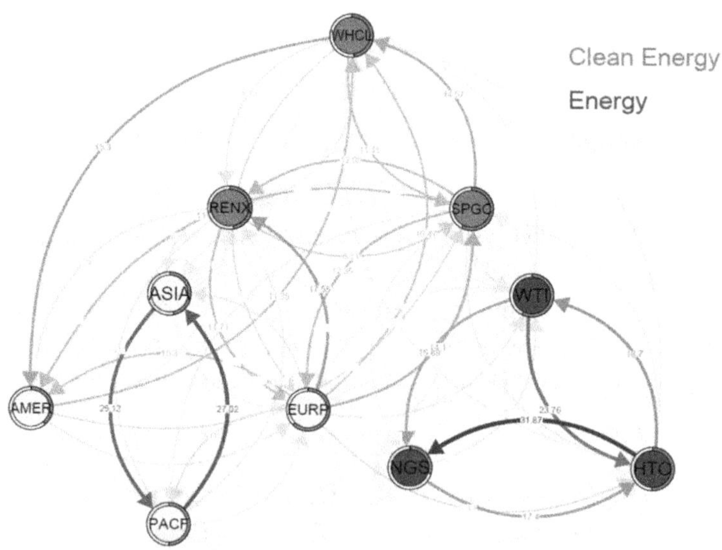

Notes: This figure shows the network connectedness among clean energy, energy, and regional stock markets using the DCC-GARCH connectedness framework. The red color in node represents the spillover from one market to all others in the system.

Figure 6. Network connectedness using DCC_GARCH model — global financial crisis.

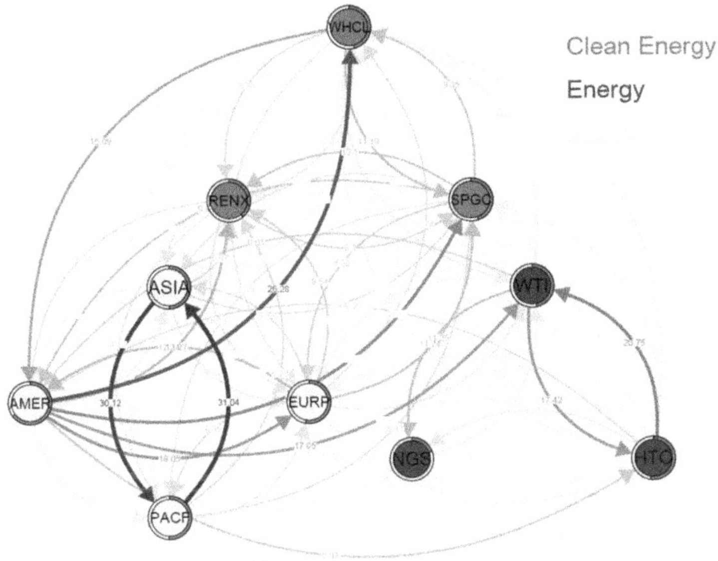

Notes: This figure shows the network connectedness among clean energy, energy, and regional stock markets using the DCC-GARCH connectedness framework. The red color in node represents the spillover from one market to all others in the system.

Figure 7. Network connectedness using DCC_GARCH model — shale oil revolution.

EURP, WTI, and HTO are net transmitters of spillovers whereas WHCL, RENX, ASIA, and PACF are transmitting moderate spillovers. Meanwhile, AMER and NGS are net receivers of spillovers which indicate that these markets can offer diversification potential for other markets during times of uncertainty. Similar findings are reported by Handika (2021), Balli *et al.* (2019) and Naeem *et al.* (2020) who reported intense spillovers among markets in the face of economic collapse during global financial crisis.

Concurrently, Fig. 7 exhibits network connectedness during Shale oil revolution which highlights strong interconnectedness of clean energy and regional stock markets whereas modest spillovers are shaped with conventional energy markets. During Shale Oil Crisis, AMER is transmitting strong spillovers to WHCL whereas ASIA and PACF are strongly connected with each other. Overall, the system-wide connectedness denotes that AMER, EURP, and HTO are transmitting sound spillovers whereas ASIA, PACF, WTI, WHCL, and SPGC are transmitting moderate spillovers. The important takeaway during Shale oil crisis reveal that regional stock markets are net transmitters whereas clean energy and conventional energy markets are net recipients of spillovers with few exceptions. It is also emphasized that shale oil crisis primarily initiated from AMER market which spread across various regional and energy markets. Therefore, regional stock markets are transmitting spillovers to other markets stressing their net contribution in shaping the network connectedness.

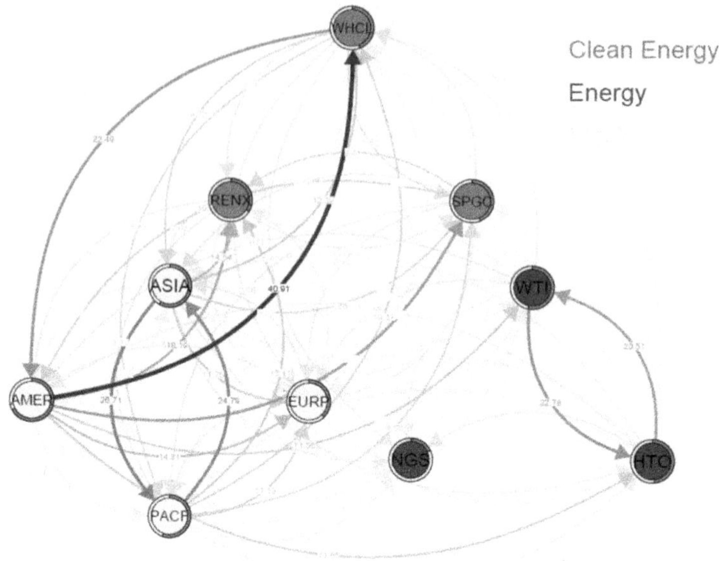

Notes: This figure shows the network connectedness among clean energy, energy, and regional stock markets using the DCC-GARCH connectedness framework. The red color in node represents the spillover from one market to all others in the system.

Figure 8. Network connectedness using DCC_GARCH model — COVID-19 crisis.

NGS showed strong disconnection from the network in line with Farid *et al.* (2021) which highlights its diversification potential in providing risk cushions when markets are experiencing high volatilities.

Figure 8 presents network connectedness of clean energy, conventional energy, and regional stock markets during the global pandemic of COVID-19 which corroborates the findings given in Figs. 6 and 7, where AMER is leading the spillovers in the network with highest transmission of volatility to WHCL. The complex network connectedness asserts that markets have shown strong connectedness during the crisis period of COVID-19. Since the COVID-19 pandemic is not originally a financial or economic crisis point, the severity of the pandemic spread across the globe eventually after an emergency situation was declared worldwide. Among all these markets, NGS again showed strong disconnection from other markets confirming its diversification potential for rest of the markets. However, our findings are in line with Adekoya and Oliyide (2020), Naeem *et al.* (2021a,b), and Shahzad *et al.* (2021) who reported that spillovers are intense during the pandemic of COVID-19.

In summary, our findings narrate that RENX and AMER are net transmitters of spillovers whereas remaining markets are net recipients of spillovers. Time-varying connectedness manifests that TCI reaches up to 80% during GFC and COVID-19 pandemic. Further, sub-sample analysis also validates similar findings when GFC, SOR, and COVID-19 periods are considered specifically.

5. Conclusion and Policy Implications

This study investigated the connectedness of clean energy markets with conventional energy and regional stock markets for the period spanning January 1, 2004 to August 31, 2021. For analysis purposes, we employed the volatility connectedness using dynamic conditional correlation (DCC-GARCH) technique and estimated the network, time-varying, and total connectedness of clean energy, conventional energy and regional stock markets. In the meantime, we also analyzed sub-samples of global financial crisis (2007–2009), shale oil revolution (2014–2015), and COVID-19 pandemic (2019–2020). Our findings pertaining to network connectedness for the whole sample period manifest that RENX is the net transmitters of spillovers followed by AMER whereas moderate spillovers are transmitted from the markets of SPGC, ASIA, EURP and PACF. In return, WTI, HTO, NGS, and WHCL are net recipients of spillovers. Strong disconnection of conventional energy markets emphasizes their less exposure to uncertainties and risks. Time-varying dynamics illustrate a sharp incline in spillovers during the aftermaths of Argentina's economic collapse (2001–2003), Global Financial Crisis (2007–2009), Eurorpean Debt Crisis (2010–2012), Shale oil crisis (2014–2015), Chinese market crash (2015–2016), Brexit referendum (2016–2017), US interest rate hike (2017–2018), and COVID-19 pandemic (2019–2020).

Further, time-varying net connectedness reiterates that RENX and AMER are net transmitters of spillovers whereas conventional energy markets are net recipients of spillovers. Sub-sample analysis demonstrates EURP, SPGC, WTI, and HTO are transmitting volatility spillovers to other markets during the global financial crisis while AMER, HTO, EURP are transmitters of spillovers during shale oil crisis. COVID-19 sub-sample analysis illustrates that AMER, WTI, ASIA, and PACF are net transmitters of risk spillovers. Overall, NGS remained slightly connected with other markets which reflects its strong integration among other financial markets and less susceptibility to shocks which ultimately offers diversification to the remaining markets.

Our findings are of higher importance particularly for regional stock markets and their respective policymakers, governments, regulators of regional markets, investors, and portfolio managers. Policymakers of regional markets such as Asia and Pacific can take up the findings based on their economic backgrounds and relevant GDPs in terms of encouraging the investments in clean energy markets. Besides, Europe and America are excelling in their clean energy initiatives as they are developed nations among other regions. Meanwhile, policymakers can reap the benefits of the study by encouraging various governments to introduce financing in clean energy and renewable investments for climate-friendly concerns as proceeds of these investments are solely attributed toward clean ecosystem. Moreover, policymakers and governments can lead the role in clean and green investments to reduce carbon emission. By reassessing the current policies and devising updated strategies, regulatory bodies can also play their key role in introducing the clean and renewable energy markets for investment purposes as these avenues will facilitate developing clean climate and net-zero emission economy.

Since International Renewable Energy Agency (IRENA) mainly devises policies for GCC region, other regional markets can also take benefit of their sound policies for transitioning the dirty energy into sustainable energy to boost clean energy initiatives in their respective countries. Investors and portfolio managers can stipulate useful implications from the study in terms of carefully examining the investment streams and choosing the investments with lower risk and higher profitability. Subsequently, markets are susceptible to economic pressures and uncertainties where conventional energy markets can offer diversification avenues for other regional and clean energy markets. Thus, the current study outlines several investment potentials and low-risk investments for portfolio managers while designing their portfolios considering the unexpected circumstances of markets and global economy.

Pertaining to future avenues of the study, it is recommended to employ various other stock markets such as G7 markets or other emerging markets stock indices to get a clearer picture of how clean energy initiatives are being carried out in their respective regions. Moreover, future studies can employ several unique methodologies, for instance, cross-qunatilogram, quantile assessment, etc. to examine the connectedness of the markets at various quantiles. In this way, there are multiple future recommendations underlining the current study that could be considered by research scholars and academicians.

References

Abid, A, F Abid and B Kaffel (2020). CDS-based implied probability of default estimation. *The Journal of Risk Finance*, 21(4), 399–422, https://doi.org/10.1108/JRF-05-2019-0079.

Adekoya, OB and JA Oliyide (2020). How COVID-19 drives connectedness among commodity and financial markets: Evidence from TVP-VAR and causality-in-quantiles techniques. *Resources Policy*, 70, 101898.

Alkathery, MA and K Chaudhuri (2021). Co-movement between oil price, CO2 emission, renewable energy and energy equities: Evidence from GCC countries. *Journal of Environmental Management*, 297, 113350.

Arif, M, M Hasan, SM Alawi and MA Naeem (2021a). COVID-19 and time-frequency connectedness between green and conventional financial markets. *Global Finance Journal*, 49, 100650.

Badaye, HK and J Narsoo (2020). Forecasting multivariate VaR and ES using MC-GARCH-Copula model. *The Journal of Risk Finance*, 21(5), 493–516, https://doi.org/10.1108/JRF-06-2019-0114.

Balli, F, MA Naeem, SJH Shahzad and A de Bruin (2019). Spillover network of commodity uncertainties. *Energy Economics*, 81, 914–927.

Blundell-Wignall, A (2012). Solving the financial and sovereign debt crisis in Europe. *OECD Journal: Financial Market Trends*, 2011(2), 201–224.

Bollerslev, T, RF Engle and JM Wooldridge (1988). A capital asset pricing model with time-varying covariances. *Journal of Political Economy*, 96(1), 116–131.

Bouri, E, O Cepni, D Gabauer and R Gupta (2021). Return connectedness across asset classes around the COVID-19 outbreak. *International Review of Financial Analysis*, 73, 101646.

Caporin, M, MA Naeem, M Arif, M Hasan, XV Vo and SJH Shahzad (2021). Asymmetric and time-frequency spillovers among commodities using high-frequency data. *Resources Policy*, 70, 101958.

Chuliá, H, D Furió and JM Uribe (2019). Volatility spillovers in energy markets. *The Energy Journal*, 40(3), 173–197.

Diebold, FX and K Yılmaz (2014). On the network topology of variance decompositions: Measuring the connectedness of financial firms. *Journal of Econometrics*, 182(1), 119–134.

Diebold, FX and K Yilmaz (2012). Better to give than to receive: Predictive directional measurement of volatility spillovers. *International Journal of Forecasting*, 28(1), 57–66.

Dimpfl, T and D Elshiaty (2021). Volatility discovery in cryptocurrency markets. *The Journal of Risk Finance*, 22(5), 313–331, https://doi.org/10.1108/JRF-11-2020-0238.

Elsayed, AH, S Nasreen and AK Tiwari (2020). Time-varying comovements between energy market and global financial markets: Implication for portfolio diversification and hedging strategies. *Energy Economics*, 90, 104847. https://doi.org/10.1016/j.eneco.2020.104847.

Engle, RF and K Sheppard (2001). Cambridge, MA: National Bureau of Economic Research.

Engle, R (2002). Dynamic conditional correlation: A simple class of multivariate generalized autoregressive conditional heteroskedasticity models. *Journal of Business & Economic Statistics*, 20(3), 339–350.

Farid, S, GM Kayani, MA Naeem and SJ Shahzad (2021). Intraday volatility transmission among precious metals, energy, and stocks during the COVID-19 pandemic. *Resources Policy*, 72, 102101.

Ferrer, R, SJH Shahzad and P Soriano (2021). Are green bonds a different asset class? Evidence from time-frequency connectedness analysis. *Journal of Cleaner Production*, 292, 125988.

Gabauer, D (2020). Volatility impulse response analysis for DCC-GARCH models: The role of volatility transmission mechanisms. *Journal of Forecasting*, 39(5), 788–796.

Hammoudeh, S, AN Ajmi and K Mokni (2020). Relationship between green bonds and financial and environmental variables: A novel time-varying causality. *Energy Economics*, 92, 104941.

Handika, R (2021). Contagions in interconnected power markets. *The Journal of Risk Finance*, 22(3/4), 296–311, https://doi.org/10.1108/JRF-01-2021-0002.

Hansen, PR and A Lunde (2005). A forecast comparison of volatility models: Does anything beat a GARCH (1, 1)? *Journal of Applied Econometrics*, 20(7), 873–889.

Hernandez, JA, SJH Shahzad, GS Uddin and SH Kang (2019). Can agricultural and precious metal commodities diversify and hedge extreme downside and upside oil market risk? An extreme quantile approach. *Resources Policy*, 62, 588–601. Accessed date: 13 September, 2021.

Hoffmann, I and CJ Börner (2020). Tail models and the statistical limit of accuracy in risk assessment. *The Journal of Risk Finance*, 21(3), 201–216, https://doi.org/10.1108/JRF-11-2019-0217.

International Energy Transitions (2021). https://www.iea.org/news/pathway-to-critical-and-formidable-goal-of-net-zero-emissions-by-2050-is-narrow-but-brings-huge-benefits.

Ji, Q, BY Liu, WL Zhao and Y Fan (2020). Modelling dynamic dependence and risk spillover between all oil price shocks and stock market returns in the BRICS. *International Review of Financial Analysis*, 68, 101238.

Kang, SH, R McIver and SM Yoon (2017). Dynamic spillover effects among crude oil, precious metal, and agricultural commodity futures markets. *Energy Economics*, 62, 19–32.

Kang, S, JA Hernandez, P Sadorsky and R McIver (2021). Frequency spillovers, connectedness, and the hedging effectiveness of oil and gold for US sector ETFs. *Energy Economics*, 99, 105278.

Karim, S (2021a). An investigation into the remuneration-CSR nexus and if it can be affected by board gender diversity, *Corporate Governance*, 21(4), 608–625, https://doi.org/10.1108/CG-08-2020-0320.

Karim, S (2021b). Do women on corporate boardrooms influence remuneration patterns and socially responsible practices? Malaysian evidence, *Equality, Diversity and Inclusion*, 40(5), 559–576, https://doi.org/10.1108/EDI-07-2020-0213.

Karim, S, MA Naeem, AA Meero and MR Rabbani (2021a). Examining the role of gender diversity on ownership structure-sustainable performance nexus: Fresh evidence from emerging markets. *Environmental Science and Pollution Research*, 1–16.

Karim, S., Lucey, B. M., Naeem, M. A. and Uddin, G. S. (2022a). Examining the interrelatedness of NFTs, DeFi Tokens and cryptocurrencies. *Finance Research Letters*, 102696.

Karim, S, MA Naeem, N Mirza and J Paule-Vianez (2022b). Quantifying the hedge and safe-haven properties of bond markets for cryptocurrency indices. *The Journal of Risk Finance.*

Karim, S and MA Naeem (2021). Clean energy, Australian electricity markets, and information transmission. *Energy RESEARCH LETTERS*, 3(Early View), 29973.

Liu, N, C Liu, B Da, T Zhang and F Guan (2021). Dependence and risk spillovers between green bonds and clean energy markets. *Journal of Cleaner Production*, 279, 123595.

Mensi, W, R Nekhili, XV Vo, T Suleman and SH Kang (2021). Asymmetric volatility connectedness among U.S. stock sectors. *North American Journal of Economics and Finance*, 56, 101327.

Naeem, MA, M Hasan, M Arif, F Balli and SJH Shahzad (2020). Time and frequency domain quantile coherence of emerging stock markets with gold and oil prices. *Physica A: Statistical Mechanics and Its Applications*, 553, 124235.

Naeem, MA, I Mbarki, M Alharthi, A Omri and SJH Shahzad (2021). Did COVID-19 impact the connectedness between green bonds and other financial markets? Evidence from time-frquency domain wih portfolio implications. *Frontiers in Environmental Science*, 9, 180.

Naeem, MA, TTH Nguyen, R Nepal, QT Ngo and F Taghizadeh–Hesary (2021b). Asymmetric relationship between green bonds and commodities: Evidence from extreme quantile approach. *Finance Research Letters*, 208, 101983.

Naeem, MA, MR Rabbani, S Karim and SM Billah (2021c). Religion vs ethics: Hedge and safe haven properties of Sukuk and green bonds for stock markets pre-and during COVID-19. *International Journal of Islamic and Middle Eastern Finance and Management.*

Naeem, MA and S Karim (2021). Tail dependence between bitcoin and green Financial assets. *Economics Letters*, 110068.

Nguyen, TTH, MA Naeem, F Balli, HO Balli and XV Vo (2020). Time-frequency comovement among green bonds, stocks, commodities, clean energy, and conventional bonds. *Finance Research Letters*, 101739.

Raghutla, C, M Shahbaz, KR Chittedi and Z Jiao (2021). Financing clean energy projects: New empirical evidence from major investment countries. *Renewable Energy*, 169, 231–241.

Rufino, CC (2018). Long-run linkages of ASEAN+ 3 floating currencies. *Business & Economics Review*, 27, 1–14.

Saeed, T, E Bouri and H Alsulami (2021). Extreme return connectedness and its determinants between clean/green and dirty energy investments. *Energy Economics*, 96, 105017.

Shahzad, SJH, E Bouri, L Kristoufek and T Saeed (2021). Impact of the COVID-19 outbreak on the US equity sectors: Evidence from quantile return spillovers. *Financial Innovation*, 7(1), 1–23.

Shaikh, I (2021). Impact of COVID-19 pandemic on the energy markets. *Economic Change and Restructuring*, 1–52. DOI: https://doi.org/10.1007/s10644-021-09320-0.

Taghizadeh-Hesary, F, A Mortha, N Yoshino and H Phoumin (2021a). Utilising green finance for sustainability: Empirical analysis of the characteristics of green bond markets. In *Energy Sustainability and Climate Change in ASEAN*, pp. 169–194. Singapore: Springer.

Taghizadeh-Hesary, F, N Yoshino and H Phoumin (2021b). Analyzing the characteristics of green bond markets to facilitate green finance in the post-COVID-19 world. *Sustainability*, 13(10), 5719.

Uddin, GS, ML Rahman, A Hedström and A Ahmed (2019). Cross-quantilogram-based correlation and dependence between renewable energy stock and other asset classes. *Energy Economics*, 80, 743–759.

Umar, M, S Farid and MA Naeem (2021). Time-frequency connectedness among clean-energy stocks and fossil fuel markets: Comparison between financial, oil and pandemic crisis. *Energy*, 240, 122702.

Wang, J, X Chen, X Li, J Yu and R Zhong (2020). The market reaction to green bond issuance: Evidence from China. *Pacific-Basin Finance Journal*, 60, 101294.

Womack, B (2017). International crises and China's rise: Comparing the 2008 global financial crisis and the 2017 global political crisis. *The Chinese Journal of International Politics*, 10(4), 383–401.

Xiao, B, Y Yang, X Peng and L Fang (2019). Measuring the connectedness of European electricity markets using the network topology of variance decompositions. *Physica A: Statistical Mechanics and Its Applications*, 535, 122279.

Yoon, SM, M Al Mamun, GS Uddin and SH Kang (2019). Network connectedness and net spillover between financial and commodity markets. *The North American Journal of Economics and Finance*, 48, 801–818.

https://doi.org/10.1142/9789819812783_0007

ENERGY FINANCING, COVID-19 REPERCUSSIONS, AND CLIMATE CHANGE: IMPLICATIONS FOR EMERGING ECONOMIES[**]

LINHAI ZHAO[*,§], HAYOT BERK SAYDALIEV[†,¶] and SAJID IQBAL[‡,||]

[*]*School of Economics and Finance*
Huaqiao University, China

[†]*Graduate School of Business and Entrepreneurship*
Under the Cabinet of Ministers of the Republic of Uzbekistan

[‡]*KUBEAC, University of Management & Technology*
Sialkot Campus, Pakistan
[§]*longmen168@126.com*
[¶]*h.saydaliev@rgsbm.uz*
[||]*sajidiqbal.edu@gmail.com*

This study is intended to test the role of renewable energy financing on climate change and to present the implications for the key stakeholders towards the acquisition of post-covid-recovery in the Asian and ASEAN economies. For this, data envelopment analysis (DEA) technique is applied to draw an inference between the constructs. Study finding resulted that higher energy consumption and rise in environmental pollution has brought a great change in the ASEAN and Asian economies' climate, for which, modern and renewable energy sources are suggested to use for the climate change mitigation. A sufficient amount of funds and the supply of energy finance to mitigate the climate change are eminently needed for the post-covid-recovery. Different financial institutions, banks and finance ministries of countries belonging from the both regions are suggested to play the best role. This is solely possible by pooling the funds in renewable energy sectors to enhance energy efficiency and control the climate change. This must be executed for the long-run period to get the desired outcomes. All the countries of both regions are further suggested to expedite the practices to apply strategic development goals (SDGs) for affordable and clean energy (SDG–7), climate change action (SDG–13) to achieve the national and global strategic objectives.

Keywords: Energy financing; climate change mitigation; energy efficiency; climate change economics.

1. Introduction

Energy financing for renewable energy sources is widely needed to mitigate the climate change in the structural imposed crises period like COVID-19 (Iqbal *et al.*, 2021). Such financing for renewable energy sources aimed at mitigating the climate

[||]Corresponding author.
[**]This chapter was originally published in Climate Change Economics, Vol. 13, No. 3, February 2022, published by World Scientific Publishing, Singapore. Reprinted with permission.

change has not reached to present the empirical evidences (Anh Tu *et al.*, 2021; Taghizadeh-Hesary and Yoshino, 2019). There is a need to test the role of energy financing for renewable energy sources on climate change in COVID-19 and suggest the way forwards to the policy makers (Park and Chung, 2021). However, this study aims to infer the connection between the constructs and fill the highlighted gap by studying the Asian and ASEAN economies. This is the study motivation.

Renewable energy financing is a key factor of climate change. COVID-19 climate friendly power improvement is frequently connected openly and strategy conversations to climate change alleviation since it is the essential way to diminishing fossil fuel byproducts in the energy area. However, the outcomes of climate change are currently obvious at provincial and nearby levels, the subject of climate change itself, and particularly what to do about it, remains profoundly politicized in the world. Renewable energy financing for COVID-19, regardless of its association with the polarizing subject of climate change, has moderately expansive public and political allure (Titley *et al.*, 2021). All things considered, climate friendly power has seen steep paces of development in the Asian and ASEAN countries, in spite of the fact that its significant development in renewables does not really dislodge petroleum products determined fuel sources, however rather adds to them. Individuals from general society and political pioneers from across the political range support less-expanded utilization of climate friendly power for an assortment of reasons not identified with climate change, for example, air quality, public energy security, and monetary turn of events (Elavarasan *et al.*, 2020).

Renewable's energy will be key in a low carbon future during and after the COVID-19. To meet the climate objective, the portion of climate friendly power in the last energy utilization should increment from 19% in 2017 to 65% by 2050 (Shahbaz *et al.*, 2020). By then, at that point, the portion of climate friendly power in power age ought to be generally 85%, up from an expected 25% in 2017. The actual effects of climate change are among the difficulties that renewables should confront, as they have suggestions for the dependability and execution of the energy framework (Vakulchuk *et al.*, 2020). Beginning examinations on this point tended to the weakness of the energy area according to an interest viewpoint; however, there are a developing number of studies breaking down impacts on supply too (Gielen *et al.*, 2019). Transmission lines and different regions along the worth chain of the energy area can likewise be influenced. One reason why the energy area has gotten such a lot of consideration in the writing is a direct result of the long life expectancy of energy framework post COVID-19 (Harjanne and Korhonen, 2019). Inside the energy area, sustainable age is the focal point of most examinations, because of the way that its primary asset is straightforwardly connected to climate factors like precipitation, temperature, light or wind. Water is a key variable, as its accessibility influences hydroelectric force plants, yet additionally any age plant that relies upon water for a piece of its interaction, including warm age (Finance, 2018) or even carbon catch and capacity (Finance, 2017).

The objective of this paper is to test the impact of renewable energy financing on climate change and present the implications for the post-COVID-19 era. Despite methodological contrasts and local varieties, the creators consider this helpful not exclusively to specialists and general society area, yet in addition to policy specialists attempting to join climate impacts into energy area dynamic cycles all throughout the planet. The accompanying segment gives a portrayal of the extension and technique of this paper. This paper closes with some conversation and finishing up comments for policy makers and theorists. This study contributes by enhancing the literature through this research topicality. This is the theoretical contribution of the contemporary investigation. On such theoretical insights study also shown the empirical verifications and guided the way forwards for key associates to apply effectively for the prudent acquisition of strategic objectives. This is the practical contribution of current research.

2. Background

Energy financing under COVID-19 for the climate change mitigations is perceived as the most basic risk confronting mankind and lopsidedly influencing the rustic poor in networks where versatile limit is altogether low. For roughly 100 million of these people, expanding hazard from climate change infers that they could be dove considerably more profound into outrageous destitution from 2030 (Todaro *et al.*, 2021). This inclination of climate change to cause and in fact sustain destitution is an immense worry for worldwide pioneers and countries trying to seek after green development. We live in a profoundly arranged existence where different drivers of climate change hazard interface, as do the actual risks (Skurka *et al.*, 2018). Associations among renewable energy financial, natural, and mechanical frameworks communicate hazard starting with one framework or area then onto the next, making new risks or fueling existing ones. For instance, a risky atmospheric devotion of 2 C above pre-mechanical levels is projected to decrease worldwide yields of staple harvests by 5–20%. Ozone depleting substance alleviation alternatives can likewise build food uncertainty if bioenergy crops dislodge food crops or can prompt biodiversity misfortune from land use change for editing and afforestation.

For instance, the Intergovernmental Panel on Climate Change (IPCC) ordinarily partitions its evaluation into three separate working gatherings zeroed in on actual climate change; climate effects, weakness, and variation reactions (by area and district); and emanations relief (by area). This methodology is helpful for orchestrating a huge number of order explicit investigations and furthermore mirrors the generally sectoral approach of numerous legislatures (Robertson, 2021). Cross-working-bunch IPCC appraisals, for example, extraordinary reports on dealing with the risk of outrageous occasions and calamities to propel climate change transformation (SREX), an Earth-wide temperature boost of 1.5 C, seas and cryosphere, and climate change and land, help us to foster more incorporated ways to deal with hazard. Notwithstanding, by having a tendency to separate risk evaluation into singular areas, districts, resource classes, or sorts of reaction alternatives, appraisals can miss significant communications that produce climate change hazard. Numerous material and calculated limits exist that can compel the appraisal of climate change hazard.

Four significant sorts are sectorial, worldly, spatial, and reaction alternative limits (Iturbide *et al.*, 2020). Connections across these limits frequently enhance or diminish hazard comparative with when associations are disregarded. Undoubtedly, late proof shows how probably the most serious climate change impacts, like those from lethal warmth or abrupt biological system breakdown, are unequivocally affected by associations across different sectoral, territorial, and reaction alternative limits. Essentially, how administration or institutional frameworks executing climate change reactions act across these limits likewise influences the idea of hazard. While sometimes these communicating impacts may have little effects, by and large the risks cannot be perceived without thinking about these connections (Viner *et al.*, 2020). For example, many water offices' long-range speculation plans are substantially more helpless against the cooperation of climate change with other financial elements than to the actual effects of a changing climate all alone (Mukherjee *et al.*, 2020). Representing these numerous intricacies is vital for appraisals entrusted with advising public governments on climate change chances, just as for comprehension and overseeing chances at more neighborhood scales, like urban communities, or across scales in the private area. In this viewpoint, we integrate ongoing work portraying complex climate change hazard — like ideas of compound, associated, and falling collaborations — and ponder the ramifications for hazard evaluation and reaction (Gibson *et al.*, 2020).

3. Literature Review

Energy utilization is a fundamental piece of day by day life and is critical across various areas, including business, transportation, and private clients, with the last burning-through 40% of the energy delivered worldwide (Lange *et al.*, 2020). Be that as it may, with the continuous infiltration of electric vehicles into the market, the transportation area's energy utilization is required to increment considerably (Ahmad and Zhang, 2020). As indicated by the United Nations (UN), the total populace will arrive at 9.7 billion by 2050. To fulfill the developing need for energy assets without the utilization of — draining — petroleum products that produce ecologically destructive fossil fuel byproducts, a few activities have been carried out internationally (Sedlmeir *et al.*, 2020). The 1987 Montreal Protocol, pointed toward decreasing the utilization of ozone-exhausting substances, prompted a significant recuperation of the ozone layer (Amasyali and El-Gohary, 2018). Additionally, the 1997 Kyoto Protocol obliged nations to put resources into efficient power energy advancements (Robinson *et al.*, 2017).

This was subsequently supplanted in 2015 by the Paris Agreement/COP21 (Conference of the Parties), in light of which resulting energy arrangements and plans have been detailed. Increment the creation of climate friendly power energy innovations, for example, sun-based, wind, and biomass. Feasible Renewable Energy (RE) accompanies a few different benefits, like contribution choices, in this manner differentiating energy assets and assisting with accomplishing energy security. Furthermore, RE can give simple admittance to energy, add to social and financial turn of events and, in particular, alleviate climate change and diminish its related natural and wellbeing impacts (Zappa *et al.*, 2019). The change from petroleum products to RE is fundamental to accomplishing a cleaner future, and insightful arrangements are expected to conquer the perplexing issues that arise in this progress, for example, the decoupling from wasteful and conventional techniques while addressing energy needs (Moriarty and Honnery, 2020).

The move from petroleum derivative-based fuel sources towards RE sources is named the Renewable Energy Transition (RET). To accomplish a powerful RET, a colossal measure of capital will be required. Albeit the general expenses identifying with RE creation have diminished fundamentally lately because of mechanical progressions (Capellán-Pérez *et al.*, 2018), there has been no comparing expansion in venture. Financial backers are less able to take speculation hazard because of changes in arrangements and the measure of capital included, making financing the RET seemingly perhaps the most serious issue of the 21st century.

Renewable energy activities and audit the methodologies utilized worldwide to defeat these deterrents. This work presents and examines the current acts of nations that are effectively going through the RET (Hosseini, 2020). An audit of the current writing is given, and a framework is introduced dependent on the holes made, either by data not being tended to in past examinations or by suggestions that were let alone. This paper distinguishes boundaries to the RET that have not been recently thought of in the writing encompassing the execution of RE activities, like predispositions against RE and the monetary states of society (Selmi *et al.*, 2021). Albeit a few examination works exist on financing the RET, these either center around one geological area or talk about just a particular arrangement or technique. In the interim, cross-provincial investigations of the RET are scant in the writing. In this manner, to best address the momentum scene of financing RE activities, a few exploration and survey articles from different locales are thought of, and a broad best in class audit of the current writing on RET financing procedures is directed.

However, a sectarian separation actually exists for renewable energy financing mentalities, and this gap is more extensive when estimating support for sustainable power strategy measures contrasted and general climate friendly power support during COVID-19. Further examination is expected to enlighten the manners in which partisanship shapes (and eases back) the energy progress, to expect touch points that could fortify existing polarization, and to recognize strategies to relieve this polarization. In this examination, we look at the connection among partisanship and hardliner personality, climate change convictions, and sustainable power support (Nelson *et al.*, 2018). Climate information and a risky atmospheric devotion science are validated since "the 'hockey stick' an Earth-wide temperature boost statement has been undermined and climate scaremongers' carbon dioxide-related a worldwide temperature alteration speculation can't represent the current decline in worldwide temperatures". However, the state passed a goal in 2018 that perceived the presence of climate change, Utah's political chiefs keep on discussing whether climate change is an after effect of human exercises, and regardless of whether ozone harming substances ought to be relieved by emanations decreases approaches and procedures (renewable energy financing and climate change) (Kahn *et al.*, 2019).

The COVID-19 climate friendly power could be decreased by contemptuousness about climate change and more extensive political polarization over the issue if such perspectives lead to strategy constraints on climate friendly power improvement or diminish the opportunity that people will embrace family sustainable power establishments. However, numerous researchers have proposed that giving climate friendly power a role as a climate moderation system, or connecting sustainable power to climate change in any capacity, will keep on enlarging the current hardliner hole (Gissi *et al.*, 2020). Additionally, in an evolving climate, the view of what individuals accept as an ordinary climate is moving too due to COVID-19, with the climate experienced as of late being a vital determinant of individuals' climatic pattern rather than the more extended authentic periods (Pugnaire *et al.*, 2019). According to a mental point of view, a psychological portrayal of a theoretical state, for example, a 30-year climate normal should be developed in an asset concentrated computational interaction that is probably not going to be routinely applied by people with restricted intellectual assets (Hassanzadeh *et al.*, 2020).

It ought to rather be normal that singular impression of climate change is driven by components of the current circumstance, rather than changes comparative with verifiable midpoints, and therefore ought to be displayed as an element of the current climate circumstance. This reasoning is more on top of what we think about the psychological systems' basic human judgment and dynamic which depend essentially on promptly accessible data without depending on complex mental elaborations (Brandão *et al.*, 2019). Simultaneously, exchange networks interface far off food frameworks together and would thus be able to make up for scaled down food security, yet they can likewise make new risks of worldwide effects, like numerous breadbasket disappointment; more quick spread of infection, bothers, and other obtrusive species; and new risks to neighborhood food security from changes in item costs brought about by strategy decisions made somewhere else (Beckage *et al.*, 2018). These cooperation incorporate both those risks brought about by climate change of COVID-19 and those including reactions to climate change through variation and alleviation (from now on the whole named climate change hazards), where hazard is perceived to allude to the potential for negative or positive results for human or natural frameworks.

Despite the fact that hazard evaluation moves toward that consider such collaborations and organizations are starting to be utilized, numerous climate change hazard appraisals regularly overlook communications partially or in full. In doing as such, they may altogether misestimate hazard, like when single area models of food creation distort the course, greatness, and spatial example of hazard contrasted and examinations that consider cross-sectoral connections. Nonetheless, for comfort and manageability, experts and administrators will in general break hazard appraisals into storehouses, regularly taking a segment situated, instead of collaboration arranged, see Elavarasan *et al.* (2020).

A broad paradigm of financing for sustainable electricity for climate change mitigation, COVID-19, demonstrates the distinctiveness of this study. Despite the growing body of literature, the empirical discussion on energy finance and climate change remains fragmented, under-researched, and based on COVID-19 tests. This study, on the other hand, exemplifies this idea by putting the study structures to the test following the purpose for this study.

4. Research Methodology

4.1. *Study data*

This research was performed in Asian and ASEAN countries to compare and contrast the findings. This study included Japan, China, Indonesia, India, Pakistan and Bangladesh among Asian countries. On the other side, Singapore, the Philippines, Malaysia, Vietnam, Thailand, and South Korea have been selected. Earlier to the Asian financial crisis of 1997, the Six Asian Tiger countries' success was ascribed to output strategies and robust capacity — building. These economies have high levels of equitable income distribution and maintained fast development. Eventually, the emergence and persistence of coronavirus made all such Asian and ASEAN economies as economically destabilized and financially fragile. Due to this, energy sector, financial institutions and climate control organizations faced a structural hit. Therefore, such economies need a viable solution to cope up with modern energy-economic-environmental challenges. Therefore, we selected these economies to investigate in recent study. The quarterly data were obtained for the period 2016 to 2020 from the World Development Indicators (WDI) and the Economic Intelligence Unit (EIU). This quarterly data have been converted by the researchers into annual data. To ensure uniformity, logarithms of all variables have been used.

4.2. *Empirical estimation technique*

The DEA approach is a non-parametric mathematical tool for evaluating different evaluations of judgment call units (DMU). We use this model by taking the total factor and environmental factor as the pivotal estimating method (Li *et al.*, 2021). The initial step is to choose the indicators. Indicators have selected measures comparison of the relative relevance and data availability. Using the composite measure, the region's utility is estimated between around 0 and 1 in combination with environmental and energy indicators; whereas the second model used many different configurations to assess energy input (work input, green funding, and industrial output) of selected countries (Geng *et al.*, 2019). We evaluated results using both methods to identify biased data or nation rankings (Iqbal *et al.*, 2021).

4.3. *Empirical design*

Let us suppose, j is equal to $1, \ldots, n$, each of them a country L is an energy input, whereas L is a non-energy input (per capita CO2, energy consumption, and work) (Asmild *et al.*, 2004). The aim is to optimize output by utilizing as little input as possible in a production process. In the whole production process, renewable energy (coal, gas and oil) as an energy input generates undesired production. We should thus predict the use of energy or encourage conservation to enhance atmospheric efficiency and decrease leakage. However, the reduction of contaminants is not allowed in traditional probability distributions (Sueyoshi and Goto, 2012). There are a number of ways to this issue, including using unpleasant incentives for results, using unwanted outcomes as that of an input (labor and energy consumption) and turning unwanted results into acceptable, categorized goods. Unwanted production is often generated in this study via the usage of fossil fuels that may be a significant obstacle to ecological sustainability. Thus, the quantity of fuel burned is lowered if electricity consumption is decreased or efficiency is increased throughout the production process,

$$E_1 = \min \theta$$

s.t.

$$\sum_{j=1}^{n} \lambda_j X_{ij} + S_i^{x-} = X_{ij0}, \quad i = 1, \ldots, m, \tag{1}$$

$$\sum_{j=1}^{n} \lambda_j e_{lj} + S_l^{e-} = \theta e_{lj0}, \quad l = 1, \ldots, L, \tag{2}$$

$$\sum_{j=1}^{n} \lambda_j y_{rj} + S_r^{y+} = y_{rj0}, \quad r = 1, \ldots, S, \tag{3}$$

$$\sum_{j=1}^{n} \lambda_j b_{kj} = \theta b_{kj0}, \quad k = 1, \ldots, K, \tag{4}$$

$$\lambda_j,\ S_i^{x-},\ S_l^{e-},\ S_r^{y+} \geq 0, \quad \text{for all } j, I, l. \tag{5}$$

The model (1) stands for the undesired generation of products with electrical energy and a specific quantity of non-energy input at the intended output with a “Co” amplitude between 0 and 1. A higher absolute value indicates a greater reduction in energy usage or emissions of pollutants. If this is not the case, the nation in issue is ecologically ineffective. Evaluation of energy efficiency is biased since the comparison utilizes various energy types. Extending energy efficiency and environmental radiation needs various techniques,

$$E_2 = \min \frac{1}{2} \left(\frac{1}{L} \sum_{l=1}^{L} \theta_l^e + \frac{1}{K} \sum_{k=1}^{K} \theta_k^b \right)$$

s.t.

$$\sum_{j=1}^{n} \lambda_j X_{ij} + S_i^{x-} = X_{ij0}, \quad i = 1, \ldots, m, \tag{6}$$

$$\sum_{j=1}^{n} \lambda_j e_{lj} + S_l^{e-} = \theta_l^e e_{lj0}, \quad l = 1, \ldots, L, \tag{7}$$

$$\sum_{j=1}^{n} \lambda_j y_{rj} - S_r^{y+} = y_{rj0}, \quad r = 1, \ldots, S, \tag{8}$$

$$\sum_{j=1}^{n} \lambda_j b_{kj} = \theta_k^b b_{kj0}, \quad k = 1, \ldots, K, \tag{9}$$

$$\lambda_j, S_i^{x-}, S_l^{e-}, S_r^{y+} \geq 0, \quad \text{for all } j, I, l. \tag{10}$$

Model (2) defines industrial structure to the Green Funding function by utilizing undesired output (compared to the energy industry's input) as input industrial structure proxy output, obtained from green financing models. This approach thus guarantees both industrial structure and green funding. Model (2) uses non-proportional (not proportional) to find the highest possible energy and environmental efficiency in the highlighting countries with unified efficiency. Consolidated green funding equation is based on whether to priorities of the labor productivity: green financing. In such a scenario, a country would be considered environmentally aware and electricity if and only if all models' slackness equals zero (i.e., $E_2 = 1$). (2) This study utilized a framework in order to evaluate the total environmental efficiency and energy of highlighted countries (2).

This technique utilizes a simple moving idea to get an efficiency measure each week or every month for each DMU. The same study framework for Vietnam's developing nation with a series of overlays and years, the research evaluates the changes of efficiency in many nations during 2000–2019. The Charnel and Cooper (Liu *et al.*, 2013b) software provides changing and cross-cutting data for dynamic evaluations of effects. The windshield had the remarks it saw. There is a limited chance to deal with this big problem. For efficiency measurement, it was found that the width of a window is 3 or 4 cycles, to generate good and electricity results (imagine window of width three). Thus, for the first session these three years (2010–2012) were utilized. Our next window will last for one year and this procedure will continue till the window is over. For each country a radius of impact may be calculated using applying DEA on the basis of window analysis.

5. Results and Discussion

5.1. *Empirical findings*

The study empirical deducted the renewable energy financing framework with the climate change mitigation indicators in the context of Asian and ASEAN economies to assess the matter of the fact that what and how such countries are less emitting in climate as being moderate source of finance and research and development. Knowledge of green energy financial indexes resulted to may improve governments, institutions and private investors' capacity to take strategic choices to decrease the climate change risk, as a base for evaluating reductions in carbon hazards — another source to measure climate change matter. For the treated set of the countries the overall figures are fairly comparable. But one key point worth noting is that, even though the identical observations are made, the means vary in numbers very much; their renewable energy finance and climate change mitigation methods have improved significantly in the treated nations. The score shows a substantial improvement in climate change after therapy. Equally high are the average GDP per capita, foreign direct investment and domestic credit for private sector involvement. Naturally, renewable energy finance has a very low mean. On the other hand, the treated nations have a higher mean value for the variables covering the different aspects of climate change mitigation.

Table 2 presents factual evidence that emerging countries, such as those in Asia and the ASEAN region, are the fastest-growing economy in the world in terms of CO2 emissions. Wealthy countries are more likely to pollute the environment per capita than developing countries, and this has become a major societal concern. Countries contribute to CO2 emissions through power and production from fossil fuels in a variety of ways. An indicator termed as the Kuznets curve (Grossman and Krueger, 1995) shows that the connection between environmental pollution and financial aid is not

Table 1. Climate change index.

Regions	Country name	2016	2017	2018	2019	2020
Asian Countries	Japan	0.189	0.081	0.117	0.147	0.625
	China	0.198	0.014	0.396	0.044	0.562
	Indonesia	0.291	0.142	0.121	0.059	0.296
	India	0.359	0.330	0.023	0.448	0.243
	Pakistan	0.329	0.207	0.189	0.279	0.203
	Bangladesh	0.212	0.113	0.337	0.656	0.113
ASEAN Countries	Singapore	0.497	0.111	0.343	0.407	0.248
	Philippines	0.248	0.296	0.561	0.097	0.258
	Malaysia	0.178	0.303	0.345	0.046	0.844
	Vietnam	0.440	0.105	0.123	0.172	0.184
	Thailand	0.691	0.191	0.024	0.028	0.958
	South Korea	0.142	0.256	0.491	0.256	0.789

Table 2. Renewable energy finance role on climate change.

Regions	Country name	2016	2017	2018	2019	2020
Asian Countries	Japan	0.756	0.356	0.111	0.377	0.648
	China	0.279	0.449	0.271	0.357	0.751
	Indonesia	0.697	0.199	0.836	0.031	0.237
	India	0.277	0.288	0.781	0.492	0.495
	Pakistan	0.277	0.238	0.661	0.507	0.645
	Bangladesh	0.112	0.566	0.788	0.649	0.219
ASEAN Countries	Singapore	0.491	0.324	0.263	0.049	0.855
	Philippines	0.707	0.256	0.1637	0.746	0.897
	Malaysia	0.426	0.443	0.616	0.357	0.119
	Vietnam	0.433	0.327	0.655	0.441	0.662
	Thailand	0.172	0.295	0.295	0.514	0.512
	South Korea	0.272	0.699	0.256	0.035	0.816

linear (EKC). This is consistent with the findings of Hafner and his colleagues (2020). There is a quasi to the trailing effect in the United States, according to Adegbite *et al.* (2019). As a result, a wide range of discrepancies are discovered, with contextual dynamics and environmental variables among the most likely culprits (Hanif *et al.*, 2019). It may be argued that large-scale private renewable energy investment from a range of investors is needed to keep global warming 'less than two degrees Celsius' under control.

In Australia, the lowest carbon index values is 0.98, but in Malta, the reduced carbon index is 0.71. As a result of the results, Australia appears to be well-positioned in terms of renewable energy financing and carbon reduction. European countries have a higher than 0.90 score, whilst Asian countries like Bahrain have a score close to Malta's. The green finance index is also significant to governments, major shareholder, investment firms, and asset owners.

To a greater extent than may be shown by cost-type signals and benefits, the greater the energy finance index value for renewable energy. Index values over 100 indicate significant progress in green energy infrastructure improvement in these countries or organizations. The higher the index number, the more likely these countries are to have lower emissions and to be able to integrate more renewable energy into their energy mix. Globally, the energy sector, as a dynamic business, should actively encourage economic development by reducing economic disparities between ASEAN and Asian countries. The ultimate concern for building a worldwide strategy for energy sustainability should be addressing current, medium and long-term demands for energy while remediating environmental harm (Mohsin *et al.*, 2019).

The usage of renewable energy outputs, R&D investment, and renewable output may mitigate climate change in low-score countries. These countries would be environmentally friendly and efficient if they implemented renewable sources of energy

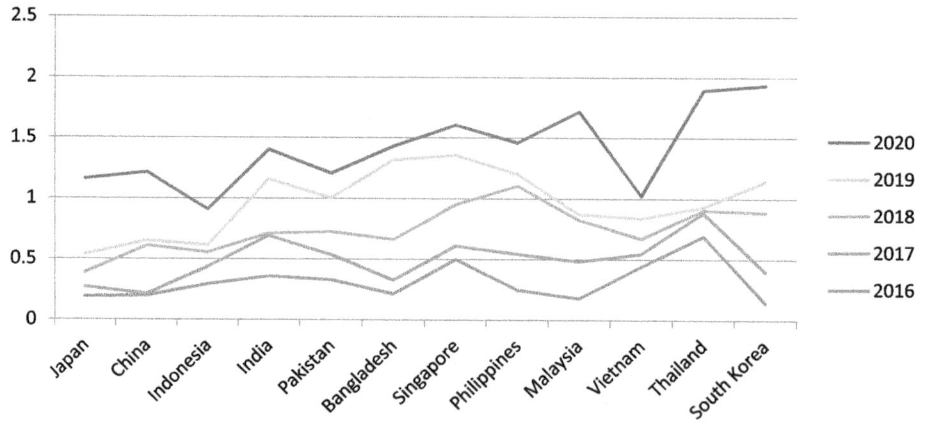

Figure 1. Climate change performance of Asian and ASEAN economies.

like wind, solar, and hydropower (Tian, 2018). According to the findings, a transition to low-carbon development will need 2 to 3 percent of GDP in the years between 2011 and 2030. Poor countries, on the other hand, are hindered by insufficient subsidies, inadequate carbon improvement support mechanisms through banking firms, and a lack of knowledge of how to implement low-carbon initiatives, as illustrated in Figs. 1 and 2.

Table 3 shows the DEA findings with covariate control. In our research, we found a strong correlation between GDP per capita and US dollar buying power parity in 2016, 2017, 2018, and 2019. On the other hand, the degree of renewable energy consumption is critical in assessing the attractiveness of climate change treatment countries' energy financing in their individual economies. Throughout the same vein, research and development (R&D) is critical to garnering financial support for green energy projects in Asia. This variable makes it possible to discover new data, which in turn draws investment in the energy system from both local and international sources, therefore

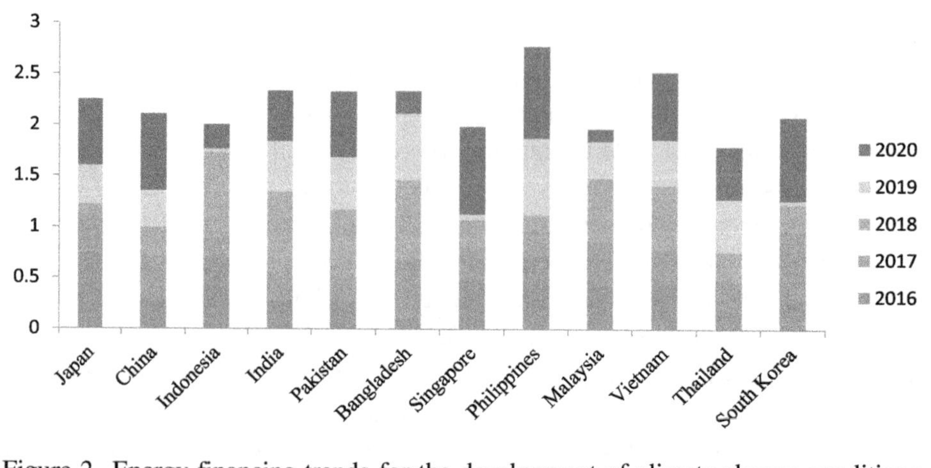

Figure 2. Energy financing trends for the development of climate change conditions.

Table 3. Changes in energy efficiency finance and climate change during 2016–2020.

		Renewable energy financing			Climate change economics		
Regions	Country name	Mean	Change	Rank	Mean	Change	Rank
Asian Countries	Japan	0.1167	0.006877	4	0.0844	0.0354	17
	China	0.0535	0.018168	1	0.7823	0.7277	24
	Indonesia	0.3421	−0.00878	15	0.4295	0.0349	36
	India	0.0208	0.007641	27	0.0284	0	0
	Pakistan	0.0434	0.004017	32	0.0381	0	0
	Bangladesh	0.0142	0.030975	18	0.0669	0.2497	21
ASEAN Countries	Singapore	0.0441	−0.0173	16	0.0693	0.0357	14
	Philippines	0.0416	0.011368	13	0.2057	0.0448	13
	Malaysia	0.5145	−0.01231	38	0.05443	0.0294	12
	Vietnam	0.1814	−0.00526	30	0.34617	0.0413	16
	Thailand	0.0112	−0.00355	14	0.2004	0.0401	15
	South Korea	0.1528	0.014735	9	0.0825	0.0367	33

fostering climate change (see Table 2 and Fig. 3). R&D is important if the multilateral development banks are to attract the right investment in the Asian and ASEAN climate change mitigation industries. Over the last nine years, the six MDBs have invested $237 billion in renewable energy funding (Tanner and Horn-Phathanothai, 2019). R&D has been shown in studies by Ndlovu and Inglesi-Lotz (2020) to be a catalyst for technological improvement since it gives fresh knowledge that ultimately improves the process of energy production and consumption.

There is a probable impact on the Asian countries' climate change under study with energy access of 36%, as shown in Table 1 and Fig. 4. However, with a positive mean 25.17%, energy efficiency finance affects the Asian countries under study, proving zero impact of the energy financing in renewables at 25.17% and at 27.91% in ASEAN countries. All the covariates suggest an impact on Asian and ASEAN countries' climate change is significant due to energy efficiency finance with means. Energy-related emissions have a 7% likelihood of impacting the environment through climate change factors. A possible variation in the percentage of one unit is suggested through the

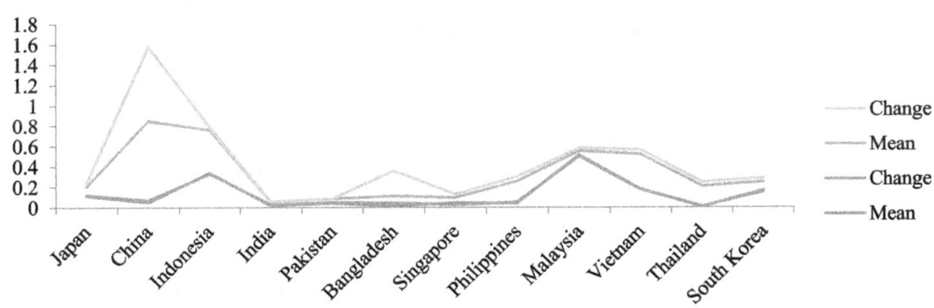

Figure 3. Climate change threshold and variations of renewable energy finance.

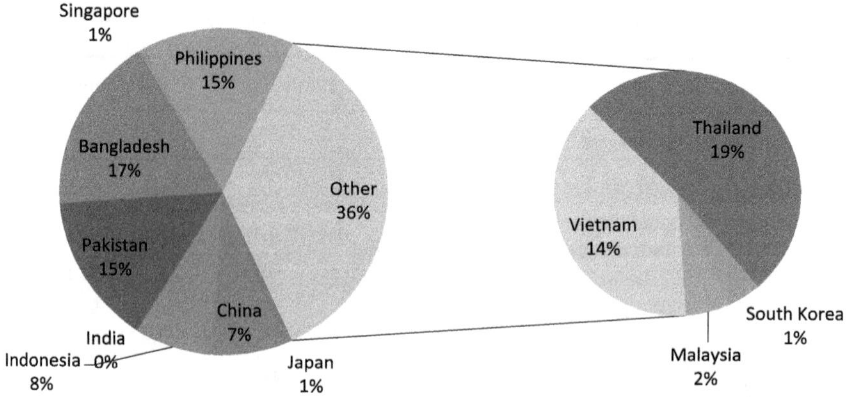

Figure 4. Sensitivity analysis of renewable energy finance role in climate change.

change in the other variable unit through the marginal effect results. A 0.184% decrease in climate change has been occurred in our sample data with a unit change in the percentage energy access variable. A high mean of around 3% probable impact on climate change of the ASEAN countries can be identified in through energy efficiency finance and gross domestic product (GDP).

Table 4 shows that the results of the research are solid, and their sensitivity analysis is shown in Fig. 4. Business as usual will be negatively affected by climate change, according to this pioneering study. Tide and storms may create floods in 54% of Asian nations, although just 29% of ASEAN countries are at danger from other areas. The report also reveals the flow of funding for energy efficiency in the sample Asian and ASEAN nations. In nations like India, Singapore, Vietnam, the Philippines, Pakistan, South Korea, and Bangladesh, the majority of the world's population is concentrated.

Table 4. Dynamics of climate change: Robustness analysis.

Regions	Country name	2016	2017	2018	2019	2020
Asian Countries	Japan	−0.00109	0.009743	−0.02183	−0.01387	−0.0048
	China	0.007808	−0.01107	−0.00996	−0.01231	−0.00098
	Indonesia	−0.0085	−0.00075	0.025915	0.014649	−0.00197
	India	0	0.012326	0.019555	−0.00726	0.014728
	Pakistan	−0.01659	−0.01408	0.003679	0.014857	−0.00096
	Bangladesh	−0.01935	−0.0285	−0.00772	−0.00506	0.000472
ASEAN Countries	Singapore	−0.00066	0.001056	−0.02275	−0.02264	−0.01584
	Philippines	−0.01651	0.024116	0.00973	−0.01322	−0.00035
	Malaysia	0.002341	0.007447	0.011071	0.015691	0.010758
	Vietnam	0.015366	−0.02448	0	−0.00065	0
	Thailand	−0.02061	0.024507	0.004398	−0.00417	0
	South Korea	−0.00172	−0.0062	−0.00242	0.001981	−0.00364

Despite having a larger population, its GDP is lower than that of China. The large population has also resulted in a rise in demand for renewable energy. It accounts for 37% of the worldwide market share (Padhan *et al.*, 2018). This Chinese trade policy's worldwide aspect may be shown by looking at its geographic scope. There is a broader range of participants when Chinese companies and other local businesses are involved in host nations.

5.2. *Discussion*

In order to develop quickly and stay healthy, a huge amount of renewable energy financing is needed. This implies that every economy has a responsibility to provide safe, adequate, and affordable energy to producers and consumers. A research based on real data has revealed that China has the highest overall rank in the environmental and energy rankings. It is likely that this is linked to the continuance of China policies on both energy and the environment. Although China imports a growing quantity of energy, she has imposed strict tariffs and has created efficient and clean and green energy consumption programs. To give another example, the Chinese government has taken steps to decrease pollution levels to 80% by 2050 (Mushtaq *et al.*, 2018). Carbon emissions produced by transportation are one of the largest contributors to the UK's energy consumption, and a key goal of the government's Clean Air Strategy is to decrease 40% of that pollution by 2020 while decreasing 46% by 2030. To reduce carbon emissions by 80% by the year 2050, China adopted a new climate change legislation in 2008.

Environmental efficiency is improved when a sustainable economic structure is adopted that helped in mitigating climate change in such Asian and ASEAN economies with good numbers; comparatively Asian countries need to take more best effort in very time. Additionally, for improved environmental conditions, there is a significant function to perform with respect to energy efficiency and energy intensity. More efficient utilization of conventional and renewable energy is needed for this specific purpose. Energy financing may aid with energy efficiency and energy intensity by assisting to develop innovative technology in the production or usage of energy. Increased energy efficiency results in decreasing CO_2 emissions and establishing the greatest energy market strategies for the future. To put it another way, this study focuses on market reforms and policies to reduce the production of greenhouse gases. This increasing emphasis on the concept of energy efficiency has emerged from the significance of energy consumption in the modern world. It is obvious that energy is a crucial element in the development of an economy and societal well-being.

For nearly a decade, energy prices have risen at a slower pace than the EU's consumer price index (Iqbal *et al.*, 2021). Towards the conclusion of this time, the affordability index for energy efficiency increased for everyone in the country (Li *et al.*, 2021). The resumption of rising fuel prices may end this era of decreasing real expenses. Governance organizations will have to be prepared to surrender efficiency profit produced from reforms to customers if they want ongoing public support of energy reforms plans and future integration to succeed.

Policy tools should have binding capabilities for carbon trading markets to be established. The efficacy of these efforts to mitigate climate change with green energy financing is possible in the current context of rapid change and national borders. The tightening of fiscal borders and restricted money movement has tangible national as well as international diplomatic repercussions. Moreover, time is running out for ASEAN leaders to execute, evaluate, and record other planned actions, such as the ASEAN green energy fund COVID-19, to reduce climate change for future epidemics. This fund has been set up by the ASEAN Plus 3 (Japan, South Korea, and China); however supply chain disruptions and slow asset flow have temporarily hampered the purchase of some medical goods and distribution equipment in countries with weak health systems. To improve the energy business and reduce climate change, this collaboration may be extended.

However, ASEAN's collaborative capability is still being built. This year's ASEAN Special Summit Statement on Coronavirus Disease included seven key measures agreed upon by member states to improve future cross-border co-operation. For example, maintaining energy supply chain connection, developing multi-partner, multi-sectoral and comprehensive responses to COVID-19 and future energy-financing crises, and providing appropriate assistance to pandemic-affected persons. After a year, the ASEAN government still shows little support. Significant and timely regional collaboration is required to address major issues related to the energy sector and the global environment. Truth and nation support are needed now, and governments must work together to prepare the future.

6. Conclusion and Practical Implications

It was the goal of this research to uncover the link between renewable energy financing and climate change in Asian and ASEAN nations as a critical component of reforming oil markets and boosting national economic development. Modernity and urbanization in these nations have substantially increased energy usage, and the production of environmental problems caused by energy usage is a worldwide issue. Energy efficiency research in the provinces of these nations might be used as a foundation for making decisions about energy and climate laws and changes in policy in these nations. It is possible to overcome the obstacles to an effective migration to renewable electricity because of the increase in renewable power and political ramifications detailed in this paper. According to this research, the overall energy and environmental efficiency factor in six Asian nations and seven ASEAN nations is evaluated using an envelope-based data package model, which includes both positive output (GDP) and negative output (CO_2 or SO_2) in addition to total energy consumption (labor and capital stock). It also uses DEA frame analysis methods for the aim of computing the efficiency rating for the period of 2010–2014 research using longitudinal and data-variant data. These nations' Eastern regions are more economic and ecological efficient than the West, according to scientific evidence.

All three aspects of effectiveness are similar, and in most cases, the energy and environmental efficiency of these nations has improved marginally. The Eastern region outperforms the Central and Western areas in terms of energy use, economy, and environmental impact. With lower pricing for future gas market, these nations promote market reforms. The findings are important enough to justify further policy consideration.

- Energy efficiency can still be improved in 28 nations and their regions, and increase in production and CO2 emission reductions are still encouraging. The non-parameter test findings suggest that there are three key avenues of financing for energy efficiency. These nations are distinct in terms of geography and economic development. The East-Middle-West and East are more efficient than the Central and Western areas, and this disparity is widening. Combining pollution and sustainable efficiency in three areas is advantageous.
- According to a 2014 assessment of the environmental costs and regulatory costs across all provinces, most provinces have environmental regulatory costs, and their economic development is heavily dependent on environmental capacity, with serious environmental costs. As a result, it is critical to alter economic development and environmental quality. The imbalance in economic development may not be to blame for the disparity in efficiency across the three regions.
- These nations may be able to achieve high energy and environmental efficiency via their economic growth strategy. A decade of effective energy and environmental regulations may have led to a better energy and environmental performance. Improved power conservation and much more reliable statistics throughout different policy periods are two benefits of reforming the Asia-Pacific electrical market. A variety of policy adjustments and actual benefits are now underway in these areas. High-tech, low-energy cellphones have gained in export proportion since 2010, and the importance of the state economy has decreased as the private sector has developed.
- There is also a current international movement toward sustainable and green energy consumption, which has a direct impact on APE's power generation goals.

References

Ahmad, T and D Zhang (2020). A critical review of comparative global historical energy consumption and future demand: The story told so far. *Energy Reports*, 6, 1973–1991.

Amasyali, K and NM El-Gohary (2018). A review of data-driven building energy consumption prediction studies. *Renewable and Sustainable Energy Reviews*, 81, 1192–1205.

Beckage, B *et al.* (2018). Linking models of human behaviour and climate alters projected climate change. *Nature Climate Change*, 8(1), 79–84.

Brandão, M *et al.* (2019). Quantifying the climate change effects of bioenergy systems: Comparison of 15 impact assessment methods. *GCB Bioenergy*, 11(5), 727–743.

Capellán-Pérez, I *et al.* (2018). Renewable Energy Cooperatives as an instrument towards the energy transition in Spain. *Energy Policy*, 123, 215–229.

Elavarasan, RM *et al.* (2020). A comprehensive review on renewable energy development, challenges, and policies of leading Indian states with an international perspective. *IEEE Access*, 8, 74432–74457.

Gibson, K *et al.* (2020). The mental health impacts of climate change: Findings from a Pacific Island atoll nation. *Journal of Anxiety Disorders*, 73, 102237.

Gielen, D *et al.* (2019). The role of renewable energy in the global energy transformation. *Energy Strategy Reviews*, 24, 38–50.

Gissi, E *et al.* (2020). A review of the combined effects of climate change and other local human stressors on the marine environment. *Science of the Total Environment*, 775, 142564.

Harjanne, A and JM Korhonen (2019). Abandoning the concept of renewable energy. *Energy Policy*, 127, 330–340.

Hassanzadeh, P *et al.* (2020). Effects of climate change on the movement of future landfalling Texas tropical cyclones. *Nature Communications*, 11(1), 1–9.

Hayhoe, K, DJ Wuebbles, DR Easterling, DW Fahey, S Doherty, J Kossin, W Sweet, R Vose, and M Wehner (2018). *Our Changing Climate. Impacts, Risks, and Adaptation in the United States: The Fourth National Climate Assessment*, Reidmiller, DR, CW Avery, DR Easterling, KE Kunkel, KLM Lewis, TK Maycock and BC Stewart (eds.), U.S. Global Change Research Program, Washington, DC, USA, Volume II, pp. 72–144, doi: 10.7930/NCA4.2018.CH2.

Hosseini, SE (2020). An outlook on the global development of renewable and sustainable energy at the time of COVID-19. *Energy Research & Social Science*, 68, 101633.

Iturbide, M *et al.* (2020). An update of IPCC climate reference regions for subcontinental analysis of climate model data: Definition and aggregated datasets. *Earth System Science Data*, 12(4), 2959–2970.

Kahn, ME *et al.* (2019). Long-term macroeconomic effects of climate change: A cross-country analysis, National Bureau of Economic Research.

Kenney, MA, AC Janetos and MD Gerst (2020). A framework for national climate indicators. *Climatic Change*, 163, 1705–1718.

Lange, S *et al.* (2020). Digitalization and energy consumption. Does ICT reduce energy demand? *Ecological Economics*, 176, 106760.

Liu, JS, LY Lu, WM Lu and BJ Lin (2013). Data envelopment analysis 1978–2010: A citation-based literature survey. *Omega*, 41(1), 3–15.

Moriarty, P and D Honnery (2020). Feasibility of a 100% global renewable energy system. *Energies*, 13(21), 5543.

Mukherjee, S *et al.* (2020). Compound drought and heatwaves at a global scale: The role of natural climate variability-associated synoptic patterns and land-surface energy budget anomalies. *Journal of Geophysical Research: Atmospheres*, 125(11), e2019JD031943.

Nelson, G *et al.* (2018). Income growth and climate change effects on global nutrition security to mid-century. *Nature Sustainability*, 1(12), 773–781.

Pugnaire, FI *et al.* (2019). Climate change effects on plant-soil feedbacks and consequences for biodiversity and functioning of terrestrial ecosystems. *Science Advances*, 5(11), eaaz1834.

Robertson, S (2021). Transparency, trust, and integrated assessment models: An ethical consideration for the Intergovernmental Panel on Climate Change. *Wiley Interdisciplinary Reviews: Climate Change*, 12(1), e679.

Robinson, C *et al.* (2017). Machine learning approaches for estimating commercial building energy consumption. *Applied Energy*, 208, 889–904.

Sedlmeir, J *et al.* (2020). The energy consumption of blockchain technology: Beyond myth. *Business & Information Systems Engineering*, 62(6), 599–608.

Selmi, R *et al.* (2021). The energy transition, Trump energy agenda and COVID-19. *International Economics*, 165, 140–153.

Shahbaz, M *et al.* (2020). The effect of renewable energy consumption on economic growth: Evidence from the renewable energy country attractive index. *Energy*, 207, 118162.

Skurka, C *et al.* (2018). Pathways of influence in emotional appeals: Benefits and tradeoffs of using fear or humor to promote climate change-related intentions and risk perceptions. *Journal of Communication*, 68(1), 169–193.

Titley, MA *et al.* (2021). Global inequities and political borders challenge nature conservation under climate change. *Proceedings of the National Academy of Sciences*, 118(7), e2011204118. DOI: 10.1073/pnas.2011204118.

Todaro, NM *et al.* (2021). The influence of managers' awareness of climate change, perceived climate risk exposure and risk tolerance on the adoption of corporate responses to climate change. *Business Strategy and the Environment*, 30(2), 1232–1248.

Vakulchuk, R *et al.* (2020). Renewable energy and geopolitics: A review. *Renewable and Sustainable Energy Reviews*, 122, 109547.

Viner, D *et al.* (2020). Understanding the dynamic nature of risk in climate change assessments — A new starting point for discussion. *Atmospheric Science Letters*, 21(4), e958.

USGCRP (2017). Climate Science Special Report: Fourth National Climate Assessment, Wuebbles, DJ, DW Fahey, KA Hibbard, DJ Dokken, BC Stewart and TK Maycock (eds.), Volume I, U.S. Global Change Research Program, Washington, DC, USA, 470 pp.

Zappa, W *et al.* (2019). Is a 100% renewable European power system feasible by 2050? *Applied Energy*, 233, 1027–1050.

https://doi.org/10.1142/9789819812783_0008

TACKLING CARBON INTENSITY WITH GREEN FINANCE: STUDY OF OECD ECONOMIES[‡‡]

LIJING LU[*,¶], HAIYANG ZHENG[†,‖], MEILAN CHEN[‡,**] and HINA NAJAM[§,††]

[*]*Hebei University of Economics and Business*
Shijiazhuang 050067, P. R. China

[†]*HSBC Business School, Peking University*
Shenzhen 518055, P. R. China

[‡]*Guangdong University of Finance & Economics*
Guangzhou 510320, P. R. China

[§]*School of Business Administration, Iqra University*
Islamabad, Pakistan
[¶]*lijinglu79@heuet.edu.cn*
[‖]*hyzheng@phbs.pku.edu.cn*
[**]*meilanchen@gdufe.edu.cn*
[††]*hinanajam27851@iqraisb.edu.pk*

Green financing has been examined in the literature. However, its impact on carbon intensity has not been fully investigated. This research sets out to fill this gap by using the dimensions of green loans, securities, insurance, and investment. In exploring the connections between green financing, nonfossil energy use, and carbon intensity, we utilized data from 2016 to 2020 to run an advanced quantile modeling. We applied the decision-making unit-method of data envelopment analysis for analyses. Our main findings are as follows. Rapid advances in the green finance sector in Organisation for Economic Co-operation and Development countries were coupled with an increase in nonfossil energy usage, resulting in a decline in carbon intensity. When the growth in nonfossil energy consumption was reduced, green investment was put on hold, and the green financing industry would be negatively impacted. The role of green financing and carbon intensity in nonfossil energy use is coupled with strong government policy interventions. Nonetheless, the effects of green finance initiatives often lag. Moreover, these effects are inconsistent. This research suggests new methods to increase the use of nonfossil energy, build a carbon trading market, and increase the consumption of green financing policies post COVID-19.

Keywords: Green financing; COVID-19; carbon intensity; quantile modeling; OECD countries.

1. Introduction

Power generation is a fundamental approach to sustainable development and energy security. Companies may suffer financial difficulty (Anh Tu *et al.*, 2021), and

---

[**]Corresponding author.
[‡‡]This chapter was originally published in Climate Change Economics, Vol. 13, No. 3, April 2022, published by World Scientific Publishing, Singapore. Reprinted with permission.

challenges securing money from financial organizations make it harder to implement energy-saving technologies or programs (Li *et al.*, 2021a). Thus, this study seeks to examine the effect of green financial constraints on companies' energy intensity and their choice of energy-saving technology (Alemzero *et al.*, 2021). The decline in energy intensity over the past years has been accompanied by improvements in economic development and living standards. For example, Organisation for Economic Co-operation and Development (OECD)'s energy intensity has dropped significantly due to tremendous efforts by the OECD government in its 11th, 12th, and 13th five-year plans to reduce energy consumption and improve energy efficiency. Between 1991 and 2002, OECD energy intensity fell by an average of 7.96% per year (Zhang *et al.*, 2021; Iqbal and Bilal, 2021a). The average yearly decrease was 4.72% between 2006 and 2018, which was a great accomplishment. However, OECD's energy intensity is still higher than the rest of the globe. For example, it is 1.5 times higher than that in High Income Countries (HIC). It is twice as high as high-medium-income countries (Li *et al.*, 2021).

OECD, as a developing nation, has not completed industrialization and urbanization. As shown in Fig. 1, there is a significant difference in economic development between OECD and HIC. According to earlier research, economic growth and energy intensity are related to various economic phases (e.g., Iqbal *et al.*, 2021). During the industrialization period, energy consumption has increased quickly to meet the requirement to build, urbanize and reorganize infrastructure, resulting in higher energy intensity (Ma and Stern, 2008). In the following stage, economic development will lead to progress in technologies and improve energy-saving materials and energy efficiency (Cornillie and Fankhauser, 2004). OECD's energy consumption must continue to rise and stay inflexible to accomplish its economic development goal. By 2020, the central government has established significant targets for a carbon peak by 2030 and carbon neutrality by 2060, showing that OECD would invest enormous money and effort to improve energy efficiency (Zeng *et al.*, 2014). It is fair to expect that energy intensity reduction and the improvement of efficiency in various

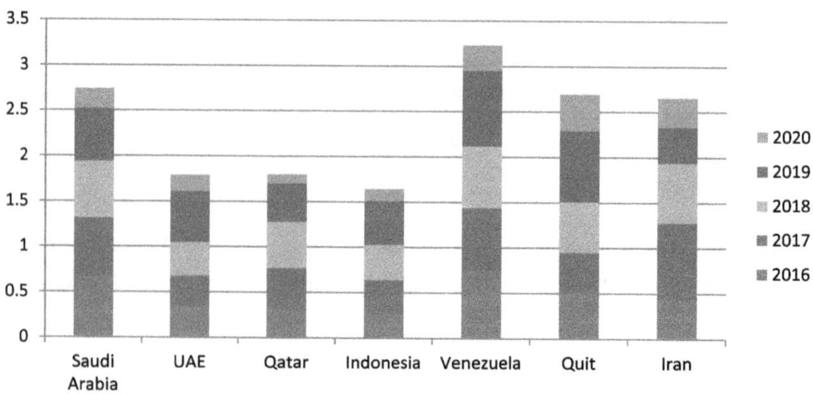

Figure 1. Carbon intensity of the countries during the sample period (2016–2020).

measures will continue to be significant issues for OECD (Feng *et al.*, 2009; Iqbal *et al.*, 2021a).

The causes of carbon intensity structural issues, technology spillover from international commerce, external direct investment and financial development, and non-economic variables must be recognized to balance economic growth and protection for the environment (Yang and Su, 2019). The connection between energy intensity and financial development is directly connected to this research (Canh *et al.*, 2020; Taghizadeh-Hesary *et al.*, 2021). Economic expansion and technological advancement in this study are two primary methods that affect energy intensity via financial development. However, the impact of these channels may be counter-intuitive and may result in conflicting empirical findings in prior research (Pan *et al.*, 2019). Therefore, more research is needed to link financial considerations with energy intensity to preserve energy security and the environment (Hussain *et al.*, 2020; Adom *et al.*, 2020).

Over the past decades, governments and the public sector have paid much attention to severe environmental issues. Many countries have passed different sustainable awareness legislations to minimize business carbon emissions and reduce the environmental effects of company operations (Aller *et al.*, 2018; Tran, 2021). In early 1997, the Kyoto Protocol created a carbon cap and emissions trading market for each nation to decrease carbon emissions efficiently. The United Kingdom developed this program to reduce its carbon emissions by 1.2 million tons per year by 2020. OECD has also taken many measures as one of the world's primary pollutants, and its Ministry of the Environment has warned companies that cannot upgrade and decrease emissions to achieve the objective of emission reduction (Zhang *et al.*, 2021a; Aydin and Onay, 2020). Under such tremendous environmental pressure, OECD firms have stepped up their output by investing in green technology, exacerbating its financial limitations. Enterprises with poor credit ratings and high default risk struggle to secure financing from conventional banks in developing nations. This may hinder and discourage these companies from addressing environmental or sustainability problems through a lack of financial means (Fathizadeh *et al.*, 2020; Tu and Rasoulinezhad, 2021).

To encourage green investment by businesses and deal with their financial challenges, banks have financed green loans worldwide (Jamalpuria, 2017; Shahbaz *et al.*, 2013a). The Green Climate Fund (GCF) is a type of green financial service for investment in projects and efforts for sustainable development that is targeted to encourage green investment in businesses. The distinctive feature of GCF is that it is subject to stringent emission restrictions or constraints. The objective of GCF is to assist enterprises to make green operational improvements and comply with environmental monitoring standards, which is a fundamental condition for a loan. It should be emphasized that GCF is quite different from the banking finance cap-and-trade system since it needs no significant funding (Ozturk and Acaravci, 2013). Typically, GCF is achieved via certain harsh environmental performance measure restrictions. An important green financial strategy is the investor portfolio decarburization in which businesses are funded within the restriction of their environmental impact. For instance, the funding and investment of BNP Paribas were linked to the Paris Carbon Agreement (Sadorsky, 2010; Faber *et al.*, 2010). If businesses fail to comply with their emission requirements, the bank stops the financing. For example, BNP Paribas backed Danone as long as Danone was able to provide its future carbon intensity target via clear documentation and align its actions with the Paris Agreement objectives. BNP Paribas Asset Management has also strengthened its green funding strategy for energy-producing businesses (Cao *et al.*, 2021; Dargahi and Khameneh, 2019).

Three contributions are made. This research highlights, first and foremost, the mechanism at the company level through which funding restrictions affect energy intensity, unlike most previous studies on macro-financial development (Shahbaz *et al.*, 2013b). The access of high-financial development nations to international financing may be a barrier. In our research, financial pressure is assessed by whether companies are given loans as an indication of the difficulty in obtaining external financing from financial institutions such as banks (Shah *et al.*, 2020). Our empirical study will thus overcome the consistent effect on all financial development companies. Second, our study incorporates factors of technological investment and environmental regulation in the determination of the technical channel via which financial limitations influence energy intensity.

Financial development refers to access to finance and money in a nation or region (Huang *et al.*, 2017). A mature funding system may minimize R&D investment risks and promote investments in eco-friendly and energy-saving technologies or projects. However, financial growth may also lead to more output and consumption (Bashir *et al.*, 2021), thus increasing the usage of energy (Li *et al.*, 2021b). The conflicting impacts of financial development on energy intensity may explain past research studies with inconsistent results. Huang and Chen (2020) identified the channel that uses the term mediating effect, where the nation's total productivity factor level is used as a measure of technological development. In contrast, we utilize the R&D indicator at the company level; see Table 1 for detailed literary support. We also include environmental control in our empirical model, which may differ between the impact of technological development and other channels (Chen *et al.*, 2019).

This research utilizes the Green Financial Development Index to empirically examine the connection between green finance (GF), nonfossil energy use and carbon intensity in OECD between 2016 and 2020. The study uses the concept to assess in three different ways. First, financial development rather than GF was the main emphasis of previous research, with few investigations examining the links between green financing and carbon intensity. With green funding rapidly increasing in recent decades and OECD becoming the world's biggest carbon producer, this research investigated the link between GF and carbon intensity and analyzed the third principal energy variable, which is nonfossil energy consumption. Second, this research developed a GF Index based on government data, the first time that such an effort has been undertaken to the best of our knowledge. The data envelopment analysis (DEA) provides extra

Table 1. Main studies related to this study.

Source	Title of study	Findings
Ren *et al.* (2020)	Nexus between green finance, nonfossil energy use, and carbon intensity: Empirical evidence from OECD based on a vector error correction model	The study findings revealed a significant role of green financing on carbon intensity. This effect is also significant on energy consumption and nonfossil fuel energy use
Ionescu (2021)	Leveraging green finance for low-carbon energy, sustainable economic development, and climate change mitigation during the COVID-19 pandemic	The study explained that green financing has significant nexus with climate change mitigation and lowers the carbon-based energy pollution emission under COVID-19 crises
Nawaz *et al.* (2021)	Nexus between green finance and climate change mitigation in N-11 and BRICS countries: Empirical estimation through difference in differences (DID) approach	The study highlighted that green financing has an immense role in climate change mitigation in N-11 and BRICS economies. Moreover, the study warranted to test the connection between GF and carbon intensity
Muganyi *et al.* (2021)	Green finance, fintech and environmental protection: Evidence from OECD	The study extended the debate with this topicality and elaborated that green financing and fintech has are significant predictors of climate protection that manage carbon intensity
Khan *et al.* (2021)	Does green finance really deliver what is expected? An empirical perspective	The study found that GF is significant for climate-related indicators and suggested estimating the relationship with carbon intensity

benefits in the identification of causal links in addition to analyzing long-term balance links.

2. Literature Review

Many studies have investigated the connection between financial growth and CO_2 emissions. While various techniques have been utilized, empirical analysis has been done in the OECD, Kuwait, Malaysia, mid-income nations, mid-income countries, high-income economies, and Southern Asian economies (Mengistu and Adhikary, 2011). However, these effects were shown by other case studies. A total of 46 sub-Saharan African nations, for example, discovered financial growth from 2000 to 2015 that would boost carbon emissions. Similarly, a case study in Turkey has shown that financial growth significantly increases CO_2 emissions, second only to economic growth and urban development (Shahbaz *et al.*, 2015). A similar scenario was discovered in 24 countries in the Middle East and North Africa (MENA), where financial indicators (e.g., percentage of domestic private sector credit assessed by real gross domestic product (GDP)) have not been acknowledged (Wu *et al.*, 2016).

In addition, there must exist preconditions for a significant connection between financial expansion and CO_2 emissions (Ulucak and Khan, 2020; Tu *et al.*, 2020). Financial variables only serve to mitigate emissions to medium-sized economies such as the OECD in high-level liberalization and financial-sector growth periods, which have less effect on carbon mitigation than other per-capita income output indicators, indicating a pressing policy. Various financial variables have different impacts on CO_2 emissions due to the variety of definitions of financial development (Andersson and Karpestam, 2013). A comprehensive study by the OECD Panel indicates that the financial development size and market value of the listed companies are variables that reduce CO_2 emissions, while financial development efficiency and stock volume play a significant role in avoiding carbon mitigation (Dar and Asif, 2017). Similar results were also obtained from another research in examining the impact on CO_2 traded emissions of financial development: expansion in the financial scale showed an increase in emissions while financial efficiency and financing reduced emissions of traded goods and services (Dogan and Seker, 2016).

CO_2 emission drivers were found to be associated with financial concerns (Zhang, 2011). The effect of CO_2 emissions on financial development is minimal compared to renewable energy use (Abbasi and Riaz, 2016). It has been shown, for instance, that renewables use in the MENA area may reduce CO_2 emissions effectively, but financial growth has no major impact. In addition, financial considerations have shown that financial developments in MENA nations may contribute to a worsening of environmental quality by decreasing the usage of renewable energy. This requires a favorable financial resource deployment in the MENA area (Haseeb *et al.*, 2018). Empirically, an important impact of financial development is also shown in the reduction of carbon intensity and energy consumption intensity. For instance, financial developments in the local OECD areas have shown that carbon intensity (measured by carbon dioxide emissions per GDP unit) is rising, while carbon intensity in neighboring provinces has decreased substantially, with global effects reducing carbon intensity (Riti *et al.*, 2017).

Contrary to this optimistic outcome, Fang *et al.* (2020) suggested that OECD's financial scale, both in the short term and long term, is positively correlated with carbon intensity, which increases carbon emissions; the authors argued that continued financial development needs to be promoted in OECD to seek ways to reduce CO_2 emissions (Iqbal and Bilal, 2021b; Huang *et al.*, 2021; Zhang *et al.*, 2021; Sun *et al.*, 2022; Ahmad *et al.*, 2021). The reasons may be because this research utilizes different financial variables definitions while the data formats and techniques used vary. Fang *et al.* (2020) utilized the deposit-to-GDP ratio as financial development, whereas Liu and Song (2020) used the loan-to-GDP ratio of financial institutions. Fang *et al.* (2020) also utilized a distributed lag approach to create an autoregressive error correction model using time series data while building a spatial econometrics data panel set (Lu, 2018).

Another study utilized carbon limitations as a profit mechanism, i.e., to cut the anticipated profit if the emissions of the business exceeded the limit (Lo, 2016).

A cap-and-trade system, for example, assesses operational choices in a two-tier supply chain. Two system coordination contracts have been examined, and the two-part tariff contracts have resulted in lower carbon emissions and higher profitability (Jin and Kim, 2018). This is also examined under a cap-and-trade system and shows that the business only supports capacity growth when its investment capacity is relatively cheap and that a marginal profit is high enough (Jiang *et al.*, 2021). The issue of production and price has been explored by means of a cap-and-trade system where the manufacturer makes two products and sells them to one single monopoly dealer (Brown and Corbera, 2003). Unlike predictions, scientists have discovered that the output amount dropped below the carbon limit under some circumstances (Dhakal, 2010). Under the cap-and-trade law, a low-carbon supply chain comprising of a manufacturer and two rival stores has invested in green technology (Ebeling and Yasué, 2008). The authors observed that carbon emissions were lower than decentralized under the centralized system. As stated above, the aforementioned research has taken a greater account of carbon limit operational alternatives, but it has not considered potential capital restrictions in supply chains (Umar *et al.*, 2021).

In recent years, many studies have started to focus on the effect of green loans on decision-making and corporate governance (Boutabba, 2014). Some studies, for example, analyze the impact on business and societal welfare of green loans and government aid (Shen *et al.*, 2021; Saud *et al.*, 2019). Green credit resembles a company subsidy bank. This literature group aims to assess the appropriate circumstances for various incentive methods and offers references to the government's development and implementation of subsidy programs (Godil *et al.*, 2021). There is also some research on the effect of green loans on the efforts of firms to decrease pollution (2020). The following study analyzes the effect of green loans on deterministic demand for companies (Ibrahiem, 2020). In contrast, this essay analyzes the effect of corporate finance choices on random demand fluctuations and focuses on choosing various kinds of funding from the corporate viewpoint (Salahuddin *et al.*, 2015). Some articles investigate the requested green credit. In contrast, our study takes the green credit entry barrier into consideration, i.e., the restricted green credit limit (Jalil and Feridun, 2011; Anser *et al.*, 2020).

3. Methodology

3.1. *Theoretical background*

Income growth, industrialization, and social reform have all advanced significantly in OECD during the last few decades. As a result, environmental damage and resource overuse have grown more significant. Carbon dioxide (CO_2) emissions in OECD climbed from 1455 million tonnes (Mt) in 1978 to 9839 Mt in 2017, as per statistics provided by the Intergovernmental Panel on climate change Atlas. OECD has been the world's foremost generator of dioxide since 2006, surpassing the United States. Even though OECD's carbon intensity has declined in recent years, it remains substantially greater than other nations' carbon emissions per unit of GDP. For instance, OECD's carbon intensity in 2010 was 1.79 kg/USD, which was 11 times more than France's carbon intensity of 0.16 kg/USD at that time (Anh Tu *et al.*, 2021). As a result, green financing is a logical path for OECD to take (Li *et al.*, 2021a). To sum it up, GF's primary goal is to offer financial support for environmentally friendly initiatives via investments, financing, operational money, and other sources of capital.

The "Equator Principles" were signed by the world's top 10 banks on June 4, 2003, in London. These cooperative guidelines are intended to solve financial concerns that have a negative impact on the environment or society as a whole. Since the adoption of GF rules by the OECD government in 2015, OECD's green financial system has been steadily improving. In Table 1, these policies and their consequences are laid forth. In 2018, countries accounted for 18% of worldwide issuance of GF bonds that fulfill regulations, making it the world's second-biggest supplier of these assets behind the United States. As the chart shows, securities are a major source of funding for green investment green credit granted by 21 major OECD banks totaled 8.29 trillion yuan in 2017 alone. With 6.2 billion yuan in sales volume at the end of 2018, the overall primary and secondary spot market transaction volume for the national carbon trading pilot period was 282 Mt.

3.2. *Data sources*

This research seeks to determine how green funding spins off carbon intensity in the COVID-19 crisis period and what impacts shift carbon intensity the greatest. The Worldwide Input–Production Database (WIOD) collects carbon emission, manufacturing net production and combustion statistics for power consumption (WIOD, 2019). The data set provided includes industrial data by 2020. In addition, between 2000 and 2016, this may reveal carbon emissions both before and after the financial crisis. This research thus examines the variations in carbon intensity from 2016 to 2020. In order to prevent inflation, the gross economic production in 2010 has been reduced to the norm. Including these, World Bank Indicator database and OECD database were also used for data collection.

3.3. *Carbon intensity and green financing measures*

We use the following measures to compute the carbon intensity:

$$\mathrm{CI} = \sum_{1} \frac{C_I}{E_i} * \frac{E_i}{O_i} * \frac{O_i}{O}, \tag{1}$$

$$D_{\mathrm{CET}}{}^{t+1} = \mathrm{EXP}\left(\sum_{i=1}^{N} Wj^{S-V} \ln \frac{\mathrm{CE}_I^{t+1}}{\mathrm{CE}_I^{T+1}} \right), \tag{2}$$

$$D_{\mathrm{EIT}}{}^{t+1} = \mathrm{EXP}\left(\sum_{i=1}^{N} Wj^{S-V} \ln \frac{\mathrm{EI}_I^{t+1}}{\mathrm{EI}_I^{T+1}} \right), \tag{3}$$

$$D_{\mathrm{OST}}{}^{t+1} = \mathrm{EXP}\left(\sum_{i=1}^{N} Wj^{S-V} \ln \frac{\mathrm{OS}_I^{t+1}}{\mathrm{OS}_I^{T+1}}\right). \tag{4}$$

In Eq. (2), it is indicated that CE_i shows the carbon emission ratio and the factor i indicates the net consumption of energy resources in a certain period of time t with per unit economic outlay of an i economy or a country. The OS_i further indicate the net economic outlay ratio of the energy industry in an i energy-economic system. Using such indicators and their measures, a multi-dimensional logarithmic mean Divisia index (LMDI) term structure for international carbon intensity is disclosed and applied in this study. Time-wise, the base year is highlighted as t and the mark or goal fiscal year is shown as $t+1$ as indicated in the study equations (see Eq. (3)).

$$D_{\mathrm{CE}}^{0,T} = \sum_{t=1}^{T} D_{\mathrm{CE}t}{}^{t+1}, \tag{5}$$

$$D_{\mathrm{EI}}^{0,T} = \sum_{t=1}^{T} D_{\mathrm{EI}t}{}^{t+1}, \tag{6}$$

$$D_{\mathrm{OI}}^{0,T} = \sum_{t=1}^{T} D_{\mathrm{OI}t}{}^{t+1}. \tag{7}$$

On the basis of Eqs. (2)–(4), this study constructs the single-time breakdown analysis to assess the influence of green financing on carbon intensity year-wise. Extending to this, it uses the entire sample period of the study (e.g., 2016–2020), where the study also used multi-time decomposition analysis, which is a pivotal and complementary portion of this research to show the desired estimation role among the constructs. Thus, for multi-period analysis, the following equations were used to compute and estimate the subject matter as conceptualized above.

For carbon intensity computation, using Eqs. (5)–(7), the LMDI breakdown method is further applied, which is calculated as follows:

$$\mathrm{CI} = \sum_{1} \frac{C_I}{E_i} * \frac{E_i}{O_i} = \mathrm{CE}_i * \mathrm{EI}_i, \tag{8}$$

$$\Delta\mathrm{CI}_i = \mathrm{CI}_i^{t+1} - \mathrm{CI}_i^t = \Delta\mathrm{CI}_i^{\mathrm{CE}(t+1)} + \mathrm{CI}_i^{\mathrm{CE}(t)}, \tag{9}$$

$$\Delta\mathrm{CI}_i^{\mathrm{CE}} = \sum_{i}^{t} (\mathrm{CI}_t^{t+1} \cdot \mathrm{CI}_i^t) \ln\left(\frac{\mathrm{CI}_t^{t+1}}{\mathrm{CI}_i^t}\right), \tag{10}$$

$$\Delta\mathrm{CI}_i^{\mathrm{CE}} = \sum_{i}^{t} (\mathrm{CI}_t^{t+1} \cdot \mathrm{CI}_i^t) \ln\left(\frac{\mathrm{EI}_t^{t+1}}{\mathrm{EI}_i^t}\right), \tag{11}$$

$$\Delta\mathrm{CI}_i^{\mathrm{CE}} = \sum_{i}^{t} (\mathrm{CI}_t^{t+1} \cdot \mathrm{CI}_i^t) \ln\left(\frac{\mathrm{OS}_t^{t+1}}{\mathrm{OI}_i^t}\right). \tag{12}$$

A study of worldwide CO_2 emissions breakdown allows us to determine the main causes of changes in carbon intensity. There are nevertheless large variations across sectors in terms of emissions of carbon, economic development, etc. Therefore, important causes of variations in industry total emissions must be further investigated. The LMDI techniques of additive deconstruction are coupled (see Eqs. (9)–(15), respectively).

OECD nations' green financing plans involve a number of follow-up efforts to guarantee that fixed goals are fulfilled. A sub-differential model (SDID) was used to evaluate our main assumption. SDID is ideally suited to evaluate nonexploratory panel information driven treatment effects with many rounds of policy actions. The average treatment effect (ATT) may be expressed for OECD countries

$$\text{ATT} \equiv (Y1_{t\_}Y0_t \,|\, dt = 1), \tag{13}$$

$$E = \left[\frac{Y_t - Y_z}{P(d_t = 1)} * \frac{d_{t-\pi(x_t)}}{1 - \pi(x_t)}\right], \tag{14}$$

$$P(d_t = 1) > 0 \text{ and } \pi(x_t) < 1. \tag{15}$$

ATT indicates the ecological variance after GF connected rules are included in the outcome at time t and $Y0_t$ signifies the identical capricious, formerly the conduct effect, and dt expresses whether a city espoused a GF linked procedure at time t.

3.4. *Empirical estimation method*

Decision-making unit (DMU) performance is assessed nonparametrically (DMU). This is done by utilizing the Chames, Cooper and Rhodes (CCR) model of Data Envlopment Analysis (DEA). In this part, we will utilize the indicators (inputs, desired outputs, unwanted outputs) (inputs, desirable outputs, undesirable outputs) in Fig. 1. According to the main goal and data availability, such a technique for estimation is considered for the application to deduct the results. Briefly stated, we utilized two models: Model (1), which utilizes divergent configurations to quantify various input and outputs for CO_2 intensity; and Model (2), which uses Eqs. (13)–(15) to assess GF input (Anh Tu *et al.*, 2021). We also considered ranking nations based on their efficacy (Iqbal *et al.*, 2021b). The advantages of this method include (i) among its many advantages is the method's flexibility in handling a wide range of inputs and outputs, and (ii) efficiency may be increased or decreased by taking returns into account while calculating it, which makes it an advantageous tool.

4. Results and Discussion

4.1. *Empirical results*

Many governments have already considered post-pandemic economic growth plans with trillions of dollars in economic incentives. Massive economic programs will also boost carbon emissions. Due to the financial crisis in 2008, several nations have

Table 2. Descriptive statistics.

Unit	Green financing	Carbon intensity	Energy consumption	GDP
Min	27.92	20.76	44.81	32.18
Max	278.4	319.2	701.6	573.5
Kurt	11.14	5.89	2.19	1.893
SD	579.86	50.51	21.78	45.78
Mean	444.23	129.8	752.5	211.7
Variance	3.91	1.22	4.29	0.179

sought restoration. The government spending introduced excessive ease by boosting the availability of money or equity capital that is highly available, sometimes as a credit (Zhang *et al.*, 2021b). In particular, emerging nations such as OECD have devoted attention to budgetary policies (Weber *et al.*, 2008). The onset of the credit collapse has impacted OECD's product exports severely. As a result, OECD has shifted to consumer spending via higher tax rebates and reduced buying taxes. These measures have made the rebuilding industry a focus while taking less care of energy usage and carbon emissions. Developed nations have been quick to withstand the financial crisis. Initially, to address the economic meltdown, the American Government implemented a targeted monetary and fiscal policy as well as unconventional measures to interfere in the financial market. It also adopted a financial strategy to cut taxes to support the overall economy.

The following measures have encouraged economic development and partially alleviated the banking crisis. Economic growth after extreme events is in particular linked to energy use and carbon emissions, which in addition has an effect on carbon intensity. Indeed, the recovery in carbon dioxide emissions concerns both researchers and policymakers. The successful research on the breakdown of the rebounding post-COVID greenhouse gases has shown that the fast rise in total emissions has significantly affected global leadership rebound after 2008.

Table 2 tabulates the findings with the minimum value of GF as 27.92, carbon intensity with 20.76, energy consumption with 44.81 and GDP with 32.18. The maximum value of GF is 9845.11, carbon intensity as 2013.7, energy consumption as 200.80, and GDP as 6667.0. Similarly, the lowest standard deviation (SD) value holds the GDP with 45.87 and the highest value belongs to green financing with 579.86. The variance of the green financing with 3.91, carbon intensity has 1.22, energy consumption with 4.29, and GDP with 0.179.

Table 2 shows a specific collection of facts in a simple manner by using data sets. The chart illustrates how the signal values, including the lowest, highest, bias, standard error, average and variation, were displayed for the benefit of the viewers. The results show a comparable study consisting of several distinct indicators that are merged to create a single index. The scale is intended to record complex concepts that cannot be

Table 3. Carbon intensity.

	2016	2017	2018	2019	2020
Saudi Arabia	0.68	0.64	0.62	0.58	0.22
UAE	0.34	0.34	0.37	0.56	0.18
Qatar	0.31	0.46	0.51	0.42	0.10
Indonesia	0.27	0.37	0.39	0.48	0.13
Venezuela	0.76	0.68	0.68	0.83	0.28
Kuwait	0.51	0.44	0.56	0.78	0.40
Iran	0.44	0.84	0.66	0.39	0.32

evaluated with a simple signal. In order to create an efficient price measure, the ranking generation technique must be open to the public so that future investigations can replicate, modify and critique the measurement. On the basis of the application of specific criteria, a relevant compound signal must be created. By examining the data, the power efficiency and environmental problems may be clearly described. With the use of these indicators, researchers and decision-makers will be able to examine and understand trends and situations in Asia Pacific countries and the impact of nation electro-reforms. Secondary industries have “more energy and less pollution” from a combination of secondary and tertiary sectors. The result is less energy consumption and much less environmental damage.

Table 3 shows that OECD countries, such as Saudi Arabia, Qatar, and Indonesia, are fully aware of their capacity to implement electricity measures effectively. In comparison, however, many countries inhabit the lowest power locations in the main data set; other states have worse energy efficiencies between places. Such results are interesting and extremely helpful to nations like South Asia, who want to pursue more responsible types of energy efficiency in the future. With respect to the above-mentioned energy efficiency, a small minority of countries were called upon to implement such reforms and to monitor them diligently to ensure compliance. Under this hypothesis, these nations took significant measures linked to the reform of the power sector and constantly monitored the implications of energy efficiency changes, which are exemplary of countries like Qatar and Iran. Many countries have taken steps to deregulate the entire energy sector. Generally, countries that follow the phases but do not retain their efficiency ratings see changes in their overall performance. The major results on the execution of the electricity reformation and protracted security correspond to prior research on the subject (Lee *et al.*, 2021a). Figure 1 indicates that, except for Indonesia and Venezuela, energy efficiency has improved throughout the sample period. The worldwide fuel efficiency is constant with generally equal energy methods.

Financial stability policy has a major role to play in lending to companies and state firms in regions where financial ecosystems are less established. OECD is a leader in sustainable credit risk management globally. Technology and existing relationships

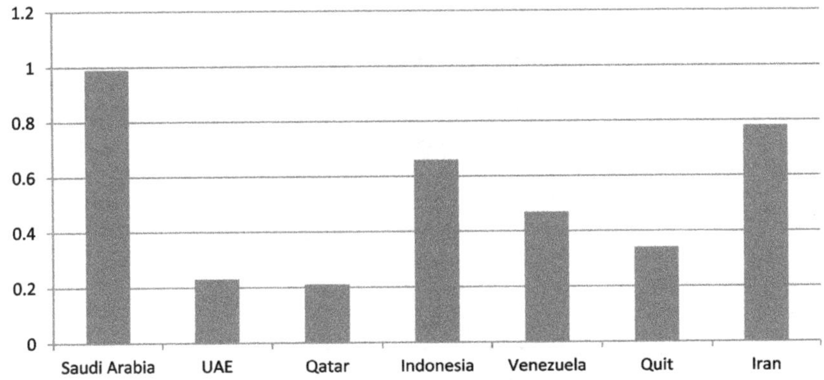

Figure 2. Overall green financing score.

between banks and businesses must be used in GF strategies. Green funding schemes based on strict carbon emission regulations can offer a win–win scenario for manufacturers and suppliers. GF strategies can benefit the manufacturing sector (see Table 4). The positive link between GF and innovation in companies is further shown. We can conclude that GF may play a key role in OECD's industrial transformation in a smart and sustainable way (see Fig. 2). Green bond inspection on the global capital markets helps to build a more dynamic ecosystem of sustainable banking in OECD.

Financial stability initiatives are effective depending on the extent of economic development in most emerging nations, including OECD. Developed regions are more highly impacted by green financing activities. GF is essential for sustainable and clean manufacturing in the economy. By enhancing the integrity of GF systems, governments can achieve sustainable development. Green funding methods need collaboration across all parties involved, which is not always the case, to improve productivity and guarantee sustainability. Similarly, recent research explained the coherent findings from the OECD context.

Table 4. Green financing score and carbon intensity nexus.

Countries	Green financing score
Saudi Arabia	0.99
UAE	0.23
Qatar	0.21
Indonesia	0.66
Venezuela	0.47
Kuwait	0.34
Iran	0.78

Table 5. Sensitivity analysis.

No.	DMU	Score
1	Saudi Arabia	0.44
2	UAE	0.68
3	Qatar	0.38
4	Indonesia	0.22
5	Venezuela	0.84
6	Kuwait	0.45
7	Iran	0.84

4.2. *Sensitivity analysis*

The study performed a sensitivity search to determine how steady clean energy uses a new data set of 15% variance (see Table 5). Policy signals that can be issued due to incorrect design or misunderstanding of full input collections. The data in Table 4 shows that the input variables affect total efficiency enormously. Table 4 shows results that are extremely close to the original efficiency value calculated from the original data set, suggesting that our results are highly strong and stable.

The DEA employs the comparative efficiency score to evaluate the efficiency of a stock. At the same time, the limitations need not be defined in advance because they may perform both input and output analyses at the same time. The DEA offers a framework that will help users choose metrics and DEA model features. DEA is a powerful performance evaluation and benchmark tool for systems in which the Decision Making Units "(DMU)" is the exact act for the creation of products or services based upon convex (and even linear) technologies that may be used to analyze a cost function in live time.

4.3. *Discussion*

As stated in the theoretical premise, the effects of trade opening on carbon intensity. This research thus classifies 104 countries into three income categories: high income, high medium incomes, and poor households, based on the classification criteria from the World Bank. In various nation groupings, we examined the link between productivity growth and carbon intensity individually. The findings are shown in Table 4 and Fig. 2. First, the thresholds effects of various income levels, and the double test the limits of the OECD economies got that the linear impact of trade opening affects the carbon intensity of different income categories. In this research, the primary expression is that the coefficient in the high-income group is positive and indicates that trade openness in these countries leads to a decrease in carbon intensity.

In comparison, the coefficient is positive for the second category, indicating that trade openness adds to carbon intensity. The regression coefficient for the low-income group, the technical progress and austerity brought about by trade developments make the reduction of carbon emissions simpler. Furthermore, compared to the lower-middle-income category, the other two income brackets have a much more substantial effect on trade openness carbon dioxide emissions, as also indicated in the findings. As stated in the theoretical hypothesis, the economic phase of the nation is influenced by the impact of trade openness on carbon intensity. This research thus classifies the OECD nations into three income categories: high income, high medium incomes and low-middle income groups, based on the categorization criteria from the World Bank. In various nation groupings, we examined the link between trade openness and carbon intensity individually. The findings are shown in Table 4 and Fig. 3.

First, various income groups have the cutoff points and the three countries have a double threshold impact, showing that the nonlinear impact of trade openness affects the carbon intensity of different income categories. In this research, the primary expression is that the coefficient in the high-income group is negative and indicates that international trade in these countries leads to a decrease in carbon intensity. In contrast, the coefficient is positive for the middle-income group, indicating that international trade adds to carbon intensity. The coefficient is negative for the low-income group, and the technical progress and structural adjustment brought about by trade developments make the reduction of carbon emissions simpler. Furthermore, compared to the lower-middle-income group, the other two income groups have a more substantial effect on trade openness carbon dioxide emissions, as also indicated in the findings.

International trade has a larger effect on carbon concentration as a threshold variable under the influence of foreign direct investment. GDP holds a significant influence on the effect on the carbon intensity of free trade. We examine two major causes for this. In the first place, the economic scale continues to grow with the development of international commerce, particularly in less developed nations. Although it has actively promoted international commerce and economic growth, it has also led to excessive natural resource use and to continued environmental degradation such as increasing emissions. In addition, the worldwide labor division is improved and international economic cooperation is common in the framework of global economic integration. When nations compete internationally, they make effective use of their own resources and advantages to progressively alter their industrial structure. GDP encourages a shift from the developed to less-developed nations of smog sectors, leading to increased emissions of carbon from OECD countries.

The coal penalty implies that an abundance of coal and oil will be linked to more intense emissions growth. Studied 41 nations and demonstrate that those with the highest CO_2 economy are also consistently wealthy in coal, oil or natural gas, as assessed by carbon dioxide emissions per unit of GDP. The carbon curse is thus a specific version of the "brain drain", a well-studied notion that links resource wealth to the negative social, political and economic consequences. The coal curse expands it via total emissions to include negative environmental consequences. Friedrichs and Inderwildi (2013) suggested four fundamental processes which make it difficult for countries that are wealthy in fossil fuels to escape the carbon curse and offer prime evidence. First, extractive pollutants, particularly from oil and gas, from the energy-intense nature of the production of fossil energy. Second, energy congestion in the energy mix and industrial profile of nations. With respect to energy, the availability of cheaper high carbon fossil fuels will tend to push out the home electricity production of lower emissions resources. For businesses, petroleum and gas wealth may generate a Netherlands disease or other resource curses which impede industrial development. This would limit the concentration of the emissions. Simultaneously, if prevented, a competitive edge would be available for energy-intensive sectors that utilize fossil fuels immediately to increase carbon concentrations. Third, owing to their relative shortage of energy, fuel-rich nations will have less incentive to invest in renewable energy. Lastly, countries that are wealthy in fossil fuels (especially the oil-rich ones) are expected to face increasing public pressure to give consumer incentives to promote wasteful use of energy. These factors interact in various ways, depending on a particular resource profile, to make it extremely difficult for those wealthy with fossil energy to escape a dioxide design process. Yet, it is not impossible: a tiny number of outliers like Qatar, while fuel-rich, have achieved low-carbon intensity development.

5. Conclusion and Policy Implications

In recent years, OECD's energy needs have been met by fossil fuels that emit a large amount of CO_2. In general, OECD's energy association and regulatory authorities have done little to manage sustainable energy. Our study was one of the first to demonstrate how to improve energy sustainability by reducing carbon emissions and energy usage. As a result of the COVID-19 outbreak, energy consumption may be reduced by using creative and advanced technology to replace fossil fuels with renewable and/or green energy sources. Carbon emissions are significantly reduced by using renewable and green energy sources. The COVID-19 pandemic has shown the structural impact of current energy consumption and carbon emission research. COVID-19 has a negative impact on energy consumption and carbon emissions. The study's hypothesis coefficient alpha of growth regression shows the findings. In essence, the pandemic has reduced energy use and carbon emissions. COVID-19 has extended the lockdown and isolated the whole world. This decreased the power consumption load, resulting in substantial reductions in energy consumption and carbon emissions. No energy player can be convinced, and this is the intrinsic attitude of energy usage. OECD's primary energy sources are oil and fossil fuels, which account for the majority of energy production and consumption.

As previously predicted, this type of energy will be prohibited in the future. Alternative energy sources must be explored and planned to stabilize energy consumption and reduce pollution. COVID-19 may be an opportunity to reorganize OECD's energy business as energy usage and the commercial sector drop. We agree with the results as a model that is country-specific but warn that energy consumption fluctuation and the COVID-19 pandemic may affect comparability. Many policy efforts have been supported by our research. Following OECD's price game and energy consumption, the reaction to the COVID-19 oil price breakout and decreased oil requirements should be managed.

COVID-19 is projected to continue to result in major shocks, such as extended health crises, simultaneous drops in oil prices, and decreased energy income as a result. We suggest for energy regulators create contingency measures to improve operational effectiveness during and after COVID-19 in order to meet the threshold level for energy usage. When the limit is reached, renewable energy sources must take over. With COVID-19, we think the energy sector can revitalize, rebuild, and reconfigure energy consumption patterns.

During COVID-19, we also saw some harsh truths in OECD's energy sector. On the one hand, a lack of emphasis on reducing energy use, oil costs, and income shortages have been questioned. Second, OECD's energy regulators need to be more innovative and active. None of these regulatory agencies have a COVID-19 action plan. In implying that regulatory agencies are like sleeping rabbits, if they do not wake up in time, energy chaos is likely to ensue.

To extend the debate on this study's topicality, we suggest some future research directions to investigate. We suggest testing the role of economic stability of OECD countries on climate risks and climate change mitigation to encounter carbon intensity. Moreover, identifying the role of fiscal gaps on carbon intensity and climate change mitigation can uncover more novel insights. Extending to it, studying green productivity acquisition and its impact on CO_2 emission mitigation through green fiscal policies can also contribute to the academic literature and industry practice.

Acknowledgment

Dr. Lu's research is supported by the Social Science Foundation of Hebei Province of China with HB17YJ069 "strategies on vegetable cold-chain logistics in Hebei Province from the perspective of institutional change".

References

Abbasi, F and K Riaz (2016). CO_2 emissions and financial development in an emerging economy: An augmented VAR approach. *Energy Policy*, 90, 102–114.

Adom, PK, MO Appiah and MP Agradi (2020). Does financial development lower energy intensity? *Frontiers in Energy*, 14(3), 620–634.

Ahmad, B, S Iqbal, M Hai and S Latif (2021). The interplay of personal values, relational mobile usage and organizational citizenship behavior. *Interactive Technology and Smart Education*.

Alemzero, DA, N Iqbal, S Iqbal, M Mohsin, NJ Chukwuma and BA Shah (2021). Assessing the perceived impact of exploration and production of hydrocarbons on households perspective of environmental regulation in Ghana. *Environmental Science and Pollution Research*, 28(5), 5359–5371.

Aller, C, MJ Herrerias and J Ordóñez (2018). The effect of financial development on energy intensity in OECD. *The Energy Journal*, 39(Special Issue 1), 25–38.

Andersson, FN and P Karpestam (2013). CO_2 emissions and economic activity: Short-and long-run economic determinants of scale, energy intensity and carbon intensity. *Energy Policy*, 61, 1285–1294.

Anh Tu, C, F Chien, MA Hussein, Y Ramli MM, MSS Psi MM, S Iqbal and AR Bilal (2021). Estimating role of green financing on energy security, economic and environmental integration of BRI member countries. *The Singapore Economic Review*.

Anser, MK, Z Yousaf, K Zaman, AA Nassani, SM Alotaibi, H Jambari, A Khan and A Kabbani (2020). Determination of resource curse hypothesis in mediation of financial development and clean energy sources: Go-for-green resource policies. *Resources Policy*, 66, 101640.

Aydin, C and RD Onay (2020). Does energy intensity affect the relationship between financial development and environmental pollution? *BRAIN. Broad Research in Artificial Intelligence and Neuroscience*, 11(1), 144–156.

Bashir, MF, MA Benjiang, M Shahbaz, U Shahzad and XV Vo (2021). Unveiling the heterogeneous impacts of environmental taxes on energy consumption and energy intensity: Empirical evidence from OECD countries. *Energy*, 226, 120366.

Behera, S and SR Behera (2018). District-wise comparative study of banking penetration and financial inclusion in Odisha. *Emerging Economy Studies*, 4(2), 129–146.

Boutabba, MA (2014). The impact of financial development, income, energy and trade on carbon emissions: Evidence from the Indian economy. *Economic Modelling*, 40, 33–41.

Brown, K and E Corbera (2003). A multi-criteria assessment framework for carbon-mitigation projects: Putting 'development' in the centre of decision-making. Tyndall Centre for Climate Change Research Working Paper 29.

Canh, NP, SD Thanh and MA Nasir (2020). Nexus between financial development & energy intensity: Two sides of a coin? *Journal of Environmental Management*, 270, 110902.

Cao, S, L Nie, H Sun, W Sun and F Taghizadeh-Hesary (2021). Digital finance, green technological innovation and energy-environmental performance: Evidence from OECD's regional economies. *Journal of Cleaner Production*, 327, 129458.

Chen, C, J Huang, H Chang and H Lei (2019). The effects of indigenous R&D activities on OECD's energy intensity: A regional perspective. *Science of the Total Environment*, 689, 1066–1078.

Cornillie, J and S Fankhauser (2004). The energy intensity of transition countries. *Energy Economics*, 26(3), 283–295.

Dar, JA and M Asif (2017). Is financial development good for carbon mitigation in India? A regime shift-based cointegration analysis. *Carbon Management*, 8(5–6), 435–443.

Dargahi, H and KB Khameneh (2019). Energy intensity determinants in an energy-exporting developing economy: Case of Iran. *Energy*, 168, 1031–1044.

Dhakal, S (2010). GHG emissions from urbanization and opportunities for urban carbon mitigation. *Current Opinion in Environmental Sustainability*, 2(4), 277–283.

Dogan, E and F Seker (2016). The influence of real output, renewable and non-renewable energy, trade and financial development on carbon emissions in the top renewable energy countries. *Renewable and Sustainable Energy Reviews*, 60, 1074–1085.

Ebeling, J and M Yasué (2008). Generating carbon finance through avoided deforestation and its potential to create climatic, conservation and human development benefits. *Philosophical Transactions of the Royal Society B: Biological Sciences*, 363(1498), 1917–1924.

Faber, N, R Jorna and JO Van Engelen (2010). The sustainability of "sustainability" — A study into the conceptual foundations of the notion of "sustainability". In *Tools, Techniques and*

Approaches for Sustainability: Collected Writings in Environmental Assessment Policy and Management, pp. 337–369. Singapore: World Scientific.

Fang, J, G Gozgor, MK Mahalik, H Padhan and R Xu (2021). The impact of economic complexity on energy demand in OECD countries. *Environmental Science and Pollution Research*, 28(26), 33771–33780.

Fathizadeh, H, M Nonejad, A Haghighat and A Aminifard (2020). The relationship between economic growth, energy intensity and financial development in sectors of Iranian economy. *Quarterly Journal of Economic Growth and Development Research*, 10(40), 76–55.

Feng, T, L Sun and Y Zhang (2009). The relationship between energy consumption structure, economic structure and energy intensity in OECD. *Energy Policy*, 37(12), 5475–5483.

Godil, DI, P Ahmad, MS Ashraf, S Sarwat, A Sharif, S Shabib-ul-Hasan and K Jermsittiparsert (2021). The step towards environmental mitigation in Pakistan: Do transportation services, urbanization, and financial development matter? *Environmental Science and Pollution Research*, 28(17), 21486–21498.

Haseeb, A, E Xia, MA Baloch and K Abbas (2018). Financial development, globalization, and CO_2 emission in the presence of EKC: Evidence from BRICS countries. *Environmental Science and Pollution Research*, 25(31), 31283–31296.

Huang, J and X Chen (2020). Domestic R&D activities, technology absorption ability, and energy intensity in OECD. *Energy Policy*, 138, 111184.

Huang, J, D Du and Q Tao (2017). An analysis of technological factors and energy intensity in OECD. *Energy Policy*, 109, 1–9.

Huang, J, X Wang, H Liu and S Iqbal (2021). Financial consideration of energy and environmental nexus with energy poverty: Promoting financial development in G7 economies. *Frontiers in Energy Research*, 9, 666.

Hussain, HI, B Slusarczyk, F Kamarudin, HMT Thaker and K Szczepańska-Woszczyna (2020). An investigation of an adaptive neuro-fuzzy inference system to predict the relationship among energy intensity, globalization, and financial development in major ASEAN economies. *Energies*, 13(4), 850.

Ibrahiem, DM (2020). Do technological innovations and financial development improve environmental quality in Egypt? *Environmental Science and Pollution Research*, 27(10), 10869–10881.

Ionescu, L (2021). Leveraging green finance for low-carbon energy, sustainable economic development, and climate change mitigation during the COVID-19 pandemic. *Review of Contemporary Philosophy, (20)*, 175–186.

Iqbal, S and AR Bilal (2021a). Energy financing in COVID-19: How public supports can benefit? *OECD Finance Review International.*

Iqbal, S and AR Bilal (2021b). Investment performance: Emotional beasts are dragging into the darkness of the castle. *Global Business Review*, 09721509211044309.

Iqbal, S, AR Bilal, M Nurunnabi, W Iqbal, Y Alfakhri and N Iqbal (2021a). It is time to control the worst: Testing COVID-19 outbreak, energy consumption and CO_2 emission. *Environmental Science and Pollution Research*, 28(15), 19008–19020.

Iqbal, S, F Taghizadeh-Hesary, M Mohsin and W Iqbal (2021b). Assessing the role of the green finance index in environmental pollution reduction. *Studies of Applied Economics*, 39(3), 12.

Jalil, A and M Feridun (2011). The impact of growth, energy and financial development on the environment in OECD: A cointegration analysis. *Energy Economics*, 33(2), 284–291.

Jamalpuria, A (2017). Environmental regulatory efficacy in India: An inter-state comparison. *Journal of Environmental Assessment Policy and Management*, 19(03), 1750016.

Jiang, Q, SI Khattak, M Ahmad and P Lin (2021). Mitigation pathways to sustainable production and consumption: Examining the impact of commercial policy on carbon dioxide emissions in Australia. *Sustainable Production and Consumption*, 25, 390–403.

Jin, T and J Kim (2018). What is better for mitigating carbon emissions – Renewable energy or nuclear energy? A panel data analysis. *Renewable and Sustainable Energy Reviews*, 91, 464–471.

Khan, MA, H Riaz, M Ahmed and A Saeed (2021). Does green finance really deliver what is expected? An empirical perspective. *Borsa Istanbul Review*.

Li, W, F Chien, CC Hsu, Y Zhang, MA Nawaz, S Iqbal and M Mohsin (2021a). Nexus between energy poverty and energy efficiency: Estimating the long-run dynamics. *Resources Policy*, 72, 102063.

Li, W, F Chien, QT Ngo, TD Nguyen, S Iqbal and AR Bilal (2021b). Vertical financial disparity, energy prices and emission reduction: Empirical insights from Pakistan. *Journal of Environmental Management*, 294, 112946.

Lo, AY (2016). Challenges to the development of carbon markets in OECD. *Climate Policy*, 16(1), 109–124.

Lu, WC (2018). The impacts of information and communication technology, energy consumption, financial development, and economic growth on carbon dioxide emissions in 12 Asian countries. *Mitigation and Adaptation Strategies for Global Change*, 23(8), 1351–1365.

Ma, C and DI Stern (2008). OECD's changing energy intensity trend: A decomposition analysis. *Energy Economics*, 30(3), 1037–1053.

Mengistu, AA and BK Adhikary (2011). Does good governance matter for FDI inflows? Evidence from Asian economies. *Asia Pacific Business Review*, 17(3), 281–299.

Muganyi, T, L Yan and HP Sun (2021). Green finance, fintech and environmental protection: Evidence from OECD. *Environmental Science and Ecotechnology*, 7, 100107.

Nawaz, MA, U Seshadri, P Kumar, R Aqdas, AK Patwary and M Riaz (2021). Nexus between green finance and climate change mitigation in N-11 and BRICS countries: Empirical estimation through difference in differences (DID) approach. *Environmental Science and Pollution Research*, 28(6), 6504–6519.

Ozturk, I and A Acaravci (2013). The long-run and causal analysis of energy, growth, openness and financial development on carbon emissions in Turkey. *Energy Economics*, 36, 262–267.

Pan, X, MK Uddin, C Han and X Pan (2019). Dynamics of financial development, trade openness, technological innovation and energy intensity: Evidence from Bangladesh. *Energy*, 171, 456–464.

Ren, X, Q Shao and R Zhong (2020). Nexus between green finance, non-fossil energy use, and carbon intensity: Empirical evidence from OECD based on a vector error correction model. *Journal of Cleaner Production*, 277, 122844.

Riti, JS, Y Shu, D Song and M Kamah (2017). The contribution of energy use and financial development by source in climate change mitigation process: A global empirical perspective. *Journal of Cleaner Production*, 148, 882–894.

Sadorsky, P (2010). The impact of financial development on energy consumption in emerging economies. *Energy Policy*, 38(5), 2528–2535.

Salahuddin, M, J Gow and I Ozturk (2015). Is the long-run relationship between economic growth, electricity consumption, carbon dioxide emissions and financial development in Gulf Cooperation Council Countries robust? *Renewable and Sustainable Energy Reviews*, 51, 317–326.

Saud, S, S Chen and A Haseeb (2019). Impact of financial development and economic growth on environmental quality: An empirical analysis from Belt and Road Initiative (BRI) countries. *Environmental Science and Pollution Research*, 26(3), 2253–2269.

Shah, SAR, SAA Naqvi and S Anwar (2020). Exploring the linkage among energy intensity, carbon emission and urbanization in Pakistan: Fresh evidence from ecological modernization and environment transition theories. *Environmental Science and Pollution Research*, 27(32), 40907–40929.

Shahbaz, M, QMA Hye, AK Tiwari and NC Leitão (2013a). Economic growth, energy consumption, financial development, international trade and CO_2 emissions in Indonesia. *Renewable and Sustainable Energy Reviews*, 25, 109–121.

Shahbaz, M, S Khan and MI Tahir (2013b). The dynamic links between energy consumption, economic growth, financial development and trade in OECD: Fresh evidence from multivariate framework analysis. *Energy Economics*, 40, 8–21.

Shahbaz, M, SA Solarin, R Sbia and S Bibi (2015). Does energy intensity contribute to CO_2 emissions? A trivariate analysis in selected African countries. *Ecological Indicators*, 50, 215–224.

Shen, Y, ZW Su, MY Malik, M Umar, Z Khan and M Khan (2021). Does green investment, financial development and natural resources rent limit carbon emissions? A provincial panel analysis of OECD. *Science of the Total Environment*, 755, 142538.

Sun, L, S Fang, S Iqbal and AR Bilal (2022). Financial stability role on climate risks, and climate change mitigation: Implications for green economic recovery. *Environmental Science and Pollution Research*, 1–12.

Taghizadeh-Hesary, F, N Yoshino, E Rasoulinezhad and C Rimaud (2021). Power purchase agreements with incremental tariffs in local currency: An innovative green finance tool. *Global Finance Journal*, 50, 100666.

Tran, QH (2021). The impact of green finance, economic growth and energy usage on CO_2 emission in Vietnam – A multivariate time series analysis. *OECD Finance Review International*.

Tu, CA and E Rasoulinezhad (2021). Energy efficiency financing and the role of green bond: Policies for post-COVID period. *OECD Finance Review International*.

Tu, CA, E Rasoulinezhad and T Sarker (2020). Investigating solutions for the development of a green bond market: Evidence from analytic hierarchy process. *Finance Research Letters*, 34, 101457.

Ulucak, R and SUD Khan (2020). Relationship between energy intensity and CO_2 emissions: Does economic policy matter? *Sustainable Development*, 28(5), 1457–1464.

Umar, M, X Ji, N Mirza and B Naqvi (2021). Carbon neutrality, bank lending, and credit risk: Evidence from the Eurozone. *Journal of Environmental Management*, 296, 113156.

Weber, CL, GP Peters, D Guan and K Hubacek (2008). The contribution of OECD exports to climate change. *Energy Policy*, 36(9), 3572–3577.

WIOD, (2019). https://www.rug.nl/ggdc/valuechain/wiod/?lang=en.

Wu, J, Q Zhu and L Liang (2016). CO_2 emissions and energy intensity reduction allocation over provincial industrial sectors in OECD. *Applied Energy*, 166, 282–291.

Yang, X and B Su (2019). Impacts of international export on global and regional carbon intensity. *Applied Energy*, 253, 113552.

Zeng, L, M Xu, S Liang, S Zeng and T Zhang (2014). Revisiting drivers of energy intensity in OECD during 1997–2007: A structural decomposition analysis. *Energy Policy*, 67, 640–647.

Zhang, D, M Mohsin, AK Rasheed, Y Chang and F Taghizadeh-Hesary (2021a). Public spending and green economic growth in BRI region: Mediating role of green finance. *Energy Policy*, 153, 112256.

Zhang, L, F Huang, L Lu, X Ni and S Iqbal (2021b). Energy financing for energy retrofit in COVID-19: Recommendations for green bond financing. *Environmental Science and Pollution Research*, 1–12.

Zhang, YJ (2011). The impact of financial development on carbon emissions: An empirical analysis in OECD. *Energy Policy*, 39(4), 2197–2203.

https://doi.org/10.1142/9789819812783_0009

PUBLIC SPENDING AS A NEW DETERMINANT OF SUSTAINABLE DEVELOPMENT GOALS AND GREEN ECONOMIC RECOVERY: POLICY PERSPECTIVE ANALYSIS[§]

ZHEN LIU* and TONG YIN†

School of Business, Nanjing Normal University,
No. 1 Wenyuan Road Qixia District, Nanjing, P. R. China
**zhenliu_cn@yahoo.com*
†18106328528@163.com

AHMAD ROMADHONI SURYA PUTRA‡

Faculty of Animal Science, Universitas Gadjah Mada Jl.
Fauna 3 Bulaksumur, Yogyakarta 55281, Indonesia
‡ahmadromadhoni@ugm.ac.id

MUHAMMAD SADIQ

Taylor University, Malaysia
muhammad.sadiq@taylors.edu.my

Green economy talks about combing final mechanisms that have ecological and macroeconomic system gains. Likewise, this research piece examined the effects of increased spending on fiscal policies and tightening fiscal policies concerning greening the economic activity as the globe reclaims itself from the COVID-19 in China. Analysis was done applying the China longitudinal data for the period 2008–2018. We utilized the ordinary least square as well as the quantile regression equation to meticulously approximate the influences of increased fiscal spending policies in addition to tightening fiscal policies has on greening the economic system acts as the countries reclaim themselves from the pandemic via a formulated green performance indicator of China nations. The findings indicate a rather exciting pattern by saying a percentage growth in fiscal policy led to nearly 6.5% growth, that is, less than 0.5 growth in the minimum carbon dioxide polluting vaporous from energy suppliers, such as natural gas, and a 0.2% less than 0.01 cuts in the midway carbon dioxide polluting liquefied energy suppliers, that is, hydrocarbon byproducts and a nonsignificant expansion of 0.2%, more significant than 0.5 in the entire case scenario coming from polluting dense energy suppliers, that is, from coal byproduct sources. At the same time, a 1% expansion in fiscal policy reduces cumulative carbon dioxide pollution to 0.2%, less than 0.05%. On this score, the presence of the environmental hypothesis was authenticated in all scenarios analyzed. Furthermore, the causality test indicated a dual movement causative correlation between fiscal policy and carbon dioxide pollution and one-way movement concerning the fiscal policy to energy use.

‡Corresponding author.

§This chapter was originally published in Climate Change Economics, Vol. 13, No. 3, March 2022, published by World Scientific Publishing, Singapore. Reprinted with permission.

The findings demonstrated that China witnessed a rising switch to green advancement in China; their Green Economic Efficiency increased steadily.

Keywords: Public expenditure; green economy; econometric estimation; China.

1. Introduction

Ecological destruction, energy use, and economic system activity expansion have attracted scholarly works in recent years. More so, it has been widely agreed that the themes of green economy and environmental have assumed a greater dimension, as well as the imperative to thoroughly switch to more efficient generation sources to avert climate change and its consequences (Mohsin *et al.*, 2018, 2021). Now, the preference amongst economic progress and ecological self-maintaining continues to be a global difficulty; besides, from the beginning of the manufacturing revolution in the 18th century, the world's economy has grown on the back of ecological progress due to the overconsumption of traditional energy sources used in manufacturing goods (Ali Shah *et al.*, 2021). Hence, economic advancement, energy use as well as ecological value connote a triple multifaceted challenging structure (Yang *et al.*, 2021; He *et al.*, 2020; Mohsin *et al.*, 2020).

Energy use depends mainly on the generation and application of conventional energy due to the invention of the original steam engine in the UK before the upscaling of the sector. Nonetheless, the number of people living in an area, economic advancement, and technological advancements have grown the requirements for energy in the 21st century (Tiep *et al.*, 2021). That is quite unparalleled, signifying that globally, the unabated consumption of conventional energy sources is a climate crisis (Bagherzadeh, 2021). This crisis culminated in the promulgation of the United Nations Framework Convention on Climate Change, a voluntary grouping of nations around the globe on ecological issues adopted in 1992 and enforced in 1994, after ratifying the required number of countries (Taherzadeh, 2021).

The key aim of the United Nations Framework Convention on Climate Change was to control the amount of human activity that causes the release of greenhouse gases (GHGs) pollution to the point that they are not destructive to the environment (Lei *et al.*, 2021; De Matos *et al.*, 2021). Subsequently, following the hills of the framework was the Kyoto convention, which instituted goals for emerging nations that are compulsory lawfully and the formation of the Paris Accord in 2015, which reduced the lawful compulsory goals that came into being in 2016 (Cojoianu *et al.*, 2020; Wang, 2020). In addition, the international panel on climate change's fifth assessment study additional underlies the importance to cut GHGs pollution, stating the future environmental effects of sustained world temperature increases even under the 1.5% temperature (IPCC, 2018). This ignites the concern to harmonize energy and ecological policies on the comprehensive fiscal policy framework — to engender ecological sustainability whilst attaining energy security (Cojoianu *et al.*, 2020).

Macroeconomic policies such as fiscal, monetary and commercial policies act as a catalyst in growing cumulative requirements and economic expansion, even though this occurrence comes with costs concerning externalities (Sun *et al.*, 2020a; Baloch *et al.*, 2020). Also, the impact of fiscal expenditure on environmental ruin relies on whether emissions are produced through the generation and utilization of merchandise and services. Shaw and Fu (2020) and Yang (2020) detected ways whereby public expenditure affects ecological value within the scenario of generation-induced effluence: (1) earnings impact, (2) structure impact, (3) technique impact, and (4) magnitude impact. In the first case, the earnings effect describes a situation where increased earnings levels grow the requirements for advanced ecological value (Al-Qahtani *et al.*, 2020). Next, the structure impact depicts a setting where the expansion in fiscal spending causes humans, instead of physical capital, concentrated actions that are relatively not harmful to the ecology (Barbier, 2020). Then, the technique effect connotes an economic situation that expanded expenditure on education and healthcare advances the effectiveness and output of the laborlore, thus, reducing ecological destruction (Li *et al.*, 2020). Ultimately, the magnitude impact means a spike in public expenditure produces environmental emissions at particular gross domestic product (GDP) staged.

Nonetheless, destruction of this nature relies on the correlation between fiscal expenditure and climate change (Rana, 2020). Given the background of utilization-induced emissions, more significant sector centered expenditure grows the long term and present earnings of customers and negatively influence ecological value (Kurukulasuriya *et al.*, 2011). Given this increase in public expenditure promotes the advancement and consolidation of institutions in support of ecological issues whilst concurrently expanding the effectiveness, implementation as well as operation of ecological rules backing a sustainable future (Sun *et al.*, 2020a, 2020b, 2020c).

In summary, the scale and latitude of ecological rules plus earnings programs ascertain the cumulative effect on utilization centered emissions. For instance (Agrawala *et al.*, 2020) discovered relative to unconstitutional cultures, on constitutional cultures, strict obedience to ecological rules inclines to dent the harmful impacts of earnings to abating emissions levels.

For this analysis, we determine the green economy indicators that consider the widely acclaimed expanse method. Variations in economic progress and particular ecological settings plus resources have been considered when the indicators were being formulated. The indicators' figures were through the entire study period. Also, we investigated the impact of public education, research, and expenditure on green development in addition to a two generalized methods movement to estimate. The findings showed the impact was supported and direct, signifying the presence of structural and technological impacts.

Regarding the dual situation, the structural effects are more than the technological effect. Our study equally investigated the impacts of green economic advancement on significant government investment policies. The findings revealed that government spending regarding education could kindle manufacturing sectors' reliance on human resources. In the interim, government investments in research and innovation would drive technological advancements (Engström *et al.*, 2020).

Because of this, the analysis adds to knowledge in five ways: One way is that we control for the dual impact of fiscal growth policy and tightening fiscal policy (TFP) on greening economic system activity build back a better approach via a specified econometric equation. The impacts of fiscal policy on greening economic system activity could be scientifically proven about China's novel energy importation category. Again, we applied a new empirical analysis to study impacts of fiscal policy on carbon dioxide pollution on the majority of carbon dioxide emission solid types, such as coal, the midway carbon dioxide emission releasing liquified sources, that is, natural gasoline and diesel in addition to the minimum carbon dioxide producing vaporous energy types, that is, natural gas. Doing this is essential to measure the different features, the effects of fiscal policy on diverse conventional energy types, plus throw more light on the fiscal policy on carbon dioxide pollution connection in China. Besides, the endogenous one-unit break analysis and the Langrage multiplier endogenously dual unit root analysis are deployed concurrently to investigate the series' stationarity properties. Another critical point is that applying the cointegration, various structural disruption approaches, and the possible misrepresenting impacts of structural disruptions on the cointegration correlation is sidestepped. The nonstatic ordinary least square (OLS) approach is deployed to ascertain the extended variables of the fiscal policy of different energy types of carbon dioxide connection, whereas regulating on the structural disruptions.

Finally, we give essential awareness of the research area and theoretical comprehension concerning fiscal growth policy and TFP. First, there is no specific research on the study area despite fiscal growth policy and fiscal reduction policy altering economic activity. After having analyzed the work empirically, we discovered the effects of greening economic activity evidentially. The analysis reveals the direct association between expanded fiscal spending and green economic advancement. More so, the analysis highlights that the study nations depict varied features of resource availability. Accordingly, different advancement policies concerning varied nations ought to be enclosed to profit government spending about greening economic activity expansion.

The remaining aspects of the analysis are structured as follows. The rest of this study is as follows. Greening economic activity via building back a better literature review is done in Sec. 2. Data and methodology are done in Sec. 3. Results and discussion are presented in Sec. 4. Ultimately, conclusions and recommendations are given in Sec. 5.

2. Green Economic Recovery

The term green economy has attracted global, subregion, and domestic prominence due to the financial crisis. The greening of economic activity is characterized by the efficient utilization of resources plus a less carbon-intensive economy and inclusive societal progress (Chandio *et al.*, 2020; Sun *et al.*, 2020b). The participation of private and public sectors' financings in economic activity, green infrastructure, plus possessions could eliminate CO_2 emissions, improve energy and resource effectiveness, and eschew the demise of biodiversity and environment services push expansion and earnings in a green economy (Parida *et al.*, 2020). Globally, nations worldwide witnessed a decline in pollution levels due to the coronavirus disease 2019 (COVID-19) and its consequences of the economic shutdown. Nonetheless, an essential reduction in carbon dioxide pollution is seen in China, India, the United States, in addition to Brazil. China, as of today, is the world's largest carbon dioxide emitter by volume globally, in the region of fourteen billion metric tons of carbon dioxide generated in 2019 (Sarfraz *et al.*, 2021). During the economic shutdown in China due to the pandemic, a 10.3% cut in carbon dioxide pollution in the initial 25% of 2020 was detected relative to a similar time in 2019 (Li *et al.*, 2020). Economic shutdowns entail the ban on travel around and economic activities and social gatherings. Shutdown includes shutting down airports for cross country travels and domestic travels, banning social gatherings and other forms of activities, closing all global movement of people. In other countries, essential services such as food, restaurant and related services are allowed to function.

The objective of a shutdown is to cut down the number of people who gather to reduce infections in large areas (Tian *et al.*, 2021). It is an indisputable fact that the COVID-19 contagion soothed companies, reduced economic activities, and hindered social activities. Through the period of the COVID-19 contagion in China, traffic reduced substantially (Dai *et al.*, 2020). Even though the COVID-19 contagion brought about a slight expansion in methane pollution levels via varied reductions in agricultural and fisheries undertakings (Paital *et al.*, 2020), the contagion essentially was benign to the ecology. The COVID-19 pandemic has significantly made the globe achieve ecological quality, which eluded the globe in some years (Aljadani *et al.*, 2021). The globe would become better off if governments around the world include in their recovery plans green plans and the type of reorientation vital to achieve ecological objectives' emissions reductions, inclusion and a robust economic advancement post the pandemic. The People's Republic of China experienced about a 42% cut in aggregate power use in the initial 1/4 of 2020 due to COVID-19 contagion. India's power sector generation plummeted to 65 GW; while China had its coal power demand from power sources reduced drastically. Equally, crude use fell due to the economic downturn in the world's production and the transport sectors (Paital, 2020; Ghenai and Bettayeb, 2021; Shan *et al.*, 2021). The International Energy Agency indicated the 2020 energy requirements other than the renewable energy sources (RES) contract vitally in excess above that was seen during the past 10 years.

Similarly, the United Nations contends carbon pollution has to reduce to 7.6% yearly by 2030 to make the world's temperature stay within 1.5°C pre-industrial levels. Connoisseurs on economic issues forecasted that if economic system activities start to pick up by mid-June 2020, the reduction will be within 4%. Nevertheless, if it continues to the end of 2020, 7% will decline further. Wind and solar will make up 40% of power production, according to a forecast from the International Energy Agency (Nižetić, 2020). The effects of the COVID-19 contagion shutdown on the ecology seem profound. Table 1 depicts the restraints on air–land, and seat movements advanced air value due to significant cuts in CO_2 and nitrogen oxide pollution alongside growth in other zone gases when juxtaposed to 2019 degrees of similar years (Earth Matters, 2020). Even though ozone was detected to expand that elucidated due to reduced titration of O_3 to nitrate oxide because of substantial cuts in local nitrate oxide pollution by road transport, there was a basic cut in nitrate oxide and particulate matter (Perre *et al.*, 2020).

In the interim, the impact of government spending on research and innovation on green economic system development has not been amply researched. Temporarily, Smith *et al.*, (2021) contended green formation impact on research and development (R&D). Ultimately, the gains of economics due to cuts in the carbon dioxide pollution on the world's economy can be approximated to increasing the aggregate cuts of carbon dioxide in tons on the global social cost of carbon. Within the next months beginning from January 1, 2020 to July 2020, the aggregate world cuts in carbon dioxide pollution are reported at 1551 million tons of carbon dioxide. The figure of the world's social cost of carbon is 418. As a result of the outstanding cuts in carbon dioxide pollution, the world's economy gained 648 billion dollars. Paramesh *et al.* (2018) studied the effects of fiscal tools on Asian nations in a green pathway. The contended countries of Asian nations are gradualists in achieving green economy and climate goals through crafting macroeconomic policies. The proffered country tailor-made fiscal policies ought to be ascertained to attain green economy objectives.

Furthermore, many types of research on the nexus of government expenditure as well as ecological destruction have been detected in research. Nonetheless, the scholarly works are yet to discover whether government expenditure can encourage green advancement in China initiative nations. Hence, to close this study gap, this detailed analysis examined empirical findings on the subject area (Scharf *et al.*, 2020).

3. Methodology and Selection of Variables

3.1. *Model specification*

One of the widely acclaimed methods is the OLS. It is used in approximating economic and financial equations. Regarding the maximum likelihood estimation (MLE), a complete comprehension of data distribution is vital; nevertheless, for undertaking the OLS approximation, there is no need for that condition. Instead, this approach needs a specific instant produced from the initial equation (Lv *et al.*, 2019). In instances where the data gathering is identified, calculating the MLE could be challenging. Nonetheless, the estimation of the generalized method moment is quite direct. Another instance that fits the situation is the log-normal random unstable equation. An equally differentiating part of the generalized method moment approximation method highlights a particular way for these equations restricted alongside extra instances and equation variables. Hence, model five depicts a specified straight estimation equation. The existence of the fixed term correlating to the independent term is probable to the nonstatic longitudinal data equation which creates the application of conventional constant approximation approaches. Hence, our approach considers applying varied generalized method moments and system generalized method moments, as the dual variables give a roadmap of the maximum N and minimum T. This corrects the indirect consistencies of the endogenous parameters via improvising the approach. Sovacool (2017) deployed a differencing method to take away the individual impacts before building the generalized method moment approximates as well as applied the lag-designate to be improvising parameters, that is, formulated as follows:

$$\text{GEPI}_{it} = \alpha + \beta\text{GEPI}_{i,t-1} + \gamma\text{PS}_{it} + \theta X_{it} + \mu_t + V_i + \varepsilon_{it}, \tag{1}$$

where α depicts the intercept and β, γ, and θ are factor figures to be approximated. Furthermore, PS_{it} connotes the per head capita fiscal expenditure on research and innovation, meaning the per head research and advancement expenditure or per head education (EDU) expenditure. The initial lag designates of GEPI_{it}, $\text{GEPI}_{i,t-1}$ is; this was added because the green performance indicator in the past period attains a substantial impact on the present green performance indicator. For controlling the parameters, they are denoted as X_{it}. Ultimately, u_t depicts the invariant time impact, v_i depicts a single fixed-effect, and ε_{it} depicts the stochastic term. In addition, from the works of Wang *et al.* (2016), Shahbaz *et al.* (2017a, 2017b), Khan *et al.* (2019), and several scholarly, the whole parameters are changed to their normal logarithms to abridge the factor figures' explanations as well as to decrease the probable occurrence of heteroscedasticity. Hence, the factors' figure of the log-changed parameters is explained as elasticities. Log changed actual per head GDP is tallied plus combined on the equation to check the quantile estimation hypothesis. The entire numerical parameters are estimated per head figures to control the number of people living in an area impact. The following variables are presumed to have a linear correlation pattern: fiscal policy, energy, actual earnings, actual quadratic earnings, as well as carbon dioxide pollution.

3.2. *Quantile autoregressive distributive lag*

This empirical analysis applied the quantile autoregressive distribution lag (QARDL) equation mooted by Cho *et al.* (2015) to analyze long-term correlation's steadiness. For this rationale, formulating the quantile and infer a supple econometric outline to show the correlation amongst fiscal disparity and ecological emission about the countries being studied. The application of QARDL is helpful relative to the straight-line. Autoregressive distribution lag due to the QARDL equation could cause probably lopsidedness in response to fiscal disparity to encourage or cut ecological emissions in varied period phases. It is noted that the autoregressive distribution lag is formulated as $Y_t = \alpha_* + \sum_{j=1}^{p} \emptyset_{j*} Y_{t-j} + \sum_{j=0}^{q} \theta'_{j*} X_{t-j} + U_t$, where $X_t \in \mathbb{R}^k$ is the absence of unit root and ergodic pattern coupling with a population mean zero, U_t depicts the stochastic designate given as $Y_t - \mathbb{E}[Y_t[\mathcal{F}_{t-1}]$ alongside $\mathcal{F}_{t-1}$ as the minutest σ-field produced to mean $\{X'_t, Y_{t-1}, X'_{t-1}, \ldots\}$, and p and q represent lag patterns. In addition, we consider that the k parameters in X_t are not harmonized alongside one another. Ensuing this structure, we set the τth quantile of Y_t provisional on $\mathcal{F}_{t-1}$ to be given as $\alpha_*(\tau) + \sum_{j=1}^{p} \emptyset_{j*}(\tau) Y_{t-j} + \sum_{j=0}^{q} \theta'_{j*}(\tau)' X_{t-j}$ and represent this to be $Q_{Yt}(\tau Y_{t-j})$; remember we depict Y_t to be

$$Y_t = \alpha_*(\tau) + \sum_{j=1}^{p} \emptyset_{j*}(\tau) Y_{t-j} + \sum_{j=0}^{q} \theta_{j*}(\tau)' X_{t-j} + U_t(\tau). \tag{2}$$

Furthermore, this is referred to as the QARDL approach. Here, $U_t(\tau)$ is defined as $Y_t - Q_{Yt}(\tau Y_{t-j})$, according to Kim *et al.* (2003). Then, it is reconstructed in Eq. (1) to examine the QARDL device

$$Y_t = \alpha_*(\tau) + \sum_{j=0}^{q-1} W'_{t-j} \delta_{j*}(\tau) X'_t \gamma_*(\tau) + \sum_{j=1}^{p} \emptyset_{j*}(\tau) Y_{t-j} + U_t(\tau), \tag{3}$$

where $\gamma_*(\tau) = \sum_{j=0}^{q} \theta_{j*}(\tau)$, $W_t = \Delta X_t$, and $\delta_{j*}(\tau) = -\sum_{j=j+1}^{q} \theta_{i*}(\tau)$. The whole variables in (18) measure the short brief and extended period correlation amongst Y_t and the X_t. Hence, it is taken in the ensuing extended-term quantile approach reconstructed in Eq. (4).

$$Y_t = \mu_*(\tau) + X'_t \beta_*(\tau) + R_t(\tau), \tag{4}$$

with

$$\beta_*(\tau) = \gamma_*(\tau) \left(1 - \sum_{i=1}^{p} \emptyset_{j*}(\tau)\right)^{-1} \text{ and } R_t = \sum_{j=0}^{\infty} W'_{t-j} \varepsilon_0, j_*(\tau) \sum_{j=0}^{\infty} \rho j_*(\tau) U_{t-j}(\tau), \tag{5}$$

where we let $\mu_*(\tau) = \alpha_*(\tau)(1 - \sum_{i=1}^{p} \emptyset_{j*}(\tau))^{-1}$ and $\varepsilon_0, j_*(\tau) = \sum_{l=j+1}^{\infty} \pi_{l*}(\tau)$, and $\{p_{0*}(\tau), p_{1*}(\tau)\}$ and $\{\pi_{0*}(\tau), \pi_{1*}(\tau)\}$ is such that $\sum_{j=0}^{\infty} \rho j_*(\tau) L^j \equiv (1 - \sum_{j=0}^{\infty} \emptyset j_*(\tau) L^j)^{-1}$ and

$$(1 - L)^{-1} \left(\frac{\sum_{j=0}^{p} \theta j_*(\tau) L^j}{1 - \sum_{j=1}^{p} \emptyset j_*(\tau) L^j} - \frac{\sum_{j=0}^{p} \theta j_*(\tau)}{1 - \sum_{j=1}^{p} \emptyset j_*(\tau)} \right) \equiv \sum_{j=0}^{\infty} \pi j_*(\tau) L^j. \tag{6}$$

The constant model, Eq. (5), is obtained from Y_ts determination (18). The remainder designate $R_t(\tau)$ denotes the gathering of successively associated stationary parameters vital to the extended-term correlation. We encapsulated this to be $\beta_*(\tau)$ and referred to as the extended variable. It is evident from the explanation that $\beta_*(\tau)$ is set to be the equation of $\gamma_*(\tau)\emptyset_*(\tau) = (\emptyset_{1*}(\tau), \ldots, \emptyset_{p*}(\tau))'$ and as it is steadily approximated to the plug-in principle and constantly approximating $\gamma_*(\tau)\emptyset_*(\tau)$. Our strong objective hinges on constructing the approximation theory for the extended period variable $\beta_*(\tau)$. Before this, we restate the QARDL in Eq. (6) to be

$$Y_t = G_t'\lambda_*(\tau) + \hat{Y}_t'\varnothing_*(\tau) + U_t(\tau) = Z_t'\alpha_*(\tau) + U_t(\tau), \tag{7}$$

where $Z_t = (G_t', \hat{Y}_t')' = (G_t', Y_{t-1}, \ldots, Y_{t-p})' = (1, W_t', \ldots, W_{t-1+1}' X_t', Y_{t-1}, \ldots, Y_{t-p})'$ and

$$\begin{aligned}\alpha_*(\tau) &= [\lambda_*(\tau)', \varnothing_*(\tau)']' = [\alpha_*(\tau), \delta_*(\tau)', \gamma_*(\tau)', \varnothing_*(\tau)']' \\ &= [\alpha_*(\tau), \delta_{1*}(\tau)', \ldots, \delta_{(q-1)*}(\tau)'\gamma_*(\tau)', \varnothing_*(\tau)']',\end{aligned}$$

where each element of $\hat{Y}_t$ in (7) has the following specific form:

$$Y_{t-i} = \mu_*(\tau) + X_t'\beta_*(\tau) \sum_{j=0}^{q-1} W_{t-j}' \varepsilon_{i,j_*}(\tau) + K_{t,i}(\tau), \quad i = 1, 2, \ldots, p \tag{8}$$

where we let $\varepsilon_{i,j_*}(\tau) = -\beta_*(\tau)$, if $i > j$; and $-\sum_{l=j+1}^{\infty} \pi_{l*}(\tau)$, otherwise, and

$$K_{t,i}(\tau) = \begin{cases} \displaystyle\sum_{j=q-i}^{\infty} W'_{t-i-j}\varepsilon_0, j_*(\tau) + \sum_{j=0}^{\infty} \rho j_*(\tau) U_{t-i-j}(\tau), & \text{if } i \le q; \\ \displaystyle\sum_{j=0}^{i-q-1} W'_{t-q-j}\beta_*(\tau) + \sum_{j=0}^{\infty} W'_{t-i-j}\pi_{j*}(\tau) + \sum_{j=0}^{\infty} \rho j_*(\tau) U_{t-i-j}(\tau), & \text{if } i > q. \end{cases}$$

(10) is the lagged version of (3). Pesaran and Shin (1998) provide a detailed derivation of (10). As (10) is iteratively applied below, we restate it additionally efficiently $\hat{Y}_t = \Gamma_*(\tau)' G_t + K_t(\tau)$ by letting

$$\Gamma_*(\tau) = \begin{bmatrix} \mu_*(\tau) & \mu_*(\tau) & \cdots & \mu_*(\tau) \\ \varepsilon_{1,0_x}(\tau) & \varepsilon_{2,0_*}(\tau) & \cdots & \varepsilon_{p,0_*}(\tau) \\ \vdots & \vdots & \ddots & \vdots \\ \varepsilon_{1,q-1_x}(\tau) & \varepsilon_{2,q-1_x}(\tau) & \cdots & \varepsilon_{p,q-1_x}(\tau) \\ \beta_*(\tau) & \beta_*(\tau) & \cdots & \beta_*(\tau) \end{bmatrix} \text{ and } k_t(\tau) = \begin{bmatrix} k_{t,1}(\tau) \\ k_{t,2}(\tau) \\ \vdots \\ k_{t,p-1}(\tau) \\ k_{t,p}(\tau) \end{bmatrix}. \tag{10}$$

Here, we give a pair of observations about the quantile reliance of the QARDL variables. To begin with, we follow the short-term and extended-term variables as quantile reliant, meaning that the QARDL variables are influenced by the innovation $U_t(\tau)$ obtained at a particular time phase and, hence, is varied across quantiles. Hence, the breaking in parameters will not change only the setting; nonetheless, it varies the magnitude and form of breaking in the allocation Y_t. In addition, Xiao (2009) reveals that the zero association amongst regressors and the randomness are vital to reliable approximate the quantile-reliant cointegrating vector. This is the primary reason why Xiao generates the quantile-dependent co — integrated variables independently using the nonstatic OLS method in past and current variables; this is absent in the given semiparametric fully modified framework. Given the autoregressive distribution lag setting, this circumstance is equal $\mathbb{E}[\Delta X_t U_t] = 0$ and $\mathbb{E}[\Delta Y_{t-j} U_t] = 0$ $(j = 1, \ldots, p)$. The expression given is ordinarily upheld on the premise that enough maximum lag methods are stated for p and q. Furthermore, it is forthright to reformulate the autoregression distribution lag process one in the ensuing error correction model (ECM) given as follows:

$$\Delta Y_t = \alpha_*(\tau) + \varsigma_*(\tau)(Y_{t-1} - \beta_*(\tau)' X_{t-1}) + \sum_{j=1}^{p-1} \theta_j^*(\tau) \Delta Y_{t-j} + \sum_{j=0}^{q-1} \theta_j^*(\tau) \Delta X_{t-j} + U_t(\tau), \tag{11}$$

where $\varsigma_*(\tau) = \sum_{i=1}^{p} \varnothing_{i*}(\tau) - 1, \theta_0^*(\tau) = \theta_{0*}(\tau)$ and $j = 1, \ldots, p-1, \theta_j^*(\tau) = -\sum_{h=j+1}^{p}$ $\varnothing_{h*}(\tau)$ and

$$\theta_j^*(\tau) = -\sum_{h=j+1}^{p} \theta_{j*}(\tau).$$

3.2.1. *Selection of variables*

The explained parameter in the analysis is the total carbon dioxide emission. About the subject of the exploratory variables, the research primarily demonstrates the expansion of the green economy which is principally influenced by the growth of fiscal policy and tightening monetary policy, whilst carbon dioxide pollution from solid, carbon pollution in liquid, carbon dioxide emission from vaporous' sources, conventional energy use, and RE consumption are the variables to be controlled. Hence, we selected growth fiscal policy (GFP) and TFP to be the main exploratory variables. The data were sourced from the WDI concerning the education variable.

The initial control parameter observed in our model is carbon dioxide from solid, carbon dioxide pollution from liquefied, carbon dioxide from vaporous sources, conventional energy use, as well as RE consumption, to be the control variables. Consequently, the entire control parameters are investigated around 2010–2018, on the same timeframe of the total carbon dioxide emissions analysis.

4. Results and Discussion

4.1. *Descriptive statistics*

Table 1 depicts descriptive statistics findings of the study parameters. This analysis individually covers the entire eight parameters — namely, lCO_2spk, lCO_2lpk, lCO_2gpk, EFP, CFP, FFC, and REC. The data were obtained on a four-week basis for

Table 1. Variables detail.

Acronyms	Detail
lCO_2spk	CO_2 emissions from solid
lCO_2lpk	CO_2 emissions from liquid
lCO_2gpk	CO_2 emissions from gaseous
EFP	Expansionary fiscal policy
CFP	Contractionary monetary policy
FFC	Fossil fuel consumption
REC	Renewable fuel consumption

the analyzed time of 2010–2018. Furthermore, the research analysis given in Table 1 affirms that the maximum nonconformity is detected in the mark of lCO_2gpk and lCO_2lpk. Ultimately, the findings of Jarque–Bera (J–B) figures have been used to investigate the normality of the data for the whole analyzed variables. Nevertheless, it is affirmed that the general propositions for corroborating the normal distribution of the data on the whole parameter are upheld at 1%, thus, corroborating a green indication for using a longitudinal system generalized method moment equation.

4.2. *Analysis of green economy recovery*

The carbon dioxide emissions reduced to 0.801%, 0.667%, 0.390%, 0.477%, as well as 0.561% as a result of a 1% spike in TFP as depicted by factor values of OLS, dynamic OLS (DOLS), fully modified OLS (FMOLS), as well as the pooled mean group (PMG), correspondingly. The world's economic system implemented TFP to control changes in prices of goods and services after missing the target to a particular degree. That is, thought to be suitable for sound economic growth and development. Likewise, other nations exercise, as a regular policy instrument, soaring costs to 2% yearly to increase economic activity. Consequently, the customer's part anticipates an increase in the costs of products in the future and inclines to soar the buying ability.

The increase in demand puts strains on production to satisfy excess demand. Given that the supplier cannot increase supply within the short term, they are likely to bloat costs to cast in with the excess demand. Other than that, there is the need to expand generation volumes by growing the labor force, which explains extra jobs and expenditure. If the economy continues on this trajectory, inflation might sky rock, proving detrimental to growth. To facilitate this state of affairs, managers of economies usually decide to swell the tax rates and reduce spending. Higher taxes create costly inputs for products; they cut down production levels, ADCSP, domestic earnings, and carbon dioxide emissions. These results are new because they explain the relationship between fiscal policy, that is, both GFP and TFP, as well as carbon dioxide emissions.

In addition, the findings of OLS, DOLS, FMOLS, as well as PMG affirm the direct long-term correlation amongst growth fiscal, monetary policy and carbon dioxide emissions. This signifies a 1% increase in TFP growths in carbon dioxide emissions to

Table 2. Descriptive statistics of studied variables.

Variable	Std. Dev.	Minimum	Maximum	J–B Statistics
lCO_2spk	0.393015	1.142272	1.820931	13.516***
lCO_2lpk	5.0646	55.00592	605.424	18.639***
lCO_2gpk	7.1071	64.37037	705.3463	15.439***
EFP	4.756	15.94412	101.6647	12.461***
CFP	0.616	0.22624	3.139174	21.615***
FREE	5.0525	60.34343	709.7434	23.562***
REC	6.042	53.44878	580.9685	26.478***

Notes: ***, ** and * denote the 1%, 5% and 10% significance level, respectively.

0.400%, 0.518%, 0.186%, 0.222%, plus 0.251%, individually. Together with seizing different approaches, the CB probably chooses to apply GFP to manage varied economic challenges in the form of poverty, joblessness, and downturn. The GFP improves the economic advancement to increasing the manufacturing and job levels, which grows the development of conventional energy use, subsequently, resulting in the upsurge of the detrimental impacts of carbon dioxide emissions. On the contrary, the coefficients of OLS DOLS, FMOLS, and the PMG divulge that the carbon dioxide emissions plunge to 0.487%, 0.669%, 0.296%, as well as 0.165% and 0.127%, correspondingly, concerning the monetary policy contraction of 1% in China. Thus, the conceivable rationale is CFP put into operation GFP in the circumstance of unbearable inflationary pressures rates emanating from disproportionate requirements for goods.

Table 3. Long-run estimates.

	OLS	DOLS	FMOLS	PMG	PMG
lCO_2spk	−0.487	−0.543	−0.351	−0.244	−0.289
	(2.11)	(1.88)	(3.77)	(3.47)	(1.77)
lCO_2lpk	−0.774	−0.554	−0.421	−0.385	−0.453
	(2.48)	(1.93)	(2.31)	(2.57)	(1.31)
lCO_2gpk	−0.879	−0.896	−0.875	−0.896	−0.654
	(3.75)	(1.88)	(1.87)	(3.56)	(1.87)
EFP	0.388	0.422	0.156	0.175	0.248
	(1.87)	(2.55)	(5.61)	(2.66)	(2.44)
CFP	−0.476	−0.563	−0.289	−0.183	−0.106
	(2.81)	(1.47)	(1.22)	(2.54)	(1.87)
FFE	0.786	0.966	0.342	0.377	0.545
	(1.60)	(1.97)	(2.11)	(2.54)	(1.66)
REC	0.852	0.664	0.546	0.760	0.324
	(2.77)	(3.32)	(7.76)	(3.54)	(2.56)
ECM					−0.654
					(3.74)
R^2	0.76	0.92	0.769	0.79	0.81

About the long-term approximators of DOLS, FMOLS, in addition to the PMG, the ADCSP likewise substantially adds on to depreciate the ecological value to growing carbon dioxide emissions. Our results show that CO_2 pollution inclines to grow to 0.769%, 0.298%, as well as 0.432%, correspondingly, because ADCSP grows to 1%. The difference is the OLS factor figures that demonstrate the nonsignificant impacts of ADCSP.

4.3. *Quantile regression analysis*

The research additionally deployed QARDL due to the expectation that fiscal disparity might influence ecological emissions via varied ways in the form of economic crisis, economic expansion, as well as general political settings in the territory being referred to geopolitical risks such as terrorists' assaults as well as wars within the study time. On September 11, 2001, terrorists assaulted the US Trade Center and the second Gulf War in 2003. Various economic system crises existed, such as the 2001 internet bubble and the 2003 economic downturn; these occurrences had profound impacts on the world's economic functioning. The use of the autoregression distribution lag might aid in comprehending the fiscal disparity's functioning on ecological emissions, taking into account the reasons above on the prevailing economic circumstances in the South Asian countries. To approximate the findings, we apply the QARDL between 2001Q to 2012Q7.

Table 4 depicts approximates for quantile that reveals fiscal disparity encourages ecological emissions meaningfully that grows around the fourth quantile. The part of fiscal disparity to grow ecological emissions within the first three quantiles is comparatively minimum about different quantiles. However, an unexpected increase was seen after the financial crunch of 2002. It is evident from the approximated findings that an increase in fiscal disparity in emerging Asian nations indicated a meaningful means to grow ecological destruction. The rationale is perhaps attributable to the ecology receiving minimal attention if the economy is faced with financial problems.

Here, in inference to the short-term findings, carbon dioxide pollution is directly correlated alongside carbon dioxide lags in the minimum and maximum quantiles. This correlation is yet direct in central to maximum quantiles alongside nonsignificant figures; within the reduced quantiles of carbon dioxide pollution, population expansion directly affects carbon dioxide pollution in the United States of America. Likewise, per head earnings directly impact economic expansion throughout the quantiles; nevertheless, this effect is nonsignificant. In addition, ecological innovations place an adverse effect on carbon dioxide pollution in reduced quantiles, nonetheless a nonsignificant adverse effect in the central to maximum quantiles of carbon dioxide pollution. As a negative emission technology, solar energy likewise extracts adverse effects on carbon dioxide pollution in the minimum quantiles. Emanating from the center to the maximum quantiles, the adverse effect of solar energy use becomes nonsignificant.

The findings emanating from the cointegration analysis in Table 5 integrate up to five structural disruptions. The scientific analysis substantiates the existence of cointegration in all models. Regarding the following equation alongside lCO_2spk to be the

Table 4. Results of QARDL.

OLS results								
Dependent variable GHGs								
	α_0	ρ_0	β_{FI}	β_{DGDP}	β_{GDP}	β^2_{GDP}	β_{EC}	β_{EI}
	0.172*	−0.272***	1.772***	1.312**	0.232***	0.275***	−1.313***	0.377***
	(0.053)	(0.051)	(0.375)	(0.711)	(0.377)	(0.023)	(0.373)	(0.122)
Quantile estimates								
(τ)	$\alpha_0(\tau)$	$\rho_0(\tau)$	$\beta_{FI}(\tau)$	$\beta_{DGDP}(\tau)$	$\beta_{GDP}(\tau)$	$\beta_{GDP^2}(\tau)$	$\beta_{EC}(\tau)$	$\beta_{EI}(\tau)$
(0.03)	0.737***	−0.773***	0.092**	0.277***	0.724***	−0.714***	1.324***	1.432*
	(0.274)	(0.172)	(0.035)	(0.714)	(0.274)	(0.213)	(0.413)	(0.435)
(0.1)	0.741***	−0.743***	0.023***	0.771**	0.327**	−0.322**	0.572**	1.777*
	(0.251)	(0.204)	(0.033)	(0.201)	(0.237)	(0.151)	(0.327)	(0.333)
(0.2)	0.327***	−0.701***	0.054**	0.272***	0.773***	−0.201	0.702***	1.031**
	(0.127)	(0.117)	(0.047)	(0.147)	(0.201)	(0.122)	(0.301)	(0.753)
(0.3)	0.350***	−0.127***	0.557***	0.122***	0.737***	−0.250***	1.003***	0.515**
	(0.072)	(0.032)	(0.354)	(0.075)	(0.271)	(0.027)	(0.727)	(0.323)
(0.4)	0.337***	−0.275***	2.013***	0.717***	0.217***	−0.155***	1.033***	1.775**
	(0.024)	(0.104)	(0.514)	(0.344)	(0.135)	(0.072)	(0.321)	(0.533)
(0.5)	0.370***	−0.322***	3.74***	0.572***	1.277***	0.442***	1.744***	2.071**
	(0.123)	(0.171)	(1.044)	(0.741)	(0.372)	(0.247)	(0.735)	(0.232)
(0.6)	0.741***	−0.744***	3.44***	0.373***	1.033***	0.441***	1.377***	0.574***
	(0.133)	(0.101)	(1.147)	(0.277)	(0.715)	(0.237)	(0.727)	(0.325)
(0.7)	0.447***	−0.457***	3.577***	0.712***	0.557***	0.322***	1.733***	0.532*
	(0.202)	(0.123)	(1.030)	(0.303)	(0.327)	(0.227)	(0.302)	(0.443)
(0.8)	0.352***	−0.375***	2.312**	0.151*	0.773	−0.317***	0.255**	0.703**
	(0.122)	(0.137)	(0.522)	(0.057)	(0.320)	(0.275)	(0.717)	(0.373)
(0.9)	0.732***	−0.257***	1.012***	0.277**	0.523*	−0.717***	0.507**	0.372**
	(0.237)	(0.133)	(0.445)	(0.172)	(0.372)	(0.321)	(0.741)	(0.172)
(0.53)	0.742***	0.174***	1.003**	0.312**	0.372***	−0.273**	0.275**	0.103**
	(0.232)	(0.033)	(0.323)	(0.134)	(0.234)	(0.121)	(0.744)	(0.072)

Notes: ***, ** and * denote the 1%, 5% and 10% significance level, respectively.
Source: Authors own calculation.

explained parameter, it is seen from the following equation that it gives meaningful proof for cointegration signifying the existence of paradigm change in the cointegration correlation. Regarding the number two-equation using lCO_2lpk to be the explained parameter, the cointegration equation proves cointegration. Within the third equation of lCO_2gpk, models 0, 2, and 3 give meaningful proof for cointegration. The cumulative CO_2 pollution is represented with lCO_2pk in equations 0, 1, and 2 of Maki empirically back the long-term association of the parameters.

Table 5. Results of the Wald test for the constancy of parameters.

Variables	Wald-statistics (EC)	Wald-statistics (CE)
P	4.635***	3.571***
	(0.000)	(0.000)
β_{ET}	7.543***	—
	(0.000)	
β_{CCT}	13.210**	—
	(0.000)	
β_{EMP}	—	6.344***
		(0.000)
β_{CMP}	—	2.334**
		(0.023)
β_{FFE}	3.033**	3.440***
	(0.001)	(0.000)
β_{REE}	2.375**	3.114***
	(0.043)	(0.000)
φ_1	2.101*	11.544***
	(0.060)	(0.000)
ω_0	1.203**	3.052***
	(0.133)	(0.000)
ω_1	—	(0.432)
		(0.632)
λ_0	0.042	2.754**
	(0.777)	(0.013)
θ_0	4.425***	4.335***
	(0.000)	(0.000)
θ_1	—	0.032
		−0.763
δ_0	5.010***	3.352***
	(0.000)	(0.000)
δ_1	0.031	—
	(0.755)	
	Cumulative short-term effect	
ω*	—	1.244
		(0.321)
θ*	—	0.374
		(0.217)
δ*	1.004	—
	(0.376)	

Notes: The table reports the quantile estimation results. The *t*-statistics are in brackets. ***, **, and * indicate significance at the 1%, 3%, and 10% levels, respectively.
Source: Author estimations.

4.4. *Robustness analysis*

Table 6 shows the results of the split OLS, DOLS, FMOLS, and PMG studies to be consistent study. In addition, the autoregression analysis two and the Sargan analysis

Table 6. Split analysis results.

	Low GDP per capita countries		High GDP per capita countries	
	OLS	DOLS	FMOLS	PMG
lCO_2spk	−0.068*	0.061***	−0.059*	−0.058*
	(0.041)	−0.011	−0.011	−0.013
lCO_2lpk	0.063***		0.014	
	(0.01)		−0.031	
lCO_2gpk				0.376**
				−0.027
EFP	−0.327***			−0.287***
	(0.101)			(0.065)
CFP	0.023			0.051
	(0.24)			(0.023)
FFE	−0.001	0.011		0.041***
	(0.017)	(0.012)		(0.017)
REC	−0.031*	−0.011		0.011*
	(0.019)	(0.012)		(0.019)
Constant	3.731***	2.692***	2.573***	2.452***
	(0.624)	(0.327)	−0.438	−0.572
Observations	112	112	112	112
Arellano–Bond AR(1)	−6.022	−5.546	−4.785	−6.765
	[0.000]	[0.000]	[0.000]	[0.000]
Arellano–Bond AR(2)	0.568	0.897	−0.032	−0.089
	[0.487]	[0.456]	[0.573]	[0.774]
Sargan test	132.654	133.522	165.568	126.882
	[0.872]	[0.874]	[0.668]	[0.844]

confirmed that the evaluation is accurate. Furthermore, countries with a minimum GDP or per head attain equitable structure and technological impact values. Within the most miniature GDP per head nations, the lCO_2spk rate is 0.057, using 1% a 1% significance level. Meanwhile, the maximum GDP rate per head countries reduced to 0.060, alongside a 5% significance level. About the nations that have the most miniature GDP per head, GFP as well as targeting fiscal policy (TFP) are 0.023 as well as 0.011, whilst in maximum GDP per head economies, the value is 0.025.

In the second model, alongside the lCO_2lpk to be explained parameter, the DOLS approximates indicate a 1% growth in fiscal policy decreases in per head carbon dioxide pollution on liquefied energy types 0.21%. This signifies that fiscal policy is directed at projects that hinder the application of liquid energy types from crude sources like petrol and diesel. Thus, a 1% expansion in energy use causes a 1.23% growth in per head carbon dioxide pollution from liquid energy types — meaning that a considerable amount of the Thai nation's economic activity relies on liquid energy types. Albeit, the fiscal policy projects ensure cutting energy consumption. The break observed in 2008 shows the time of the world's financial crisis and a time of decreased

Table 7. Industrial structure effect.

	Low GDP per capita countries	High GDP per capita countries	Full sample
log(IND)	0.0736***	0.0432***	0.0763***
	(0.032)	(0.112)	(0.021)
R&D	0.038***	0.034***	0.042***
	(0.013)	(0.011)	(0.003)
Constant	2.321***	2.221***	2.452***
	(0.312)	(0.231)	(0.232)
Control variables	Yes	Yes	Yes
Observations	264	264	264
Arellano–Bond AR(1)	−2.432	−2.47	−2.358
	[0.000]	[0.000]	[0.000]
Arellano–Bond AR(2)	0.273	−0.453	0.325
	[0.435]	[0.453]	[0.543]
Sargan test	432.56	543.556	254.465
	[0.23]	[0.565]	[0.144]

Notes: p-value in brackets and standard errors in parentheses; $^{*}p < 0.1$, $^{**}p < 0.5$, $^{***}p < 0.01$.

Table 8. Results of human capital investment effect.

	Low GDP per capita countries	High GDP per capita countries	Full sample
R&D	0.0389**	0.041***	0.0421***
	(0.011)	(0.009)	(0.007)
Constant	0.763**	1.173***	0.543***
	(0.221)	(0.243)	(0.339)
Control variables	Yes	Yes	Yes
Observations	112	112	252
Arellano–Bond AR(1)	−4.348	−3.985	−4.7362
	[0.000]	[0.000]	[0.000]
Arellano–Bond AR(2)	2.734	2.893	2.853
	[0.073]	[0.154]	[0.029]
Sargan test	83.984	78.83	76.467

Notes: p-value in brackets and standard errors in parentheses; $^{*}p < 0.1$, $^{**}p < 0.5$, $^{***}p < 0.01$.

world's energy requirements, culminating in a reduction in crude use. Also, a 1% expansion in fiscal policy grows per head carbon dioxide pollution on vaporous energy types to 6.5%. Implying that fiscal policy in Thailand is efficiently geared at a slow substitution of extra cost unpredictability and comparatively extra carbon dioxide polluting liquid energy types on the comparatively low carbon dioxide energy types, that is, natural gas. One % expansion in energy use agrees on a 6.6% expansion in carbon dioxide pollution via vaporous types. The cointegrating hypothesis is authenticated regarding per head carbon dioxide pollution from vaporous energy types. Thus, the precise impact of fiscal policy on cumulative pollution per head demonstrates an inverse correlation — as a crease of fiscal policy of 1% leads to 0.2% cuts in total carbon dioxide pollution per head. EC obtains a weak meaningful correlation alongside cumulative per head carbon dioxide pollution. This is attributable to the implementation of fiscal policy aimed at reducing carbon dioxide pollution in China.

4.4.1. *The effect of R&D in building back better*

Literature is full of proof that government spending in education is vital to the advancement of the green economy. Scholarly works indicate that financing human capital can promote greening economic system activity expansion meaningfully (Teixeira and Queirós, 2016; Gilbert and Wahl, 2001). Taking cognizance of this research, dual approaches were applied as proxies for the retaining of human capital. The analysis initially considers the fraction of junior school talents for the whole study unit as a proxy for financing human capital. Junior high school teachers were chosen due to the availability of data about them and because it was not sufficient for graduate students within the countries. Even though the plan of action about growing the ADCSP yielded results, the amounts of carbon dioxide emissions have grown concurrently. Furthermore, more so, it is additionally plausible to suggest that industrial use of conventional energy in China might cause an increase in carbon dioxide emissions. Around the world, manufacturing sectors are not likely to deploy negative emission technologies due to cost affordability and produce products to satisfy the requirements of median income earners. The analysis authenticates the present analysis done in China.

Likewise, the findings show conventional energy use interrupted carbon dioxide emission in Australia; a 1% spike in conventional energy use amplified carbon dioxide emission to 1.09% (FMOLS), 1.26% (DOLS), as well as 1.08% (canonical cointegrating regression (CCR)). An additional reason, this analysis equally authenticates the transmittal carbon dioxide-induced hypothesis, when a percentage growth in transmittals resulted in an increase in carbon dioxide emissions to 0.07% (FMOLS), 0.06% (DOLS), as well as 0.07% (CCR). The findings fall in past studies that did a similar analysis for Asian nations. Finally, the findings indicated that workforce added to abating carbon dioxide emissions in Australia, due to 1% expansion in the workforce reduced carbon dioxide emission to 0.67% (FMOLS), 0.070% (DOLS) in addition to 0.65% (CCR). The analysis implies that the workforce circuitously plays an essential part in abating carbon dioxide emissions by laboring in a low carbon-intensive sector.

Similarly, the approximated findings indicated that TFP added to reducing amounts of carbon dioxide emissions in Australia when a percentage expansion in the actual interest rate resulted in reducing carbon dioxide emissions. The findings confirmed the existing analysis undertaken in Asian nations. Last but not least, the findings affirmed the earnings-induced carbon dioxide hypothesis for Australia, when a percentage growth in GDP rises carbon dioxide emissions to 0.78% (FMOLS), 0.81% (DOLS), as well as 0.78% (CCR). The analysis is consistent with past works, in the case of Pakistan.

One percentage expansion in energy consumption results in a 0.4% expansion in carbon dioxide emissions when the carbon dioxide emissions are totaled (lCO_2pk). From the analysis, a dual meaningful structural break correlation is detected on the lCO_2pk. Also, the initial period reveals a direct intercept change that declines within the years of hydrocarbons supply inactivity — this phase occurred at the same time of demand growth in the Asian region for hydrocarbons and the plunge in the excess capacity of Saudi Arabia. The next phase of the break-in year of 2008, as well as an adverse intercept change, indicates the year of 2008 global economic downturn. Now, juxtaposing the findings of past studies, we identified that the negative correlation between fiscal policy and carbon dioxide pollution within Belt and Road Initiative is in line alongside (Katircioglu *et al.*, 2018). A negative correlation between fiscal policy as well as cumulative pollution was detected for Turkey. Nevertheless, unconformity to Ike *et al.* (2020), where a direct impact amongst fiscal policy and carbon dioxide pollution was detected for China. Likewise, the DOLS approximation shows the main diffusion instrument via which fiscal policy in Thailand abates carbon dioxide pollution in the long term. The result is obtained beyond advancing policies that promote the use of least carbon dioxide releasing sources in the form of natural gas resulting in a clear cut in cumulative carbon dioxide pollution whilst dampening the application of high-level carbon dioxide releasing types, such as hydrocarbons.

4.5. *Discussion*

The analyses of the approximate emanating from model six are displayed in the two Sargan, and AR evaluations indicate that the forecasted findings are reliable. Policy formulators control as well as expand global trade movement via commercial policy instruments (Boyes and Melvin, 2011). Countries around the globe apply commercial policy to expand aggregate trade as well as consequently encourage economic expansion. Given this, the endogenous advancement equation proffered the addition of trade to economic expansion which might differ in various economic assumptions. That is to assert, the economic importance of trade hinges on if the parameters connected to the relative gain circumstances of a nation's resources produce economic activity that brings future inclusive development. Thus, the effect of trade might vary in the stages of economic advancement (Aljadani *et al.*, 2021). Most scholarly works asserted that irrespective of its likely beneficial impacts on economic expansion, trade directness could interrupt economic expansion. Camargo-Caicedo *et al.* (2021) asserted that trade directness may reduce expansion in the future when a nation focuses on manufacturing alongside evolving relative gains characterized by likely output or where innovations in technology or learning by doing are inadequate. Thus, the practice of discriminatory safeguard is a means that technological advancement is cultivable in those nations. Even so, foreign direct investment (FDI) in an economy is encouraged by a commercial policy. Han *et al.* (2021) showed that trade directness promotes export-led FDI, whilst trade controls cause axe evasion on FDI to utilize the local market. Likewise, previous studies revealed that trade directness controls could impact FDI movement in two ways, adversely and directly. In South American nations, trade directness (free trade agreements) has mainly wooed FDI. Wang and Yi (2021) contended that FDI encourages the exchange of imports and exports and advances transitional input trade. Bampatsou and Halkos (2019), however, inversely stated that free trade agreements might expand FDI given in peculiar circumstances. Therefore, there is the likelihood of this occurring due to foreign taxes within the balance state not being very high to promote FDI or due to an economy, that is, trapped in several balances, unable to back FDI scholarly works detected scientific basis for the direct link among FDI and trade (Cheng *et al.*, 2020b).

So, nations can apply commercial policy to set in place for the first-time tax reductions in exports. This move incentivizes global behemoths and indigenous enterprises to produce extra goods at minimum costs, increasing total requirements, and economic expansion. On the other hand, nations are inclined to grow exports tariffs to grow the use of locally manufactured merchandise. Consequently, making exportation goods extra costly due to growth in export tariffs motivates customers to purchase internally manufactured merchandise. Exorbitantly cost exports make global customers look for affordable goods elsewhere, causing the reduction in the export of consumption and supply of exports.

Furthermore, nations that levy export levies relax trade tariffs abroad and grow exports and production in the chosen areas (Al Kharusi and Ada, 2018). Reductions in interruption encourage earnings benefits as well as economic progress. This is because intense rivalry domestically limits production and actual currency gain, increasing imports and tightening in other areas of the market. This circumstance leads to the reduction of industrial upscaling.

Nonetheless, an expansion in the production of before-tariffs exports plummets the world's merchandise costs. When the final impact manages the before impacts, the remaining deficit might happen to a specific nation when tariffs are relaxed. Also, larger nations with high export tariffs rates saturate the market with merchandise due to maximum efficiency gains whilst equally reducing the world's cost of the product it trades abroad. Moreover, these circumstances may lead to negative monetary costs to the rivalling nations, nonetheless importing nations could seize the opportunity of world's costs declines (Taghizadeh-Hesary and Yoshino, 2019, 2020).

Regarding the explanation above, commercial policy changes influence cumulative utilization, global trade, and manufacturing systems. Hence, it is illogical to downplay its effects on carbon dioxide emissions. Given this, no research studied the correlation between commercial policy as well as carbon emission. The analysis wants to close the study gap empirically and in theory by connecting commercial policy to carbon dioxide emissions in Australia.

Also, in bit to regulate the flow of money in an economy, monetary policy is used by CBS to achieve this aim. In addition, to attain varied macroeconomic goals, CBS craft and implement monetary policies. For instance, tightening monetary is applied to manage inflation to reduce money distribution, as CBS actual interest ratios attain unaffordable levels, subsequently creating a cut in total requirements, manufacturing activity, conventional energy use, economic expansion, as well as carbon dioxide emissions. In present days, Cheng *et al.* (2020a) scientific analysis backed the application of monetary policy as an efficient restraining to counter inflation in various economies globally. However, specific stages of changes in costs of goods and services were thought reasonable for the world's prosperity. An example, some nations often cause demand by bringing into existence a policy directive encouraging a 2% yearly growth in costs. Thus, when economists predict a cost spike in the long term, the imperative for goods grows, resulting in surplus purchases. Although CBS globally sustain an inflation goal of roughly 2% to keep a demand, high-level inflation ratios could destroy an economy in the future. As a result, the trajectory of over-purchasing because of high-level demand and long-term costs promotes enterprises to find extra income to expand their supply of merchandise (Taghizadeh-Hesary and Yoshino, 2015; Taghizadeh-Hesary *et al.*, 2021).

5. Conclusion and Policy Implications

This novel study indicated that sustainable economic advancement would not be attained, devoid of focusing on growing and sustaining a green economy. Past studies looked at the connection between government spending and pollution alone but did not consider the advancement and expansion of greening the economic system activity. So, this analysis endeavored to throw more light on this sector, as well as beyond thoroughly scrutinizing relevant empirical works and at the same time did a statistical evaluation, thus, resolves that as a result of geopolitical conspiracies of the governing parties of the country, there existed year to year variations alongside expansions and reductions in the formulated green economic indicators. However, the generalized method moment approximated findings indicate that there are dual structural and technological effects. Not only this, but also, the findings of the development signify the increment of the green economy, alongside government spending on research and innovation. However, the levels of advancements of technologies, in addition to human capital, differ amongst nations.

Our analysis approximated the reliable and consistent methods with the changing impacts of different structural breaks and exposed different fiscal policy impacts on carbon dioxide pollution via varied energy types. Whereas fiscal policy attained a direct influence on minimal carbon dioxide releasing vaporous, that is, natural gas, an adverse impact on high-level carbon dioxide releasing liquid energy types, hydrocarbon, and a directly nonsignificant impact on carbon dioxide polluting solid energy type, such as coal, were detected within the scientific findings. The findings authenticated the presence of the causality hypothesis in all models. While economic system advancement enables ecological affluence, growing the amounts of earnings levels of income has a pollution-abating impact. Referencing Oladipo (2010), Granger causality model indicates an underlying one-way movement from fiscal policy to carbon dioxide pollution and from fiscal program to energy use — signifying that fiscal policy projects in the direction energy use attain future ramifications to ecological value. The scientific analysis additionally backs the energy-induced expansion hypothesis on the Thai economy. You are implying the deployment of RES as energy-saving resources. Here, the energy transition is strongly recommended instead of the conventional energy sources. Also, there is the need for sustained financing in harmful emissions generation sources from governments and the private actors; this should be done not to hinder the energy production source of the study countries and requirements — as a result of the overly taxing of carbon-intensive sources, nevertheless, to augment the low carbon dioxide polluting and RES to a point when the volume is created in the RE segment. In this vein, fiscal policy projects ought to be sent on the way of the slow taxation of conventional energy consumption and the encouraging of inducements to financing in RE beyond tax exclusions as well as particular public loans. Due to the large infrastructural requirements of the RE segment, there is the basis for formulating a future infrastructure plan to leverage finances from emission trading systems such as carbon tax or cap and trade schemes on fossil fuel companies. Subsequently, the adverse impact of fiscal policy on cumulative carbon dioxide pollution and the slow substitution of hydrocarbon alongside natural gas to be the principal energy source ought not to be the ultimate panacea to carbon dioxide mitigation in Thailand. Nevertheless, it ought to be a midway choice. Similarly, commitment ought to be made to a snail's space substitution of conventional energy types and the achievement of net-zero pollution. Hence, this can be a path of long-term research for scholars.

Our study has policy importance for policy formulators, according to analyzes. To begin with, the findings emphasize the imperative for managers of economies to craft green commercial policies in Belt and Road initiative nations. The findings affirm that growth commercial fiscal policies result in an expansion in carbon dioxide emissions, whilst tightening commercial policies eases the reduction of carbon dioxide emissions. So, it is mooted that Australia levied maximum export tariffs on manufacturing products that applied polluting energy sources in their production process. Likewise, beyond commercial policy, the public ought to reduce export tariffs on manufacturing goods produced utilizing clean RE technologies. The green commercial policy approach will incentivize and promote the application of cleaner energy in the production processes. The next point is that it is essential to craft green and ecological focused monetary policy for the Australian market, given the differing effects of various monetary policies on carbon dioxide emissions. Regarding the individual approximates computed on this research piece, TFP limits carbon dioxide emissions. This analysis gives reliable scientific analysis proof that CBS applying monetary policy as an instrument to encourage "green and environmental focused lending propositions" within commercial banks in the Belt and Road countries. More so, taking exorbitant interest rates, commercial institutions could punish enterprises, companies, and suppliers that supply conventional energy in their manufacturing processes whilst concurrently reassuring enterprises that utilized RE via reduced interest ratios. The scheme, if implemented, is anticipated to cut carbon dioxide emissions to encourage enterprises to find RE generation sources to encourage sustainable generation.

References

Agrawala, S, D Dussaux and N Monti (2020). What policies for greening the crisis response and economic recovery? Lessons learned from past green stimulus measures and implications for the COVID-19 crisis. OECD Environment Working Papers.

Al Kharusi, S and MS Ada (2018). External debt and economic growth: The case of emerging economy. *Journal of Economic Integration*, 33(1), 1141–1157. https://doi.org/10.11130/jei.2018.33.1.1141.

Al-Qahtani, AM, WT Elgzar and HAF Ibrahim (2020). COVID-19 pandemic: Psycho-social consequences during the social distancing period among najran city population. *Psychiatria Danubina*, 32, 280–286. https://doi.org/10.24869/PSYD.2020.280.

Ali Shah, SA, C Longsheng, YA Solangi, M Ahmad and S Ali (2021). Energy trilemma based prioritization of waste-to-energy technologies: Implications for post-COVID-19 green economic recovery in Pakistan. *Journal of Cleaner Production*, 284, 124729. https://doi.org/10.1016/j.jclepro.2020.124729.

Aljadani, A, H Toumi, S Toumi, M Hsini and B Jallali (2021). Investigation of the N-shaped environmental Kuznets curve for COVID-19 mitigation in the KSA. *Environmental Science and Pollution Research*, 28, 29681–29700. https://doi.org/10.1007/s11356-021-12713-3.

Bagherzadeh, F, MJ Mehrani, M Basirifard and J Roostaei (2021). Comparative study on total nitrogen prediction in wastewater treatment plant and effect of various feature selection methods on machine learning algorithms performance. *Journal of Water Process Engineering*, 41, 102033.

Baloch, ZA, Q Tan, N Iqbal, M Mohsin, Q Abbas, W Iqbal and IS Chaudhry (2020). Trilemma assessment of energy intensity, efficiency, and environmental index: Evidence from BRICS countries. *Environmental Science and Pollution Research*, 27(27), 34337–34347. https://doi.org/10.1007/s11356-020-09578-3.

Bampatsou, C and G Halkos (2019). Economic growth, efficiency and environmental elasticity for the G7 countries. *Energy Policy*, 130, 355–360.

Barbier, EB (2020). Greening the post-pandemic recovery in the G20. *Environmental and Resource Economics*, 76(4), 685–703. https://doi.org/10.1007/s10640-020-00437-w.

Camargo-Caicedo, Y, LC Mantilla-Romo and TR Bolaño-Ortiz (2021). Emissions reduction of greenhouse gases, ozone precursors, aerosols and acidifying gases from road transportation during the COVID-19 lockdown in Colombia. *Applied Sciences*, 11(4), 1458. https://doi.org/10.3390/app11041458.

Chandio, AA, Y Jiang, A Rehman, MA Twumasi, AG Pathan and M Mohsin (2020). Determinants of demand for credit by smallholder farmers': A farm level analysis based on survey in Sindh, Pakistan. *Journal of Asian Business and Economic Studies*, 28, 225–240. https://doi.org/10.1108/jabes-01-2020-0004.

Cheng, Z, J Liu, L Li and X Gu (2020b). Research on meta-frontier total-factor energy efficiency and its spatial convergence in Chinese provinces. *Energy Economics*, 86, 104702.

Cheng, F, C Chiao, Z Fang, C Wang and S Yao (2020a). Raising short-term debt for long-term investment and stock price crash risk: Evidence from China. *Finance Research Letters*, 33, 101200. https://doi.org/10.1016/j.frl.2019.05.018.

Cho, JS, TH Kim and Y Shin (2015). Quantile cointegration in the autoregressive distributed-lag modeling framework. *Journal of Econometrics*, 188(1), 281–300.

Cojoianu, TF, E Collins, AGF Hoepner, D Magill, T O'Neill and FI Schneider (2020). In the name of COVID-19: Is the ECB fuelling the climate crisis? *Environmental and Resource Economics*, 76, 447–517. https://doi.org/10.1007/s10640-020-00450-z.

De Matos, TPV, VPV De Matos, K De Mello and RA Valente (2021). Protected areas and forest fragmentation: Sustainability index for prioritizing fragments for landscape restoration. *Geology, Ecology, and Landscapes*, 5(1), 19–31. https://doi.org/10.1080/24749508.2019.1696266.

Engström, G, J Gars, N Jaakkola, T Lindahl, D Spiro and AA van Benthem (2020). What policies address both the coronavirus crisis and the climate crisis? *Environmental and Resource Economics*, 76(4), 789–810. https://doi.org/10.1007/s10640-020-00451-y.

Ghenai, C and M Bettayeb (2021). Data analysis of the electricity generation mix for clean energy transition during COVID-19 lockdowns. *Energy Sources, Part A: Recovery, Utilization and Environmental Effects*, 1–21.

Gilbert, J and T Wahl (2001). Export restrictions, urban unemployment, and the location of processing activities. *Economics Letters*, 71(1), 105–110.

Han, P, Q Cai, T Oda, N Zeng, Y Shan, X Lin and D Liu (2021). Assessing the recent impact of COVID-19 on carbon emissions from China using domestic economic data. *Science of the Total Environment*, 750, 141688. https://doi.org/10.1016/j.scitotenv.2020.141688.

He, W, Q Abbas, M Alharthi, M Mohsin, I Hanif and X Vinh Vo (2020). Integration of renewable hydrogen in light-duty vehicle: Nexus between energy security and low carbon emission resources. *International Journal of Hydrogen Energy*, 45(51), 27958–27968. https://doi.org/10.1016/j.ijhydene.2020.06.177.

Ike, GN, O Usman and SA Sarkodie (2020). Fiscal policy and CO_2 emissions from heterogeneous fuel sources in Thailand: Evidence from multiple structural breaks cointegration test. *Science of the Total Environment*, 702, 134711. https://doi.org/10.1016/j.scitotenv.2019.134711.

Katircioglu, S, S Katircioglu and O Altun (2018). The moderating role of oil price changes in the effects of service trade and tourism on growth: The case of Turkey. *Environmental Science and Pollution Research*, 25(35), 35266–35275. https://doi.org/10.1007/s11356-018-3448-2.

Kim, TI, YH Shin and RC White-Traut (2003). Multisensory intervention improves physical growth and illness rates in Korean orphaned newborn infants. *Research in Nursing and Health*, 26(6), 424–433. https://doi.org/10.1002/nur.10105.

Kurukulasuriya, P, N Kala and R Mendelsohn (2011). Adaptation and climate change impacts: A structural ricardian model of irrigation and farm income in Africa. *Climate Change Economics*, 2(2), 149–174. https://doi.org/10.1142/S2010007811000255.

Li, Z, S Ju, M Duan and S Cai (2020). Quantitative selection of leading industries of green economy in coastal cities based on industrial relevance. *Journal of Coastal Research*, 103, 566–569. https://doi.org/10.2112/SI103-115.1.

Lv, K, X Feng, S Kelly, L Zhu and M Deng (2019). A study on embodied carbon transfer at the provincial level of China from a social network perspective. *Journal of Cleaner Production*, 225, 1089–1104.

Mendelsohn, R (2020). Integrated assessment and climate change. *Climate Change Economics*, 11, 2040004. https://doi.org/10.1142/S2010007820400047.

Mohsin, M, P Zhou, N Iqbal and SAA Shah (2018). Assessing oil supply security of South Asia. *Energy*, 155, 438–447. https://doi.org/10.1016/j.energy.2018.04.116.

Mohsin, M, F Taghizadeh-Hesary, N Panthamit, S Anwar, Q Abbas and XV Vo (2020). Developing low carbon finance index: Evidence from developed and developing economies. *Finance Research Letters*, 43, 101520. https://doi.org/10.1016/j.frl.2020.101520.

Mohsin, M, H Ullah, N Iqbal, W Iqbal and F Taghizadeh-Hesary (2021). How external debt led to economic growth in South Asia: A policy perspective analysis from quantile regression. *Economic Analysis and Policy*, 72, 423–437.

Nižetić, S (2020). Impact of coronavirus (COVID-19) pandemic on air transport mobility, energy, and environment: A case study. *International Journal of Energy Research*, 44(13), 10953–10961. https://doi.org/10.1002/er.5706.

Oladipo, OS (2010). Does saving really matter for growth in developing countries? The case of a small open economy. *International Business & Economics Research Journal*, 9(4), 87–94. https://doi.org/10.19030/iber.v9i4.556.

Paital, B, K Das and SK Parida (2020). Inter nation social lockdown versus medical care against COVID-19, a mild environmental insight with special reference to India. *Science of the Total Environment*, 728, 138914.

Paital, B (2020). Nurture to nature via COVID-19, a self-regenerating environmental strategy of environment in global context. *Science of the Total Environment*, 729, 139088.

Parida, BR, S Bar, N Singh, B Oinam, AC Pandey and M Kumar (2020). A short-term decline in anthropogenic emission of CO_2 in India due to COVID-19 confinement. *Progress in Physical Geography:Earth and Environment*, 45(4), 471–487. https://doi.org/10.1177/0309133320966741.

Rana, U (2020). Psychosocial consequences of COVID-19 on sex workers: A global perspective. *Psychiatria Danubina*, 32, 590–592.

Sarfraz, M, M Mohsin, S Naseem and A Kumar (2021). Modeling the relationship between carbon emissions and environmental sustainability during COVID-19: A new evidence from asymmetric ARDL cointegration approach. *Environment, Development and Sustainability*, 23, 16208–16226. https://doi.org/10.1007/s10668-021-01324-0.

Scharf, M, L Heide, A Grahle, AM Syré and D Göhlich (2020). Environmental impact of subsidy concepts for stimulating car sales in Germany. *Sustainability*, 12(23), 10037. https://doi.org/10.3390/su122310037.

Shan, Y, J Ou, D Wang, Z Zeng, S Zhang, D Guan and K Hubacek (2021). Impacts of COVID-19 and fiscal stimuli on global emissions and the Paris Agreement. *Nature Climate Change*, 11(3), 200–206. https://doi.org/10.1038/s41558-020-00977-5.

Shaw, D and YH Fu (2020). Climate clubs with tax revenue recycling, tariffs, and transfers. *Climate Change Economics*, 11(4), 2040008. https://doi.org/10.1142/S2010007820400084.

Smith, LV, N Tarui and T Yamagata (2021). Assessing the impact of COVID-19 on global fossil fuel consumption and CO_2 emissions. *Energy Economics*, 97, 105170. https://doi.org/10.1016/j.eneco.2021.105170.

Sovacool, BK (2017). Contestation, contingency, and justice in the Nordic low-carbon energy transition. *Energy Policy*, 102, 569–582.

Sun, L, X Cao, M Alharthi, J Zhang, F Taghizadeh-Hesary and M Mohsin (2020a). Carbon emission transfer strategies in supply chain with lag time of emission reduction technologies and low-carbon preference of consumers. *Journal of Cleaner Production*, 264, 121664. https://doi.org/10.1016/j.jclepro.2020.121664.

Sun, H, AK Pofoura, I Adjei Mensah, L Li and M Mohsin (2020b). The role of environmental entrepreneurship for sustainable development: Evidence from 35 countries in Sub-Saharan Africa. *Science of the Total Environment*, 741, 140132. https://doi.org/10.1016/j.scitotenv.2020.140132.

Sun, L, L Qin, F Taghizadeh-Hesary, J Zhang, M Mohsin and IS Chaudhry (2020c). Analyzing carbon emission transfer network structure among provinces in China: New evidence from social network analysis. *Environmental Science and Pollution Research*, 27(18), 23281–23300. https://doi.org/10.1007/s11356-020-08911-0.

Taghizadeh-Hesary, F and N Yoshino (2015). Macroeconomic effects of oil price fluctuations on emerging and developed economies in a model incorporating monetary variables. *Economics and Policy of Energy and the Environment*, 2015, 51–75. https://doi.org/10.3280/EFE2015-002005.

Taghizadeh-Hesary, F and N Yoshino (2019). The way to induce private participation in green finance and investment. *Finance Research Letters*, 31, 98–103. https://doi.org/10.1016/j.frl.2019.04.016.

Taghizadeh-Hesary, F and N Yoshino (2020). Sustainable solutions for green financing and investment in renewable energy projects. *Energies*, 13(4), 788. https://doi.org/10.3390/en13040788.

Taghizadeh-Hesary, F, E Rasoulinezhad, N Yoshino, Y Chang, F Taghizadeh-Hesary and PJ Morgan (2021). The energy-pollution-health nexus: A panel data analysis of low-and middle-income asian countries. *Singapore Economic Review*, 66(2), 435–455. https://doi.org/10.1142/S0217590820430043.

Taherzadeh, O (2021). Promise of a green economic recovery post-Covid: Trojan horse or turning point? *Global Sustainability*, 4, e2.

Teixeira, AAC and ASS Queirós (2016). Economic growth, human capital and structural change: A dynamic panel data analysis. *Research Policy*, 45(8), 1636–1648.

Tian, X, C An, Z Chen and Z Tian (2021). Assessing the impact of COVID-19 pandemic on urban transportation and air quality in Canada. *Science of the Total Environment*, 765, 144270. https://doi.org/10.1016/j.scitotenv.2020.144270.

Tiep, NC, M Wang, M Mohsin, HW Kamran and FA Yazdi (2021). An assessment of power sector reforms and utility performance to strengthen consumer self-confidence towards private investment. *Economic Analysis and Policy*, 69, 676–689. https://doi.org/10.1016/j.eap.2021.01.005.

Wang, Q and H Yi (2021). New energy demonstration program and China's urban green economic growth: Do regional characteristics make a difference? *Energy Policy*, 151, 112161. https://doi.org/10.1016/j.enpol.2021.112161.

Wang, Z (2020). Development and integration model of marine tourism resources based on sustainable development. *Journal of Coastal Research*, 103, 1030–1033. https://doi.org/10.2112/SI103-214.1.

Yang, Z, Q Abbas, I Hanif, M Alharthi, F Taghizadeh-Hesary, B Aziz and M Mohsin (2021). Short- and long-run influence of energy utilization and economic growth on carbon discharge in emerging SREB economies. *Renewable Energy*, 165, 43–51. https://doi.org/10.1016/j.renene.2020.10.141.

Yang, Z (2020). Climate change and externality. *Climate Change Economics*, 11(4), 2040007. https://doi.org/10.1142/S2010007820400072.

https://doi.org/10.1142/9789819812783_0010

MEASURING THE IMPACT OF ECONOMIC POLICIES ON CO_2 EMISSIONS IN EU: WAYS TO ACHIEVE GREEN ECONOMIC RECOVERY[||||]

WENJI HUANG[*,††], HAYOT BERK SAYDALIEV[†,‡‡], WASIM IQBAL[‡,§§] and MUHAMMAD IRFAN[§,¶,||,**,¶¶]

[*]*School of Political Science and Public Administration*
Neijiang Normal University, Neijiang 641112, China

[†]*Graduate School of Business and Entrepreneurship*
Under the Cabinet of Ministers of the Republic of Uzbekistan

[‡]*Department of Management Science*
College of Management, Shenzhen University, Shenzhen, China

[§]*Business School, Shandong Management University, Jinan 250357, China*

[¶]*European Center of Economics*
Azerbaijan State University of Economics (UNEC)
Istiqlaliyyat Str. 6, Baku, Azerbaijan

[||]*Advanced Research Centre European University of Lefke*
Lefke, Northern Cyprus, TR-10 Mersin, Turkey

[**]*School of Business Administration, ILMA University*
Karachi 75190, Pakistan
[††]*scdxhwj@163.com*
[‡‡]*h.saydaliev@rgsbm.uz*
[§§]*wasimiqbal01@yahoo.com*
[¶¶]*irfansahar@sdmu.edu.cn*

Regional attempts to reduce pollution levels emerging from the European Union (EU) relative to 2010 are contrasted with unique policies of individual member countries' aims to achieve a 10% reduction per country. Given this scenario, this research expands on the topic by developing a novel framework that links macroeconomic policies, total national expenditure per person, traditional energy use, renewable energy use, and CO_2 emissions levels in EU countries from 1990 to 2016. The study utilizes the second generation cross-sectional-autoregressive-distributed lag (CS-ARDL) panel data method. According to the study's findings, the monetary instruments of growth exacerbated the adverse effects of CO_2 emissions, and by tightening monetary policy, the harmful effects of CO_2 emissions levels have been reduced. Further, the Granger causality test indicates a bidirectional causality between monetary policy and CO_2 emissions levels, and unidirectional causality from the policy assessment for energy use. The finding confirms that the assessment policy recommendations on energy consumption have future effects on ecological value.

[¶¶]Corresponding author.

[||||]This chapter was originally published in Climate Change Economics, Vol. 13, No. 3, March 2022, published by World Scientific Publishing, Singapore. Reprinted with permission.

Keywords: Sustainable development; CO_2; monetary policy; cumulative consumption expenditure; green economic recovery; European Union.

1. Introduction

Sustainability is about establishing the right balance between environmental, social, and governance concepts that ensure intergenerational equity (Razzaq *et al.*, 2021; Ahmad *et al.*, 2021a). Due to the company's slow and stimulating approach to sustainability, the first three bottom line (TBL) concepts laid the foundation for the application of the concept of sustainable development (Zakari and Toplak, 2021). COVID-19 has caused severe damage to world economic activities and triggered serious monetary consequences (Zhang *et al.*, 2021; Iqbal *et al.*, 2021a; Chien *et al.*, 2021; Iqbal *et al.*, 2019b), such as expanded GDP costs of nations, entrenching poverty as well as the quest for food around the world (Berger and Marinacci, 2020; Irfan *et al.*, 2020a; Elavarasan *et al.*, 2021). Consequently, the world's healthcare challenges presented by the COVID-19 grievously retards the pace to a sustainable future (Irfan *et al.*, 2020b,f; Ahmad *et al.*, 2021b).

Fortmann *et al.* (2020) stated that the negative impact of the pandemic might lead to inhumane efforts to achieve 12 of the 17 UN Sustainable Development Goals (SDGs) within a decade. Leal Filho *et al.* (2020) discovered the contagion as an important danger to executing the SDGs by watering down the importance of the SDGs as nations are concerned with handling the pandemic challenges but with limited resources. Thus, there has been a commitment worldwide to contain the contagion. The issue of sustainability after the contagion's phrase ought not to be swept under the carpet (Razzaq *et al.*, 2020; Yang *et al.*, 2021). Indeed, building back better entails taking the issue of sustainability seriously than the world ever did (Abbas *et al.*, 2021; Hou *et al.*, 2019; Yu *et al.*, 2021).

Despite the numerous parameters that influence the ecological value that has been studied in the more than past 10 years, this study takes a different angle by considering monetary policy as a novel parameter and evaluates the casual factors of environmental destruction based on the ensuing factors (Mohsin *et al.*, 2021; Khokhar *et al.*, 2020a; Fu *et al.*, 2021). Managers of national economies execute financial policies via spending and levies to manage changes in prices of goods and services, joblessness, and a steady sustainable GDP increase. In this case, green finance has emerged as an important strategy for the financial sector and a point of reference for government policies in the face of environmental issues such as climate change and biodiversity loss. Green finance arose from the ashes of the 2008 global financial crisis and is rooted in private financial sector strategies. As Taghizadeh-Hesary and Yoshino (2019) argue, it represents the financial industry's first concerted approach: "Green finance represents the global financial community's first structured attempt to join financial performance and positive environmental impact."

In the public debate on green finance, the financial industry and its partners, as well as transnational corporate leaders, are prominent players. There is a good reason for this. Green finance provides the financial industry with new profit opportunities (Abbas *et al.*, 2021). Public policy initiatives in the fields of green finance, green recovery, green growth, and monetary policy have recently gained traction (Sun *et al.*, 2020a,b; Taghizadeh-Hesary and Yoshino, 2020; Taghizadeh-Hesary *et al.*, 2021). The European Parliament, in collaboration with the European Commission and the European Union (EU) Technical Expert Group (TEG), has proposed a taxonomy that is expected to improve the effectiveness of green finance (Baloch *et al.*, 2020; Iqbal *et al.*, 2019b,c; Latif *et al.*, 2021; Mohsin *et al.*, 2021). The European Commission released a strategy for financing the transition to a sustainable economy. Furthermore, a debate has erupted at the central bank level (e.g., the European Central Bank's climate action plan, the People's Bank of China's Guidelines for Establishing Green Finance) with the goal of proposing strategies for dealing with climate change and the role of finance and monetary policy in this regard (Taghizadeh-Hesary and Taghizadeh-Hesary, 2020). There are also international initiatives, such as UNCTAD's proposal for a Global Green New Deal and numerous national initiatives to boost green finance. Furthermore, there is a significant trend toward green finance in the field of development finance.

In addition, the reduction of ADCSP due to tax expansion reduces the company's ability to produce large quantities of goods and services because of slow demand. In response to this situation, the company reduced manufacturing and traditional energy use in the manufacturing system, thereby reducing carbon dioxide emissions (Shaw *et al.*, 2021). The rise in taxes through TFP reduces aggregate domestic consumption spending per capital, manufacturing activity, conventional energy use, and reduces carbon dioxide emissions. As the EU nations apply the monetary policy to be an important instrument to encouraging sustainable progress, FDI, and innovation, it warrants assessing its usefulness to bettering carbon dioxide emissions levels Iqbal *et al.* (2021b, 2019c); Anser *et al.* (2020). The opinions concerning the efficiency and efficacy of tax programs aimed at cutting pollution levels have been one of the positions in recent times (Madurai Elavarasan *et al.*, 2021; Irfan *et al.*, 2020c,b, 2019). The concerns are what are the effectiveness of the idiosyncratic member's actions and that of joint member countries' actions in the EU (Davidovic *et al.*, 2020). Besides, the concerns of the cost of regional competitiveness were vehemently opposed by an interest group resulting in the forfeiture of the idea of the EU's proposal on putting a cost on carbon more than three decades ago (He *et al.*, 2020) and the United States attempted to influence the Kyoto Treaty of December 1997.

This paper seeks to investigate the effects of the reasonableness of growth economic policies and tightening monetary policies (TMPs) on carbon dioxide emissions levels alongside several economic parameters of the group of 20 countries. Thus, the exclusivity of the study from the past research is given below:

(i) This analysis gives the macroeconomic equation that dissects the influence of growth monetary policy (GMP) and TMP on CO_2 emission levels.
(ii) The analysis couples the presently found emission parameters through growth and tightening financial programs.
(iii) This is the first study that inculcates the dual policy tools of GFP and TFP to evaluate their correlation alongside the ecology.
(iv) Ultimately, no empirical analysis has previously investigated the influence of GMPs and TMPs and CO_2 emissions on ADCSP in the context of EU nations. The rest of the paper is structured as follows. The economic and ecological effects are given in Sec. 2. The theoretical foundation of the research is given in Sec. 3, alongside the data and methods. While Sec. 4 provides the results of the study with conclusions, policy implications and limitations.

2. The Economic and Environmental Impact of COVID-19

The COVID-19 has been likened to World War II due to its destructive nature (Irfan *et al.*, 2021d, 2021e) and is characterized as a "Black Swan" event (Gilbert *et al.*, 2020; Qiao *et al.*, 2021). The pandemic occurrence has shipwrecked the global economy like never. A section of scholars has forecasted measures taken to contain the pandemic such as economic lookdowns, ban on travels, and no movement has contributed to reducing infections and death (Li *et al.*, 2021a). Nevertheless, these measures have had drastic macroeconomic impacts in the form of economic recession and prolonged economic costs. The macroeconomic cost of the contagion is largely attributed to a drastic reduction in demand for goods and services. This is due to consumers not being available to spend on goods and services due to job losses and movement restrictions.

According to Matveevskii (2021), on 1st June 2020, the projected figure of national demand plunged, necessitated by a large scale outburst of the COVID-19 (referred to a situation of >1000 COVID-19) comparative to a without COVID-19 baseline assumption regarding a country like Bangladesh (7.70–11.55%) (Iqbal *et al.*, 2019a; Khokhar *et al.*, 2020b), next to Pakistan between 7.26% and 10.89% and then India of 6.40% and 9.60%. This evolving situation is much felt virtually in all segments of the economy (Wu *et al.*, 2021). Especially deprived of government financial assistance, airlines companies had to lay off staff to cut down expenditure (Wang *et al.*, 2021). The assertion holds for all sectors of the economy. The worry is that the economy might take a different twist, and jobless people would not be able to spend on goods and series, making the industry cut down jobs to continue to operate (Li *et al.*, 2021b). This might be a vicious circle when the pandemic persists. Shaw and Fu (2020) explain such a scenario to be the "macroeconomic flu" — a transient negative shock to demand

and production and causing reductions in productivity that rapidly recuperates, and the cost is perhaps totally recuperated.

Furthermore, Economists concur that the pandemic's havoc on the world will be felt great but did not give a crystal-clear cost of the pandemic to the world's economy (Kamensky, 2021). The Bretton Wood Institutions both forecasted that the developed economies would plunge by 7% and 6% (Al Asbahi *et al.*, 2019; Latif *et al.*, 2021; Baloch *et al.*, 2020; Hou *et al.*, 2019), correspondingly due to the drastic tightening of financial activity, pervasive socially distanced measures, and a plunge in international requirements for goods and services that reduced productivity. Regarding the gross domestic product of EDMEs, it is forecasted to reduce to 2.5% and 1.0% in 2020 due to adverse production shocks emanating from feebleness in demand from the developed countries (Chen *et al.*, 2021a), alongside disruptions from their national surges, sending hundreds of millions back to poverty and lack.

Following the hills of stark retrenchment of developed countries and the ruin of emerging nations, global gross domestic product is forecasted to plunge to 5.2%, according to the forecast of the World Bank (WB). In contrast, the International Monetary Fund (IMF) forecast a 3% plunge in the world's gross domestic product (see Table 1). Now, the undeniable conclusion is the world's GDP will fall into a deep recession since World War II, over three times the 2008/2009 financial crisis (The World Bank Annual Report 2020, 2020). As a result, the Corona pandemic already cut a greater chunk of international trade to negative 13.4% and a drastic cut in commodity prices, particularly a plunge in the crude cost of negative 47.9% in 2020 (The World Bank, 2021) (See Figure 1). Whereas the world's economy is regaining expansion at 4.2%, according to the WB, and 5.8% according to the IMF. It is anticipated that the pandemic will be overcome soon as many people are being vaccinated, restrictions

Table 1. Growth projections (real GDP, change of % annually).

	2019		2020		2021	
Regions	WB	IMF	WB	IMF	WB	IMF
World output	2.9	2.4	−3.0	−5.2	5.8	4.2
Developed Economies	1.7	1.6	−6.1	−7.0	4.5	3.9
United States	2.3	2.3	−5.9	−6.1	4.7	4
Euro Area	1.2	1.2	−7.5	−9.1	4.7	4.5
Japan	0.7	0.7	−5.2	−6.1	3	2.5
Emerging Markets and Economies	3.7	3.5	−1.0	−2.5	6.6	4.6
East Asia and Pacific	5.5	5.9	1	0.5	8.5	6.6
Europe and Central Asia	2.1	2.2	−5.2	−4.7	4.2	3.6
Latin America and the Caribbean	0.1	0.8	−5.2	−7.2	3.4	2.8
The Middle East and North Africa	1.2	−0.2	−2.8	−4.2	4	2.3
Sub-Saharan Africa	3.1	2.2	−1.6	−2.8	4.1	3.1

Source: World Bank (Europe and Central Asia Economic Update, Fall 2020: COVID-19 and Human Capital, 2020), International Monetary Fund (2020).

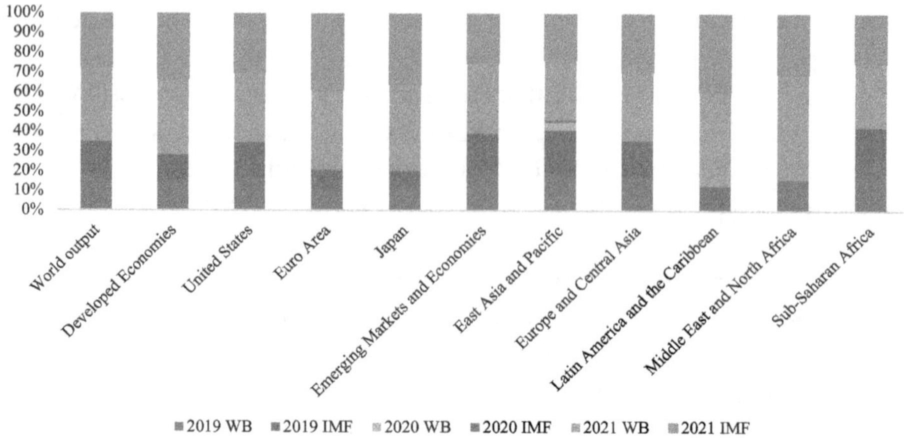

Figure 1. Growth projection.

ease, leading to the revitalization of the world's economy (MADAGASCAR: World Bank Update, 2021).

Though previous knowledge with pandemics reveals that even if the current pandemic is contained, the global economy could not recover at a faster pace, it would be gradual (Yang, 2020). This assertion implies that gross domestic product expansion to all intents and purposes would recover in the form of a U-shaped scenario, not V-shaped.

Five years ago, on the first of September, 193 nations from developed and developing nations alike formed the SDGs under the auspices of the UN. They seek to achieve a certain level of sustainable development among the nations by 2030 (Mitter and Schmid, 2021). Energy is one of the significant goals for achieving sustainable economic progress, goal seven and has gained attention worldwide (Sovacool *et al.*, 2021; Akram *et al.*, 2021; Chandio *et al.*, 2021; Irfan *et al.*, 2020a). The use of energy in the world grew by a whopping 8,588.9 million tons to 13.147.3 million tons (Mtoes) between 1995 and 2015 (Ahmad *et al.*, 2020; Dong *et al.*, 2020a). Inversely, several world's energy demand forecasts have been studied by multilateral institutions such as the World Energy Council (WEC), the Organization of Petroleum Exporting Countries, the IEA, and world mega-oil organizations (Knopf *et al.*, 2013).

Owning to a change in demand for coal to generate electricity and production of goods and services, all the known bodies anticipate a spike in energy application for the long term (Carattini *et al.*, 2019; Irfan *et al.*, 2020c, 2021g). The key effect of COVID-19 has been the issue of climate change on a global scale. It has brought down CO_2 emissions due to reduced energy consumption (Saadat *et al.*, 2020). Variations in the generation amount of gross domestic product productivity occasioned by COVID-19 led to significant differences in energy use and consumption demands. This resulted from the speedy enactment of lockdown measures shortly after the pandemic, causing the decline in energy consumption in certain sectors, such as the industrial sector. The complete shutdown for each month decreased power requirements to a mean of 20% and 1.5% on a yearly footing. For instance, China being the first nation to execute shutdown measures, power requirements plunged in the initial 6.5%. Whereas Italy, India, France, Spain, the North-Western region of the USA and the UK expected a fall in energy consumption of 15%. At the same time, Italy had a demand cut of 75% at the pinnacle of the pandemic. Besides, carbon dioxide pollution is the principal greenhouse gas emitted by the energy sector causing global warming. The fifth evaluation report of the Intergovernmental Panel on Climate Change (Charnock and Thomson, 2020) (IPCC) known as AR5, highlights the globe, is staying heated due to the growing intensity of conventional energy-focused carbon dioxide emissions (McFarland *et al.*, 2018). Truly, in line with averting global warming, 196 nations appended their signatures to form the Paris Agreement, imposing on them the responsibility to take measures to halve emission of pollution to a level within 1.5°C pre-industrial levels (Nyambuu and Semmler, 2020). Every one of the nations has a national plan to achieve this called the nationally determined contributions (NDCs), making them commit to achieving the goals of the Agreement.

Irrespective of the significant steps taken by the nations, carbon dioxide pollution is still growing around the globe (Khan *et al.*, 2021; Nuvvula *et al.*, 2022; Tanveer *et al.*, 2021), signifying that the world is at a critical juncture in this period of cutting pollution (Hao *et al.*, 2020; Mani *et al.*, 2021; Rauf *et al.*, 2021). Across the globe, carbon dioxide pollution grew by 1.7% in 2017, after nosediving in 2014 and 2016, and an additional growth to 2.7% in 2018 (Pellow *et al.*, 2020). Even though RE generation grew speedily in 2019 at the heart of decreasing costs (Hepburn *et al.*, 2020), the majority of the RE consumption was integrated alongside conventional energy, not substituting them. In contrast, land transport pollution is still rising. The nations "economic systems and the sources of revenues of many people are being endangered via growing emissions". As impending economic recession brought on by the COVID-19 pandemic, many countries across the world are witnessing a cut in carbon dioxide emissions levels in 2020 as more than 40% in the past year due to new restrictions to reduce the pandemic growth rate and manage the pandemic (Barbier, 2020; Long *et al.*, 2021).

Referencing the IEA, during the beginning of 2020, the largest carbon concentrated sources accompany the fall in energy requirements. Carbon dioxide fell additionally more after the fall in world energy requirements. The world's emission reduced to above 5% within the initial 1/4 of 2019 to 2020 principally to fall in pollution from coal to 8%, oil to 4.5%, and natural gas to 2.3%. The territories that attain the biggest pollution cuts are the United States of negative 11%, China negative 8%, and the EU negative 8%, which were the top global polluters of carbon dioxide and territories with the majority of COVID-19 infection cases. Therefore, if the world can put in abetment measures to the close of 2020, then it can achieve an 8% reduction in pollution in emissions levels compared to 2019 levels (IEA, 2020c), whereas the negative 3% forecast of the IMF for 2020 within the world's gross domestic product could result in negative 5.7% reduction of carbon dioxide emissions in 2020 (International Monetary Fund, 2020). It will be the minutest size since 2010. Ensuing the GFC, this decrease will be more than any other, six-time above the past recorded decrease of 0.4 Gt in 2009 and since the close of World War II, increases the mean figure of previous cuts (Barrett, 2020).

3. Data and Methodology

As stated in Benchimol (2014), the correlation amongst labor key-ins, capital key-ins, actual money balance, and productivity are connoted by the ensuing CD production equation

$$Y_t = AK_t^{\alpha} L_t^{\beta} [\mathrm{RCB}_t]^{\gamma}. \tag{1}$$

From the equation, Y_t connotes productivity, A depicts Solow's residuals, K_t depicts capital to produce, L_t depicts labor, and RCB_t connotes actual cash remainder. It is thought that enterprises keep the money to buy capital as well as undertake routine expenses. Hence, actual cash remainders go in the production equation that accelerates generation activities a varied economic system dealing. Also, α, β, and γ connote a direct unchanging parameter and $\gamma = 1 - \alpha - \beta$. The proponents α, β, and γ explain the electricity of the end productivity regarding capital and actual cash balance (variations in productivity for one percentage variation in the capital, labor, and monetary policy, correspondingly). Further, differences in α, β, and γ could be depicted better by the principle of returns to scale (LRS). As stated in model (1), whether key-ins, K, L, and RCB are associated with a parameter z, model (1) could be restated as

$$hY_t = AL_t^{\beta}(zK)^{\alpha}(zL)^{\beta}[\mathrm{RCB}_t]^{\gamma} \tag{2}$$

$$hY_t = Az^{\alpha+\beta+\gamma}K_t^{\alpha}L_t^{\beta}[\mathrm{RCB}_t]^{\gamma} \tag{3}$$

$$hY_t = z^{\alpha+\beta+\gamma}AK_t^{\alpha}L_t^{\beta}[\mathrm{RCB}_t]^{\gamma} \tag{4}$$

Models (2)–(4) imply the h-numbers expansion in the end productivity (Y_t). The aforementioned models explain the procedures for the LRS. Because $Y_t = AK_t^{\alpha}L_t^{\beta}[\mathrm{RCB}_t]^{\gamma}$ factor $h = z^{\alpha+\beta\gamma}$. Deducing from the correlation, inferences can be made from the LRS as follows. If $\alpha + \beta + \gamma > 1$, $h > z$, increasing returns to scale (IRS) as given by the production model. IRS depicts a state when growth or reduction in K, L, integrated with RCB results in greater growth or Y_t reduction. If $\alpha + \beta + \gamma = 1, h = z$, the generation model presents a consistent return to scale (CRS). CRS depicts a setting when growth or reduction in K, L, and RCB equates to Y_t. If $\alpha + \beta + \gamma < 1, h < z$, the production model presents a diminishing returns scale (DRS). Diminishing returns to scale shows growth or reduction in K, L, coupled to RCB connote a below increment or growth in Y_t.

To arrive at productivity, model (1) is divided by L_t:

$$\mathcal{Y}_t = AK_t^{\alpha}[\mathrm{rcb}t_t]^{\gamma}, \tag{5}$$

where $\mathcal{Y}_t = Y_t/L_t$, $k_t = K_t/L_t$ and $\mathrm{rcb}_{\ t} = \mathrm{RCB}_t/L_t$. The theory of liquidity preference states that "interest rate alters to send money distribution and demand in equilibrium". In addition, the interest rate has been one of the important instruments of monetary policy (Quinet, 2005). Hence, via monetary policy, the main bank can institute differences in the money distribution; eventually, it explicitly influences actual cash. Subsequently, the study couples "Monetary Policy (MP)" to be an input in the cumulative CD production model:

$$\mathcal{Y}_t = AK_t^{\alpha}[\mathrm{MP}_t]^{\gamma}. \tag{6}$$

Largely, affluence, particularly carbon dioxide emissions, is positively linked alongside economic system activity. Thus, relying on the approach of the carbon dioxide emission is amounted to:

$$\mathrm{CO}_2et = f(\mathcal{Y}_t). \tag{7}$$

Substituting models (6) into model (7), we arrive at the ensuing carbon dioxide pollution model:

$$\mathrm{CO}_2et = AK_t^{\alpha}[\mathrm{MP}_t]^{\gamma}. \tag{8}$$

Usually, it is asserted that all capital goods do not emit greenhouse gases that pollute the ecology. These are categorized as RE goods (RES) and conventional capital goods (CCG).

$$kt = k_{\mathrm{RCG}} + k_{\mathrm{FCG}}. \tag{9}$$

The parameter k_t is substitutable by RE use (REU) as well as conventional fossil fuels (CFF) in the model (9):

$$\mathrm{CO}_2et = A[\mathrm{REC}_t]^{\delta}[\mathrm{FFC}_t]^{\delta}[\mathrm{MP}_t]^{\gamma}. \tag{10}$$

Model (10) reproduces that REU, CFF, and MP are vital parameters for carbon dioxide emissions. Central banks formulate monetary policy to manage the total money supply. The central bank applies actual interest rates which is an important instrument in regulating the money supply. Central bank's interest influences a greater variation in a cumulative generation, consumption, global trade, FDI, financial advancement, and EG. Hence, monetary policy is an important instrument for either abating as well can increase carbon dioxide emissions. For varied aims, MP is categorized as GMP, and TMP elucidates the means via which the dual approaches of GMP (Onakoya *et al.*, 2019) as well as TMP, influence the ecology's value. GMP poses a state where the central bank expands money distribution by reducing the actual interest rate. It is rational that producers lend money from commercial institutions at reduced interest rates. From their point of view, a fall in actual interest rates grows their capacity to churn out more goods, use increased conventional energy sources, and put-up generation sources to satisfy national and global requirements. Export-led enterprises grow their production by consuming conventional fuels. To encourage global consumers, they reduce the costs, and generators depend on affordable and polluting sources. Subsequently, this increases carbon dioxide emissions levels.

From the consumer's point of view, a fall in the actual interest rate grows their earnings levels as well as ADCSP. Gleaned from the study of Xie *et al.* (2021), ADCSP comprises total expenditure on the buy of nationally generated energy and products from energy. The growth in ADCSP owning to a cut from the actual interest rate places stress on the national manufacturing sector to manufacture goods and servers at reduced costs. In confronting national free market-based activity and demand for manufacturing goods, enterprises apply polluting generating sources to manufacture goods, leading to a growth in carbon dioxide emissions. To summarize, a plunge in interest rate via growth policy causes a spike in ADCSP, production. Conventional energy use nevertheless grows carbon dioxide emissions. TMP is a state where the CB reduces the money in distribution by growing the actual interest rate.

Moreover, suppliers and producers are adamant about going for loans from the open market at higher interest rates. This is seen from the supplier's viewpoint where growth in actual interest reduces his capacity to supply more goods, thereby using a lesser amount of conventional energy and not able to increase the capacity of their generation sources. Companies that sell goods abroad equally cut down their generation from conventional fuel sources. As a result, cutting down their carbon dioxide emissions levels. From the customer's point of view, the surge in actual real interest has reduced revenue for the customer and ADCSP. The reductions in ADCSP because of a spike in actual interest rate result in cuts in manufacturing processes, conventional fuel sources, and carbon dioxide emissions levels. Overall, expansion in interest rate via TMP does not only reduce ADCSP, manufacturing process, conventional energy use; nevertheless, it reduces carbon dioxide emissions levels. In connecting GMP and TMP onto the carbon dioxide emissions levels model, we set the ensuing restraints on the variables of monetary policy, according to Raza *et al.* (2020) and Hu *et al.* (2018):

$$\mathrm{CO_2}et = A[\mathrm{REC}_t]^{\delta}[\mathrm{FFC}_t]^{\rho}[\mathrm{MP}_t]^{\gamma}\left(\Delta(\mathrm{RIR})_t > 0, \Delta\mathrm{RIR}_t^{\Phi+}\right), \left(\Delta(\mathrm{RIR})_t > 0, \Delta\mathrm{RIR}_t^{\Phi-}\right). \tag{11}$$

Here, $\Phi+$ denotes growth in RIR due to CMP; $\Phi-$ implies reductions in RIR because of growth monitory policy. Furthermore, the present analysis from Samour *et al.* (2020) says that monetary policy determines the levels of pollution on the ecology. The monetary policy comprises the government varying its expenditures levels and revenues mobilization strategies to grow or degrow ADCSP. According to differing aims, monetary policy is categorized into growth monetary policy (GFP) and tightening monetary policy (TFP). GFP elucidates the condition where public expenditure is in surplus. That is, public spending is more than its liabilities due to reduced tax levels. Reduced taxes expand workers' take-home pay and ADCSP. The growth in ADCSP resulting from a reduction in levies places stress on the national manufacturing companies to manufacture goods and services to meet increased demand due to reduced prices of goods and services. Emissions levels increase due to the race to the bottom issue connected to increased demand from the market, making firms generate their energy from conventional sources (Saidi *et al.*, 2019). In sum, a reduction in levies via GFP does not only grow ADCSP, industrial manufacturing, conventional energy use; nevertheless, it grows carbon dioxide emissions levels. Inversely, TFP demonstrates a state where public expenditure is in deficit due to reduced levies. Here, public expenditure is more than its earnings. Increased levies reduce workers' take-home pay and aggregate domestic consumption spending per capita. The diminished ADCSP resulting from a growth in taxes shrinks the enterprise's capacity to manufacture goods and services. Faced with this terrain, enterprises reduce their manufacturing and conventional energy use within the manufacturing processes and, consequently, carbon dioxide emissions levels.

To summarize, a growth in levies via TFP does not only reduce ADCSP, manufacturing processes, traditional energy use, as well as a reduction in carbon dioxide emissions. When linking GFP to TFP onto carbon dioxide emissions levels, the study sets constraints on monetary policy variables according to the approach (Cheng *et al.*, 2020). The present research takes four steps to arrive at the findings. Step one, a dual-unit root test, i.e., Levin Lin Chu (LLChu) test, in which Im Pesaran and Shin (IPShin) analysis are deployed. Step two, we deployed the Kao and Westerlund cointegration analysis to affirm a long-term association of the variables. Step four, the ordinary least square, dynamic ordinary least square, fully modified ordinary least squares, and the pooled median group (PMG) autoregressive distribution lags approaches were deployed to estimate the future correlation of the coefficient. Also, the short-run coefficients are approximated via the longitudinal error-correction model (ECM). Ultimately, the granger causality analysis is applied to investigate the long-run approximate validity (Mughal *et al.*, 2021).

3.1. *Panel unit root tests*

In conducting for the structural breaks and unit root within the model, a dual step approach was applied as done in Choi (2019). The initial approach investigates the existence of structural breaks within the series. In contrast, the next approach talks about analyzing for unit root analysis. For analyzing and knowing the significance of the break, the analysis uses the maximum F (max$F$) analysis. Here, the exogenous analysis is applied as the next approach because the setting or the existence of breaks are identified ensuing the initial approach. This approach is instructive because exogenous analyses have more statistical ability than the analysis more than the endogenous approach. Brownlees (2019) begins alongside the ensuing data producing steps that are grounded on units' illustration:

$$\mathcal{Y}_t = \delta \Delta z_t + e_t. \tag{12}$$

Now, $e_t = \beta e_t + \epsilon_t$ is known to be the standard approach in econometric estimations. The analysis did a dual unit root analysis to affirm the approximated results' cogency and consistency. To begin with, the study applies the (Levin *et al.*, 2002) unit root analysis, which makes functions as given below. The analysis has dual assumptions: the prevailing hypothesis presumes the existence of unit roots on all chosen series. Inversely, the other hypothesis posits the other variables are without unit root tests. The absence of unit root within the series tests was done using a different test called the IPShin test. The IPShin check says that the prevailing hypothesis has unit root within a section of the series. This null hypothesis is contrary to the preceding null hypothesis. Furthermore, the initial check is stronger in checking the stationarity based on permitting the different attributes of the longitudinal series coefficient (Liu *et al.*, 2020).

3.2. *Panel cointegration tests*

Furthermore, after checking the absence of unit root, the study then evaluates the long-term correlation within the analyzed parameters. Because of this, the study uses the dual cointegration checks in the form of the Kao and Westerlund checks. The residual-focused-based (Dash, 2019) check is used to analyze the nonheterogeneous long-term correlation analysis. In addition, the analysis applies the different DF and ADF measurements to analyze the null hypotheses without cointegration to the inverse hypothesis through the cointegration approach. For example, the ADF measurements are estimable according to Regis *et al.* (2021) approach. Then, the analysis applies Westerlund's (2008) cointegration check to affirm the future association within the chosen series. The essence of the check was to check for the different attributes in a wider context to ascertain the future cointegration correlation (Musah *et al.*, 2020). The principal models of the different checks connote cross-section, period, and equation residual, correspondingly. The prevailing hypothesis of the analysis signifies no-cointegration, whereas the other hypothesis shows the long-term correlation existence.

3.3. *Long-run estimators*

The study applies different approaches to approximate the long-run factor figures rather depending on one approach based on the under listed factors: (i) to derive consistent results, (ii) from eschewing uncertainties in results due to a section of scholars presume the findings of the dynamic ordinary least square seem consistent and cogent; whereas another school of thought says the results of the fully modified ordinary least square and ordinary least square are consistent, in the views of Apergis and Payne (2010). We utilized the ordinary longitudinal square, dynamic ordinary square, fully modified ordinary square analyses. Equally, the Pool Median Group Autoregressive distribution. The functional form of the longitudinal ordinary least square approach for carbon dioxide emissions is formulated below:

$$CO_{2eit} = \alpha_i + \beta_i x_{it} + e_t. \tag{13}$$

To approximate the β_i coefficients, the longitudinal ordinary least square is given below:

$$CO_{2it} = \alpha_i + \beta_i x_{it} + e_t,$$

$$\hat{\beta}_i = (x_{it} - x_i^*) + (x_{it} - x_i^*)^{2-1} \sum_{i=1}^{N} \sum_{t=1}^{T} (x_{it} - x_i^*)(CO_{2it} - CO_{2it}^t). \tag{14}$$

In addition, the ensuing model is formulated to approximate besides (Pedroni, 2004) developing β_i coefficients via the fully modified ordinary least square approach. Here, x^- depicts the arithmetic median of X, CO_{2eit}^* equivalent to $(x_{it} - x_i^*)$. Further, the concept "CO_2" carbon dioxide emissions is imbedded to remedy the challenge of anticipated serial association. To formulate the longitudinal dynamic ordinary least square approximator, Pedroni formulates the under-listed model by adding future and previous values to the nonstatic model. In estimating the short-term coefficients alongside the long-term factor figures, the study applies the ensuing model (Wang and Su, 2021). This shows γ_i is the stochastic correction factor figure, ϕ_i denotes the future coefficients, and $\tau_{ij}*$ and $\beta_{ij}*$ imply the short-term coefficients. Ultimately, the Granger causality analysis is applied to authenticate the results to study the equations series causal relationship. The ensuing parameters have been applied in the study.

3.4. *Data sources and variables*

The source of the data available for the selected parameters is from the WDI ranging from 1990 to 2016 for EU nations. The sample has the under-listed parameters: CO_2 pollution, actual interest rate, as a substitute variable for monetary policy, tax on the gross domestic product, as a substitute variable for monetary policy, conventional energy consumption (CEC), growth monetary policy (GFP), tightening monetary policy (TFP), renewable energy consumes (REC) and ADCSP that is equivalent to the total of GDP as well as exports being subtracted from imports, all over/cumulative number of people living in an area. In addition, the explanation and the units of

Table 2. System of variables.

Acronym	Description
ET	Environmental tax
CCT	Carbon capture cost
EMP	Expansionary monetary policy
CMP	Contractionary monetary policy
FFE	Fossil fuel energy
REE	Renewable energy

Table 3. Kao-cointegration test.

Test	Statistics	p-value
Dickey–Fuller (DF) t-statistics	−2.564	0.002
Unadjusted modified Dickey–Fuller (UMDF) t-statistics	−4.255	0000
Unadjusted Dickey–Fuller (UDF) t-statistics	−4.115	0000
Modified Dickey–Fuller (MDF) t-statistics	−2.422	0.001
Augmented Dickey–Fuller (ADF) t-statistics	−3.443	0.007

estimated variables are obtained from WDI. To standardize the variables, we covert the parameters into a log form. Table 2 presents the system of variables and their explanation.

4. Results and Discussion

4.1. *Co-integration analysis*

Our analysis shows an important variation amongst the maximum and minimum figures, demonstrating the noticeable differences in the equations' parameters trajectories, particularly within the variables of CMP and EMP. The stationarity analysis ensures the long-run correlation amongst the variables is determined. Because of this, the analysis applies a dual cointegration analysis, through residual-focused Kao's and Westerlund longitudinal cointegration tests as in Kao (1999) and Persyn and Westerlund (2008), correspondingly. Table 2 shows that all the analysis statistics of Kao's analysis cointegration implies not to accept the hypothesis of no cointegration of 1% importance level, excluding the t-statistic of ADF, which is supported at 5% level. On the other hand, the probability figure of Westerlund analysis from Table 3. Two equally backs the findings of Kao's analysis, signifying that carbon dioxide emissions attain the long-term correlation alongside monetary policies and other related macroeconomic parameters.

To find variables that correlated to greenhouse gas pollution, an estimation interpretation was made on the database of greenhouse pollution for each year around 2018. Different independent parameters were included, namely five per annum figures of environmental tax, variations in carbon capture cost, GMP in a nonchanging, and

Table 4. Westerlund test.

Statistics	Value	z-value	p-value
Gt	−3.874	−7.763	0000
Ga	−18.267	−8.556	0000
Pt	−9.996	−6.673	0000
Pa	−19.874	−7.564	0000

present costs and inflation. From the backward approach, only the five annum-mean of environmental tax and carbon tax parameters had an important impact, around a 5% significance level on the greenhouse gases pollution. Seeing a spike in both variables signifies growths in greenhouse gas pollution, except for nations that decouple their economic growth from energy consumption.

4.2. *Regression analysis*

The findings of long-term analysis of ordinary least square, dynamic ordinary least square analysis, fully modified ordinary least square, PMG approaches are demonstrated in Table 4. The results of ordinary least square, dynamic ordinary least square, fully modified ordinary least square, and the PMG demonstrates a 1% growth in GMP expands the rate of carbon dioxide emissions in European nations to 0.483%, 0.382%, 0.2631% and 0.321%, correspondingly. The probable elucidation is that European nations show commitment to secure long-term sustainable progress together alongside macroeconomic variables such as unemployment, inflation, etc. Even though these nations have undergone significant economic interruptions in the supply and consumption areas of their national economic activity, a recession to be exact. Correspondingly, GMP is operational in these countries through governments reducing tariffs while spending more to increase demand, promote manufacturing uptake, and cut down the actual interest rate, which is the cost to consumers.

Deducing from the analysis, the control parameter findings satisfy the anticipations of the investigation. From the viewpoint of manufacturing composition, it is revealed that in all approaches, the manufacturing composition inclines to attain an adverse and supported effect on sustainable advancement with the coefficient equivalent to negative 0.35, negative 0.29, and negative 0.28 correspondingly. The conclusion drawn from this is that the second-tier manufacturing sector emits a bulk of emissions because of its overuse of conventional energy (Shuai and Fan, 2020), that is not right for ecological advancement (Shahbaz *et al.*, 2018). The overall estimation methods reveal that the fraction of green zones within the metropolis that yield to ecological standards are supported and statistically direct, but with varying coefficients figures ranging from 0.066, 0.068, and 0.056, correspondingly. Our findings are in line with Shahbaz *et al.* (2018), where they contended that defining ecological standards and regulations ensures green economic system progress.

Furthermore, the analysis of the ordinary least square, nonstatic ordinary least square, fully modified ordinary least square, and pooled mean group connotes a supported direct correlation amongst conventional energy consumption (CFC) coupled with carbon dioxide emissions in the extended period term. This indicates 1% spike in CFC results in a growth in carbon dioxide emissions to 0.91%, 0.4517%, as well as 0.566%, correspondingly. Similar estimates are given in by Shrestha (2020), concerning ordinary least square, dynamic ordinary least square, fully modified ordinary least square, as well as a pooled mean group, results equally influence the adverse damaging consequences of CO_2 pollution in the group of 20 nations plummeted to 0.197%, 0.265%, 0.228%, as well as 0.187%, separately because of 1% expansion in RE use (REU). The analysis results strongly stake a claim for the deployment of RES such as wind, solar, hydro to decrease the pollution levels.

The socioeconomic ramifications reveal a scale of extra taxes set as a hypothetical approximates of their earnings as a fraction of gross domestic product. The approximates are depicted in Table 3 in the ensuing years of 2000, 2005, and 2010. Regarding the EU nations, a spike in 0.4% of the gross domestic product in the particular year 2000 to 2.2% in 2010. The increase is the result of a 10% reduction in the tariff rate in 2010, which is consistent with the rate of 156 US dollars per ton of CO_2 emissions or US$16 per barrel of oil equivalent cost in 1999. Relative to the cost of US $10 in 1993, it is recommended that carbon/energy should be around 2000. These approximates are in line with (Iqbal *et al.*, 2021d) for the suggested 10 dollars be carbon/energy tax, which is hypothetical nevertheless disregard any exclusions or impacts of EG and the reference line variations in economic system composition. Because of these variances in the treated and the exorbitant tariffs, the fraction is quite the same, alongside variations ratios amongst nations depicting their carbon dioxide emissions for a component of gross domestic product and the exclusions of extra levies proposal (Umit and Schaffer, 2020).

4.3. *Granger causality test*

We analyze the Granger-causality check regarding our optimum lag order chosen for the different CMP and EMP approaches. The findings are given in Table 5. Having done the Granger causality amongst the CMP and EMP of group 20 nations, the authors strengthen the analysis by adding an extended designate analysis to approximate the impact of CMP and EMP due to the Granger causality do not grant-supported coefficients. The findings of the longitudinal casualty analysis affirm the findings from pairwise Granger causality analysis designate the magnitude of the causality. All in all, the longitudinal estimation relationship amongst the equation while controlling the effect of different parameters and improvising for the endogenous variables, the longitudinal estimation check demonstrates improved financial performance in the past year results in a reduction in carbon dioxide emissions in the coming year, that is, good ecological performance. Similarly, a decrease in GHGs pollution in the past year equally results in an expansion in financial performance in the following year.

Because the endogeneity concern can obliterate the precise correlation between CMP and EMP, the authors apply improvised parameters in our longitudinal equation to surmount the constraint. Our analysis equally draws a longitudinal OLS comparative approximates to imply the significance of the econometric equation's analysis. From our findings, the longitudinal data set OLS generates the coefficients that are minimum in scale, principally nonsignificant, and vitally dissimilar from the fourth approximates. We think that the longitudinal OLS approximates are characterized by

Table 5. Main estimation results.

	OLS	DOLS	FMOLS	PMG
Variable	(1)	(2)	(3)	(4)
ET	−0.245**	−0.045***	−0.320***	−0.074**
	(0.042)	(0.021)	(0.011)	(0.013)
CCT	0.034**	0.012***		
	(0.002)	(0.011)		
EMP			0.034	0.066***
			(0.043)	(0.053)
CMP	−0.352***	−0.334***	−0.431***	−0.427***
	(0.023)	(0.046)	(0.002)	(0.002)
FFE	0.034**	0.012	0.023**	0.022*
	(0.023)	(0.013)	(0.033)	(0.017)
REE	0.037***	0.032**	0.021***	0.023*
	(0.015)	(0.015)	(0.027)	(0.014)
Constant	2.021***	2.212***	2.133***	2.543***
	(0.021)	(0.132)	(0.021)	(0.121)
Observations	278	278	278	278
Adjusted R^2	0.044		0.064	
Arellano–bond AR(1)		−5.436		−5.564
		[0.000]		[0.000]
Arellano–bond AR(2)		−0.432		−0.654
		[0.543]		[0.765]
Sargan test		273.654		281.658
		[0.702]		[0.723]

Notes: p-value in brackets and standard errors in parentheses; $^{*}p < 0.1$, $^{**}p < 0.5$, $^{***}p < 0.01$.

an endogeneity challenge within the equation. Consequently, we evaluate the probably means endogeneity. An enterprise's unseen output and its fringe prices of ecological projects are investigated to know if they are the probable source of endogeneity. The results demonstrate that peripherical costs of ecological projects are above industrious enterprises, leading to spiral inconsistency in the longitudinal least square approximation. From Table 5, the bivariate Granger causality analysis shows the absence of causality amongst pollution levels and the monetary policy instruments. In the same vein, causality was detected amongst cumulative pollution and ecological tariffs.

Analyzing the magnitude, the causality, the findings of the longitudinal causality are the same as those stated in Table 5. Hence, the findings are consistent because a comparable image of causality surfaced after deploying the many control parameters. Also, the findings of the sensitivity analysis indicate an analogous causality trend, as reported in Table 5. Still, for casual correlation amongst monetary policy and cumulative pollution, where, subsequently next to including the control parameters, the findings indicate a two-way causality amongst CMP and EMP. The longitudinal causality gives coefficients that are not found in the conventional Granger causality analysis. Therefore, the study results mean that Tobin's Q value has increased by 1%, resulting in a reduction in cumulative pollution equal to 99,800 tons of carbon dioxide.

Here, the Granger causality analysis demonstrates 1% increase in environmental tax, GTPase, and CFC results in an expansion in carbon dioxide pollution to 0.332%, 0.251%, 0.616%, and 0.566%, correspondingly. In contrast, one expansion in carbon capture tax, TFP, and REE causes a reduction in pollution to 0.56%, correspondingly. The ECM coefficient is negative 0.0665, which reveals a rapid change to the future balance.

Furthermore, the Granger causality analysis is used to investigate causal correlations between the series. The causality analysis authenticates the findings by corroborating the correlation amongst most of the parameters, as shown in Table 6. The results indicate the one-way causal relationship amongst environmental tax, carbon emissions, carbon capture tax, and carbon emissions, that go across from conventional energy sources and RES to carbon dioxide emissions (Chen *et al.*, 2021b). Nonetheless, government spending has a one-way causal impact on carbon emissions, backed by The Economy in the Time of Covid-19 (2020). Ultimately, one-way causality is ascertained amongst renewable energy and carbon emissions that turn to renewable energy sources to carbon dioxide, in conformity alongside the analysis of Asim *et al.* (2020).

4.4. *Robustness analysis*

The sensitivity analysis starts the pairwise Granger causality analysis and the longitudinal causality analysis alongside control variables for the sensitivity test. So to test for the sensitivity of the findings, we did the longitudinal check with control parameters. Then, we reapproximate the optimum lag chosen for our equations to handle the inclusion of the controls. While controlling the effects of the parameters, a novel lag was derived after including the control parameters and applied to approximate the longitudinal causality analysis (See Table 7).

The findings signify variations in CO_2 pollution Granger lead Tobin's Q and the other round. In addition, there is a one-way causality emanating from Tobin's Q to aggregate pollution and carbon dioxide pollution to GFP, meaning a variation in Tobin's Q, as well as variation in pollution Granger, triggers aggregate pollution as well as GFP, correspondingly. Referencing the aforementioned parameters, control parameters may play a vital part when approximating the causality test. Hence, the bivariate causality analysis can result in inconsistent findings. The function of the Granger causality procedure is constraint to cumulative per head carbon dioxide model to reveal the magnitude of causality between the analyzed parameters. Consequently, a structural break from the Maki cointegration analysis regarding the cumulative per head carbon dioxide model is exogenously supplemented on the

Table 6. Granger causality test.

Null hypothesis	F-statistics	The direction of the causality
ET does not Granger cause CO_2	16.433***	ET→CO_2
CO_2 does not Granger cause ET	2.432	
CCT does not Granger cause CO_2	9.184***	CCT→CO_2
CO_2 does not Granger cause CCT	2.232	
EMP does not Granger cause CO_2	12.221**	EMP→CO_2
CO_2 does not Granger cause EMP	2.183	
CMP does not Granger cause CO_2	14.374***	CMP→CO_2
CO_2 does not Granger cause CMP	1.132	
FFE does not Granger cause CO_2	4.528**	FFE→CO_2
CO_2 does not Granger cause FFE	1.332	
REC does not Granger cause CO_2	11.473***	REC→CO_2
CO_2does not Granger cause REC	1.166	
ET does not Granger cause CCT	5.284**	EFP→ADCSP
CCT does not Granger cause ET	0.332	
EMP does not Granger cause FFE	7.773***	EMP→FFE
FFE does not Granger cause EMP	1.311	
EMP does not Granger cause REC	0.331	None
REC does not Granger cause EMP	1.231	
CMP does not Granger cause REC	8.476***	CMP→REC
REC does not Granger cause CMP	1.365	
CCT does not Granger cause ET	5.673**	CCT→ET
ET does not Granger cause CCT	0.823	
CCT does not Granger cause EMP	11.037***	CCT→EMP
REC does not Granger cause CFP	0.736	
CCT does not Granger cause FFE	1.322	CCT↔FFE
CMP does not Granger cause CCT	1.552	
CCT does not Granger cause CMP	6.763**	CCT→CMP
CMP does not Granger cause CCT	0.255	
CMP does not Granger cause REC	1.232	None
REC does not Granger cause CMP	0.942	
CMP does not Granger cause FFE	1.432	None
FFE does not Granger cause CMP	0.476	
CMP does not Granger cause FFE	6.211**	CMP→FFE
FFE does not Granger cause CMP	0.476	
CMP does not Granger cause REC	0.887	None
REC does not Granger cause CMP	0.449	
ET does not Granger cause FFE	8.980***	ET↔FFE
FFE does not Granger cause ET	5.879***	
EMP does not Granger cause REC	1.736	None
REC does not Granger cause EMP	1.487	
FFE does not Granger cause REC	0.432	None
REC does not Granger cause FFE	0.887	

Table 7. Robustness analysis of main estimation results.

	One step	Two-step	One step	Two-step
Variable	(1)	(2)	(3)	(4)
ET	−0.346**	−0.034***	−0.356***	−0.324**
	(0.011)	(0.021)	(0.012)	(0.012)
CCT	0.021**	0.012***		
	(0.001)	(0.011)		
EMP				0.0546***
				(0.065)
CMP				−0.478***
				(0.001)
FFE				0.021*
				(0.012)
REE	0.032***		0.021***	0.021*
	(0.015)	(0.011)	(0.023)	(0.012)
Constant	2.011***	2.212***	2.133***	2.54***
	(0.021)	(0.132)	(0.021)	(0.121)
Observations	272	272	272	272
Adjusted R^2	0.044		0.078	
Arellano-bond AR(1)		−5.654		−5.664
		[0.000]		[0.000]
Arellano-bond AR(2)		−0.566		−0.566
		[0.776]		[0.744]
Sargan test		254.743		233.743
		[0.678]		[0.678]

Notes: p-value in brackets and standard errors in parentheses; $^{*}p < 0.1$, $^{**}p < 0.5$, $^{***}p < 0.01$.

equation to be a binary parameter to sidestep the misrepresenting influences of structural breaks in the series.

5. Conclusions and policy recommendations

The study's primary aim is to check the soundness of macroeconomic relationships amongst GMPs and TMPs, as well as carbon dioxide emissions, alongside different parameters; that is, growth and tightening policies (CMP and EMP), cumulative national spending for the head, conventional fuel use, and renewable energy use about the EU. To test for the long-term relationship of the parameters, the Kao's and Westerlund cointegration analyses were applied and affirms the presence of long-term correlation amongst the parameters. About the future term results of the ordinary least square, dynamic ordinary least square fully modified the least square, as well as a PMG, GMP reduces the value of the ecology by growing the harmful impacts of carbon emissions, whereas TMP reduces the carbon emissions. Similarly, GMP and tightening policy equally add to disrupting ecological effluence, either reducing or expanding carbon emissions, correspondingly. In addition, the findings ascertain the important direct correlation between environmental tax and carbon emissions without the ordinary least square approximator's results.

What is more, conventional energy use and renewable energy use decrease and at the same time advance carbon dioxide emissions, correspondingly. Likewise, the short-term approximates of the pooled mean group back the extended approximates concerning the reaction of carbon dioxide emissions to CMP and EMP, and RE individually. Other than that, we equally analyze the causality amongst the parameters. The Granger casualty analysis authenticated our findings by confirming the one-way connection to CMP and EMP on carbon emissions.

Beginning with the findings from the EU, the total tax rate is 156.5 ecu/tonne for connection aside from and 165.1 ecu/tonne toward unconnected policy, an expansion of 5.5%, showing that there is again designate on reduced tariffs CO_2 tariffs to obtain similar cuts in pollution, nonetheless, it is not very big. But, the span of tariffs ratios on the unconnected forecast is huge, around a ratio of 42 ecu/tonne regarding Belgium on 252 regarding Denmark, 312 on Portugal, and 356 on the Netherlands. For one reason or other, nations that attain high-level unharmonized tariffs have carbon dioxide pollution trends that seem nonreactive to actual interest growths. The span is even broader than discovered by (McFarland *et al.*, 2018), probably revealing the fact that the approximated variables alternate within the EU. Regarding the carbon dioxide pollution levels, they are precisely 10% beneath the baseline in 2010, jobs are about 1.2%, more than 1.3% unharmonized scenario, in addition to the gross domestic product of 1.4% higher than the baseline of 1.5%, the carbon dioxide outcome as if by the plan.

The greater the expansion and the jobs in the unharmonized forecast are due to greater so that there are substantial revenues to reutilize, providing an increased cut in jobs deductions coupled with high-level productivity and jobs. Point three, the direct and important correlation amongst aggregate domestic spending per capita and carbon emissions, needs to be put in instant steps by policy formulators to sustain a clean ecology in the EU countries. Managers of nations' economies should invest substantial public expenditure on scholarly studies and innovation on ecologically benign and appropriate generation sources. The development of environmentally benign generation sources developers to plug the shortfall amongst extreme production and consumption via the generation of goods might yield ecological together with economic system gains. Ultimately, the generation and burning of fossil energy depreciate the ecological quality by enhancing carbon dioxide emissions, while RE uses cause promising impacts on the ecology by impeding carbon emissions. The position demands policy formulators to make generators, particularly first-time financiers, know the economic system and ecological gains of greening technologies. Most financiers waver to deploy the modern-day generation sources due to insufficient understanding of the negative generating sources (Duan *et al.*, 2020). The next important step is that sustainable energy consumption ought to be backed by the government via the formulation of monetary policy that compensates and de-risk the renewable energy sector, giving free taxes rebates and investing more clear production sources. In addition, there is the need to monetize carbon dioxide to use the proceeds to mitigate the adverse effects of climate change caused by the consumption of fossil fuels.

The Granger causality framework demonstrates a way to move from monetary policy to carbon dioxide pollution and monetary policy to energy use — meaning the monetary policy projects aimed at energy utilization have an extended ramification for an ecological value. The scientific analysis backs the notion of the European economy's energy-induced consumption expansion hypothesis. Signifying that deploying renewable energy and efficient energy use ought to be promoted instead of energy preservation. Funding from RES ought to be supported and promoted via the right policy frameworks and incentives that de-risk the sector and make the sector attractive to the private sector. Also, an emission trading system could be developed by member countries to deter overconsumption of fossil fuels and taxing polluting companies for the externalities.

References

Abbas, Q, I Hanif, F Taghizadeh-Hesary, W Iqbal and N Iqbal (2021). Improving the Energy and Environmental Efficiency for Energy Poverty Reduction.

Ahmad, B, L Da, MH Asif, M Irfan, S Ali and MIUD Akbar (2021a). Understanding the antecedents and consequences of service-sales ambidexterity: A motivation-opportunity-ability (MOA) framework. *Sustainability*, 13(17), 9675.

Ahmad, M, N Akhtar, G Jabeen, M Irfan, MK Anser, H Wu and C Isek (2021b). Intention-based critical factors affecting willingness to adopt Novel Coronavirus prevention in Pakistan: Implications for future pandemics. *International Journal of Environemntal Research and Public Health*, 18, 6167.

Akram, R, F Chen, F Khalid, G Huang and M Irfan (2021). Heterogeneous effects of energy efficiency and renewable energy on economic growth of BRICS countries: A fixed effect panel quantile regression analysis. *Energy*, 215, 119019.

Al Asbahi, AAMH, FZ Gang, W Iqbal, Q Abass, M Mohsin and R Iram (2019). Novel approach of Principal Component Analysis method to assess the national energy performance via Energy Trilemma Index. *Energy Reports*, 5, 704–713.

Anser, MK, W Iqbal, US Ahmad, A Fatima and IS Chaudhry (2020). Environmental efficiency and the role of energy innovation in emissions reduction. *Environmental Science and Pollution Research*, 27(23), 29451–29463.

Apergis, N and JE Payne (2010). Renewable energy consumption and economic growth: Evidence from a panel of OECD countries. *Energy Policy*, 38(1), 656–660.

Asim, M, S Saleem, M Imran, MKH Leung, SA Hussain, LS Miró and I Rodríguez (2020). Thermo-economic and environmental analysis of integrating renewable energy sources in a district heating and cooling network. *Energy Efficiency*, 13(1), 79–100.

Baloch, ZA, Q Tan, N Iqbal, M Mohsin, Q Abbas, W Iqbal and IS Chaudhry (2020). Trilemma assessment of energy intensity, efficiency, and environmental index: Evidence from BRICS countries. *Environmental Science and Pollution Research*, 27(27), 34337–34347.

Barbier, EB (2020). Greening the post-pandemic recovery in the G20. *Environmental and Resource Economics*, https://doi.org/10.1007/s10640-020-00437-w.

Barrett, S (2020). Dikes versus windmills: Climate treaties and adaptation. *Climate Change Economics*, https://doi.org/10.1142/S2010007820400059.

Benchimol, J (2014). Money in the production function: A New Keynesian DSGE perspective. *Southern Economic Journal*, https://doi.org/10.4284/0038-4038-2011.197.

Berger, L and M Marinacci (2020). Model uncertainty in climate change economics: A review and proposed framework for future research. *Environmental and Resource Economics*, https://doi.org/10.1007/s10640-020-00503-3.

Brownlees, CT (2019). Hierarchical GARCH. *Journal of Empirical Finance*, https://doi.org/10.1016/j.jempfin.2019.01.009.

Carattini, S, S Levin and A Tavoni (2019). Cooperation in the climate commons.

Chandio, AA, Y Jiang, W Akram, S Adeel, M Irfan and I Jan (2021). Addressing the effect of climate change in the framework of financial and technological development on cereal production in Pakistan. *Journal of Cleaner Production*, 288, 125637.

Charnock, R and I Thomson (2020). Accounting and climate finance: Engaging with the intergovernmental panel on climate change. *Social and Environmental Accountability Journal*, https://doi.org/10.1080/0969160x.2020.1761064.

Chen, X, C Huang, H Wang, W Wang, X Ni and Y Li (2021a). Negative emotion arousal and altruism promoting of online public stigmatization on COVID-19 pandemic. *Frontiers in Psychology*, 12, 652140.

Chen, Y, E Kusuma Kumara, V Sivakumar, E Kusuma, HA In and V Sivakumar (2021b). Invesitigation of finance industry on risk awareness model and digital economic growth. *Annals of Operations Research*, 2021, 1–22.

Cheng, Z, J Liu, L Li and X Gu (2020). Research on meta-frontier total-factor energy efficiency and its spatial convergence in Chinese provinces. *Energy Economics*, 86.

Chien, FS, HW Kamran, G Albashar and W Iqbal (2021). Dynamic planning, conversion, and management strategy of different renewable energy sources: A sustainable solution for severe energy crises in emerging economies. *International Journal of Hydrogen Energy*, https://doi.org/10.1016/j.ijhydene.2020.12.004.

Choi, I (2019). Unit root tests for dependent micropanels. *Japanese Economic Review*, https://doi.org/10.1111/jere.12170.

Dash, SK (2019). Has the Feldstein-Horioka puzzle waned? Evidence from time series and dynamic panel data analysis. *Economic Modelling*, https://doi.org/10.1016/j.econmod.2019.02.015.

Davidovic, D, N Harring and SC Jagers (2020). The contingent effects of environmental concern and ideology: Institutional context and people's willingness to pay environmental taxes. *Environmental Politics*, https://doi.org/10.1080/09644016.2019.1606882.

Duan, Y, Z Han and H Mu (2020). Research on the influence of product differentiation and emission reduction policy on CO2 emissions of China's iron and steel industry. *International Journal of Climate Change Strategies and Management*, https://doi.org/10.1108/IJCCSM-06-2020-0068.

Elavarasan, RM, R Pugazhendhi, GM Shafiullah, M Irfan and A Anvari-Moghaddam (2021). A hover view over effectual approaches on pandemic management for sustainable cities — The endowment of prospective technologies with revitalization strategies. *Sustainable Cities and Society*, 68, 102789.

Europe and Central Asia Economic Update, Fall 2020: COVID-19 and Human Capital (2020).

Fortmann, L, J Beaudoin, I Rajbhandari, A Wright, S Neshyba and P Rowe (2020). Teaching modules for estimating climate change impacts in economics courses using computational guided inquiry. *Journal of Economic Education*, https://doi.org/10.1080/00220485.2020.1731383.

Fu, FY, M Alharthi, Z Bhatti, L Sun, F Rasul, I Hanif and W Iqbal (2021). The dynamic role of energy security, energy equity and environmental sustainability in the dilemma of emission reduction and economic growth. *Journal of Environmental Management*, 280.

Gilbert, F, S Poynton, J Yuen, J Kaji, B Hurley, P Devan, H Bachman, R Bhat, AG Tharakan, and N Gangopadhya (2020). Deloitte Insights — The social enterprise at work: Paradox as a path forward. 2020 Deloitte Global Human Capital Trends. Deloitte Insights.

Hao, Y, Z Gai, G Yan, H Wu and M Irfan (2020). The spatial spillover effect and nonlinear relationship analysis between environmental decentralization, government corruption and air pollution: Evidence from China. *Science of the Total Environment*, 144183.

He, P, Y Sun, H Niu, C Long and S Li (2020). The long and short-term effects of environmental tax on energy efficiency: Perspective of OECD energy tax and vehicle traffic tax. *Economic Modelling*, https://doi.org/10.1016/j.econmod.2020.04.003.

Hepburn, C, B O'Callaghan, N Stern, J Stiglitz and D Zenghelis (2020). Will COVID-19 monetary recovery packages accelerate or retard progress on climate change?*Oxford Review of Economic Policy*, https://doi.org/10.1093/oxrep/graa015.

Hou, Y, W Iqbal, GM Shaikh, N Iqbal, YA Solangi and A Fatima (2019). Measuring energy efficiency and environmental performance: A case of South Asia. *Processes*, 7(6), 325.

Hu, H, N Xie, D Fang and X Zhang (2018). The role of renewable energy consumption and commercial services trade in carbon dioxide reduction: Evidence from 25 developing countries. *Applied Energy*, 211, 1229–1244.

International Monetary Fund (2020). World Economic Outlook, April 2020: The Great Lockdown.

Iqbal, W, A Altalbe, A Fatima, A Ali and Y Hou (2019a). A DEA approach for assessing the energy, environmental and economic performance of top 20 industrial countries. *Processes*, 7(12), 902.

Iqbal, W, H Yumei, Q Abbas, M Hafeez, M Mohsin, A Fatima, MA Jamali, M Jamali, A Siyal and N Sohail (2019b). Assessment of wind energy potential for the production of renewable hydrogen in Sindh Province of Pakistan. *Processes*, 7(4).

Iqbal, W, H Yumei, Q Abbas, M Hafeez, M Mohsin, A Fatima, MA Jamali, M Jamali, A Siyal and N Sohail (2019c). Assessment of wind energy potential for the production of renewable hydrogen in Sindh Province of Pakistan. *Processes*, 7(4), 196.

Iqbal, S, AR Bilal, M Nurunnabi, W Iqbal, Y Alfakhri and N Iqbal (2021a). It is time to control the worst: Testing COVID-19 outbreak, energy consumption and CO2 emission. *Environmental Science and Pollution Research*, 28(15), 19008–19020.

Iqbal, W, YM Tang, KY Chau, M Irfan and M Mohsin (2021b). Nexus between air pollution and NCOV-2019 in China: Application of negative binomial regression analysis. *Process Safety and Environmental Protection*, https://doi.org/10.1016/j.psep.2021.04.039.

Iqbal, W, YM Tang, M Lijun, KY Chau, W Xuan and A Fatima (2021c). Energy policy paradox on environmental performance: The moderating role of renewable energy patents. *Journal of Environmental Management*, 297, 113230.

Iqbal, W, YM Tang, M Lijun, KY Chau, W Xuan and A Fatima (2021d). Energy policy paradox on environmental performance: The moderating role of renewable energy patents. *Journal of Environmental Management*, 297, 113230.

Irfan, M, Z-Y Zhao, M Ahmad and M Mukeshimana (2019). Solar energy development in Pakistan: Barriers and policy recommendations. *Sustainability*, 11(4), 1206.

Irfan, M, Y Hao, MK Panjwani, D Khan, AA Chandio and H Li (2020a). Competitive assessment of South Asia's wind power industry: SWOT analysis and value chain combined model. *Energy Strategy Reviews*, 32, 100540.

Irfan, M, ZY Zhao, M Ikram, NG Gilal, H Li and A Rehman (2020b). Assessment of India's energy dynamics: Prospects of solar energy. *Journal of Renewable and Sustainable Energy*, 12(5), 053701.

Irfan, M, ZY Zhao, H Li and A Rehman (2020c). The influence of consumers' intention factors on willingness to pay for renewable energy: A structural equation modeling approach. *Environmental Science and Pollution Research*, 27(17), 21747–21761.

Irfan, M, M Ahmad, Z Fareed, N Iqbal, A Sharif and H Wu (2021a). On the indirect environmental outcomes of COVID-19: Short-term revival with futuristic long-term implications. *International Journal of Environmental Health Research*, 1–11.

Irfan, M, N Akhtar, M Ahmad, F Shahzad, RM Elavarasan, H Wu and C Yang (2021b). Assessing public willingness to wear face masks during the COVID-19 pandemic: Fresh insights from the theory of planned behavior. *International Journal of Environmental Research and Public Health*, 18(9), 4577.

Irfan, M, RM Elavarasan, Y Hao, M Feng and D Sailan (2021c). An assessment of consumers' willingness to utilize solar energy in China: End-users' perspective. *Journal of Cleaner Production*, 292, 126008.

Irfan, M, M Ikram, M Ahmad, H Wu and Y Hao (2021d). Does temperature matter for COVID-19 transmissibility? Evidence across Pakistani provinces. *Environmental Science and Pollution Research*, 28, 59705–59719.

Irfan, M, A Razzaq, W Suksatan, A Sharif, RM Elavarasan, C Yang, Y Hao and A Rauf (2021e). Asymmetric impact of temperature on COVID-19 spread in India: Evidence from quantile-on-quantile regression approach. *Journal of Thermal Biology*, 103101.

Irfan, M, AL Shahid, M Ahmad, W Iqbal, RM Elavarasan, S Ren and A Hussain (2021f). Assessment of public intention to get vaccination against COVID-19: Evidence from a developing country. *Journal of Evaluation in Clinical Practice*, 1–11.

Irfan, M, ZY Zhao, A Rehman, I Ozturk and H Li (2021g). Consumers' intention-based influence factors of renewable energy adoption in Pakistan: A structural equation modeling approach. *Environmental Science and Pollution Research*, 28(1), 432–445.

Kamensky, E (2021). Digital technologies in the Russians' everyday life: Analysis based on the opinion surveys.

Kao, C (1999). Spurious regression and residual-based tests for cointegration in panel data. *Journal of Econometrics*, https://doi.org/10.1016/S0304-4076(98)00023-2.

Khan, I, F Hou, M Irfan, A Zakari and HP Le (2021). Does energy trilemma a driver of economic growth? The roles of energy use, population growth, and financial development. *Renewable and Sustainable Energy Reviews*, 146, 111157.

Khokhar, M, Y Hou, MA Rafique and W Iqbal (2020a). Evaluating the Social Sustainability Criteria of Supply Chain Management in Manufacturing Industries: A Role of BWM in MCDM Ocena kryteriow zrownowazonosci spol ecznej w zarzadzaniu łańcuchem dostaw w przemyśle wytwórczym: rola BWM w MCDM vol. 15.

Khokhar, M, W Iqbal, Y Hou, M Abbas and A Fatima (2020b). Assessing supply chain performance from the perspective of Pakistan's manufacturing industry through social sustainability. *Processes*, 8(9), 1064.

Knopf, B, YHH Chen, E De Cian, H Förster, A Kanudia, I Karkatsouli, I Keppo, T Koljonen, K Schumacher and DP Van Vuuren (2013). Beyond 2020-strategies and costs for transforming the European energy system. *Climate Change Economics*, https://doi.org/10.1142/S2010007813400010.

Latif, Y, G Shunqi, S Bashir, W Iqbal, S Ali and M Ramzan (2021). COVID-19 and stock exchange return variation: Empirical evidences from econometric estimation. *Environmental Science and Pollution Research*, https://doi.org/10.1007/s11356-021-14792-8.

Levin, A, CF Lin and CSJ Chu (2002). Unit root tests in panel data: Asymptotic and finite-sample properties. *Journal of Econometrics*, 108(1), 1–24.

Li, J, Y Zhao, A Zhang, B Song and RL Hill (2021a). Effect of grazing exclusion on nitrous oxide emissions during freeze-thaw cycles in a typical steppe of Inner Mongolia. *Agriculture, Ecosystems & Environment*, 307, 107217.

Li, Z, J Wang and S Che (2021b). Synergistic effect of carbon trading scheme on carbon dioxide and atmospheric pollutants. *Sustainability*13(10), 5403.

Liu, L, HR Moon and F Schorfheide (2020). Forecasting with dynamic panel data models. *Econometrica*, https://doi.org/10.3982/ecta14952.

Long, J, C Zhong, A Bilal, M Irfan and R Nazir (2021). How do green financing and green logistics affect the circular economy in the pandemic situation: Key mediating role of sustainable production. *Economic Research-Ekonomska Istraživanja*, https://doi.org/10.1080/1331677X.2021.2004437.

MADAGASCAR: World Bank Update (2021). *Africa Research Bulletin: Economic, Financial and Technical Series*, https://doi.org/10.1111/j.1467-6346.2021.09858.x.

Madurai Elavarasan, R, S Leoponraj, A Dheeraj, M Irfan, G Gangaram Sundar and GK Mahesh (2021). PV-Diesel-Hydrogen fuel cell based grid connected configurations for an institutional building using BWM framework and cost optimization algorithm. *Sustainable Energy Technologies and Assessments*, 43, 100934.

Mani, PK, A Mandal, D Mandal, M Irfan, GC Hazra and S Saha (2021). Assessment of non-carcinogenic and carcinogenic risks due to ingestion of vegetables grown under sewage water irrigated soils near a 33 years old landfill site in Kolkata, India. *Exposure and Health*, https://doi.org/10.1007/s12403-021-00407-7.

Matveevskii, SS (2021). Asian Development Bank performance assessment system. Vestnik Universiteta, https://doi.org/10.26425/1816-4277-2021-2-144-151.

McFarland, JR, AA Fawcett, AC Morris, JM Reilly and PJ Wilcoxen (2018). Overview of the EMF 32 study on U.S. carbon tax scenarios. *Climate Change Economics*, https://doi.org/10.1142/S201000781840002X.

Mitter, H and E Schmid (2021). Informing groundwater policies in semi-arid agricultural production regions under stochastic climate scenario impacts. *Ecological Economics*, https://doi.org/10.1016/j.ecolecon.2020.106908.

Mohsin, A, H Ullah, N Iqbal, W Iqbal and F Taghizadeh-Hesary (2021). How external debt led to economic growth in South Asia: A policy perspective analysis from quantile regression. *Economic Analysis and Policy*, 72, 423–437.

Mughal, YH, M Jehangir, M Khan and M Saeed (2021). Nexus between corporate social responsibility and firm's performance: A panel data approach. *International Journal of Finance and Economics*, https://doi.org/10.1002/ijfe.1956.

Musah, M, Y Kong, IA Mensah, SK Antwi and M Donkor (2020). The connection between urbanization and carbon emissions: A panel evidence from West Africa. *Environment, Development and Sustainability*, https://doi.org/10.1007/s10668-020-01124-y.

Nuvvula, RSS, E Devaraj, R Madurai, S Iman, M Irfan and K Srinivasa (2022). Multi-objective mutation-enabled adaptive local attractor quantum behaved particle swarm optimisation based optimal sizing of hybrid renewable energy system for smart cities in India. *Sustainable Energy Technologies and Assessments*, 49, 101689.

Nyambuu, U and W Semmler (2020). Climate change and the transition to a low carbon economy — Carbon targets and the carbon budget. *Economic Modelling*, https://doi.org/10.1016/j.econmod.2019.04.026.

Onakoya, A, B Johnson and G Ogundajo (2019). Poverty and trade liberalization: Empirical evidence from 21 African countries. *Economic Research-Ekonomska Istrazivanja*, https://doi.org/10.1080/1331677X.2018.1561320.

Pedroni, P (2004). Panel cointegration: Asymptotic and finite sample properties of pooled time series tests with an application to the PPP hypothesis. *Econometric Theory*, 20(3), 597–625.

Pellow, MA, H Ambrose, D Mulvaney, R Betita and S Shaw (2020). Research gaps in environmental life cycle assessments of lithium ion batteries for grid-scale stationary energy storage systems: End-of-life options and other issues.

Persyn, D and J Westerlund (2008). Error-correction-based cointegration tests for panel data. *Stata Journal*, https://doi.org/10.1177/1536867x0800800205.

Qiao, G, L Ding, L Zhang and H Yan (2021). Accessible tourism: A bibliometric review (2008–2020). *Tourism Review*, https://doi.org/10.1108/TR-12-2020-0619/FULL/XML.

Quinet, F (2005). Le rôle de la recherche dans la négociation collective centralisée. *Relations Industrielles*, https://doi.org/10.7202/028192ar.

Rauf, A, I Ozturk, F Ahmad, K Shehzad, AA Chandiao and M Irfan (2021). Do tourism development, energy consumption and transportation demolish sustainable environments? Evidence from Chinese provinces. *Sustainability*, 13, 12361.

Raza, SA, N Shah and KA Khan (2020). Residential energy environmental Kuznets curve in emerging economies: The role of economic growth, renewable energy consumption, and financial development. *Environmental Science and Pollution Research*, https://doi.org/10.1007/s11356-019-06356-8.

Razzaq, A, A Sharif, N Aziz, M Irfan and K Jermsittiparsert (2020). Asymmetric link between environmental pollution and COVID-19 in the top ten affected states of US: A novel estimations from quantile-on-quantile approach. *Environmental Research*, 191, 110189.

Razzaq, A, T Ajaz, JC Li, M Irfan and W Suksatan (2021). Investigating the asymmetric linkages between infrastructure development, green innovation, and consumption-based material footprint: Novel empirical estimations from highly resource-consuming economies. *Resources Policy*, 74, 102302.

Regis, M, P Serra and ER van den Heuvel (2021). Random autoregressive models: A structured overview. *Econometric Reviews*, https://doi.org/10.1080/07474938.2021.1899504.

Saidi, LO, P Adam, M Rahim and Rosnawintang (2019). The effect of crude oil prices on economic growth in South East Sulawesi, Indonesia: An application of autoregressive distributed lag model. *International Journal of Energy Economics and Policy*, https://doi.org/10.32479/ijeep.7322.

Samour, A, AZ Isiksal and N Gunsel Resatoglu (2020). The impact of external sovereign debt and the transmission effect of the US interest rate on Turkey's equity market. *Journal of International Trade and Economic Development*, https://doi.org/10.1080/09638199.2019.1668047.

Shahbaz, M, A Lahiani, S Abosedra and S Hammoudeh (2018). The role of globalization in energy consumption: A quantile cointegrating regression approach. *Energy Economics*, 71, 161–170.

Shaw, D and YH Fu (2020). Climate clubs with tax revenue recycling, tariffs, and transfers. *Climate Change Economics*, https://doi.org/10.1142/S2010007820400084.

Shaw, D, JC Huang, CY Lin, TY Hsu and M Tsai (2021). Estimating demand for good climate and air quality in Taiwan. *Climate Change Economics*, https://doi.org/10.1142/S2010007821500032.

Shrestha, N (2020). Detecting multicollinearity in regression analysis. *American Journal of Applied Mathematics and Statistics*, https://doi.org/10.12691/ajams-8-2-1.

Shuai, S and Z Fan (2020). Modeling the role of environmental regulations in regional green economy efficiency of China: Empirical evidence from super efficiency DEA-Tobit model. *Journal of Environmental Management*, 261.

Sovacool, BK, J Kim and M Yang (2021). The hidden costs of energy and mobility: A global meta-analysis and research synthesis of electricity and transport externalities.

Sun, H, BK Edziah, X Song, AK Kporsu and F Taghizadeh-Hesary (2020a). Estimating persistent and transient energy efficiency in belt and road countries: A stochastic frontier analysis. *Energies*, 13(15), 3837.

Sun, L, X Cao, M Alharthi, J Zhang, F Taghizadeh-Hesary and M Mohsin (2020b). Carbon emission transfer strategies in supply chain with lag time of emission reduction technologies and low-carbon preference of consumers. *Journal of Cleaner Production*, 264.

Taghizadeh-Hesary, F and F Taghizadeh-Hesary (2020). The impacts of air pollution on health and economy in Southeast Asia. *Energies*, https://doi.org/10.3390/en13071812.

Taghizadeh-Hesary, F and N Yoshino (2019). The way to induce private participation in green finance and investment. *Finance Research Letters*, https://doi.org/10.1016/j.frl.2019.04.016.

Taghizadeh-Hesary, F and N Yoshino (2020). Sustainable solutions for green financing and investment in renewable energy projects. *Energies*, https://doi.org/10.3390/en13040788.

Taghizadeh-Hesary, F, Y Chang, N Yoshino and PJ Morgan (2021). Energy insecurity, renewable energy and economic growth. *Singapore Economic Review*, https://doi.org/10.1142/S0217590821020021.

Tanveer, A, S Zeng, M Irfan and R Peng (2021). Do perceived risk, perception of self-efficacy, and openness to technology matter for solar pv adoption? An application of the extended theory of planned behavior. *Energies*, 14(16), 5008.

The Economy in the Time of Covid-19 (2020).

The World Bank Annual Report 2020 (2020).

The World Bank (2021). Labor force, total — Data.

Umit, R and LM Schaffer (2020). Attitudes towards carbon taxes across Europe: The role of perceived uncertainty and self-interest. *Energy Policy*, https://doi.org/10.1016/j.enpol.2020.111385.

Wang, W and L Su (2021). Identifying latent group structures in nonlinear panels. *Journal of Econometrics*, https://doi.org/10.1016/j.jeconom.2020.04.003.

Wang, F, Y Lu, J Li and J Ni (2021). Evaluating environmentally sustainable development based on the psr framework and variable weigh analytic hierarchy process. *International Journal of Environmental Research and Public Health*, 18(6), 1–16.

Wu, B, C Jin, A Monfort and D Hua (2021). Generous charity to preserve green image? Exploring linkage between strategic donations and environmental misconduct. *Journal of Business Research*, 131, 839–850.

Xie, N, H Hu, D Fang, X Shi, S Luo and K Burns (2021). An empirical analysis of financial markets and instruments influencing the low-carbon electricity production transition. *Journal of Cleaner Production*, https://doi.org/10.1016/j.jclepro.2020.124415.

Yang, C, Y Hao and M Irfan (2021). Energy consumption structural adjustment and carbon neutrality in the post-COVID-19 era. *Structural Change and Economic Dynamics*, 59, 442–453.

Yang, Z (2020). Climate change and externality. *Climate Change Economics*, https://doi.org/10.1142/S2010007820400072.

Yu, J, YM Tang, KY Chau, R Nazar, S Ali and W Iqbal (2021). Role of solar-based renewable energy in mitigating CO_2 emissions: Evidence from quantile-on-quantile estimation. *Renewable Energy*, 182, 216–226.

Zakari, A and J Toplak (2021). Investigation into the social behavioural effects on a country's ecological footprint: Evidence from Central Europe. *Technological Forecasting and Social Change*, 170, 120891.

Zhang, Y, M Abbas, YH Koura, Y Su and W Iqbal (2021). The impact trilemma of energy prices, taxation, and population on industrial and residential greenhouse gas emissions in Europe. *Environmental Science and Pollution Research*, 28(6), 6913–6928.

www.ingramcontent.com/pod-product-compliance
Lightning Source LLC
LaVergne TN
LVHW081230231125
825833LV00004B/242